Lady Death ORIGINS®

written by
BRIAN PULIDO

covers
RAFA LOPEZ trade paperback cover
JUAN JOSE RYP hardcover
RICHARD ORTIZ signed hardcover
DIGIKORE STUDIOS cover color

story
GABRIEL GUZMAN chapters 1-5 art
MARIANO TAIBO chapters 1-5 inks
DANIEL HDR chapters 6-8 art
ANDREW DALHOUSE chapters 1-8 color

gallery & chapter breaks
**JUAN JOSE RYP, DANIEL HDR,
GABRIEL GUZMAN** artwork
MARK SWEENEY, ANDREW DALHOUSE colors

boundless
WILLIAM CHRISTENSEN editor in chief
MARK SEIFERT creative director
JIM KUHORIC managing editor
KEITH DAVIDSEN director of sales & marketing
DAVID MARKS director of events
ARIANA OSBORNE production assistant

lady death created by **BRIAN PULIDO**

www.boundlesscomics.com

BOUNDLESS™

LADY DEATH ORIGINS VOLUME 2. October 2011. Published by Boundless Comics, a division of Avatar Press, Inc., 515 N. Century Blvd. Rantoul IL 61866. ©2010 Avatar Press, Inc. Lady Death® and all related properties TM & © Mischief Maker Media, Inc. and Avatar Press, Inc. All characters as depicted in this story are over the age of 18. The stories, characters, and institutions mentioned in this magazine are entirely fictional. Printed in Canada.

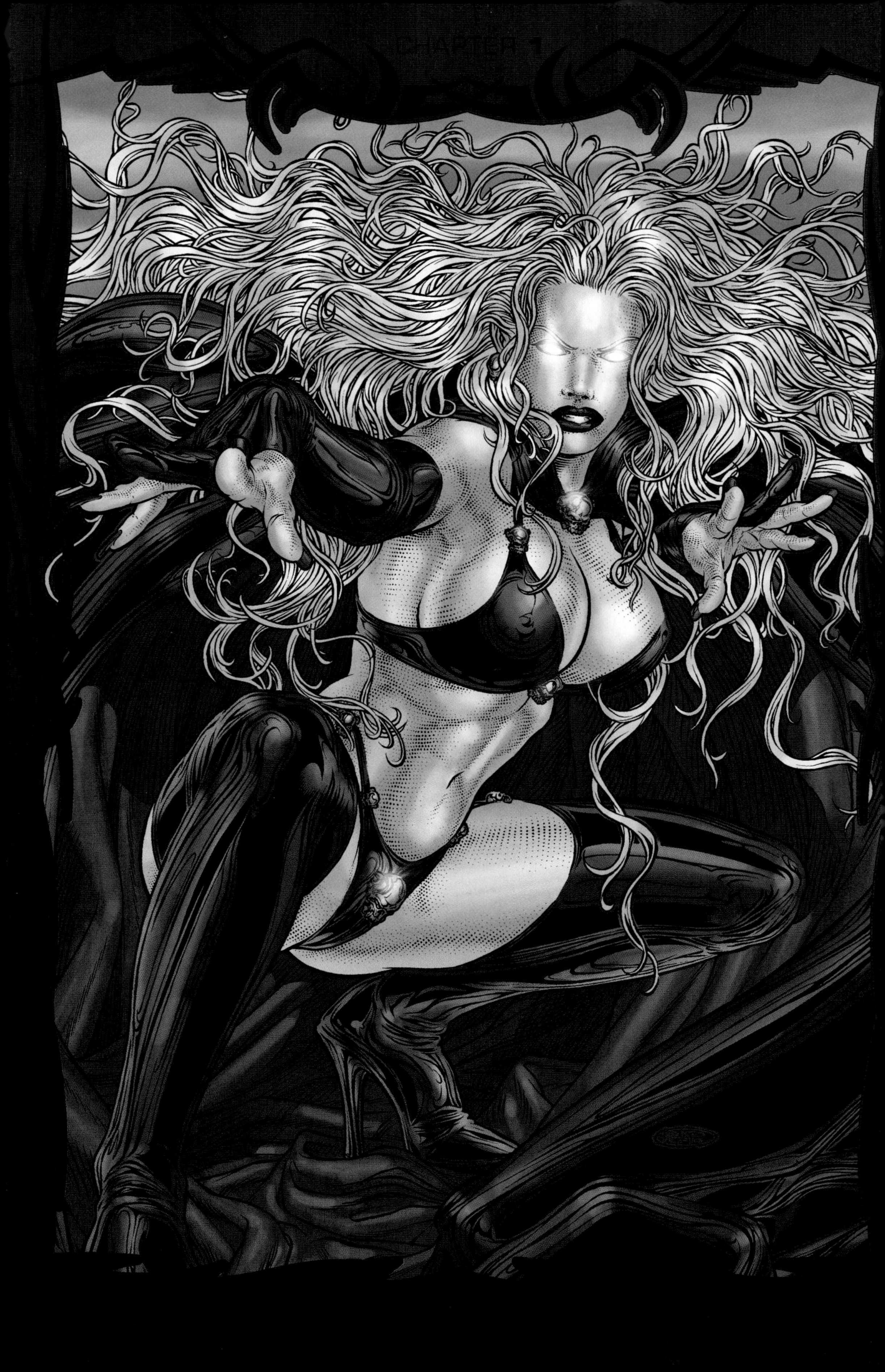
CHAPTER 1

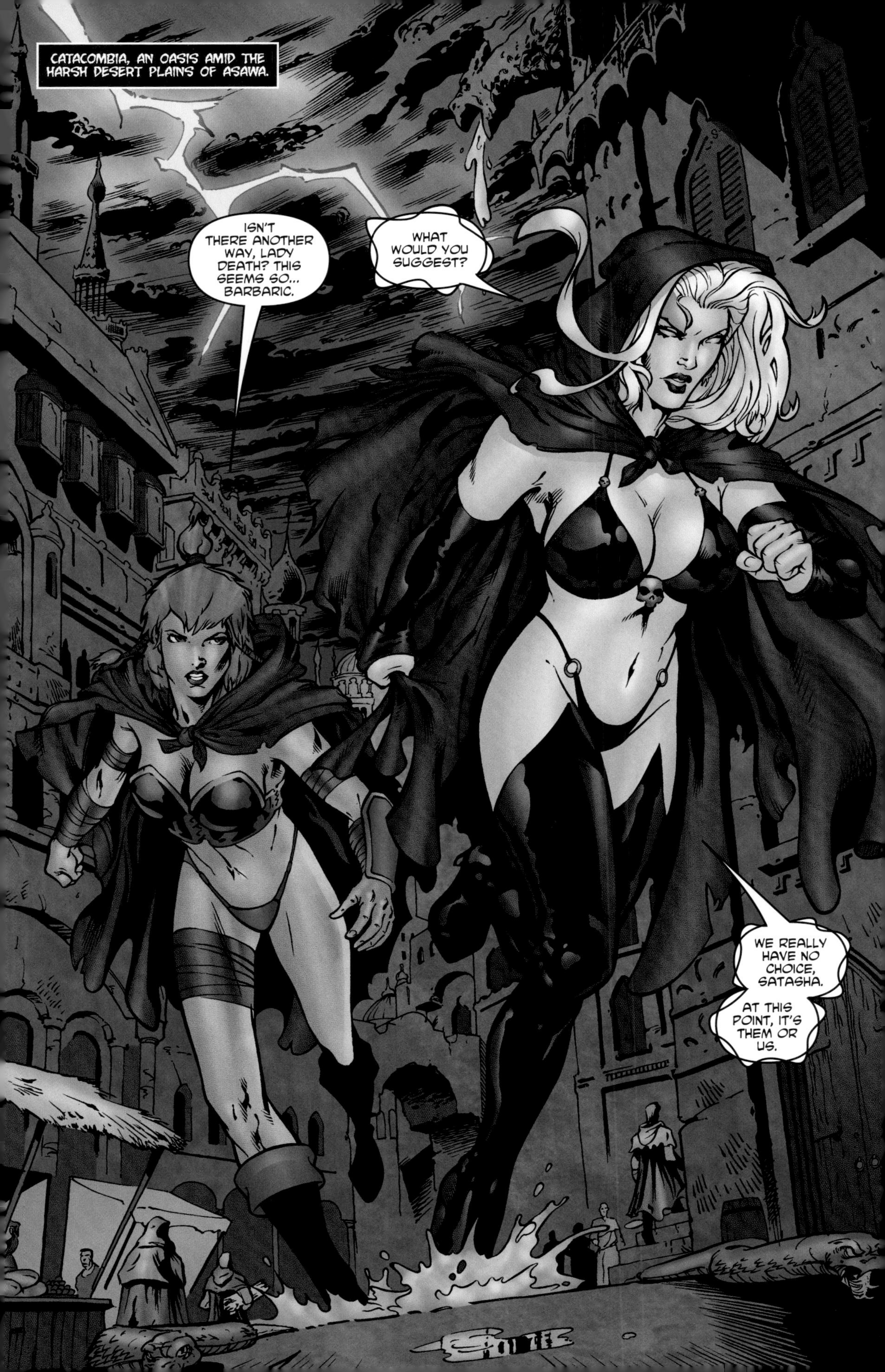
CATACOMBIA, AN OASIS AMID THE HARSH DESERT PLAINS OF ASAWA.
ISN'T THERE ANOTHER WAY, LADY DEATH? THIS SEEMS SO... BARBARIC.
WHAT WOULD YOU SUGGEST?
WE REALLY HAVE NO CHOICE, SATASHA.
AT THIS POINT, IT'S THEM OR US.

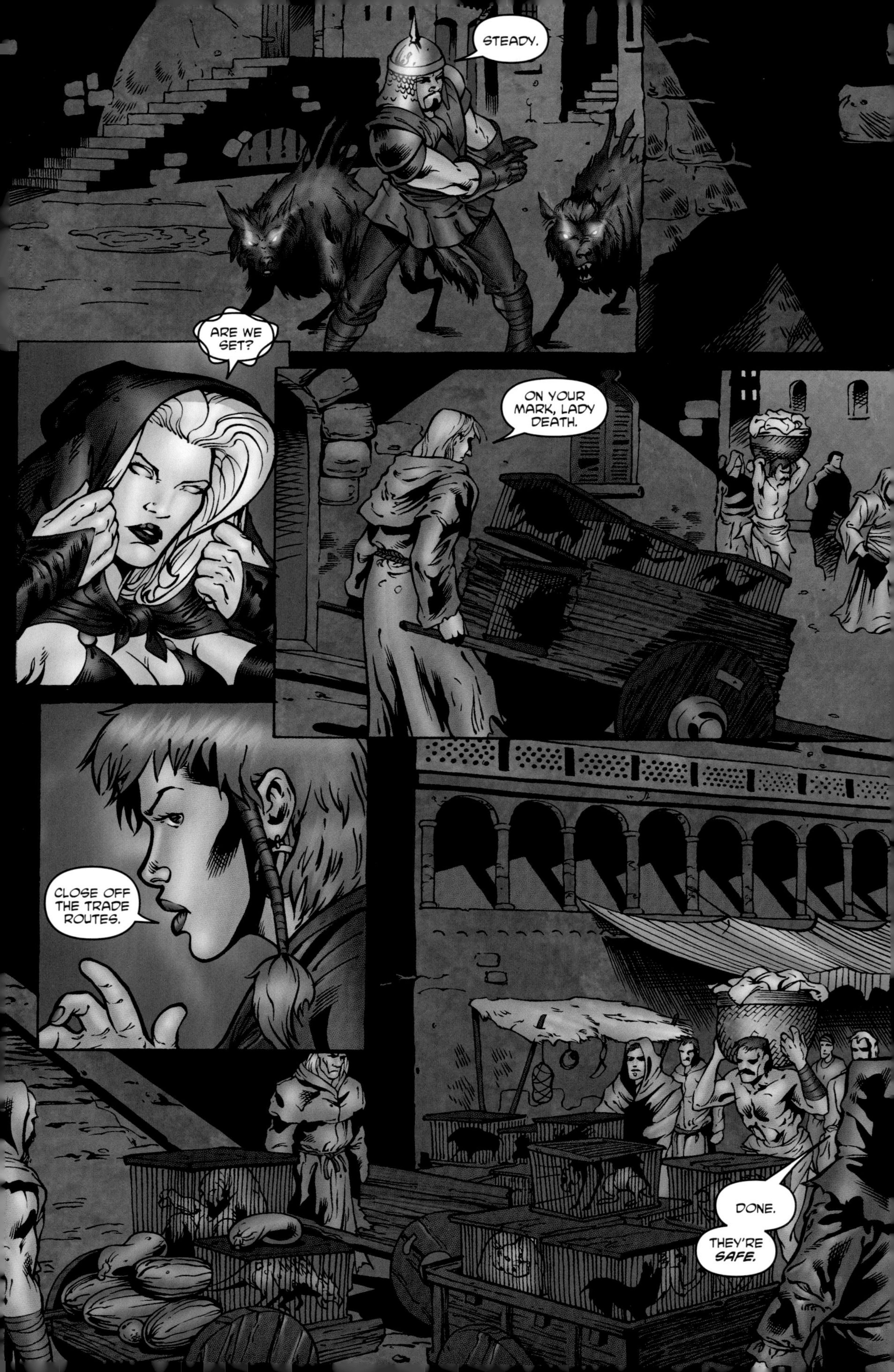
STEADY.
ARE WE SET?
ON YOUR MARK, LADY DEATH.
CLOSE OFF THE TRADE ROUTES.
DONE.
THEY'RE *SAFE.*

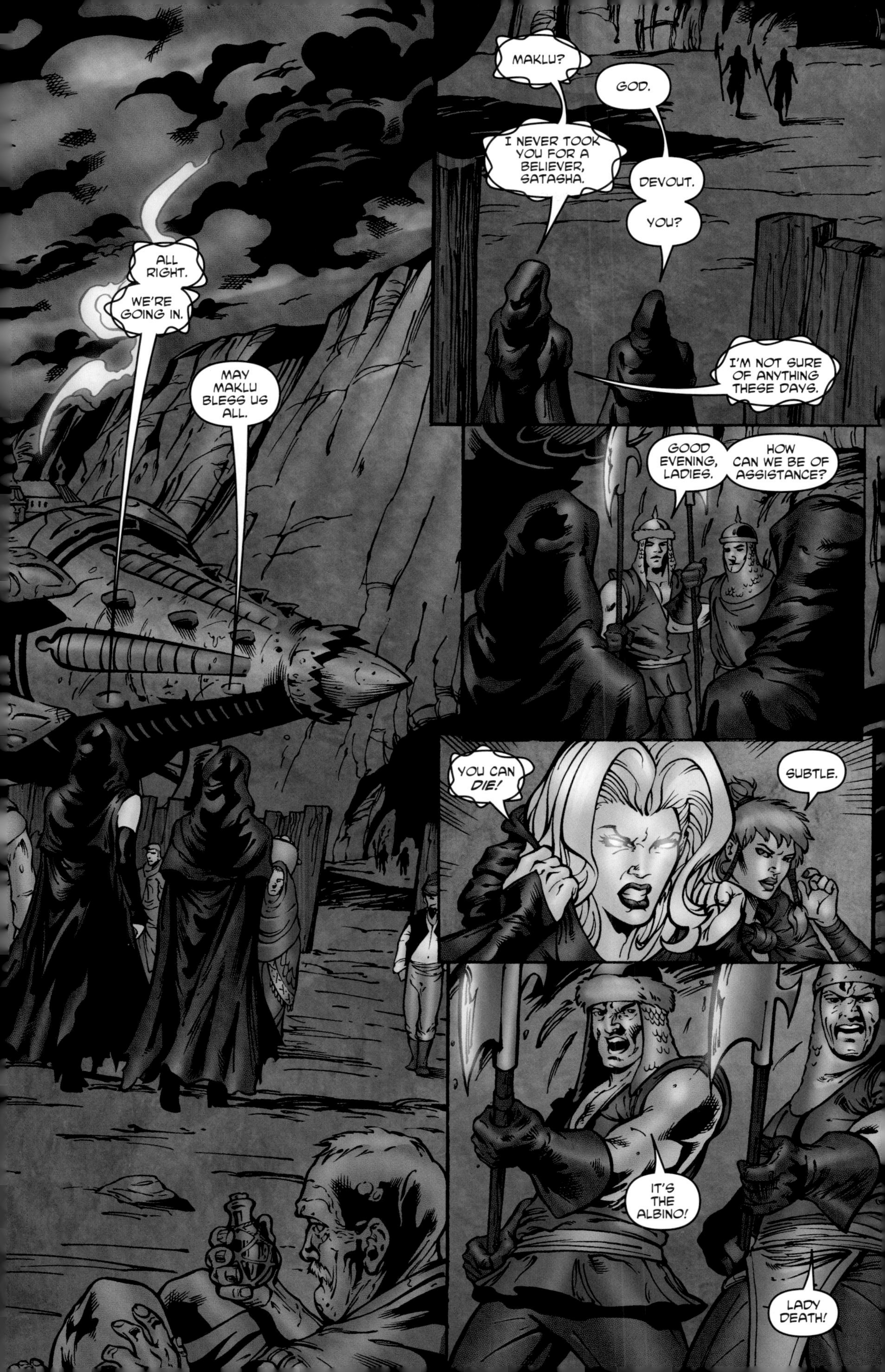
ALL RIGHT.
WE'RE GOING IN.
MAY MAKLU BLESS US ALL.
MAKLU?
GOD.
I NEVER TOOK YOU FOR A BELIEVER, SATASHA.
DEVOUT.
YOU?
I'M NOT SURE OF ANYTHING THESE DAYS.
GOOD EVENING, LADIES.
HOW CAN WE BE OF ASSISTANCE?
YOU CAN *DIE!*
SUBTLE.
IT'S THE ALBINO!
LADY DEATH!

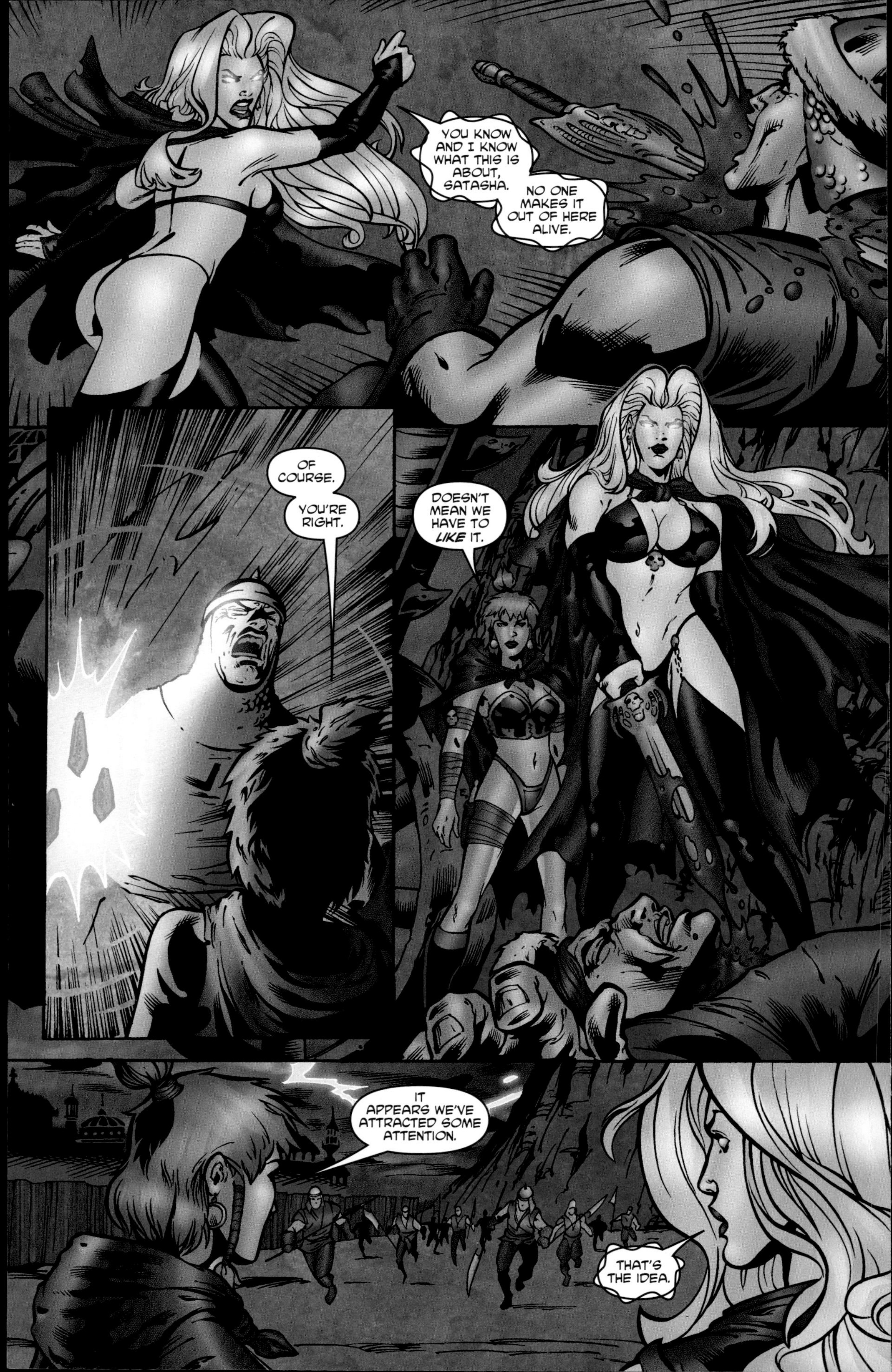
YOU KNOW AND I KNOW WHAT THIS IS ABOUT, SATASHA.
NO ONE MAKES IT OUT OF HERE ALIVE.
OF COURSE.
YOU'RE RIGHT.
DOESN'T MEAN WE HAVE TO *LIKE* IT.
IT APPEARS WE'VE ATTRACTED SOME ATTENTION.
THAT'S THE IDEA.

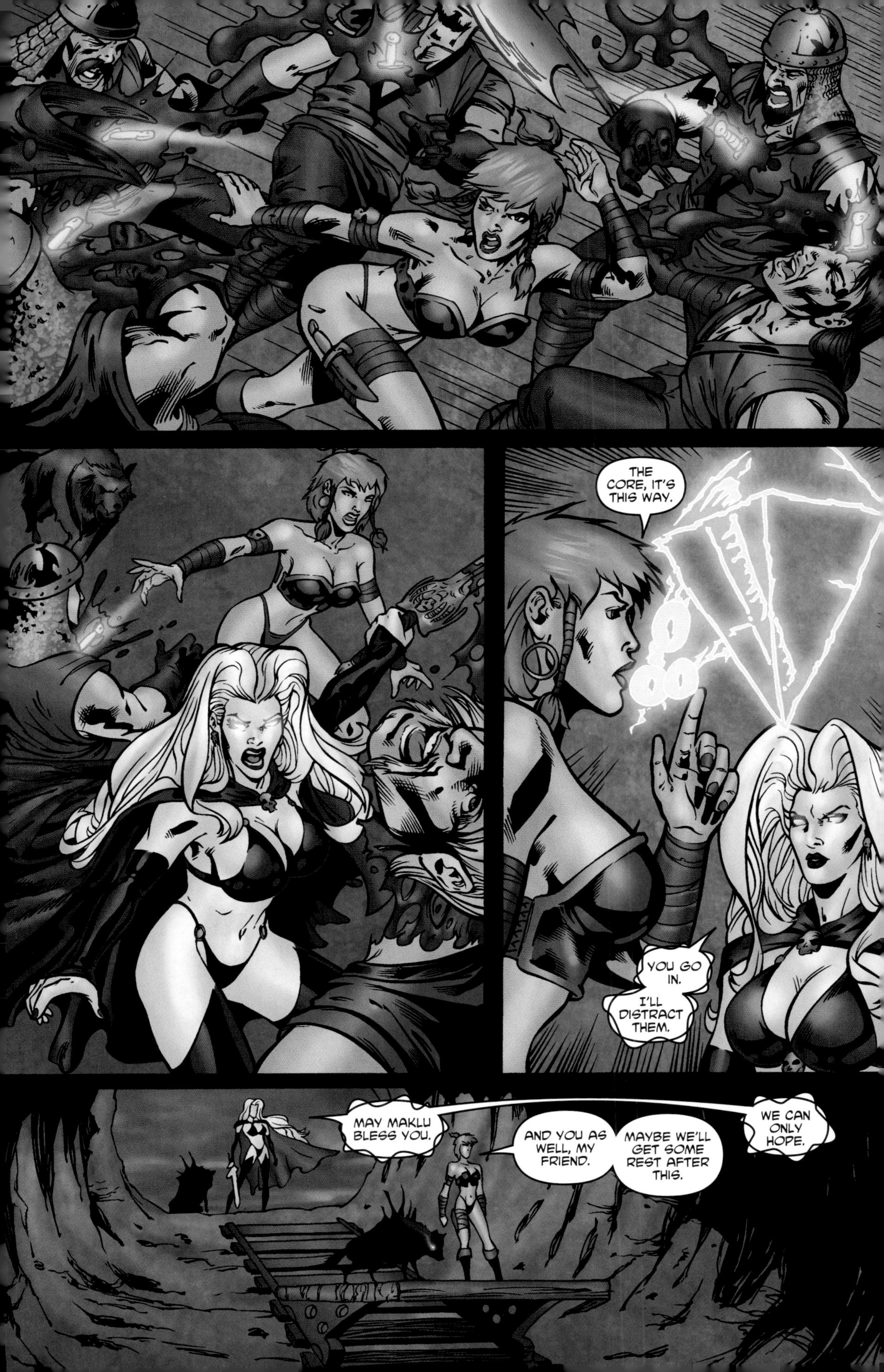
THE CORE, IT'S THIS WAY.
YOU GO IN.
I'LL DISTRACT THEM.
MAY MAKLU BLESS YOU.
AND YOU AS WELL, MY FRIEND.
MAYBE WE'LL GET SOME REST AFTER THIS.
WE CAN ONLY HOPE.

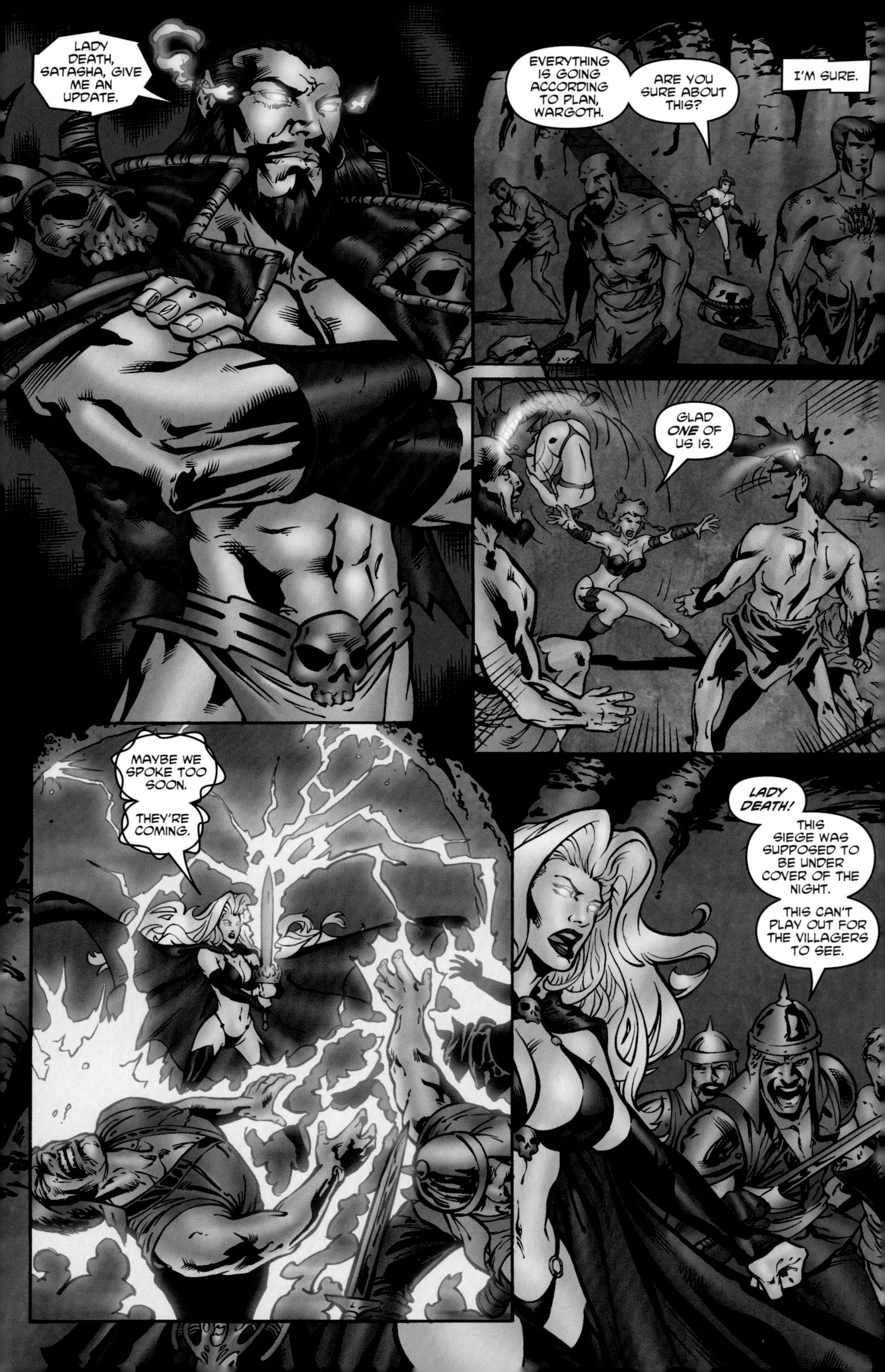
LADY DEATH, SATASHA, GIVE ME AN UPDATE.
EVERYTHING IS GOING ACCORDING TO PLAN, WARGOTH.
ARE YOU SURE ABOUT THIS?
I'M SURE.
GLAD ONE OF US IS.
MAYBE WE SPOKE TOO SOON.
THEY'RE COMING.
LADY DEATH!
THIS SIEGE WAS SUPPOSED TO BE UNDER COVER OF THE NIGHT.
THIS CAN'T PLAY OUT FOR THE VILLAGERS TO SEE.

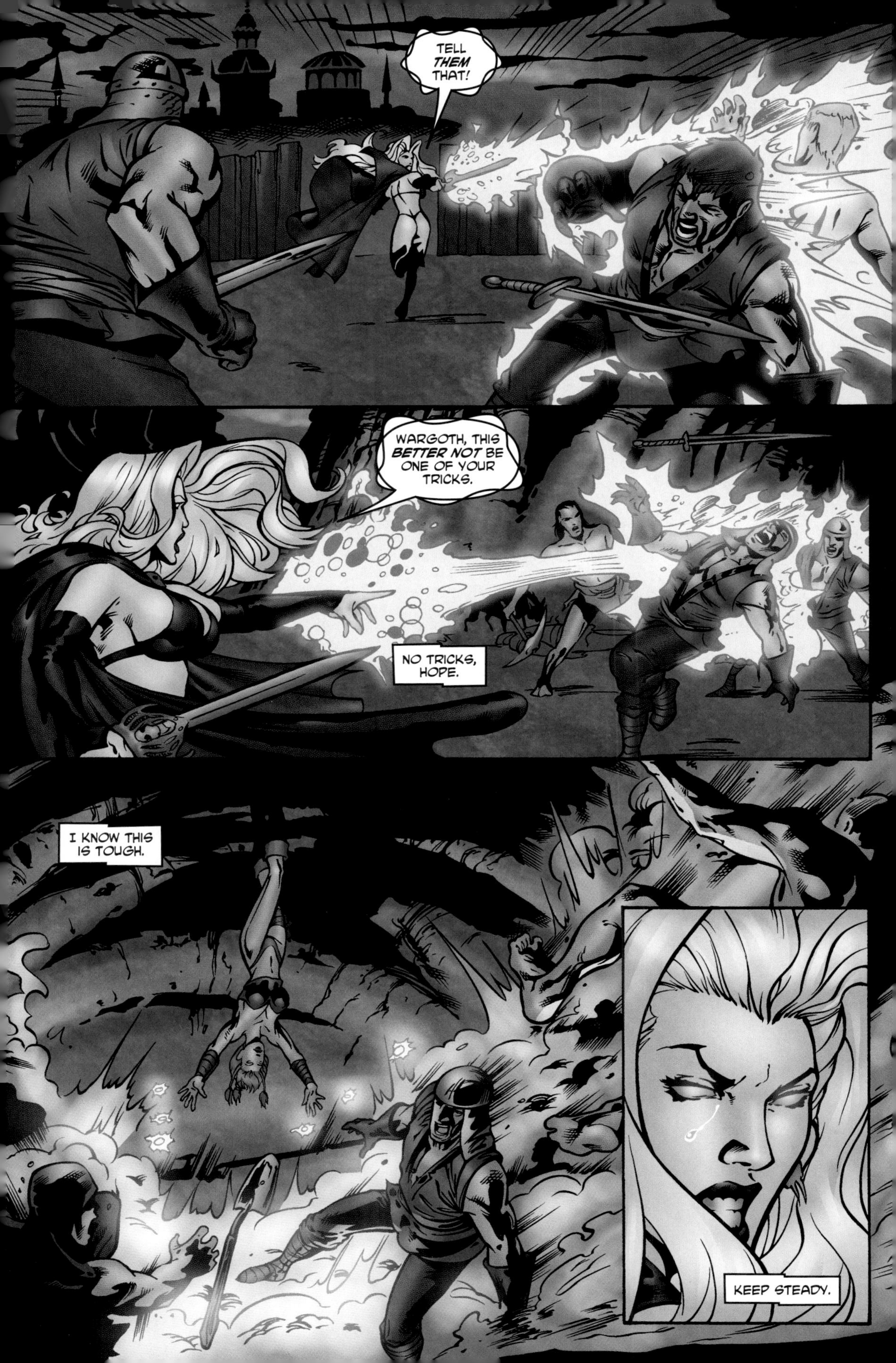
TELL *THEM* THAT!
WARGOTH, THIS *BETTER NOT* BE ONE OF YOUR TRICKS.
NO TRICKS, HOPE.
I KNOW THIS IS TOUGH.
KEEP STEADY.

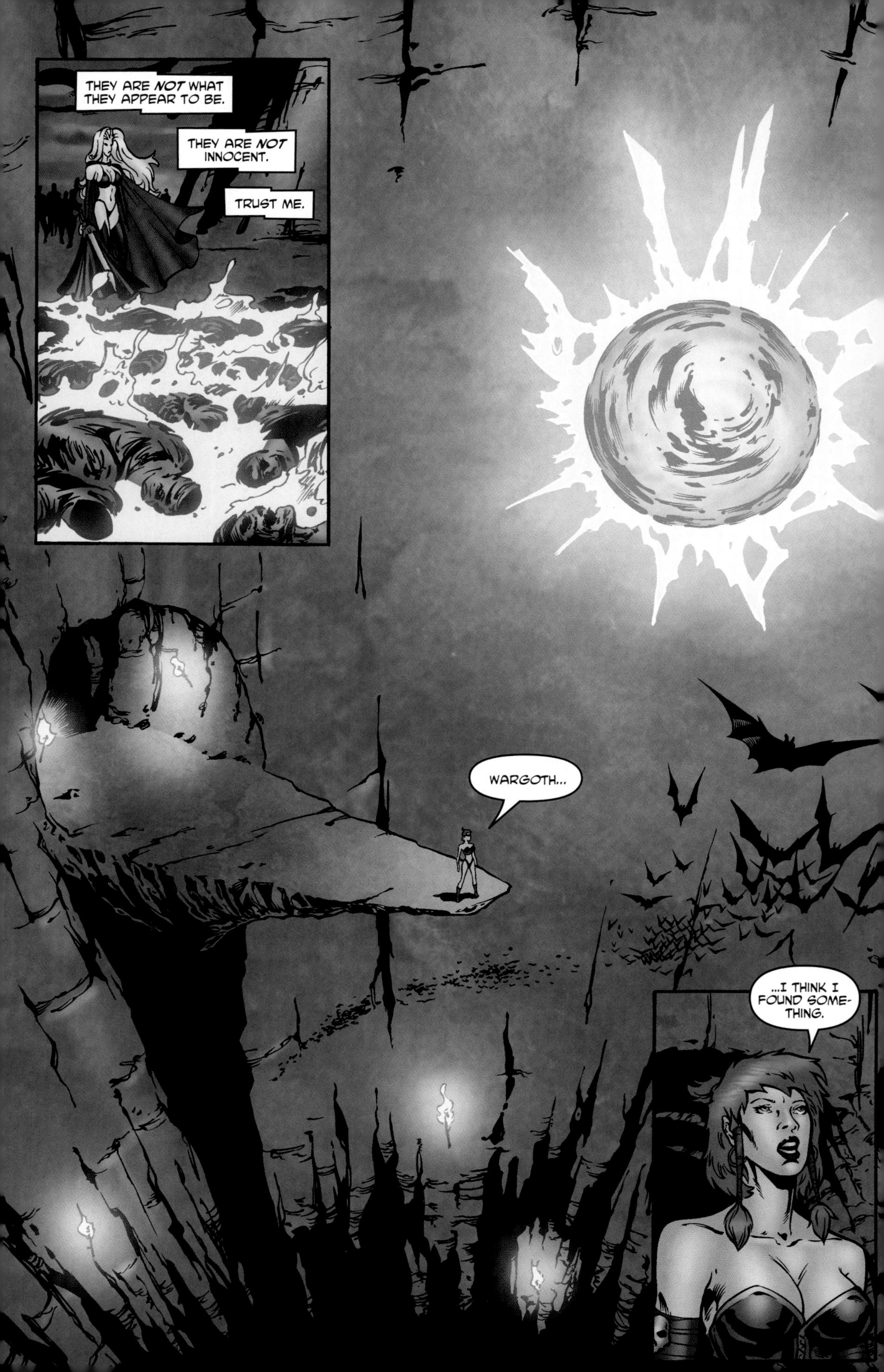
THEY ARE NOT WHAT THEY APPEAR TO BE.
THEY ARE NOT INNOCENT.
TRUST ME.
WARGOTH...
...I THINK I FOUND SOME-THING.

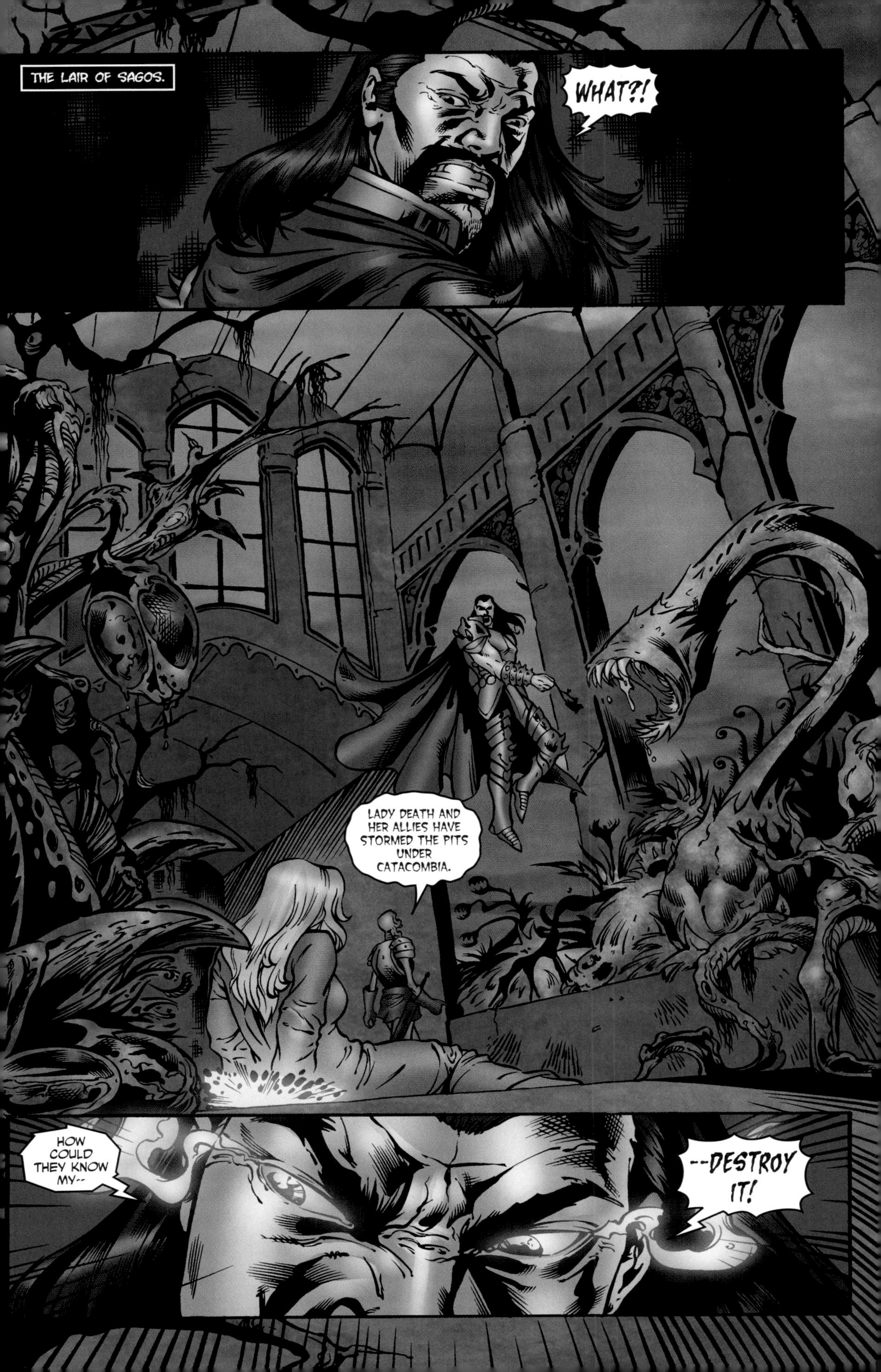
THE LAIR OF SAGOS.
WHAT?!
LADY DEATH AND HER ALLIES HAVE STORMED THE PITS UNDER CATACOMBIA.
HOW COULD THEY KNOW MY--
--DESTROY IT!

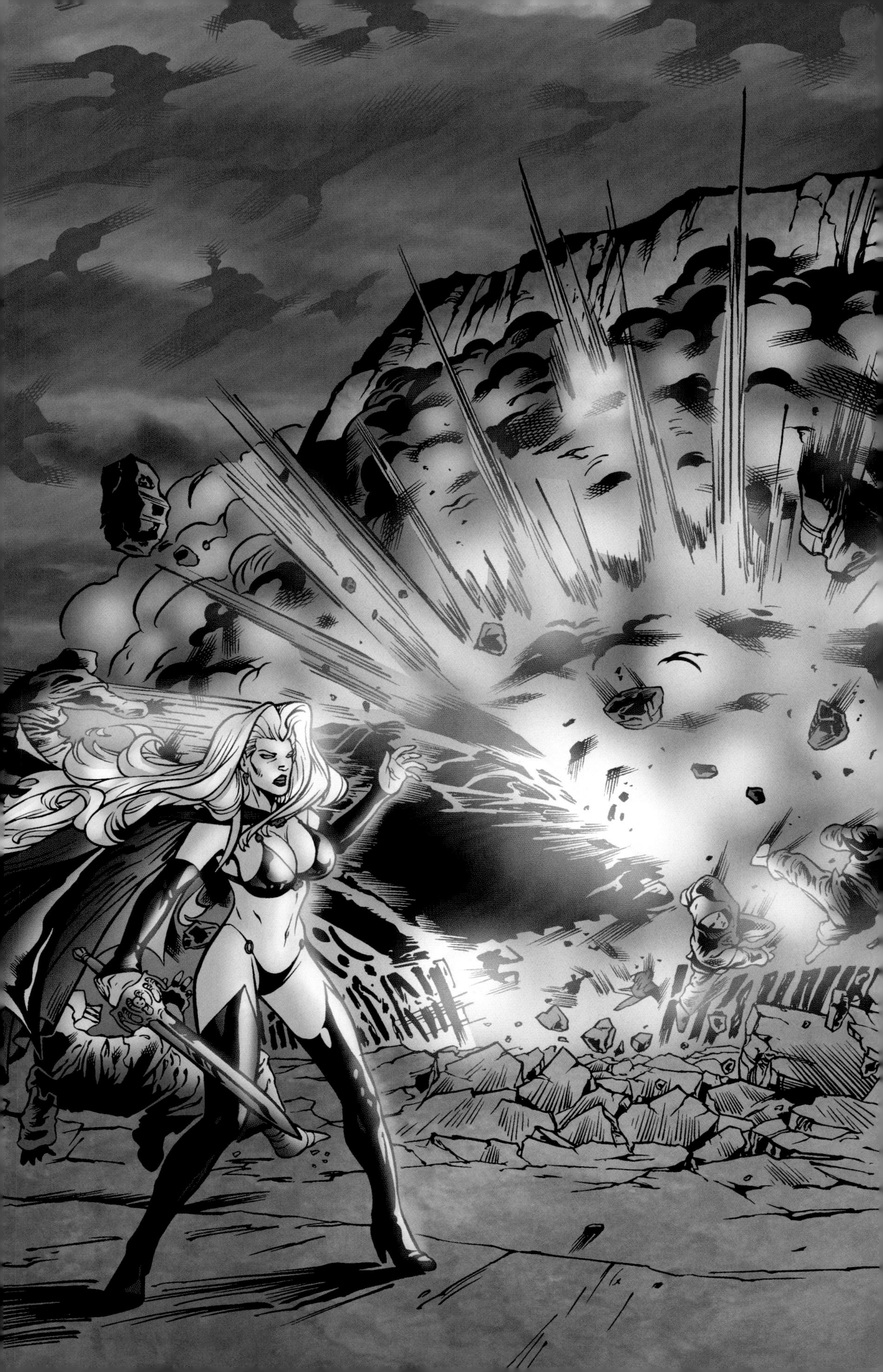

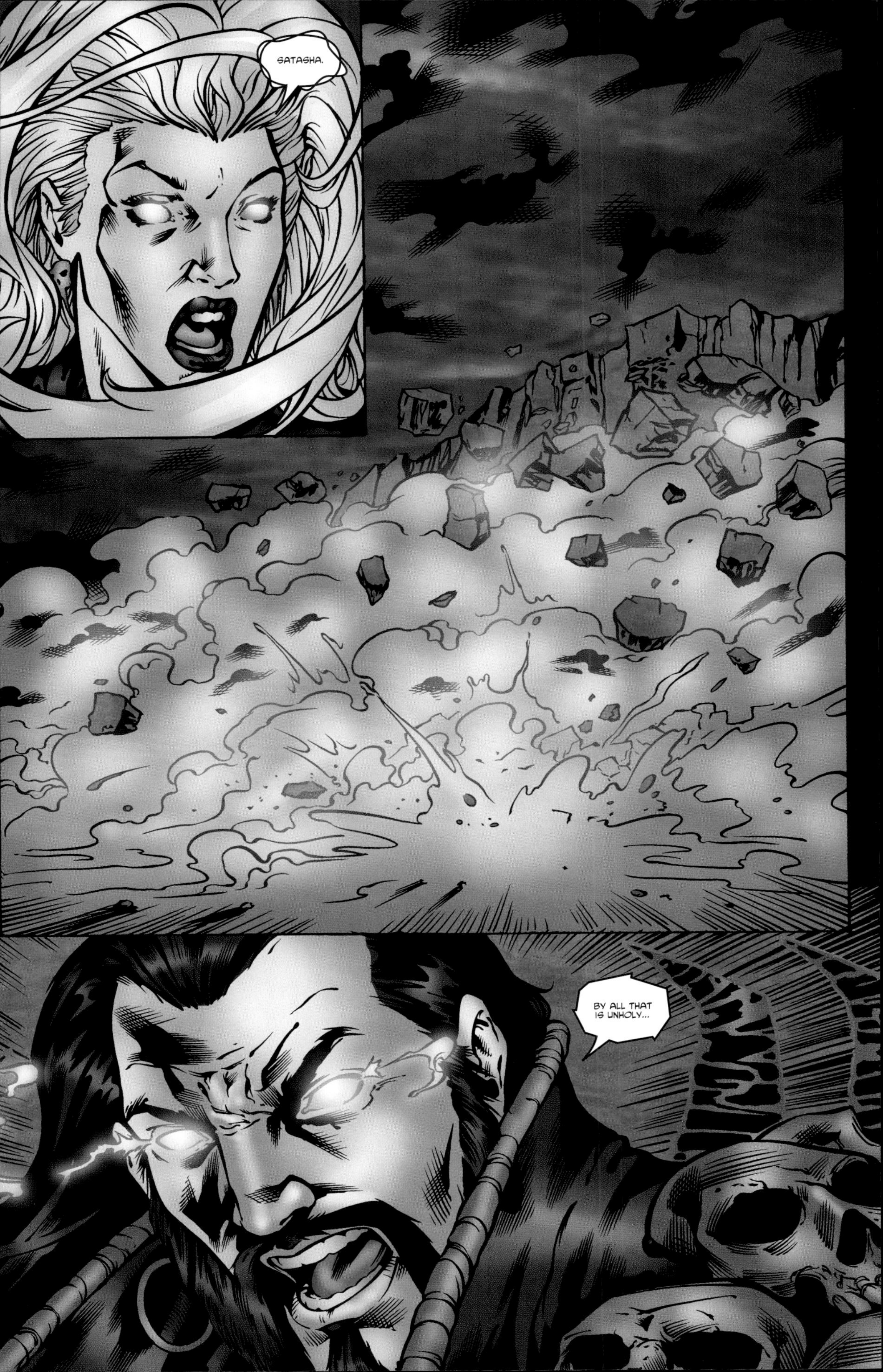
SATASHA.
BY ALL THAT IS UNHOLY...

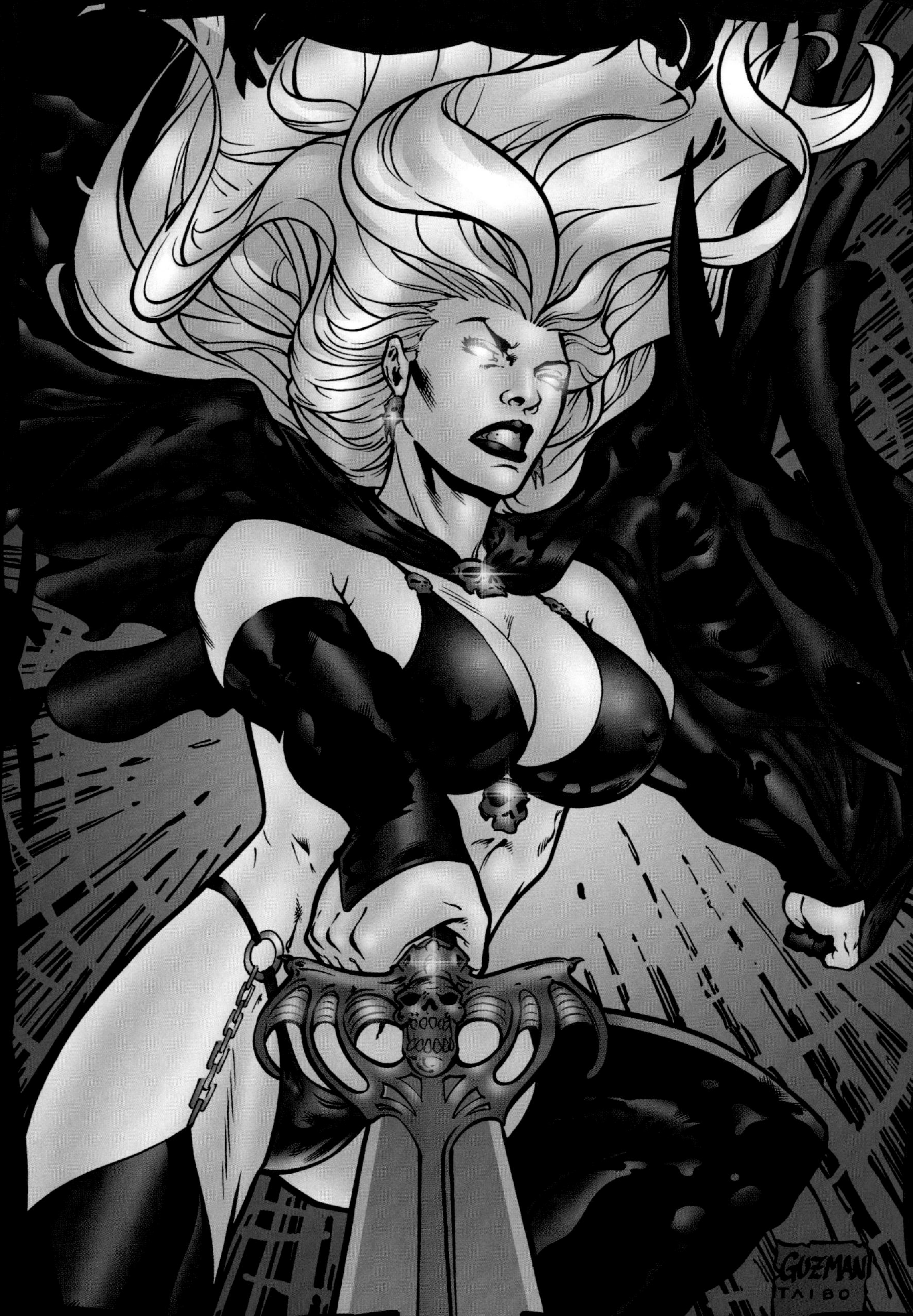
GUZMAN
TAIBO

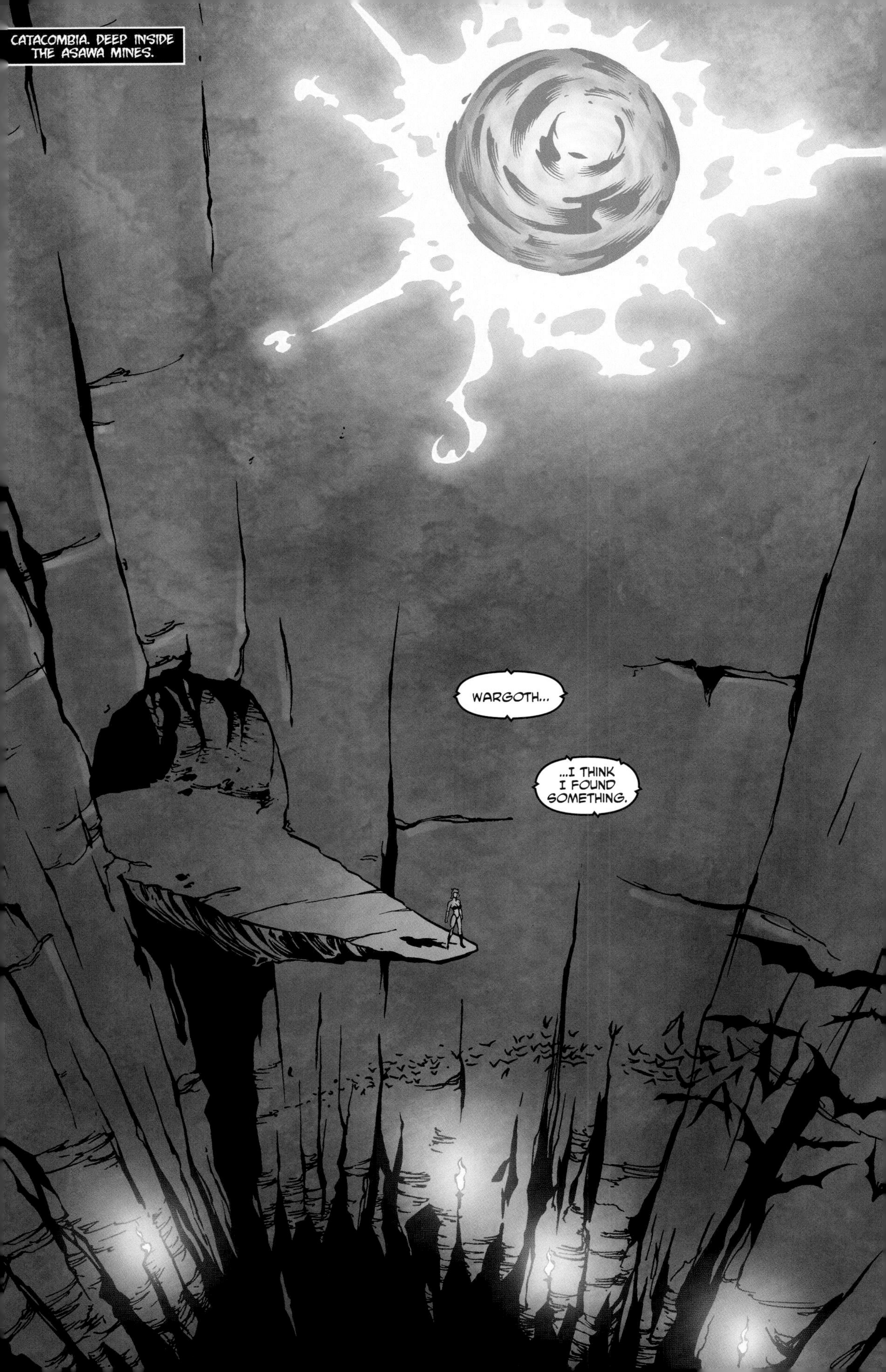
CATACOMBIA. DEEP INSIDE THE ASAWA MINES.
WARGOTH...
...I THINK I FOUND SOMETHING.

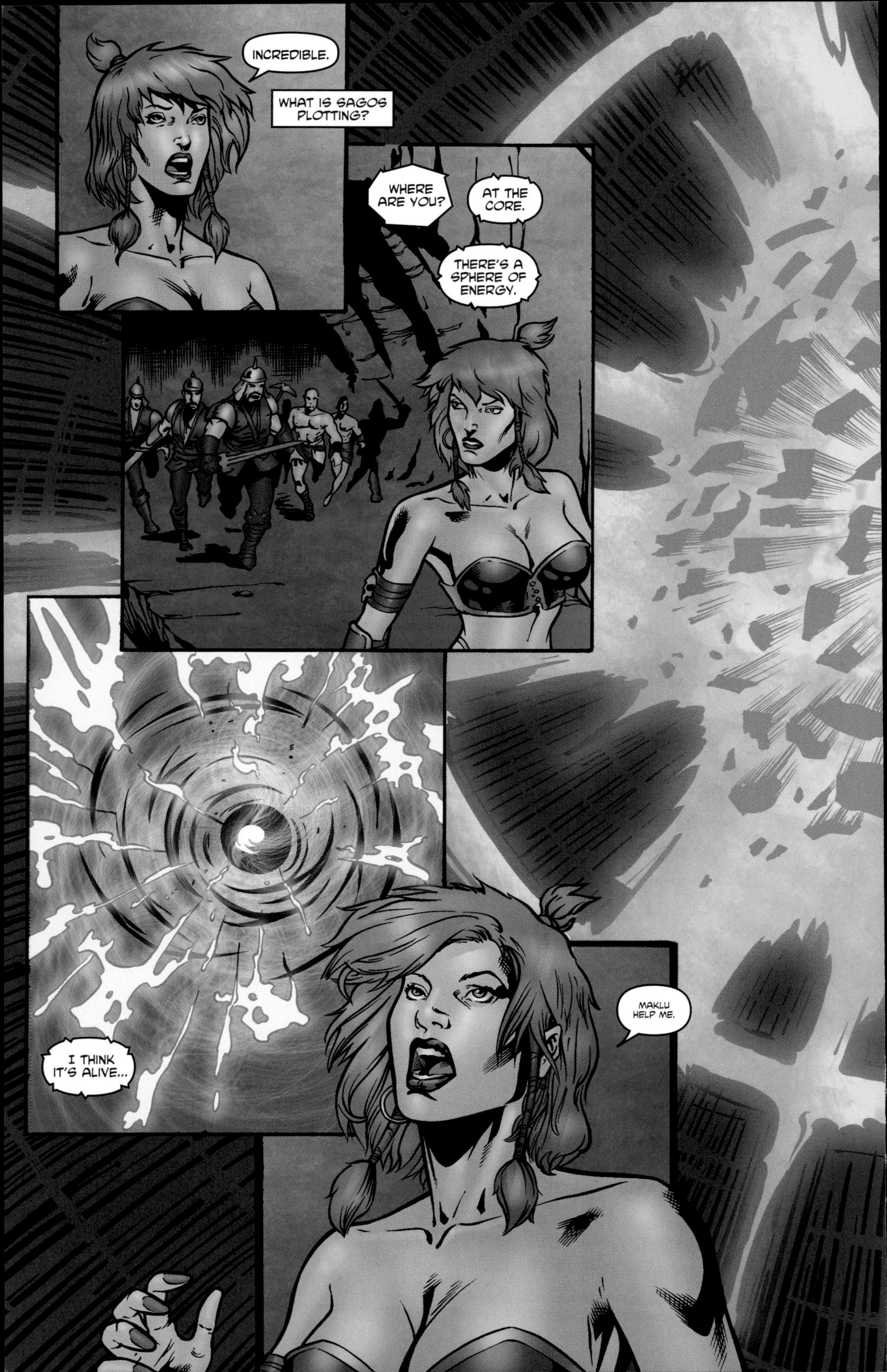
INCREDIBLE.
WHAT IS SAGOS PLOTTING?
WHERE ARE YOU?
AT THE CORE.
THERE'S A SPHERE OF ENERGY.
I THINK IT'S ALIVE...
MAKLU HELP ME.

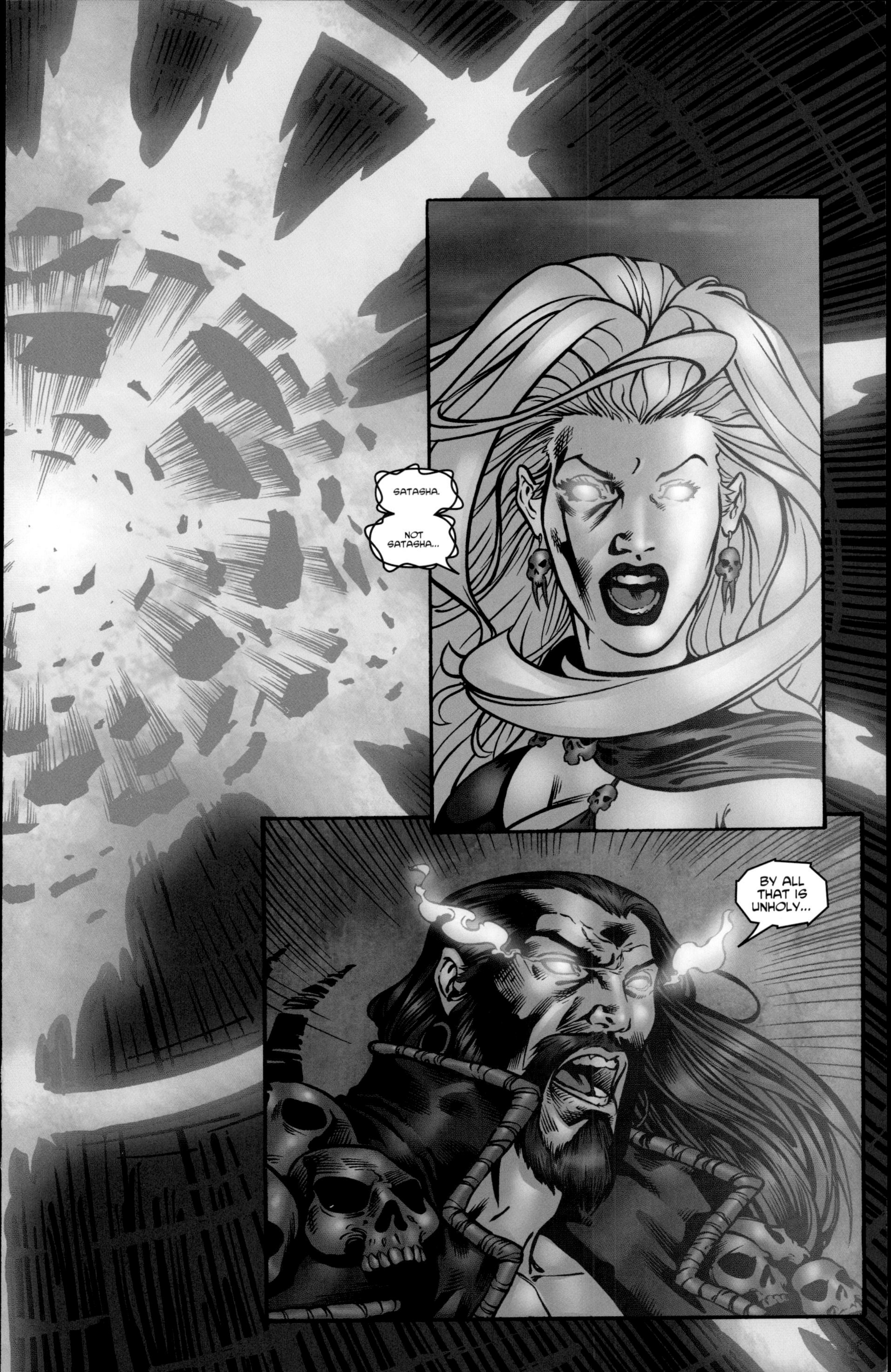
SATASHA.
NOT SATASHA...
BY ALL THAT IS UNHOLY...

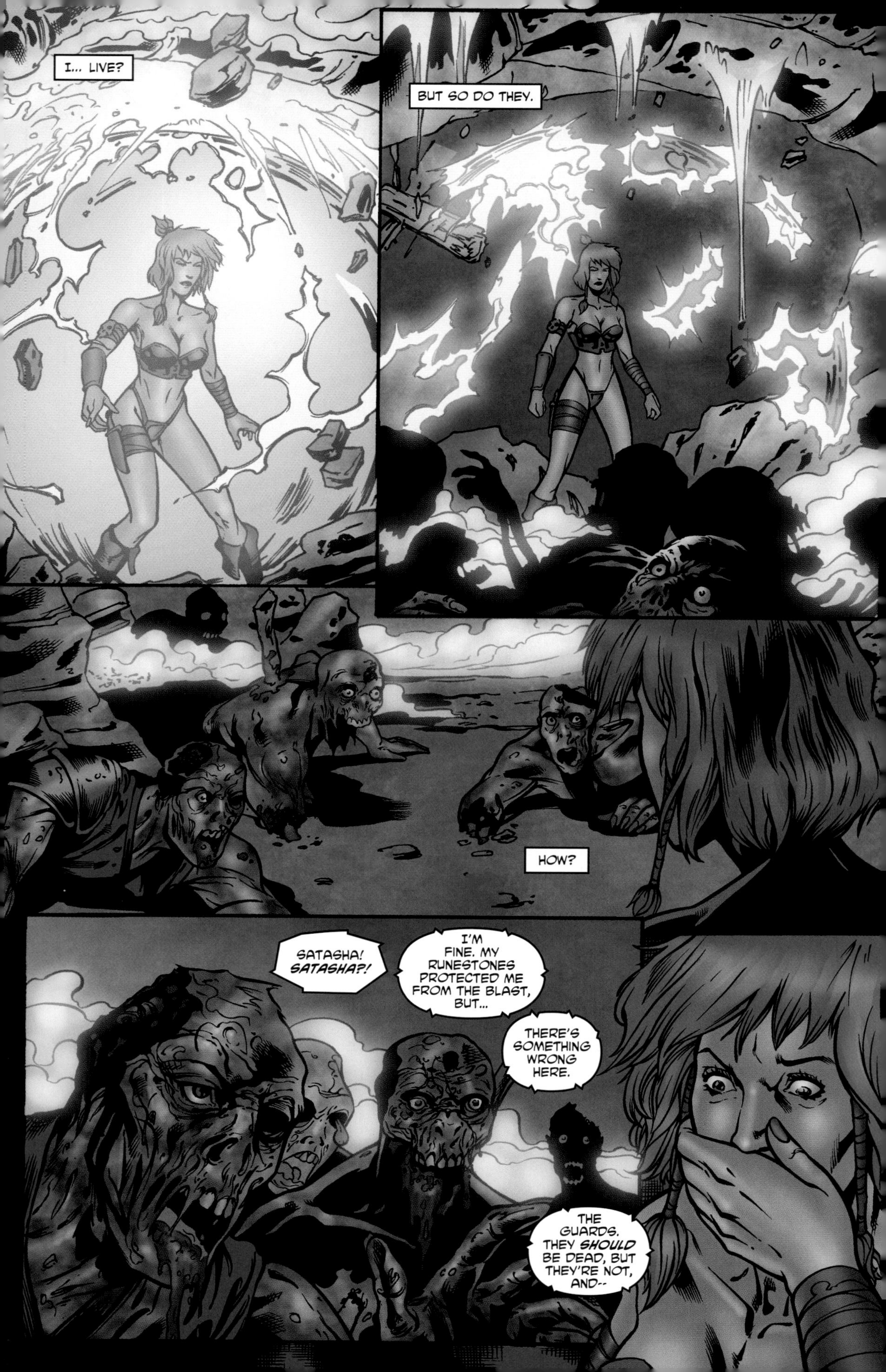
I... LIVE?
BUT SO DO THEY.
HOW?
SATASHA! SATASHA?!
I'M FINE. MY RUNESTONES PROTECTED ME FROM THE BLAST, BUT...
THERE'S SOMETHING WRONG HERE.
THE GUARDS. THEY SHOULD BE DEAD, BUT THEY'RE NOT, AND--

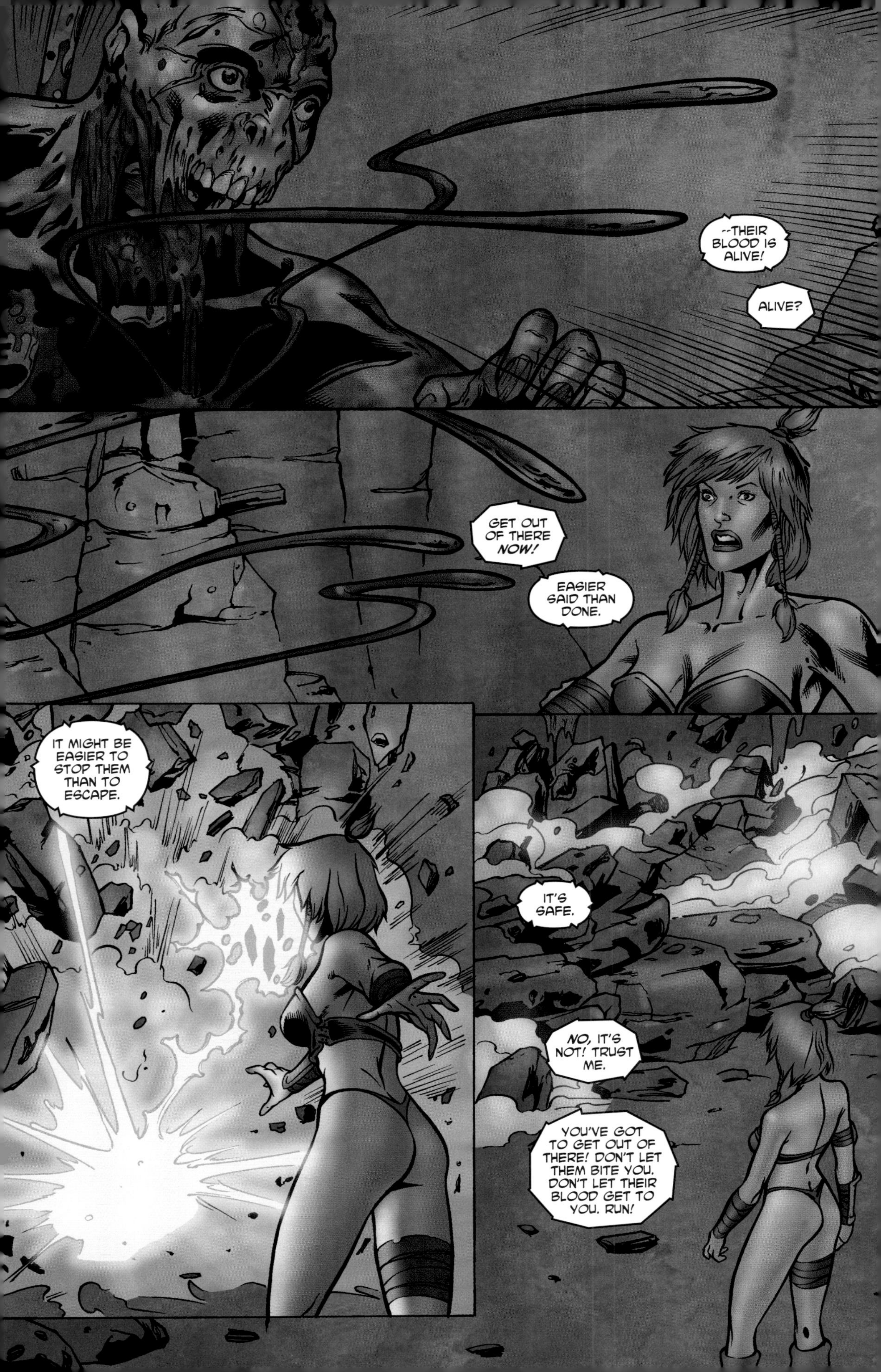
--THEIR BLOOD IS ALIVE!
ALIVE?
GET OUT OF THERE NOW!
EASIER SAID THAN DONE.
IT MIGHT BE EASIER TO STOP THEM THAN TO ESCAPE.
IT'S SAFE.
NO, IT'S NOT! TRUST ME.
YOU'VE GOT TO GET OUT OF THERE! DON'T LET THEM BITE YOU. DON'T LET THEIR BLOOD GET TO YOU. RUN!

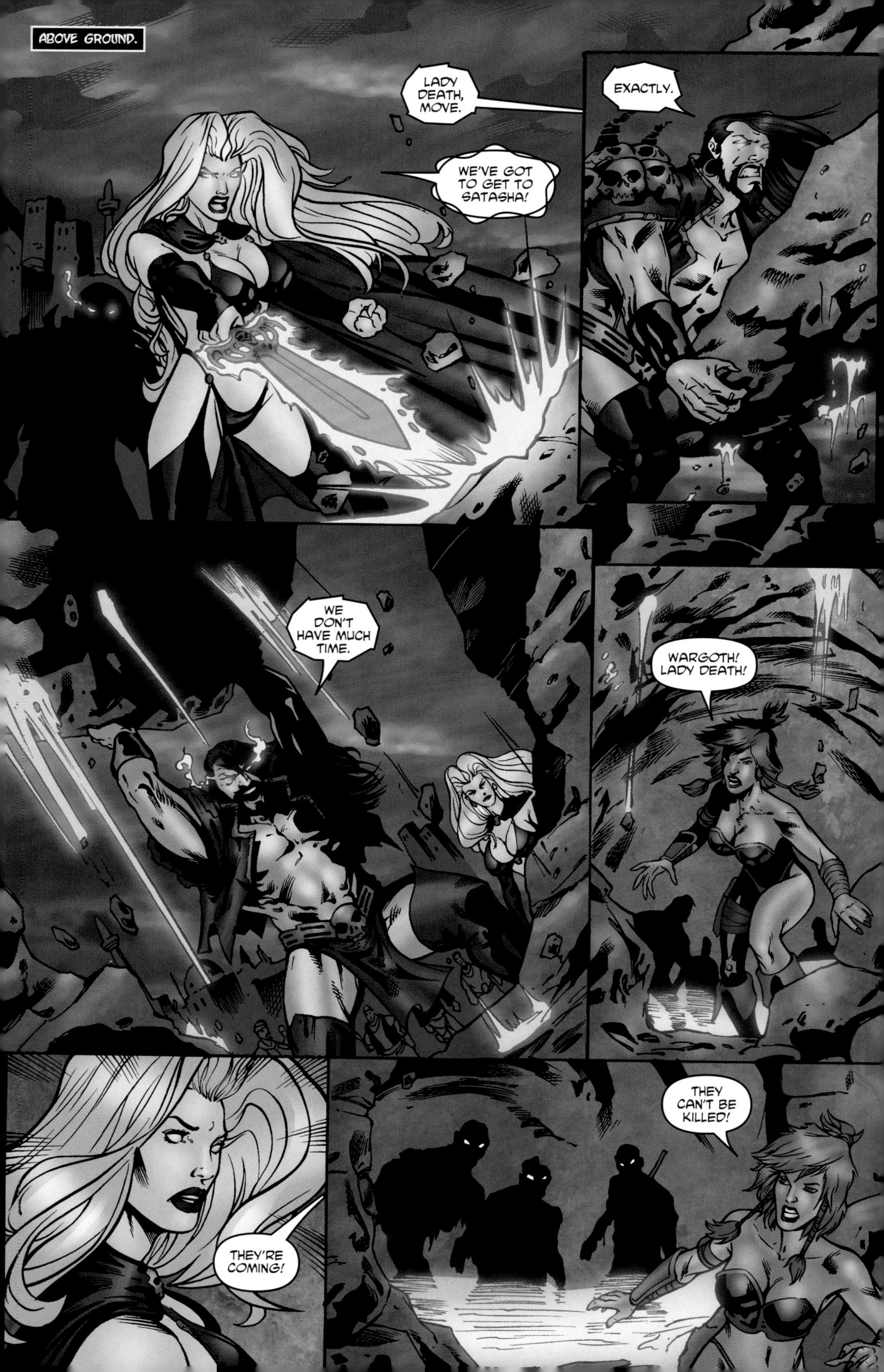
ABOVE GROUND.
LADY DEATH, MOVE.
WE'VE GOT TO GET TO SATASHA!
EXACTLY.
WE DON'T HAVE MUCH TIME.
WARGOTH! LADY DEATH!
THEY'RE COMING!
THEY CAN'T BE KILLED!

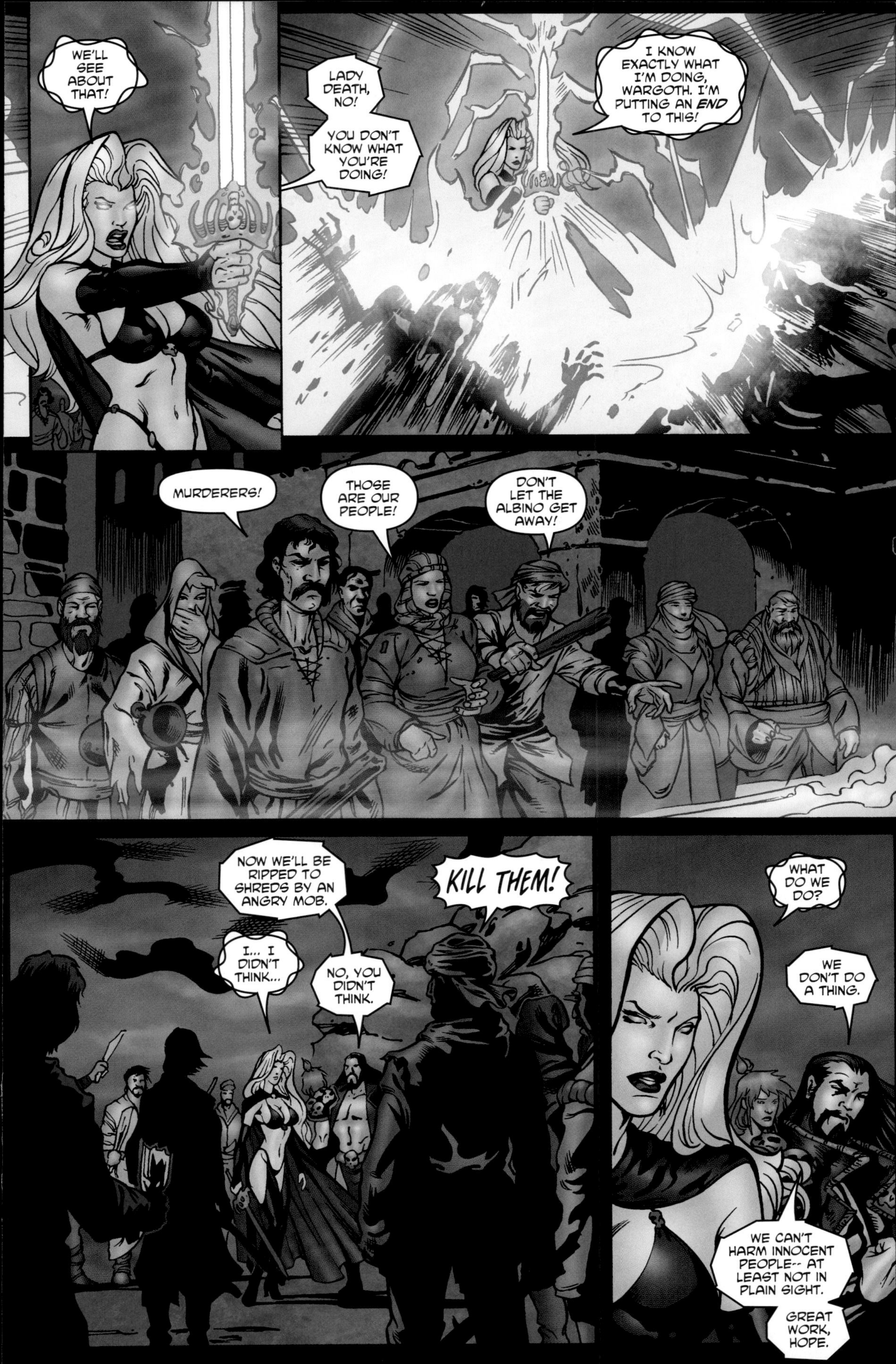
WE'LL SEE ABOUT THAT!
LADY DEATH, NO!
YOU DON'T KNOW WHAT YOU'RE DOING!
I KNOW EXACTLY WHAT I'M DOING, WARGOTH. I'M PUTTING AN *END* TO THIS!
MURDERERS!
THOSE ARE OUR PEOPLE!
DON'T LET THE ALBINO GET AWAY!
NOW WE'LL BE RIPPED TO SHREDS BY AN ANGRY MOB.
KILL THEM!
I... I DIDN'T THINK...
NO, YOU DIDN'T THINK.
WHAT DO WE DO?
WE DON'T DO A THING.
WE CAN'T HARM INNOCENT PEOPLE-- AT LEAST NOT IN PLAIN SIGHT.
GREAT WORK, HOPE.

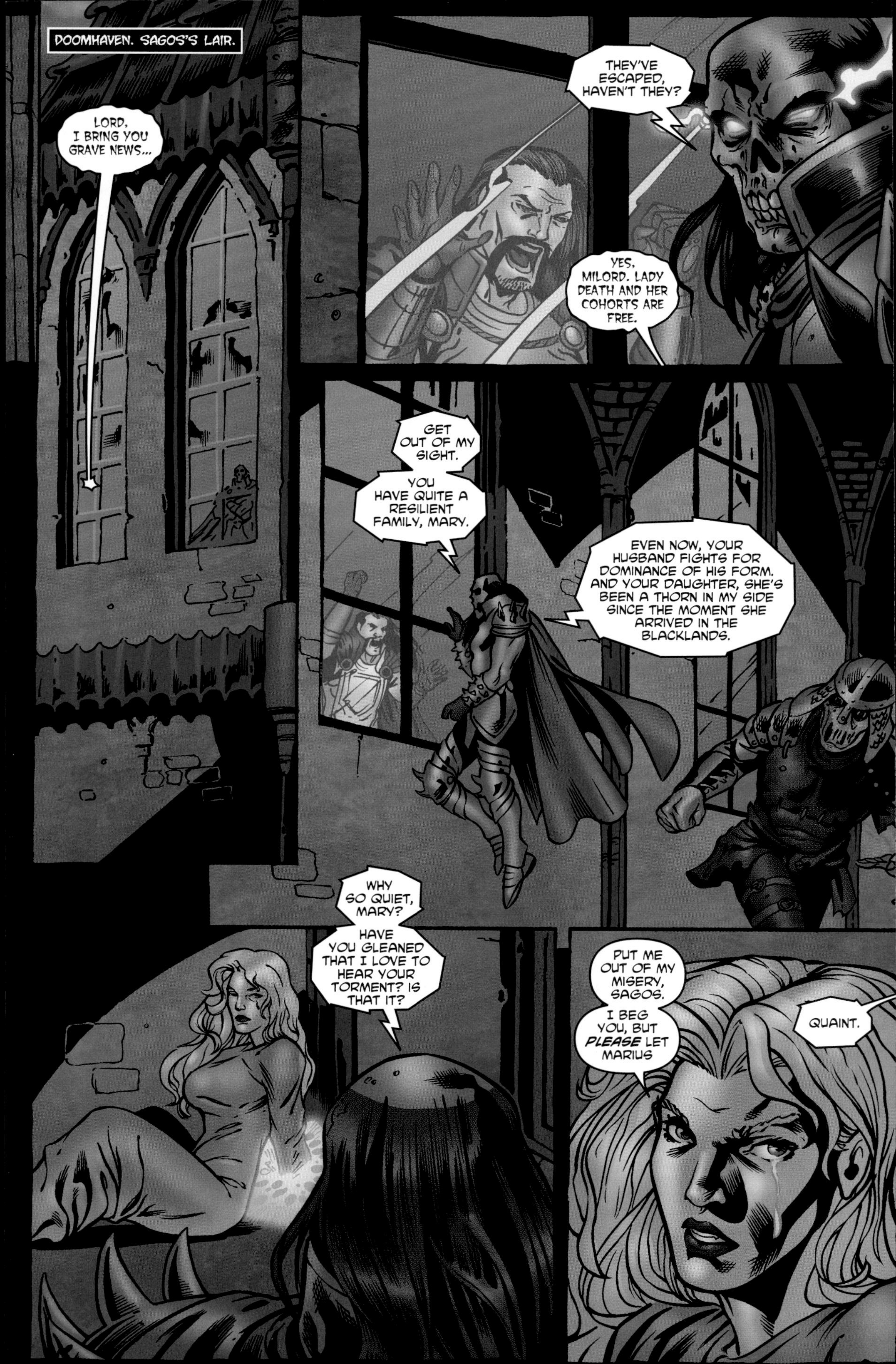
DOOMHAVEN. SAGOS'S LAIR.
LORD, I BRING YOU GRAVE NEWS...
THEY'VE ESCAPED, HAVEN'T THEY?
YES, MILORD. LADY DEATH AND HER COHORTS ARE FREE.
GET OUT OF MY SIGHT.
YOU HAVE QUITE A RESILIENT FAMILY, MARY.
EVEN NOW, YOUR HUSBAND FIGHTS FOR DOMINANCE OF HIS FORM. AND YOUR DAUGHTER, SHE'S BEEN A THORN IN MY SIDE SINCE THE MOMENT SHE ARRIVED IN THE BLACKLANDS.
WHY SO QUIET, MARY?
HAVE YOU GLEANED THAT I LOVE TO HEAR YOUR TORMENT? IS THAT IT?
PUT ME OUT OF MY MISERY, SAGOS.
I BEG YOU, BUT *PLEASE* LET MARIUS
QUAINT.

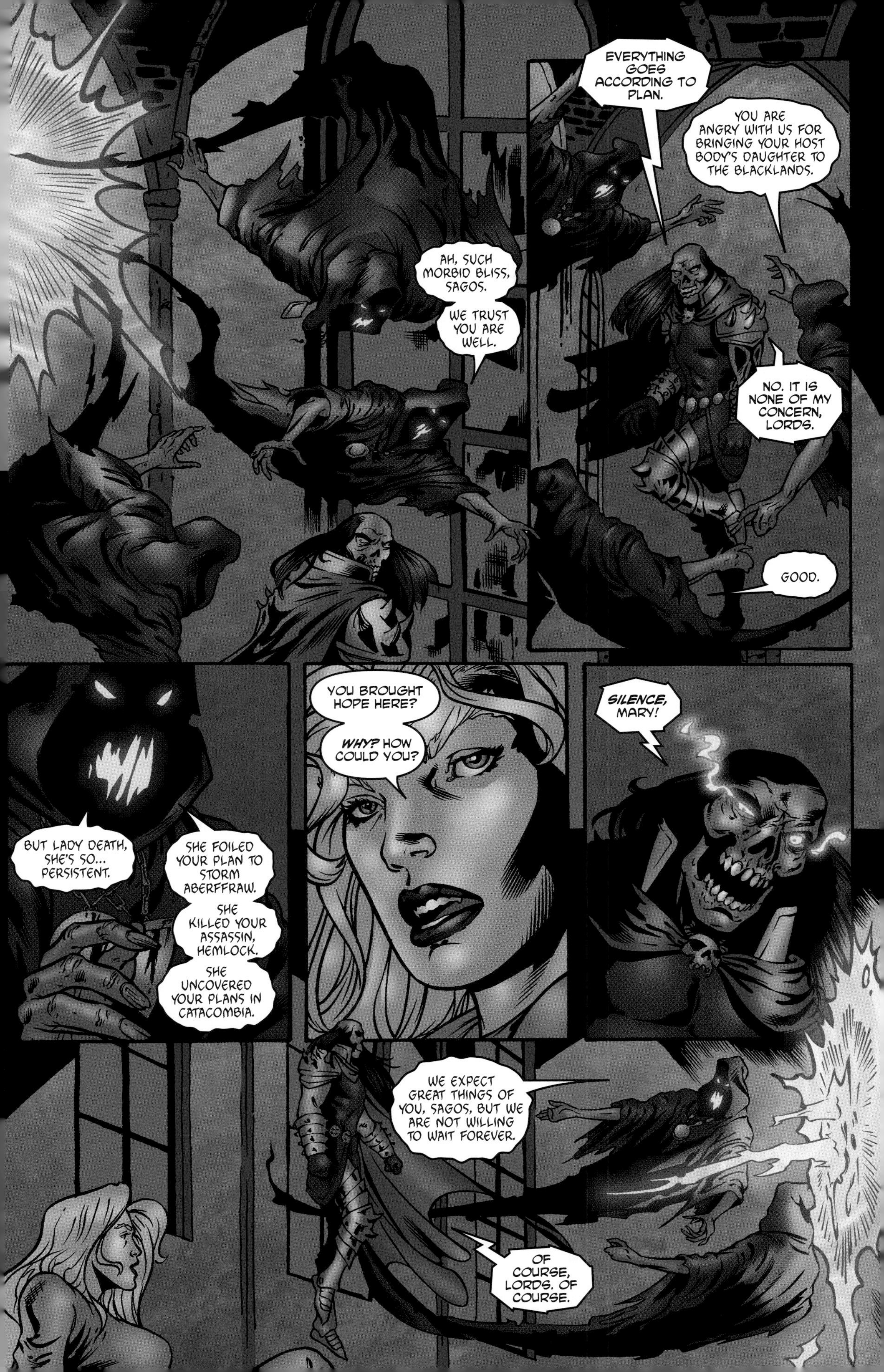
AH, SUCH MORBID BLISS, SAGOS.
WE TRUST YOU ARE WELL.
EVERYTHING GOES ACCORDING TO PLAN.
YOU ARE ANGRY WITH US FOR BRINGING YOUR HOST BODY'S DAUGHTER TO THE BLACKLANDS.
NO. IT IS NONE OF MY CONCERN, LORDS.
GOOD.
BUT LADY DEATH, SHE'S SO... PERSISTENT.
SHE FOILED YOUR PLAN TO STORM ABERFFRAW.
SHE KILLED YOUR ASSASSIN, HEMLOCK.
SHE UNCOVERED YOUR PLANS IN CATACOMBIA.
YOU BROUGHT HOPE HERE?
WHY? HOW COULD YOU?
SILENCE, MARY!
WE EXPECT GREAT THINGS OF YOU, SAGOS, BUT WE ARE NOT WILLING TO WAIT FOREVER.
OF COURSE, LORDS. OF COURSE.

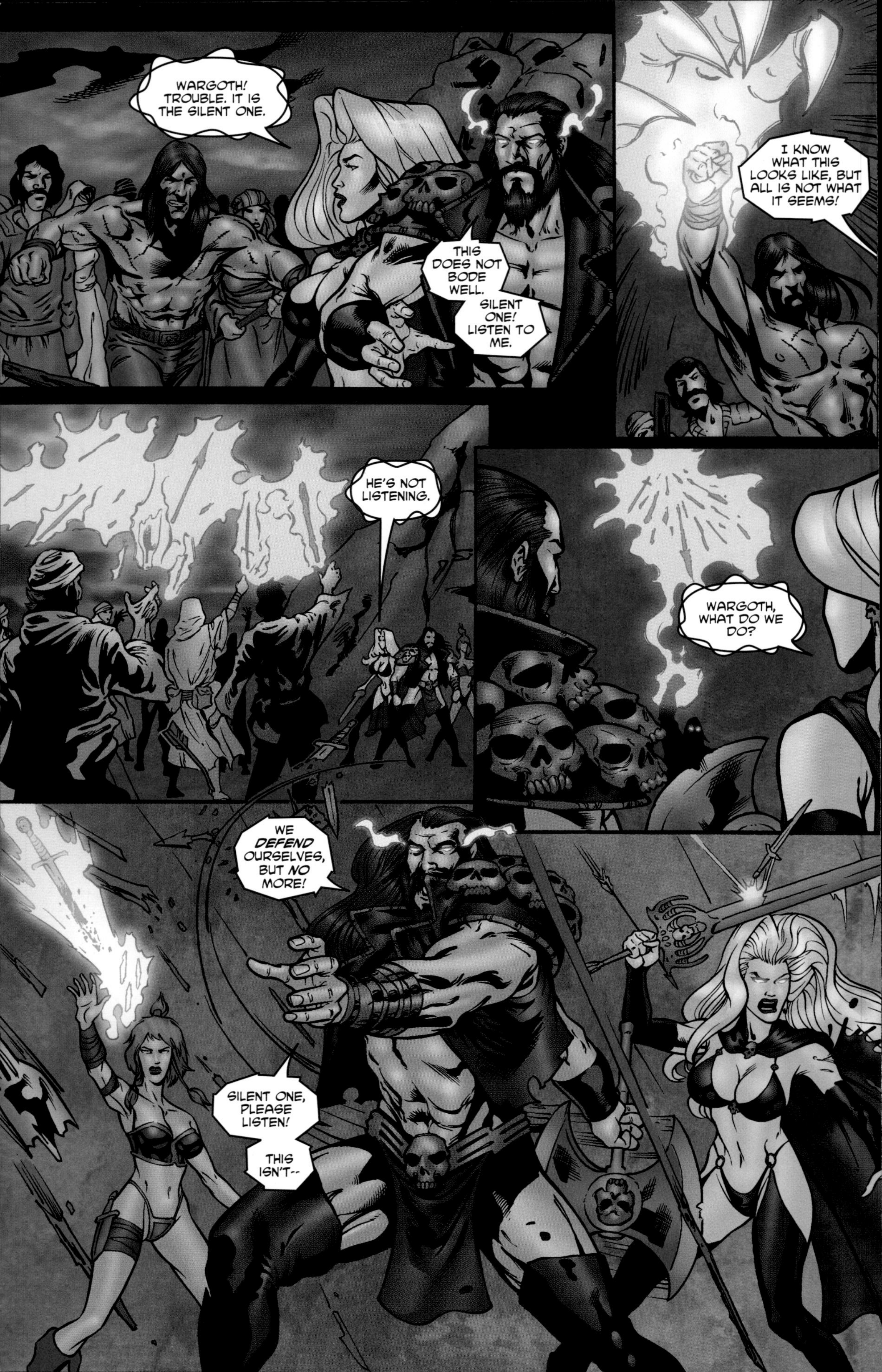
WARGOTH! TROUBLE. IT IS THE SILENT ONE.
THIS DOES NOT BODE WELL.
SILENT ONE! LISTEN TO ME.
I KNOW WHAT THIS LOOKS LIKE, BUT ALL IS NOT WHAT IT SEEMS!
HE'S NOT LISTENING.
WARGOTH, WHAT DO WE DO?
WE DEFEND OURSELVES, BUT NO MORE!
SILENT ONE, PLEASE LISTEN!
THIS ISN'T--

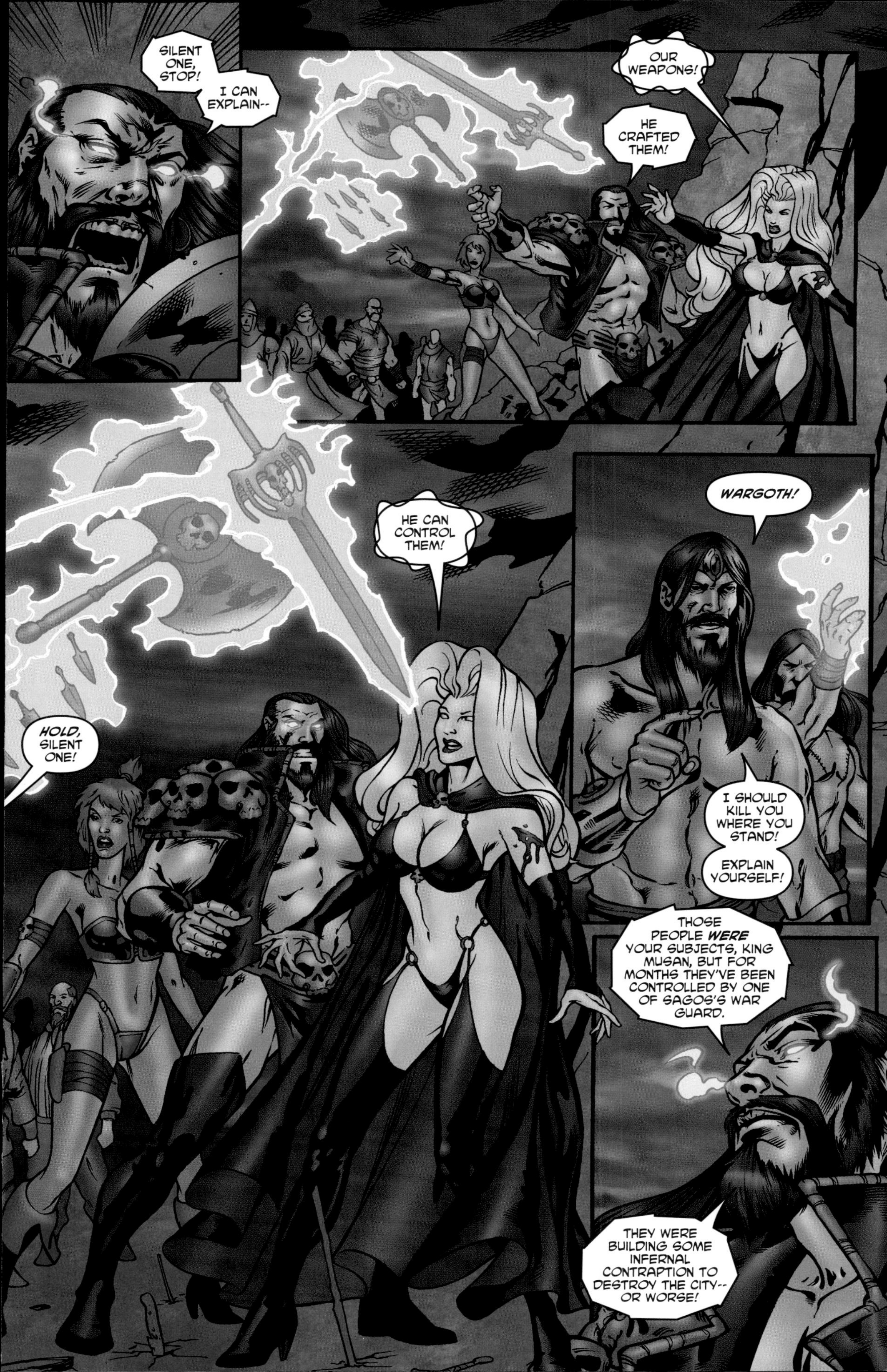
SILENT ONE, STOP!
I CAN EXPLAIN--
OUR WEAPONS!
HE CRAFTED THEM!
HE CAN CONTROL THEM!
HOLD, SILENT ONE!
WARGOTH!
I SHOULD KILL YOU WHERE YOU STAND!
EXPLAIN YOURSELF!
THOSE PEOPLE WERE YOUR SUBJECTS, KING MUSAN, BUT FOR MONTHS THEY'VE BEEN CONTROLLED BY ONE OF SAGOS'S WAR GUARD.
THEY WERE BUILDING SOME INFERNAL CONTRAPTION TO DESTROY THE CITY-- OR WORSE!

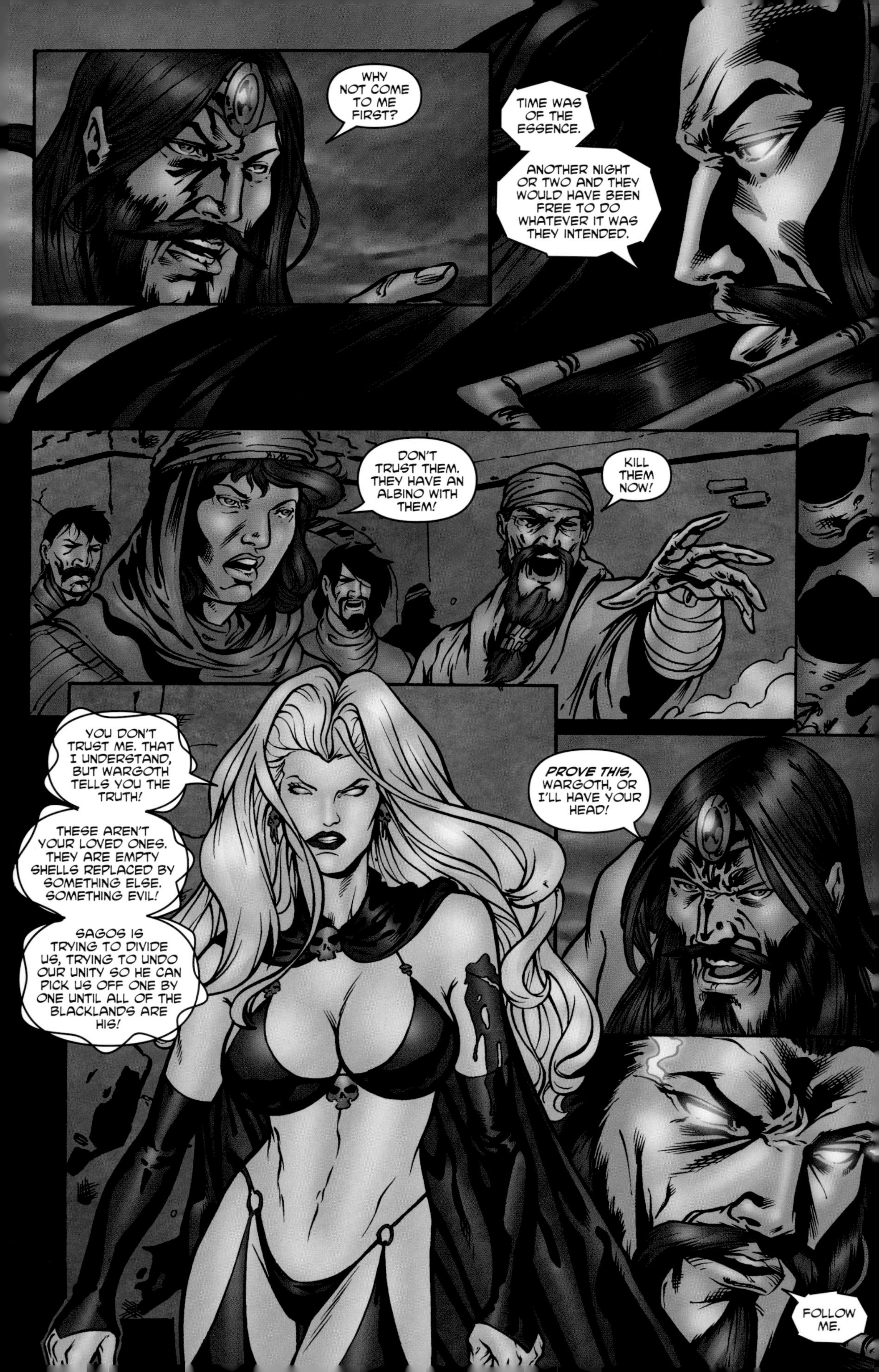
WHY NOT COME TO ME FIRST?
TIME WAS OF THE ESSENCE.
ANOTHER NIGHT OR TWO AND THEY WOULD HAVE BEEN FREE TO DO WHATEVER IT WAS THEY INTENDED.
DON'T TRUST THEM. THEY HAVE AN ALBINO WITH THEM!
KILL THEM NOW!
YOU DON'T TRUST ME. THAT I UNDERSTAND, BUT WARGOTH TELLS YOU THE TRUTH!
THESE AREN'T YOUR LOVED ONES. THEY ARE EMPTY SHELLS REPLACED BY SOMETHING ELSE. SOMETHING EVIL!
SAGOS IS TRYING TO DIVIDE US, TRYING TO UNDO OUR UNITY SO HE CAN PICK US OFF ONE BY ONE UNTIL ALL OF THE BLACKLANDS ARE HIS!
PROVE THIS, WARGOTH, OR I'LL HAVE YOUR HEAD!
FOLLOW ME.

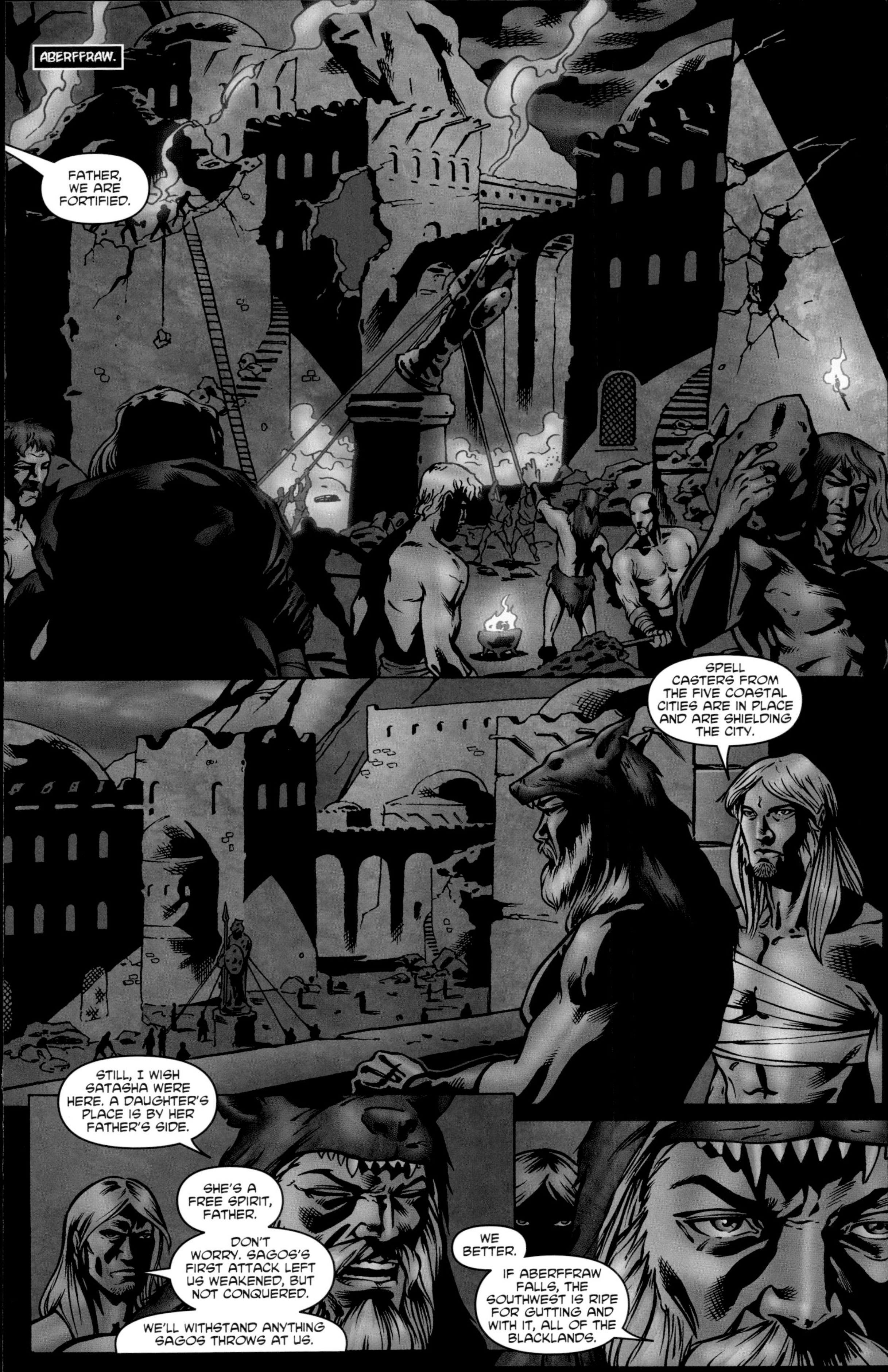
ABERFFRAW.
FATHER, WE ARE FORTIFIED.
SPELL CASTERS FROM THE FIVE COASTAL CITIES ARE IN PLACE AND ARE SHIELDING THE CITY.
STILL, I WISH SATASHA WERE HERE. A DAUGHTER'S PLACE IS BY HER FATHER'S SIDE.
SHE'S A FREE SPIRIT, FATHER.
DON'T WORRY. SAGOS'S FIRST ATTACK LEFT US WEAKENED, BUT NOT CONQUERED.
WE'LL WITHSTAND ANYTHING SAGOS THROWS AT US.
WE BETTER.
IF ABERFFRAW FALLS, THE SOUTHWEST IS RIPE FOR GUTTING AND WITH IT, ALL OF THE BLACKLANDS.

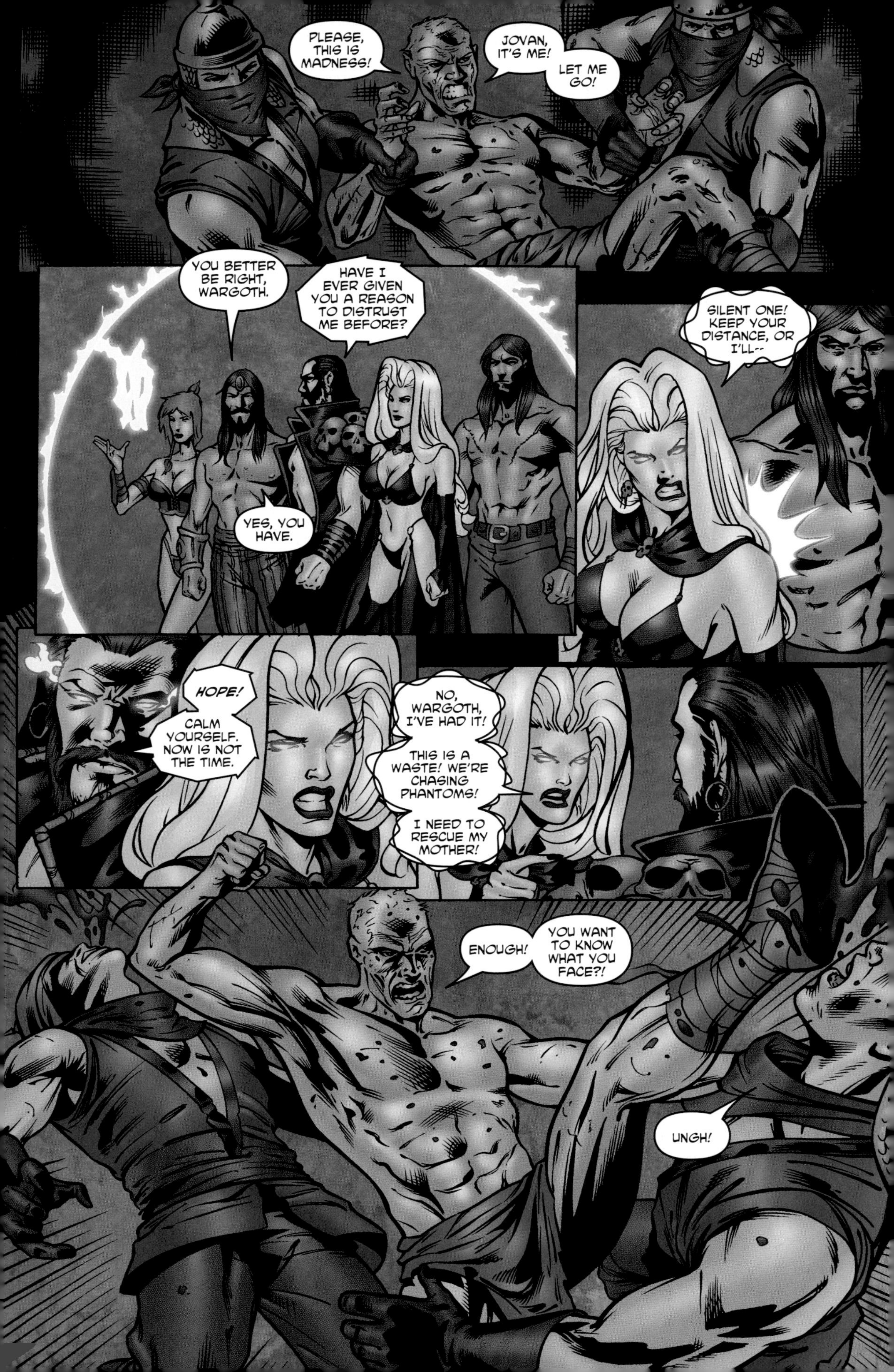
PLEASE, THIS IS MADNESS!
JOVAN, IT'S ME!
LET ME GO!
YOU BETTER BE RIGHT, WARGOTH.
HAVE I EVER GIVEN YOU A REASON TO DISTRUST ME BEFORE?
YES, YOU HAVE.
SILENT ONE! KEEP YOUR DISTANCE, OR I'LL--
HOPE!
CALM YOURSELF. NOW IS NOT THE TIME.
NO, WARGOTH, I'VE HAD IT!
THIS IS A WASTE! WE'RE CHASING PHANTOMS!
I NEED TO RESCUE MY MOTHER!
ENOUGH!
YOU WANT TO KNOW WHAT YOU FACE?!
UNGH!

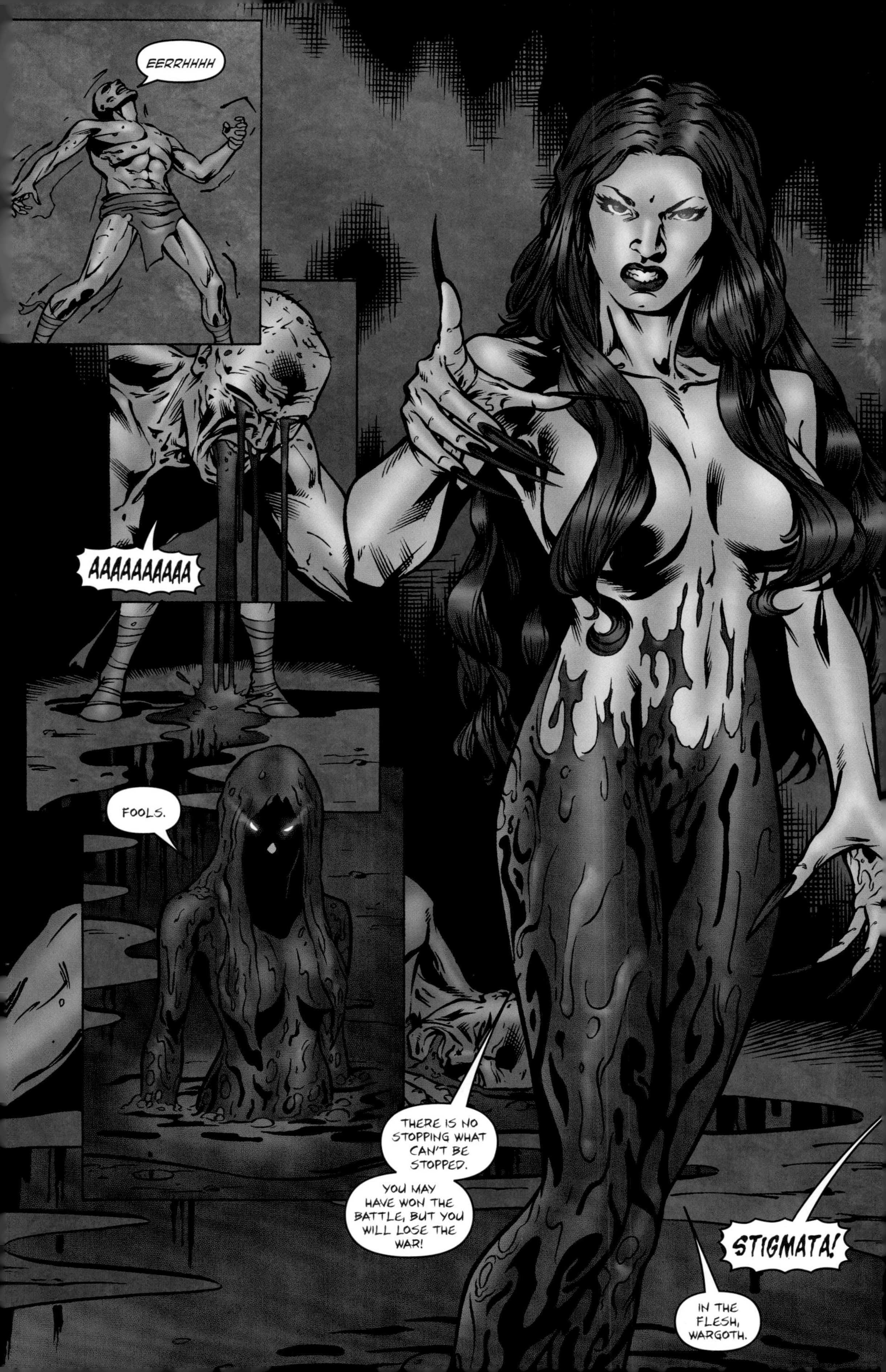
EERRHHHH
AAAAAAAAAA
FOOLS.
THERE IS NO STOPPING WHAT CAN'T BE STOPPED.
YOU MAY HAVE WON THE BATTLE, BUT YOU WILL LOSE THE WAR!
STIGMATA!
IN THE FLESH, WARGOTH.

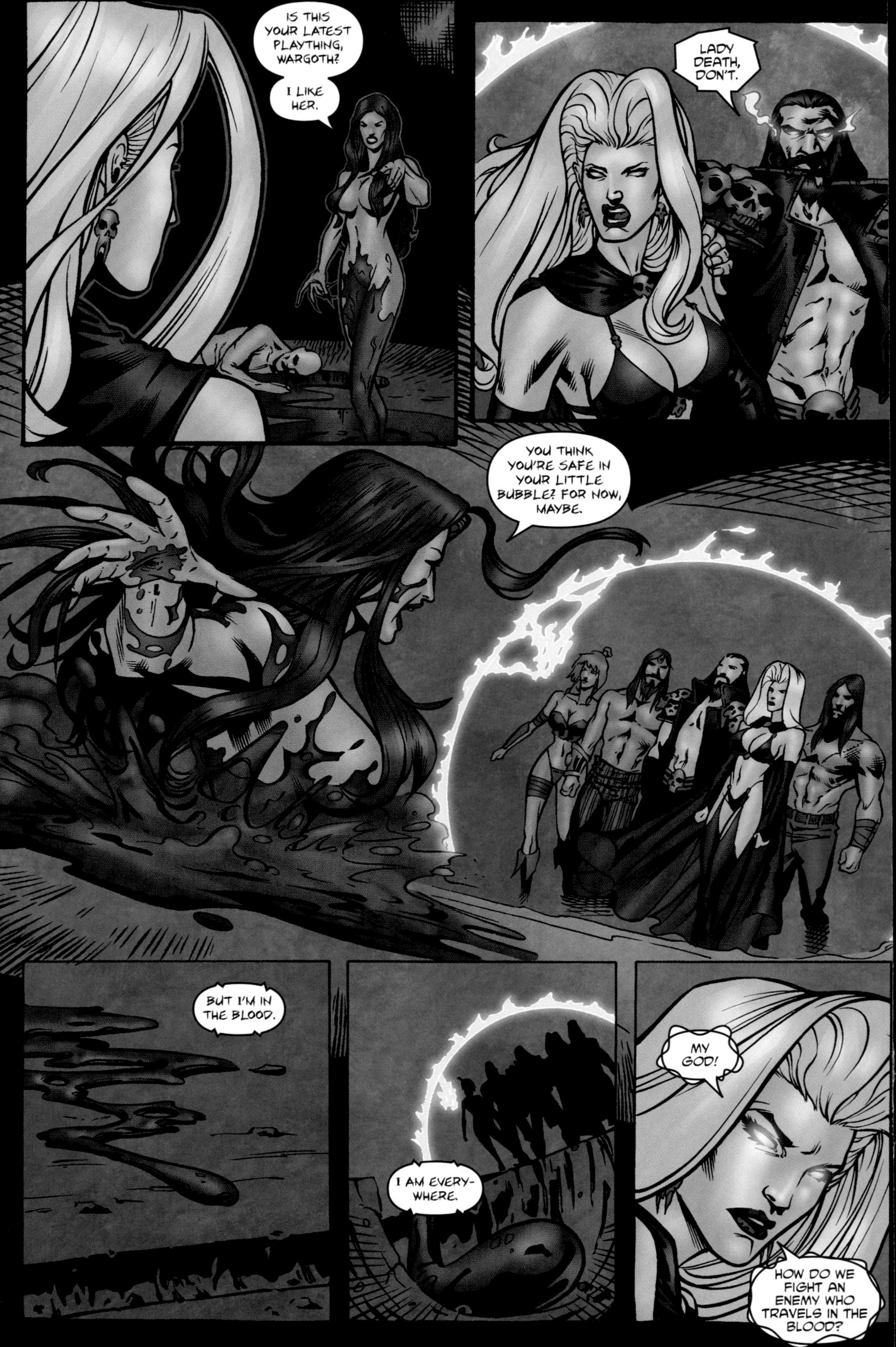
IS THIS YOUR LATEST PLAYTHING, WARGOTH?
I LIKE HER.
LADY DEATH, DON'T.
YOU THINK YOU'RE SAFE IN YOUR LITTLE BUBBLE? FOR NOW, MAYBE.
BUT I'M IN THE BLOOD.
I AM EVERY-WHERE.
MY GOD!
HOW DO WE FIGHT AN ENEMY WHO TRAVELS IN THE BLOOD?

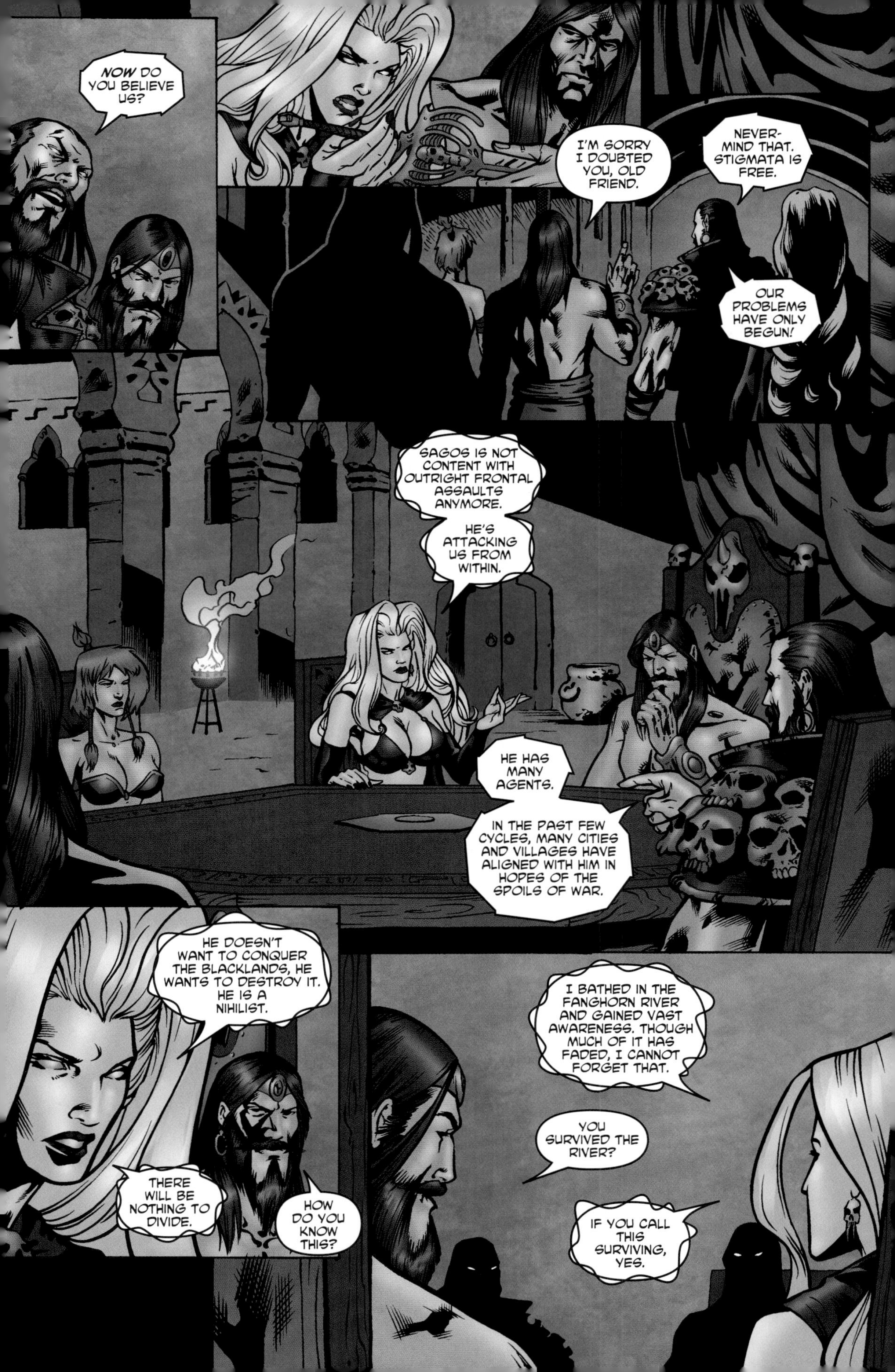
NOW DO YOU BELIEVE US?
I'M SORRY I DOUBTED YOU, OLD FRIEND.
NEVER-MIND THAT. STIGMATA IS FREE.
OUR PROBLEMS HAVE ONLY BEGUN!
SAGOS IS NOT CONTENT WITH OUTRIGHT FRONTAL ASSAULTS ANYMORE.
HE'S ATTACKING US FROM WITHIN.
HE HAS MANY AGENTS.
IN THE PAST FEW CYCLES, MANY CITIES AND VILLAGES HAVE ALIGNED WITH HIM IN HOPES OF THE SPOILS OF WAR.
HE DOESN'T WANT TO CONQUER THE BLACKLANDS, HE WANTS TO DESTROY IT. HE IS A NIHILIST.
THERE WILL BE NOTHING TO DIVIDE.
HOW DO YOU KNOW THIS?
I BATHED IN THE FANGHORN RIVER AND GAINED VAST AWARENESS. THOUGH MUCH OF IT HAS FADED, I CANNOT FORGET THAT.
YOU SURVIVED THE RIVER?
IF YOU CALL THIS SURVIVING, YES.

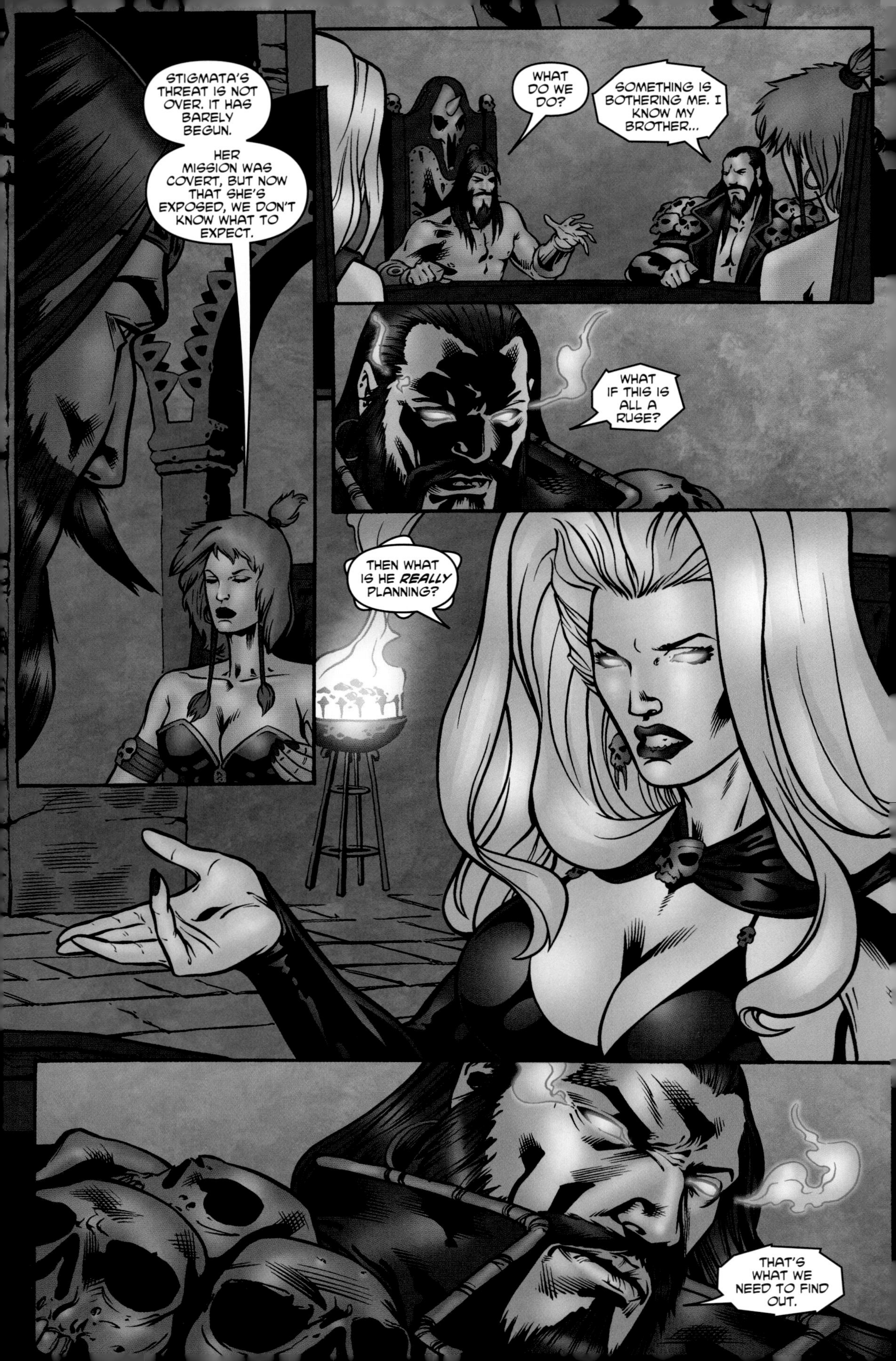
STIGMATA'S THREAT IS NOT OVER. IT HAS BARELY BEGUN.
HER MISSION WAS COVERT, BUT NOW THAT SHE'S EXPOSED, WE DON'T KNOW WHAT TO EXPECT.
WHAT DO WE DO?
SOMETHING IS BOTHERING ME. I KNOW MY BROTHER...
WHAT IF THIS IS ALL A RUSE?
THEN WHAT IS HE *REALLY* PLANNING?
THAT'S WHAT WE NEED TO FIND OUT.

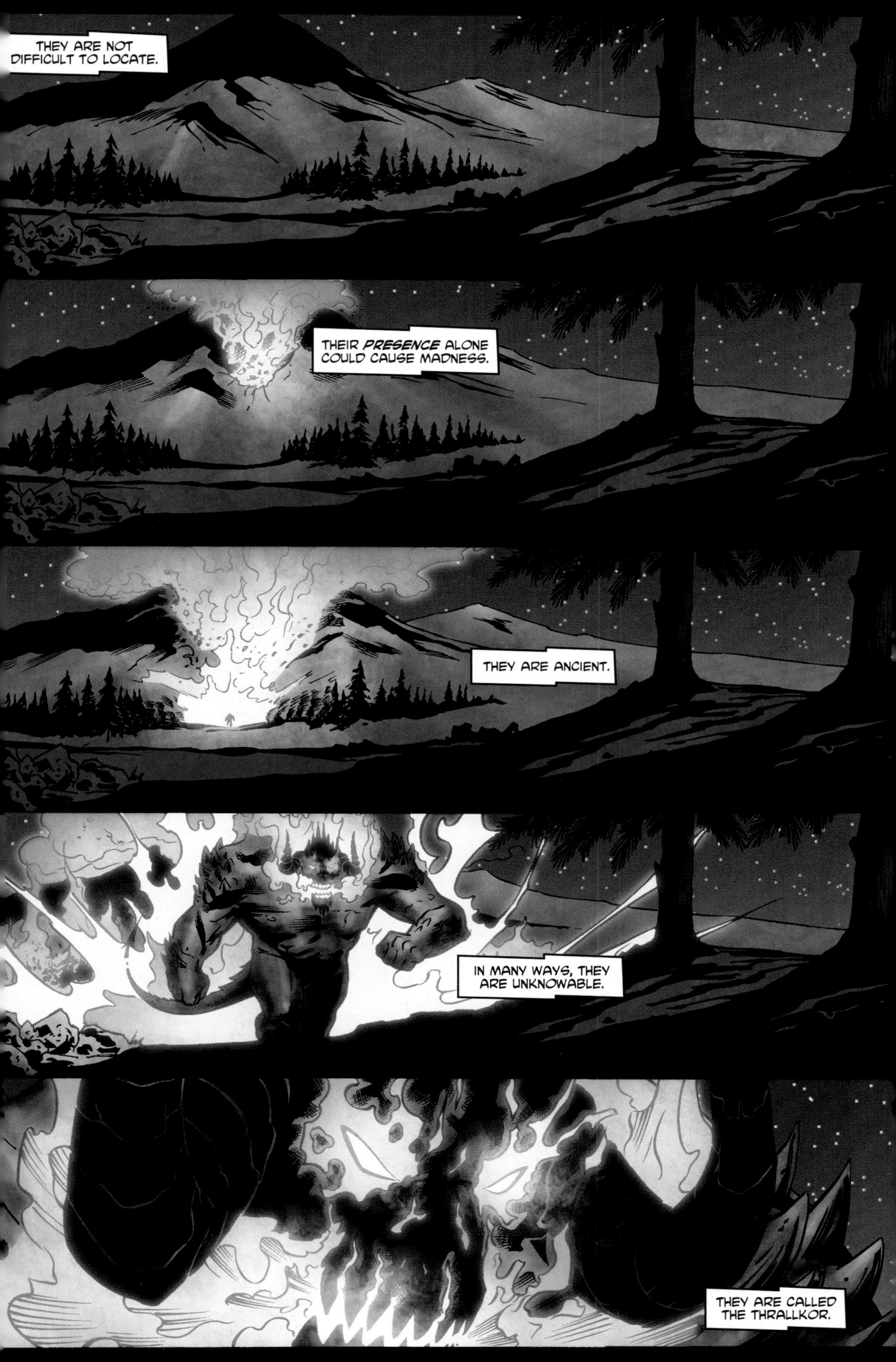
THEY ARE NOT DIFFICULT TO LOCATE.
THEIR *PRESENCE* ALONE COULD CAUSE MADNESS.
THEY ARE ANCIENT.
IN MANY WAYS, THEY ARE UNKNOWABLE.
THEY ARE CALLED THE THRALLKOR.

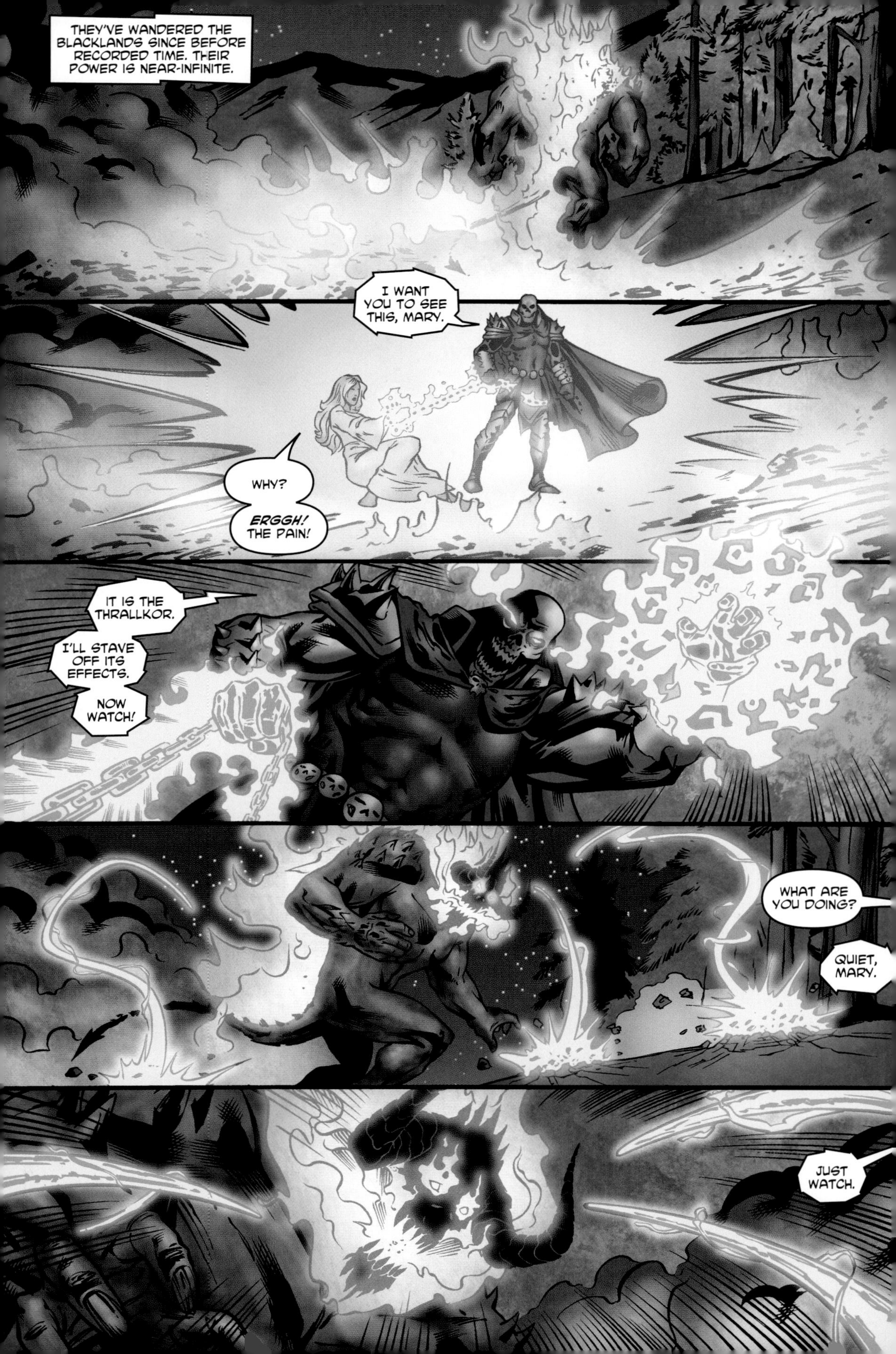
THEY'VE WANDERED THE BLACKLANDS SINCE BEFORE RECORDED TIME. THEIR POWER IS NEAR-INFINITE.
I WANT YOU TO SEE THIS, MARY.
WHY?
ERGGH! THE PAIN!
IT IS THE THRALLKOR.
I'LL STAVE OFF ITS EFFECTS.
NOW WATCH!
WHAT ARE YOU DOING?
QUIET, MARY.
JUST WATCH.

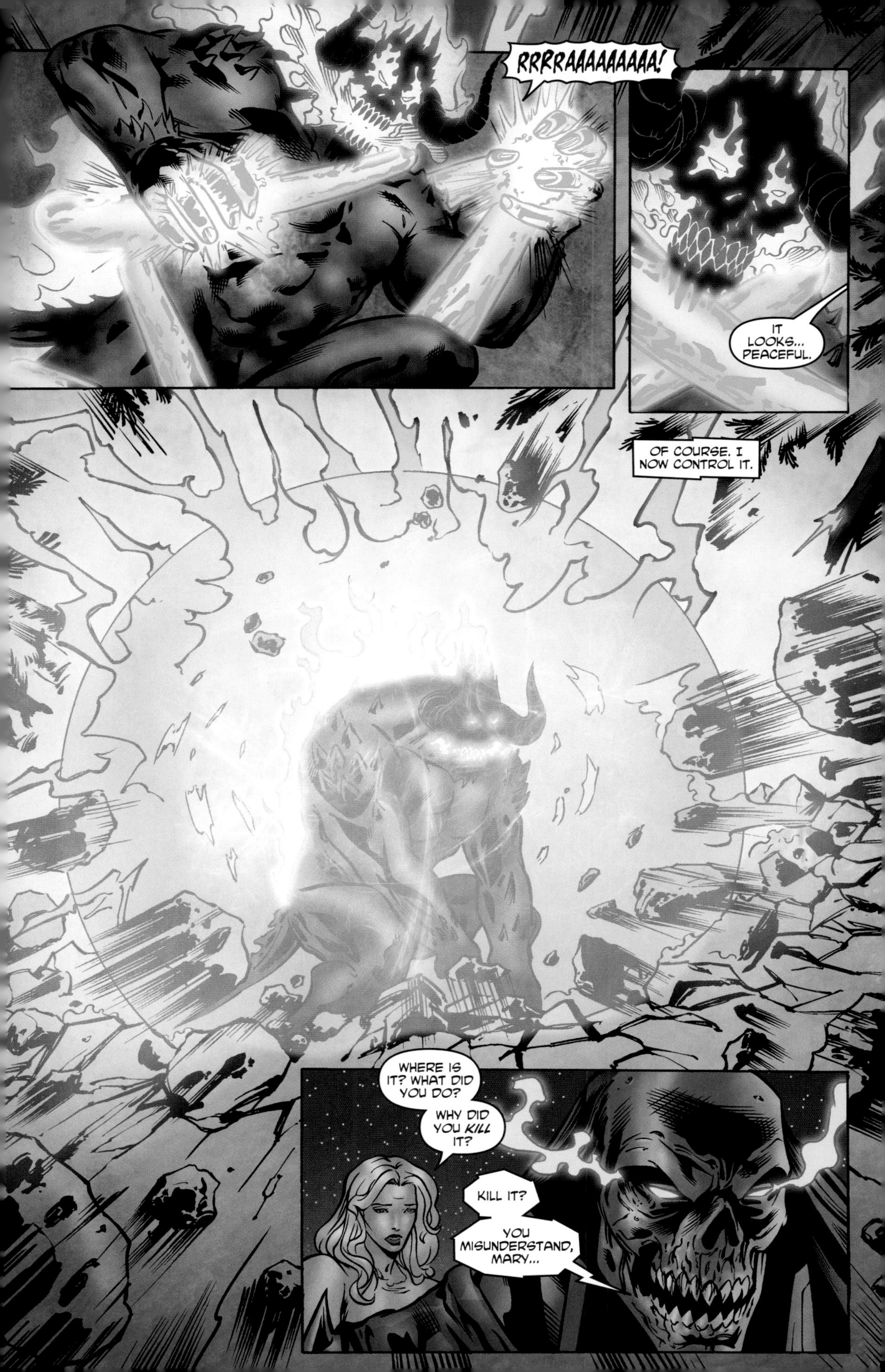
RRRRAAAAAAAAA!
IT LOOKS... PEACEFUL.
OF COURSE. I NOW CONTROL IT.
WHERE IS IT? WHAT DID YOU DO?
WHY DID YOU *KILL* IT?
KILL IT?
YOU MISUNDERSTAND, MARY...

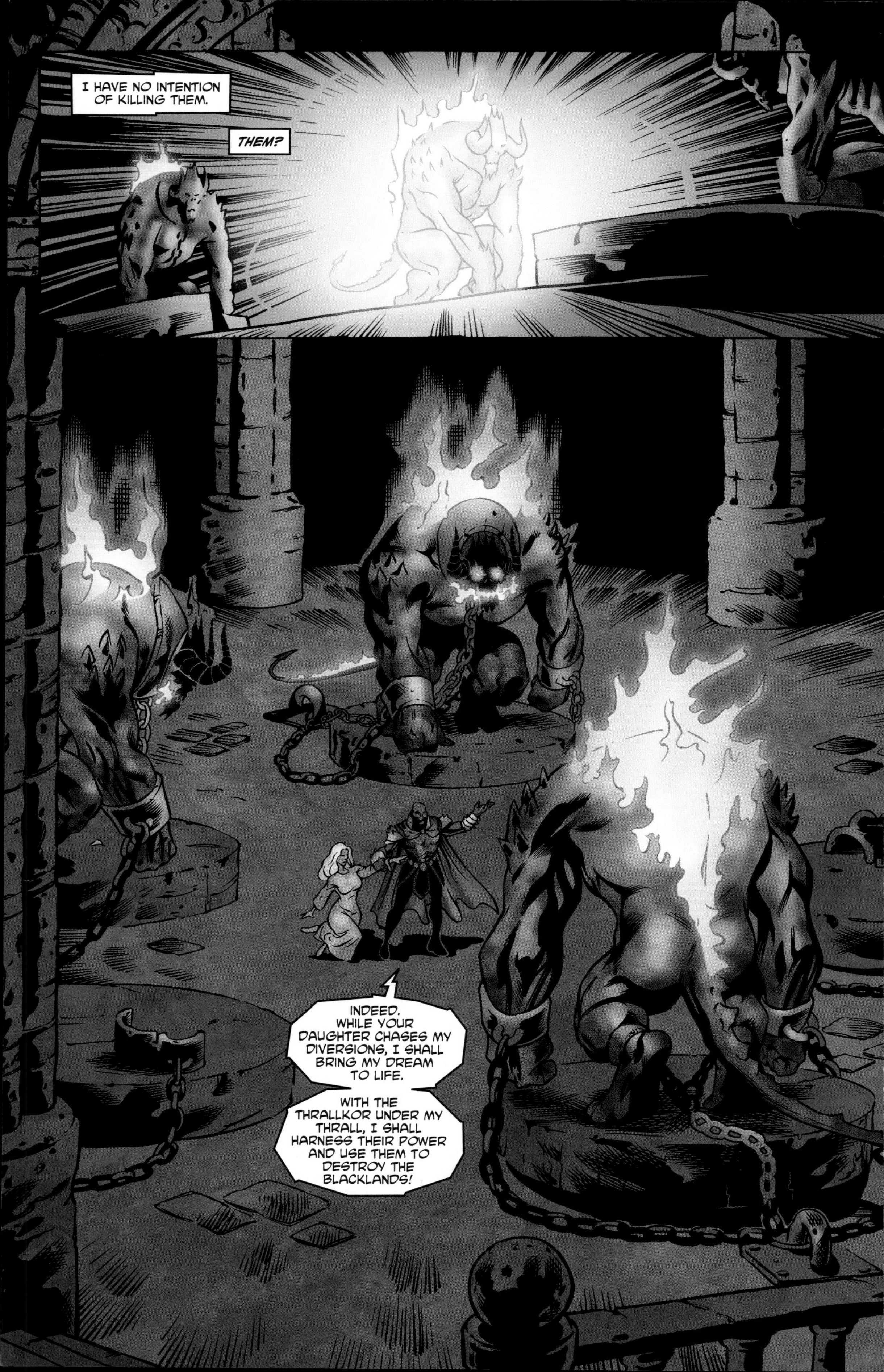
I HAVE NO INTENTION OF KILLING THEM.
THEM?
INDEED. WHILE YOUR DAUGHTER CHASES MY DIVERSIONS, I SHALL BRING MY DREAM TO LIFE.
WITH THE THRALLKOR UNDER MY THRALL, I SHALL HARNESS THEIR POWER AND USE THEM TO DESTROY THE BLACKLANDS!

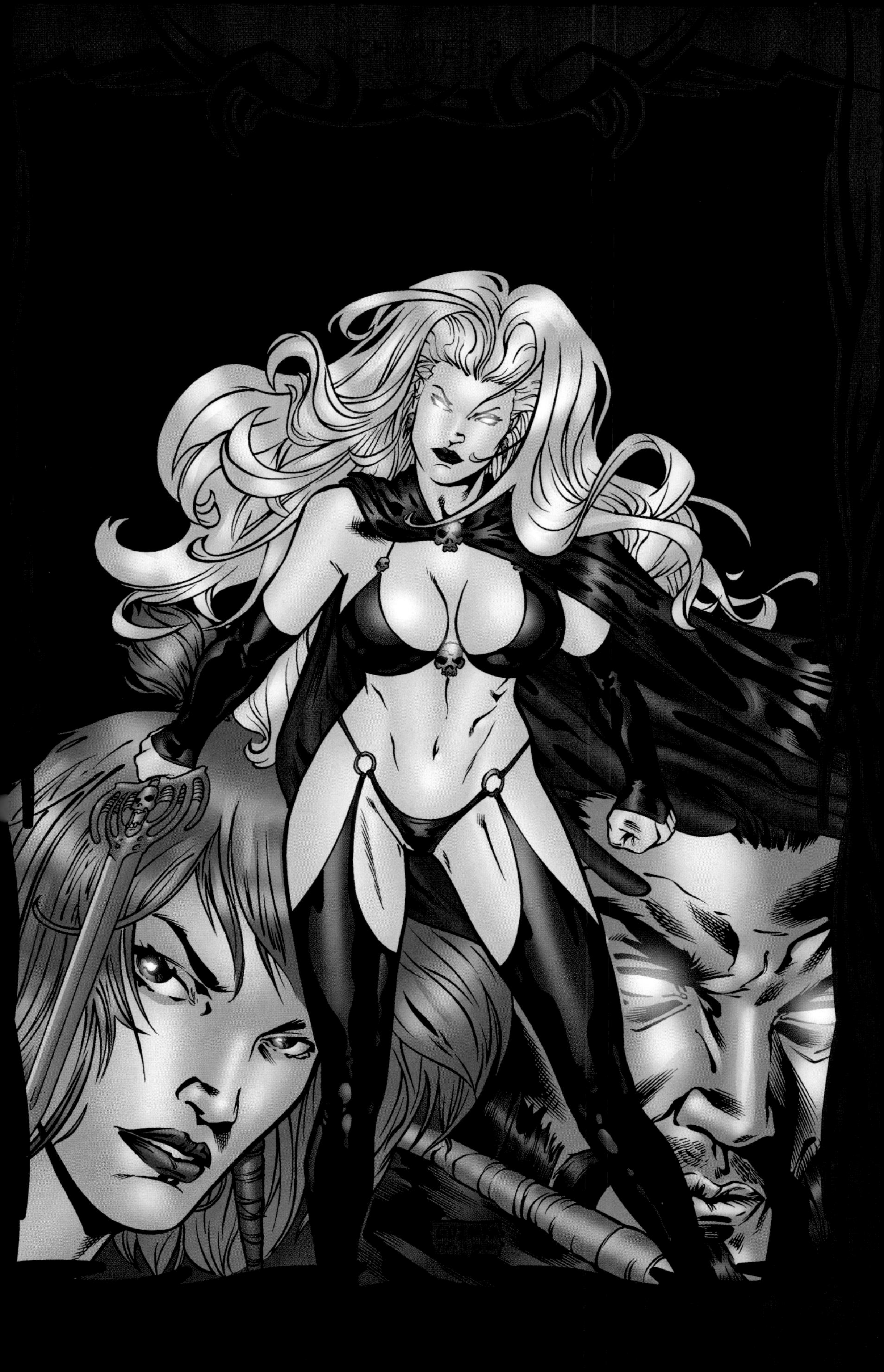
CHAPTER 3

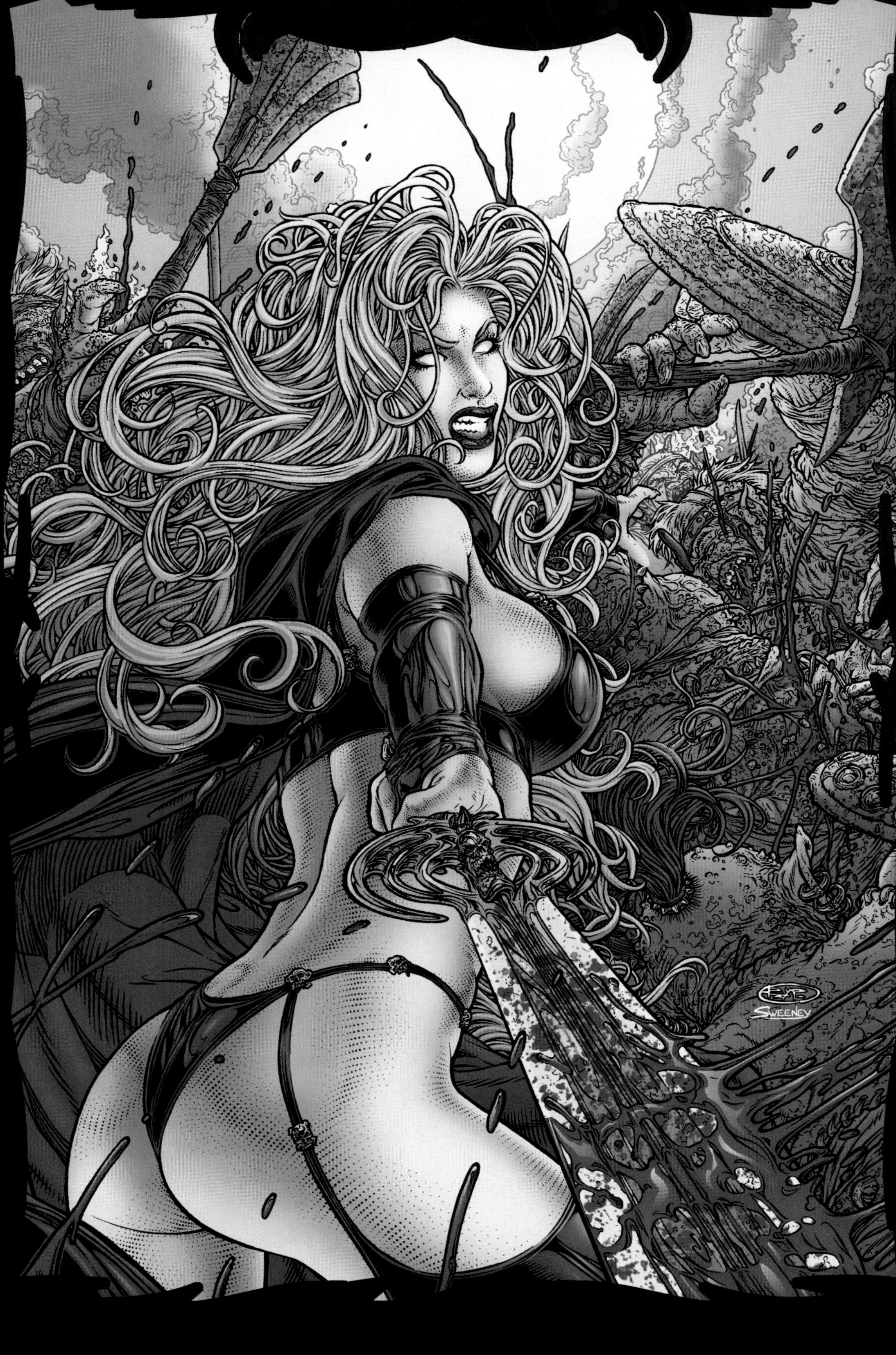
SWEENEY

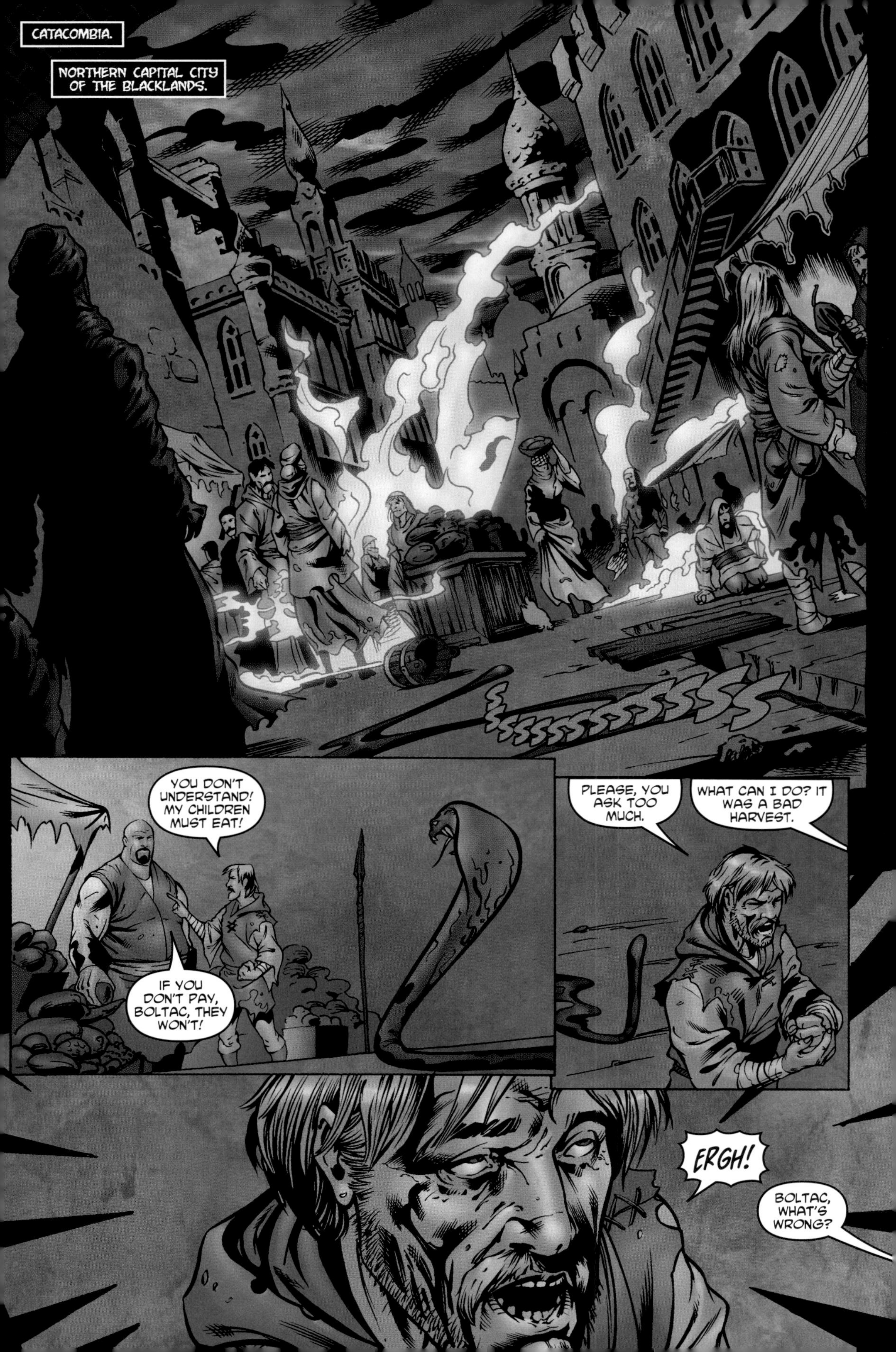
CATACOMBIA.
NORTHERN CAPITAL CITY OF THE BLACKLANDS.
SSSSSSSSSSSSSSSS
YOU DON'T UNDERSTAND! MY CHILDREN MUST EAT!
IF YOU DON'T PAY, BOLTAC, THEY WON'T!
PLEASE, YOU ASK TOO MUCH.
WHAT CAN I DO? IT WAS A BAD HARVEST.
ERGH!
BOLTAC, WHAT'S WRONG?

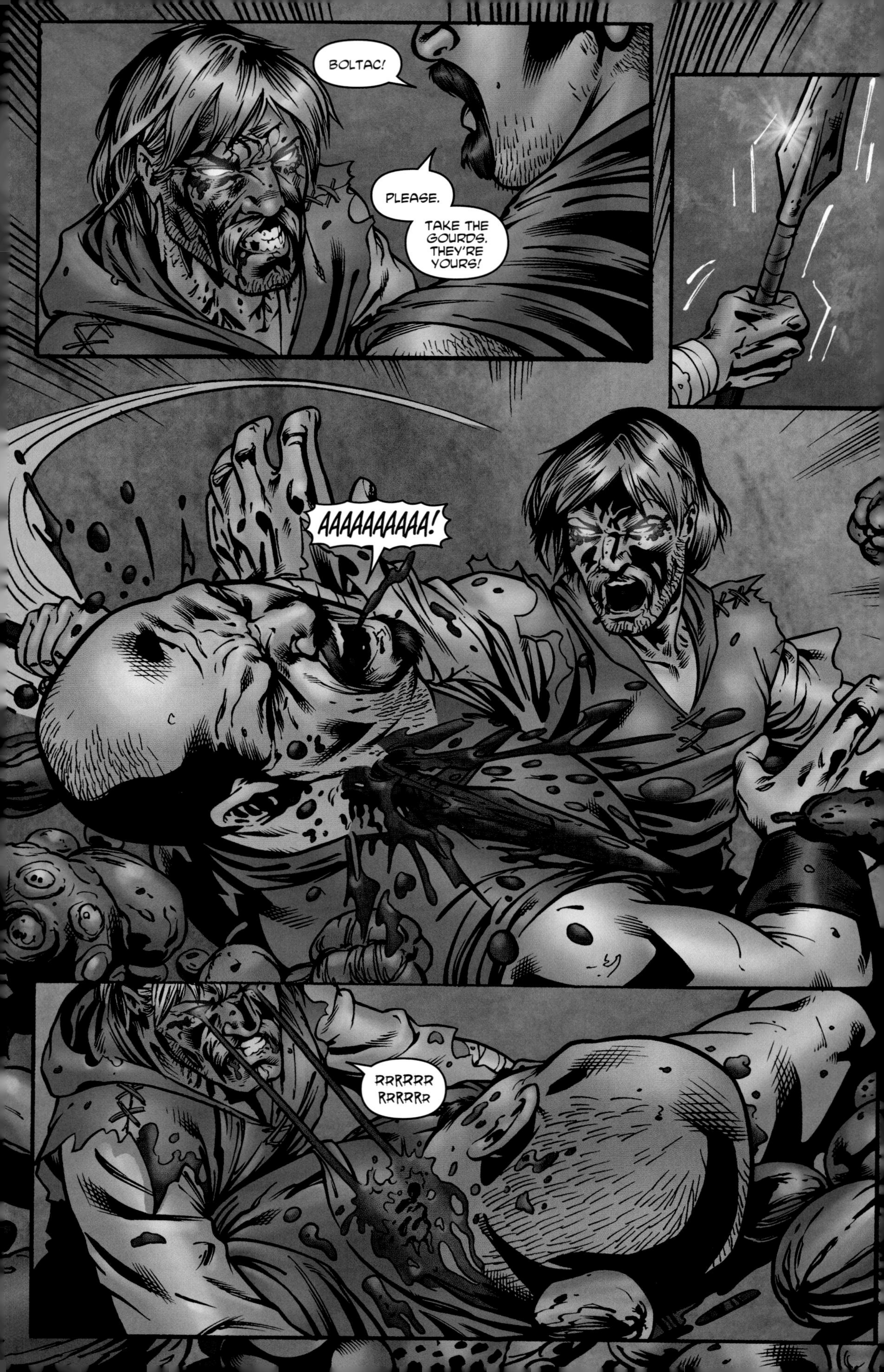
BOLTAC!
PLEASE.
TAKE THE GOURDS. THEY'RE YOURS!
AAAAAAAAAA!
RRRRRR RRRRRR

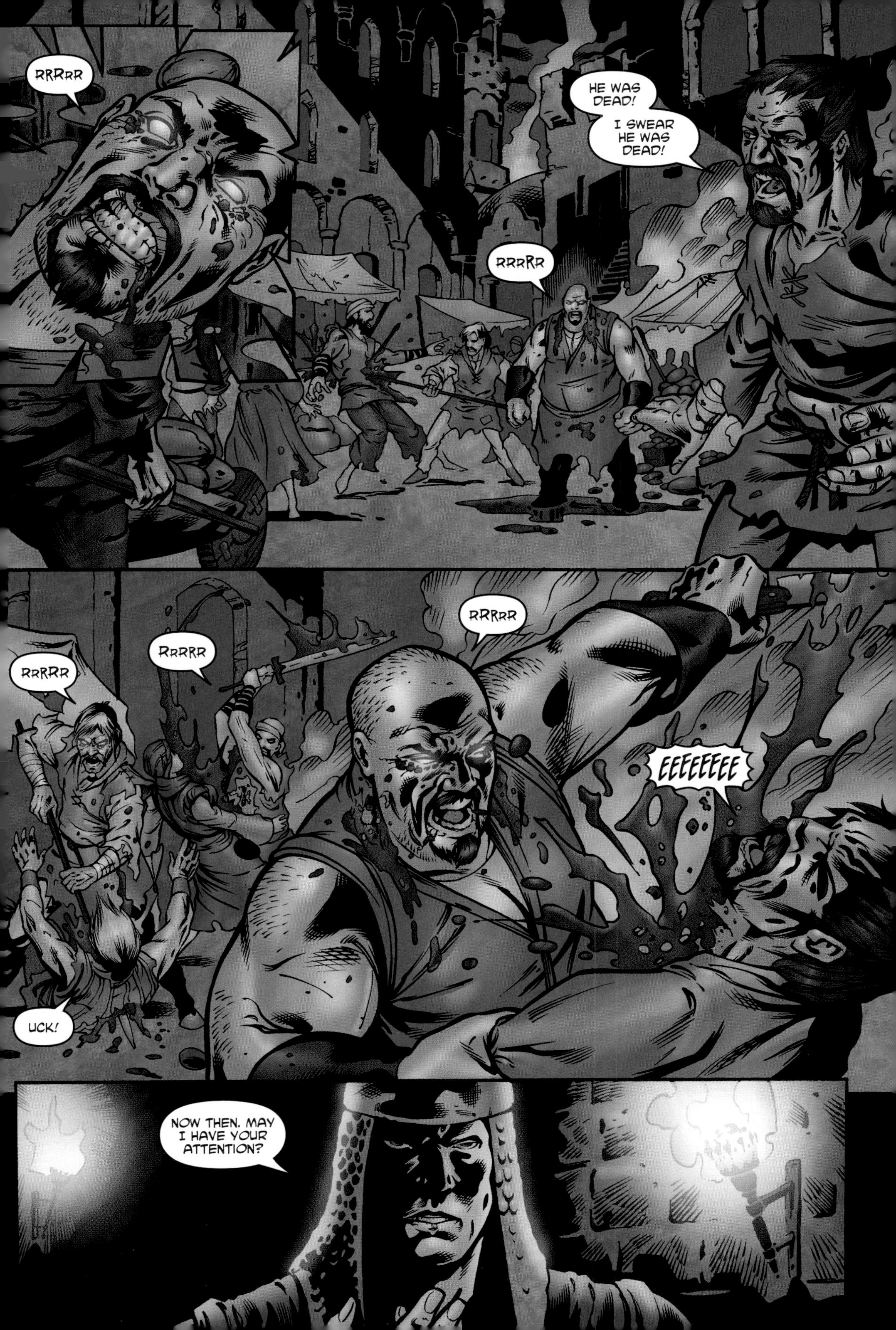
RRRRR
HE WAS DEAD!
I SWEAR HE WAS DEAD!
RRRRR
RRRRR
RRRRR
RRRRR
EEEEEEEE
UCK!
NOW THEN. MAY I HAVE YOUR ATTENTION?

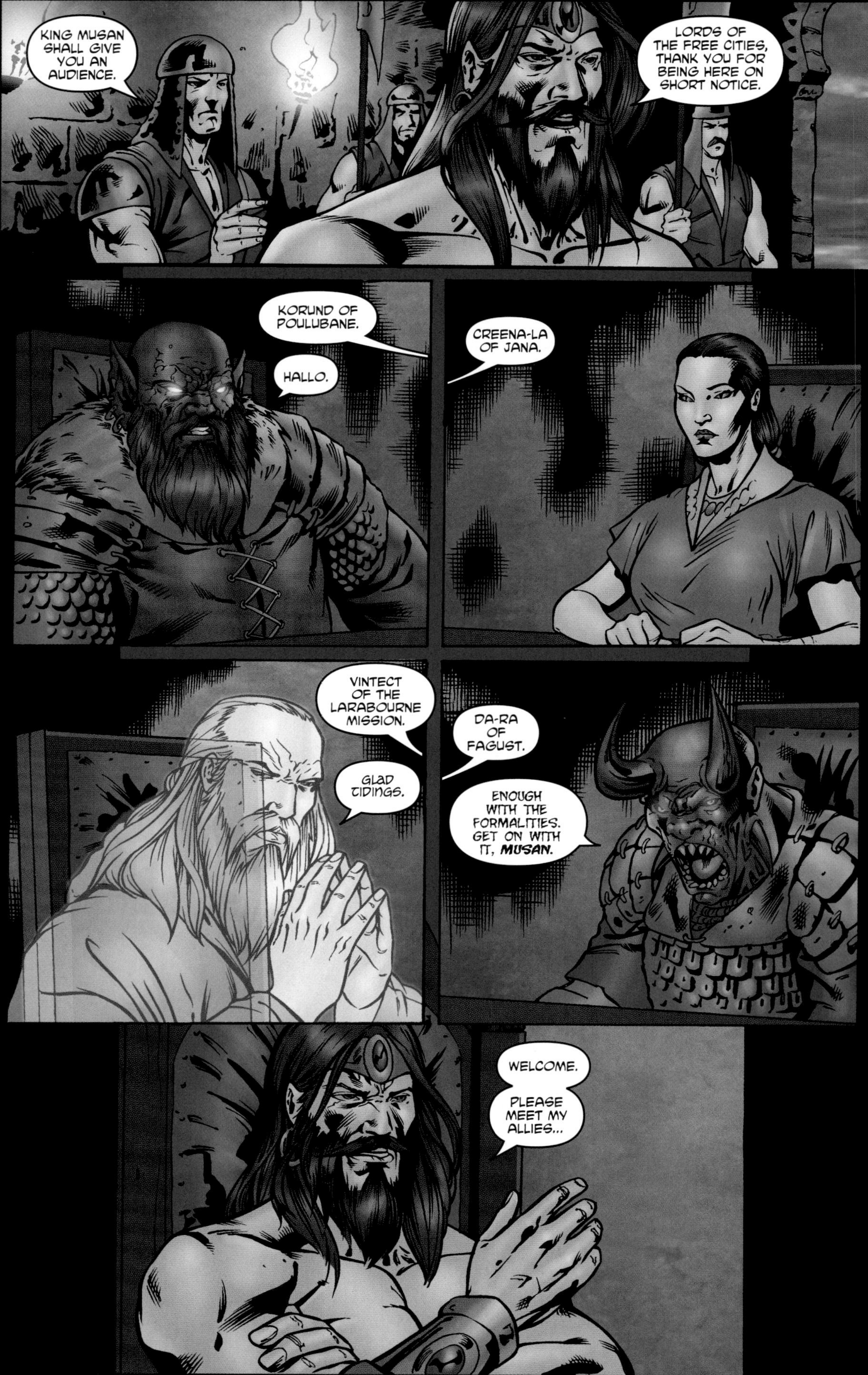
KING MUSAN SHALL GIVE YOU AN AUDIENCE.
LORDS OF THE FREE CITIES, THANK YOU FOR BEING HERE ON SHORT NOTICE.
KORUND OF POULUBANE.
HALLO.
CREENA-LA OF JANA.
VINTECT OF THE LARABOURNE MISSION.
GLAD TIDINGS.
DA-RA OF FAGUST.
ENOUGH WITH THE FORMALITIES. GET ON WITH IT, **MUSAN**.
WELCOME.
PLEASE MEET MY ALLIES...

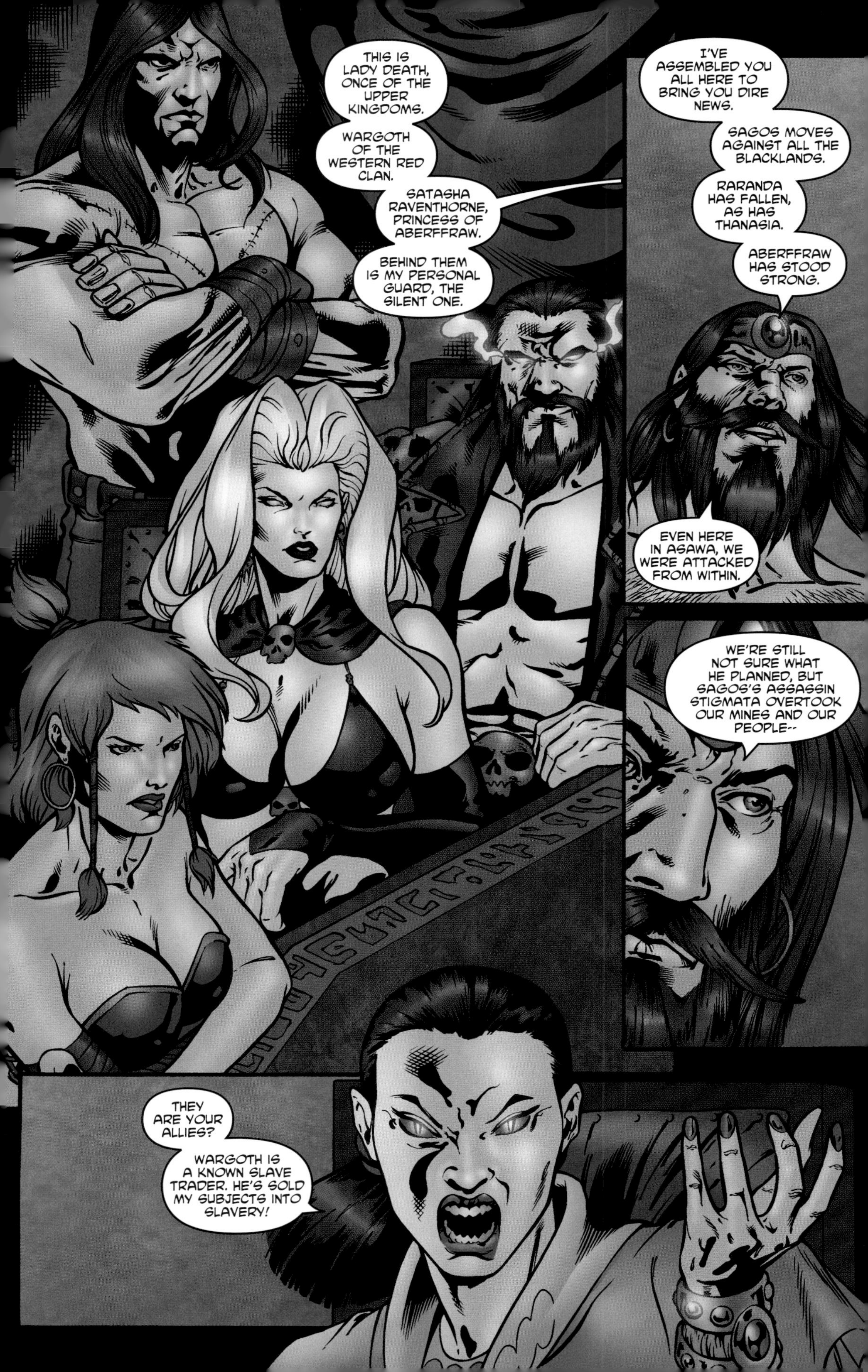

THIS IS LADY DEATH, ONCE OF THE UPPER KINGDOMS.
WARGOTH OF THE WESTERN RED CLAN.
SATASHA RAVENTHORNE, PRINCESS OF ABERFFRAW.
BEHIND THEM IS MY PERSONAL GUARD, THE SILENT ONE.
I'VE ASSEMBLED YOU ALL HERE TO BRING YOU DIRE NEWS.
SAGOS MOVES AGAINST ALL THE BLACKLANDS.
RARANDA HAS FALLEN, AS HAS THANASIA.
ABERFFRAW HAS STOOD STRONG.
EVEN HERE IN ASAWA, WE WERE ATTACKED FROM WITHIN.
WE'RE STILL NOT SURE WHAT HE PLANNED, BUT SAGOS'S ASSASSIN STIGMATA OVERTOOK OUR MINES AND OUR PEOPLE--
THEY ARE YOUR ALLIES?
WARGOTH IS A KNOWN SLAVE TRADER. HE'S SOLD MY SUBJECTS INTO SLAVERY!

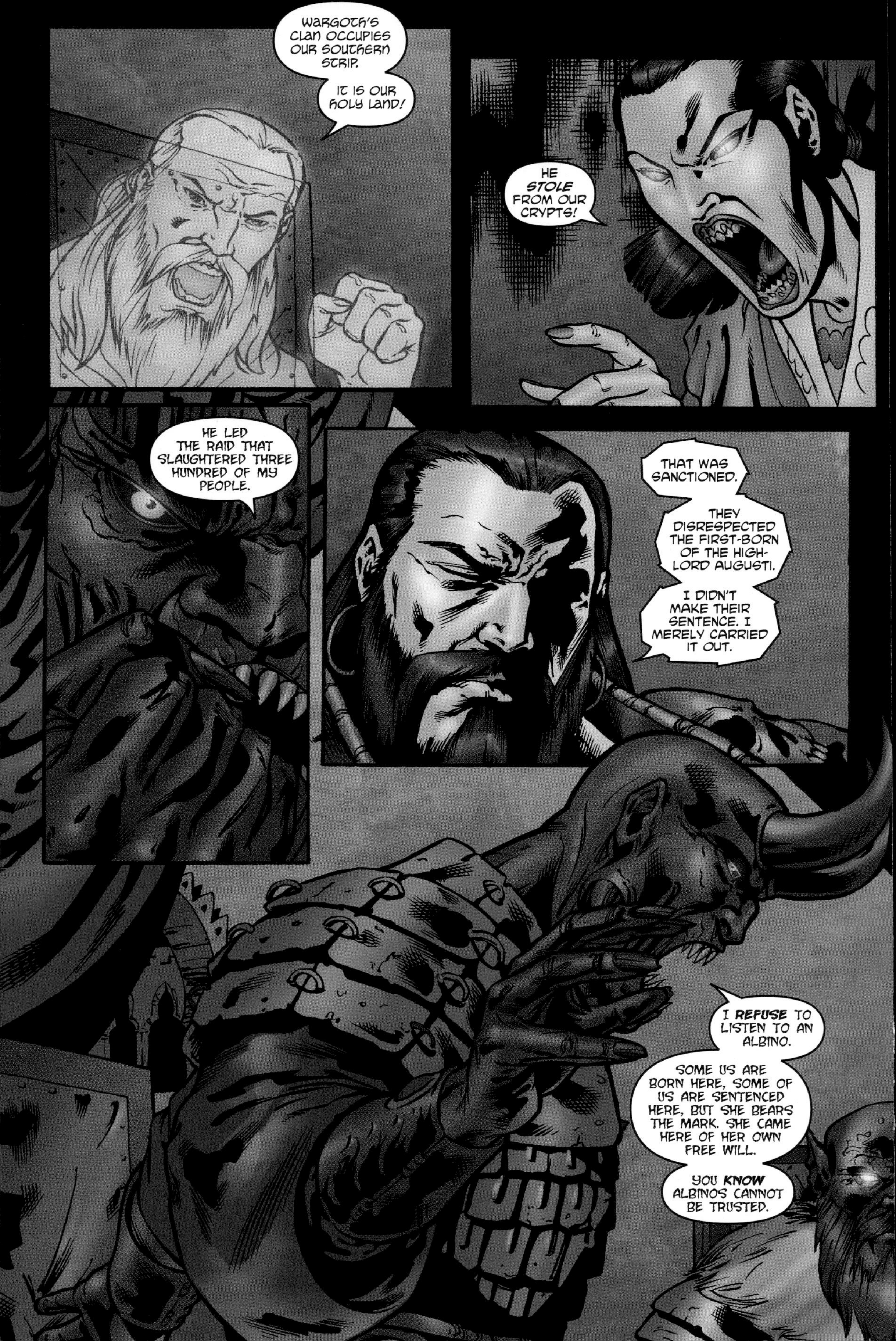
WARGOTH'S CLAN OCCUPIES OUR SOUTHERN STRIP.
IT IS OUR HOLY LAND!
HE STOLE FROM OUR CRYPTS!
HE LED THE RAID THAT SLAUGHTERED THREE HUNDRED OF MY PEOPLE.
THAT WAS SANCTIONED.
THEY DISRESPECTED THE FIRST-BORN OF THE HIGH-LORD AUGUSTI.
I DIDN'T MAKE THEIR SENTENCE. I MERELY CARRIED IT OUT.
I REFUSE TO LISTEN TO AN ALBINO.
SOME US ARE BORN HERE, SOME OF US ARE SENTENCED HERE, BUT SHE BEARS THE MARK. SHE CAME HERE OF HER OWN FREE WILL.
YOU KNOW ALBINOS CANNOT BE TRUSTED.

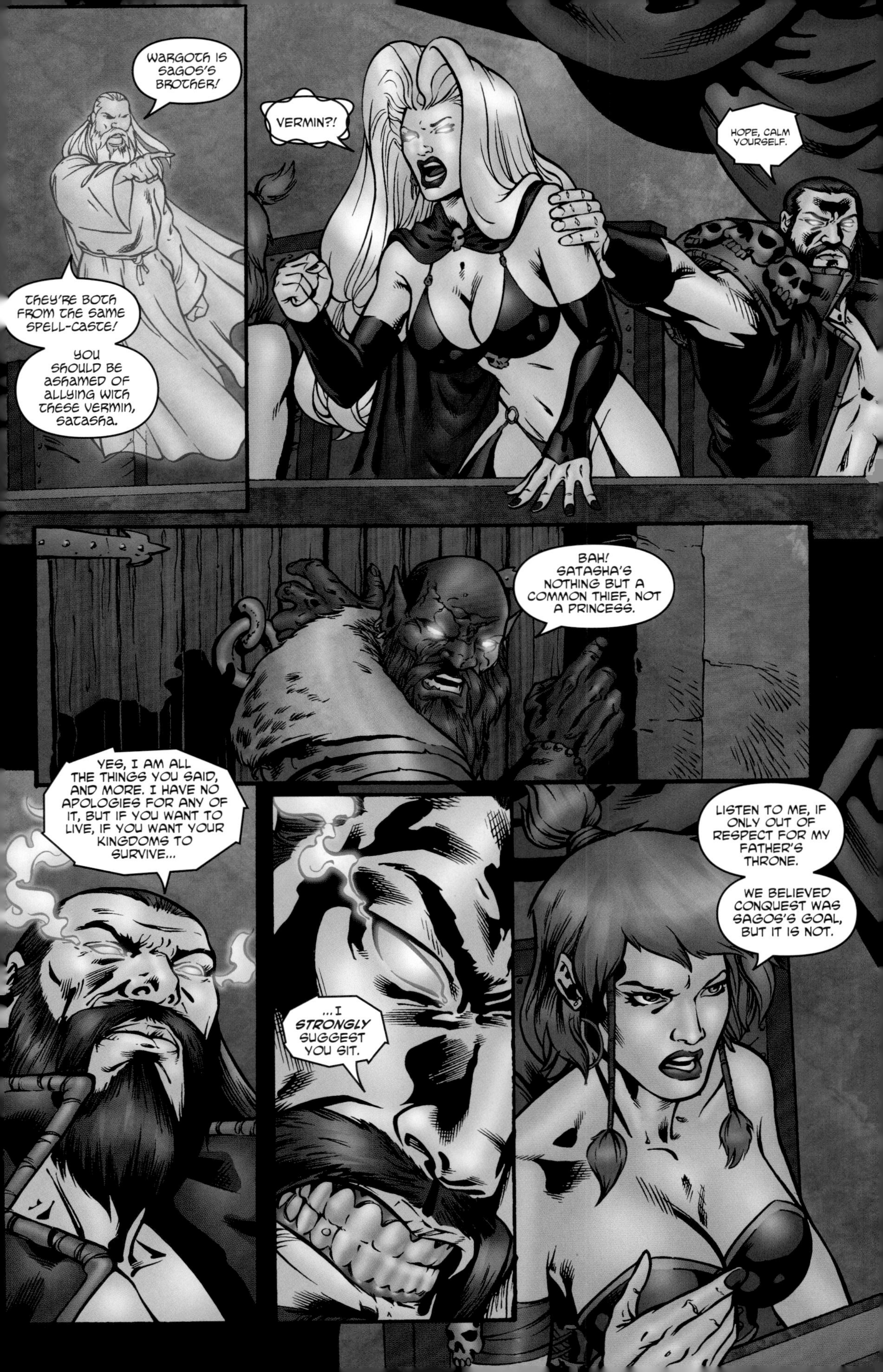
WARGOTH IS SAGOS'S BROTHER!
THEY'RE BOTH FROM THE SAME SPELL-CASTE!
YOU SHOULD BE ASHAMED OF ALLYING WITH THESE VERMIN, SATASHA.
VERMIN?!
HOPE, CALM YOURSELF.
BAH! SATASHA'S NOTHING BUT A COMMON THIEF, NOT A PRINCESS.
YES, I AM ALL THE THINGS YOU SAID, AND MORE. I HAVE NO APOLOGIES FOR ANY OF IT, BUT IF YOU WANT TO LIVE, IF YOU WANT YOUR KINGDOMS TO SURVIVE...
...I *STRONGLY* SUGGEST YOU SIT.
LISTEN TO ME, IF ONLY OUT OF RESPECT FOR MY FATHER'S THRONE.
WE BELIEVED CONQUEST WAS SAGOS'S GOAL, BUT IT IS NOT.

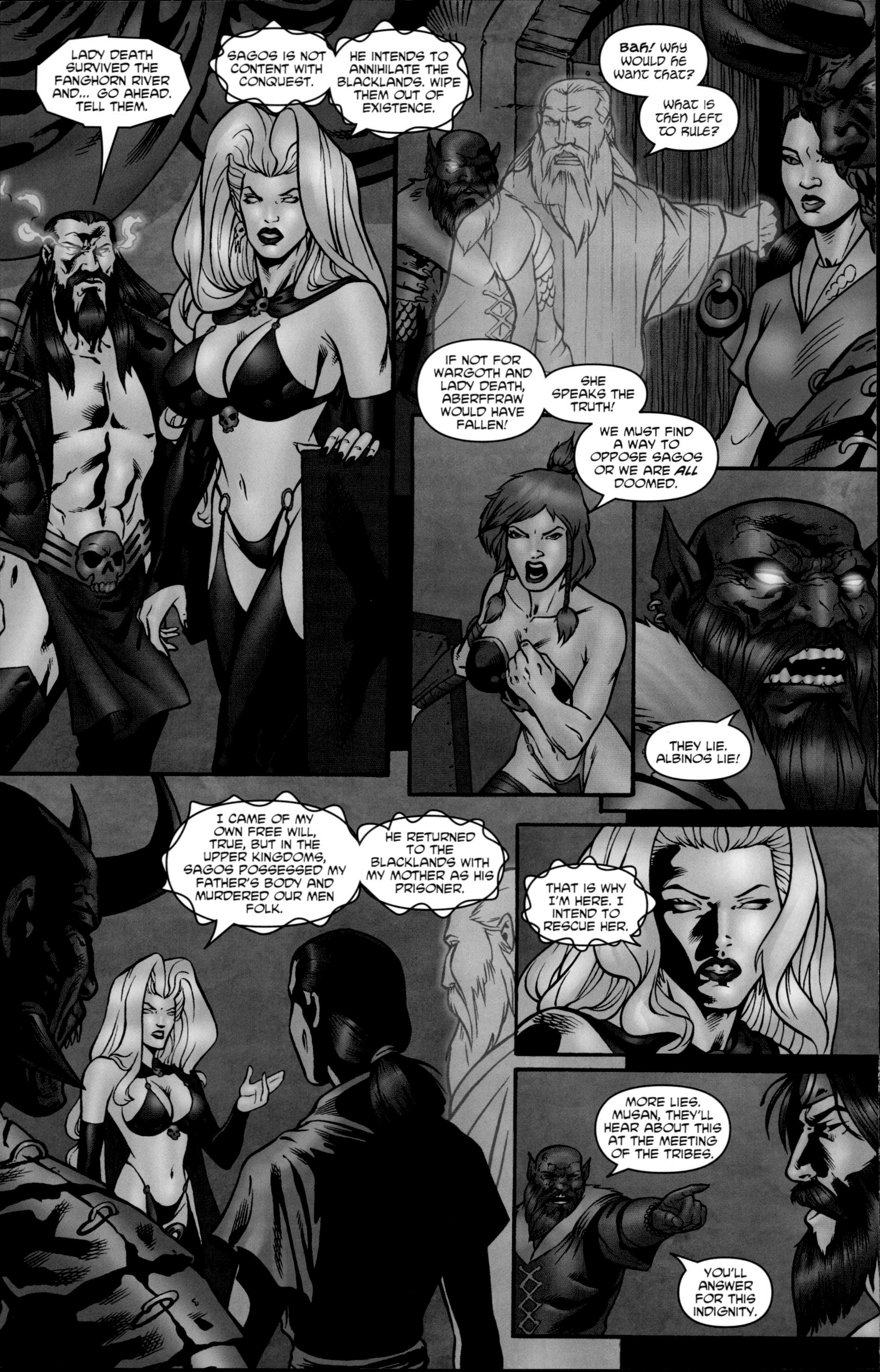
LADY DEATH SURVIVED THE FANGHORN RIVER AND... GO AHEAD. TELL THEM.
SAGOS IS NOT CONTENT WITH CONQUEST.
HE INTENDS TO ANNIHILATE THE BLACKLANDS. WIPE THEM OUT OF EXISTENCE.
BAH! WHY WOULD HE WANT THAT?
WHAT IS THEN LEFT TO RULE?
IF NOT FOR WARGOTH AND LADY DEATH, ABERFFRAW WOULD HAVE FALLEN!
SHE SPEAKS THE TRUTH!
WE MUST FIND A WAY TO OPPOSE SAGOS OR WE ARE ALL DOOMED.
THEY LIE. ALBINOS LIE!
I CAME OF MY OWN FREE WILL, TRUE, BUT IN THE UPPER KINGDOMS, SAGOS POSSESSED MY FATHER'S BODY AND MURDERED OUR MEN FOLK.
HE RETURNED TO THE BLACKLANDS WITH MY MOTHER AS HIS PRISONER.
THAT IS WHY I'M HERE. I INTEND TO RESCUE HER.
MORE LIES. MUSAN, THEY'LL HEAR ABOUT THIS AT THE MEETING OF THE TRIBES.
YOU'LL ANSWER FOR THIS INDIGNITY.

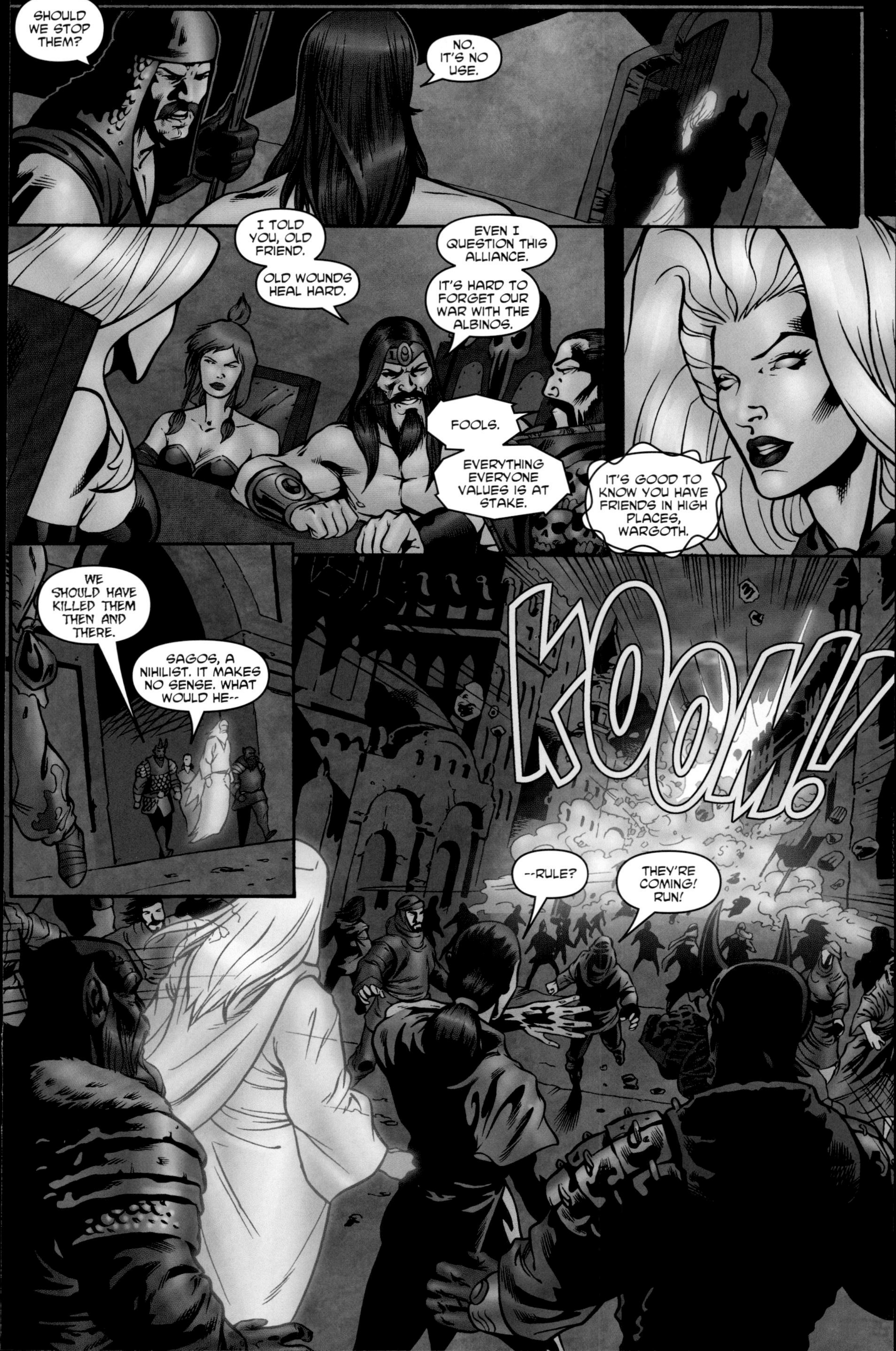
SHOULD WE STOP THEM?
NO. IT'S NO USE.
I TOLD YOU, OLD FRIEND.
OLD WOUNDS HEAL HARD.
EVEN I QUESTION THIS ALLIANCE.
IT'S HARD TO FORGET OUR WAR WITH THE ALBINOS.
FOOLS.
EVERYTHING EVERYONE VALUES IS AT STAKE.
IT'S GOOD TO KNOW YOU HAVE FRIENDS IN HIGH PLACES, WARGOTH.
WE SHOULD HAVE KILLED THEM THEN AND THERE.
SAGOS, A NIHILIST. IT MAKES NO SENSE. WHAT WOULD HE--
KROOM!
--RULE?
THEY'RE COMING! RUN!

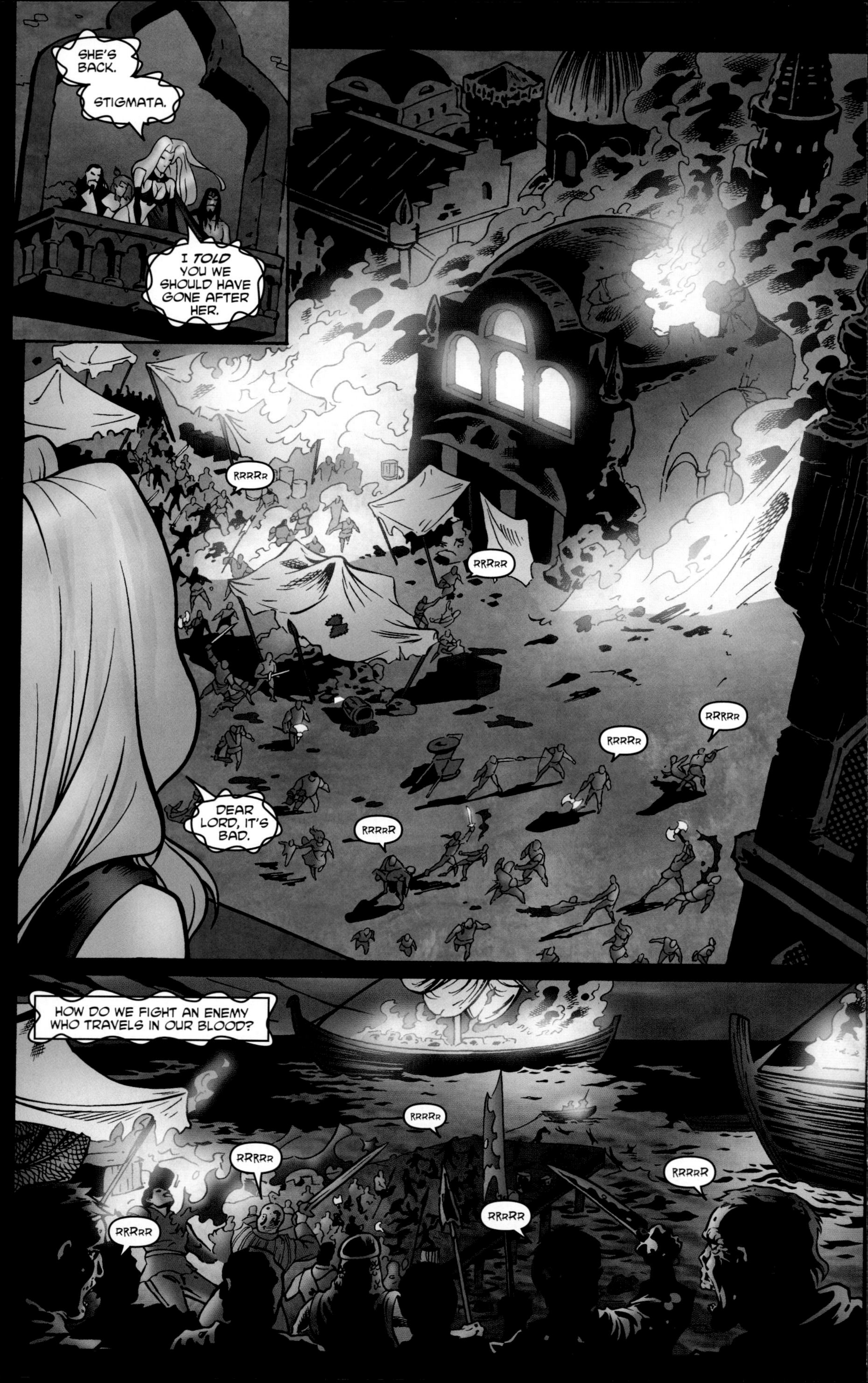
SHE'S BACK.
STIGMATA.
I TOLD YOU WE SHOULD HAVE GONE AFTER HER.
RRRRR
RRRRR
RRRRR
RRRRR
DEAR LORD, IT'S BAD.
RRRRR
HOW DO WE FIGHT AN ENEMY WHO TRAVELS IN OUR BLOOD?
RRRRR
RRRRR
RRRRR
RRRRR
RRRRR

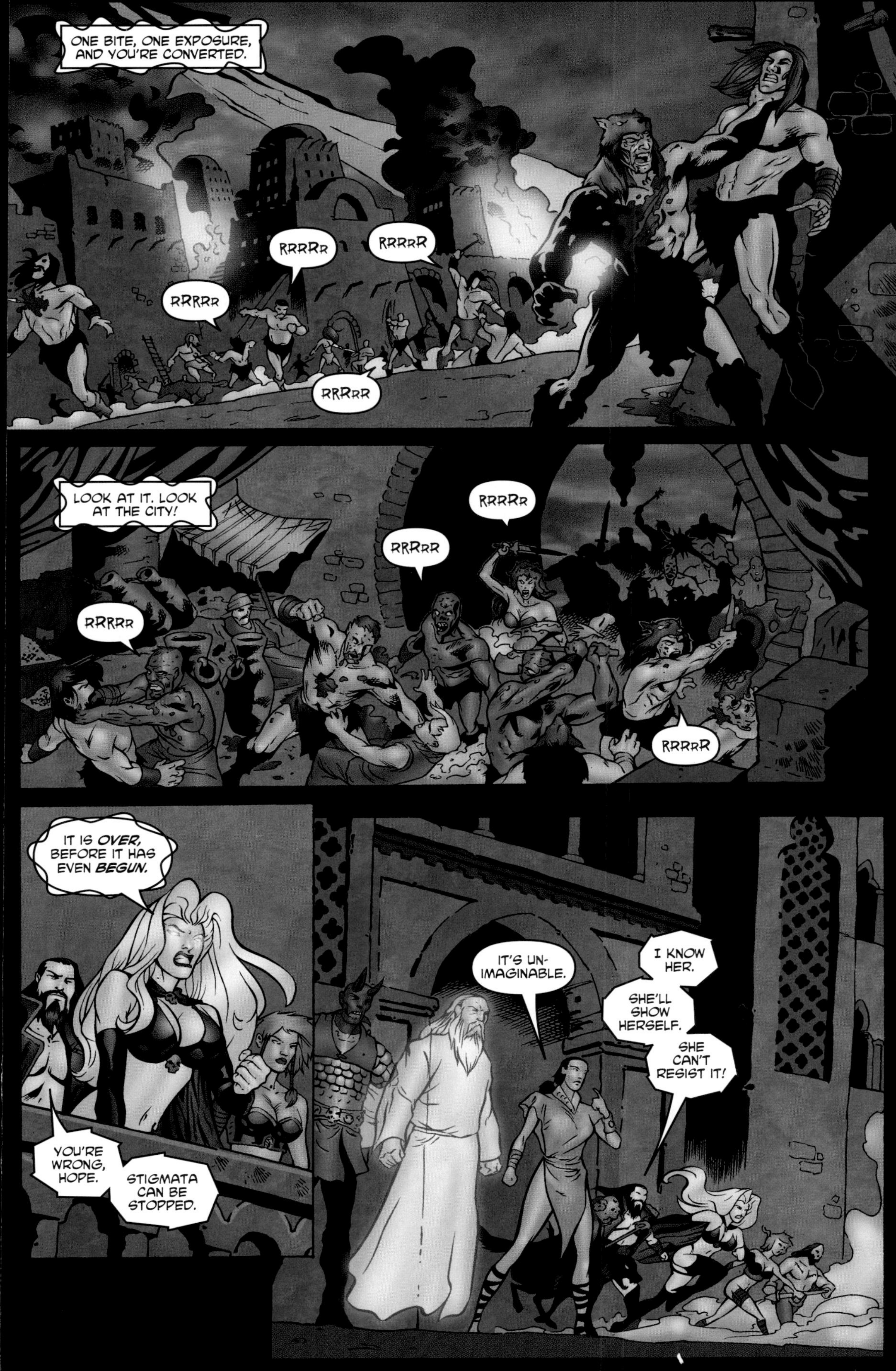

ONE BITE, ONE EXPOSURE, AND YOU'RE CONVERTED.
RRRRR
RRRRR
RRRRR
RRRRR
LOOK AT IT. LOOK AT THE CITY!
RRRRR
RRRRR
RRRRR
RRRRR
IT IS OVER, BEFORE IT HAS EVEN BEGUN.
YOU'RE WRONG, HOPE.
STIGMATA CAN BE STOPPED.
IT'S UN-IMAGINABLE.
I KNOW HER.
SHE'LL SHOW HERSELF.
SHE CAN'T RESIST IT!

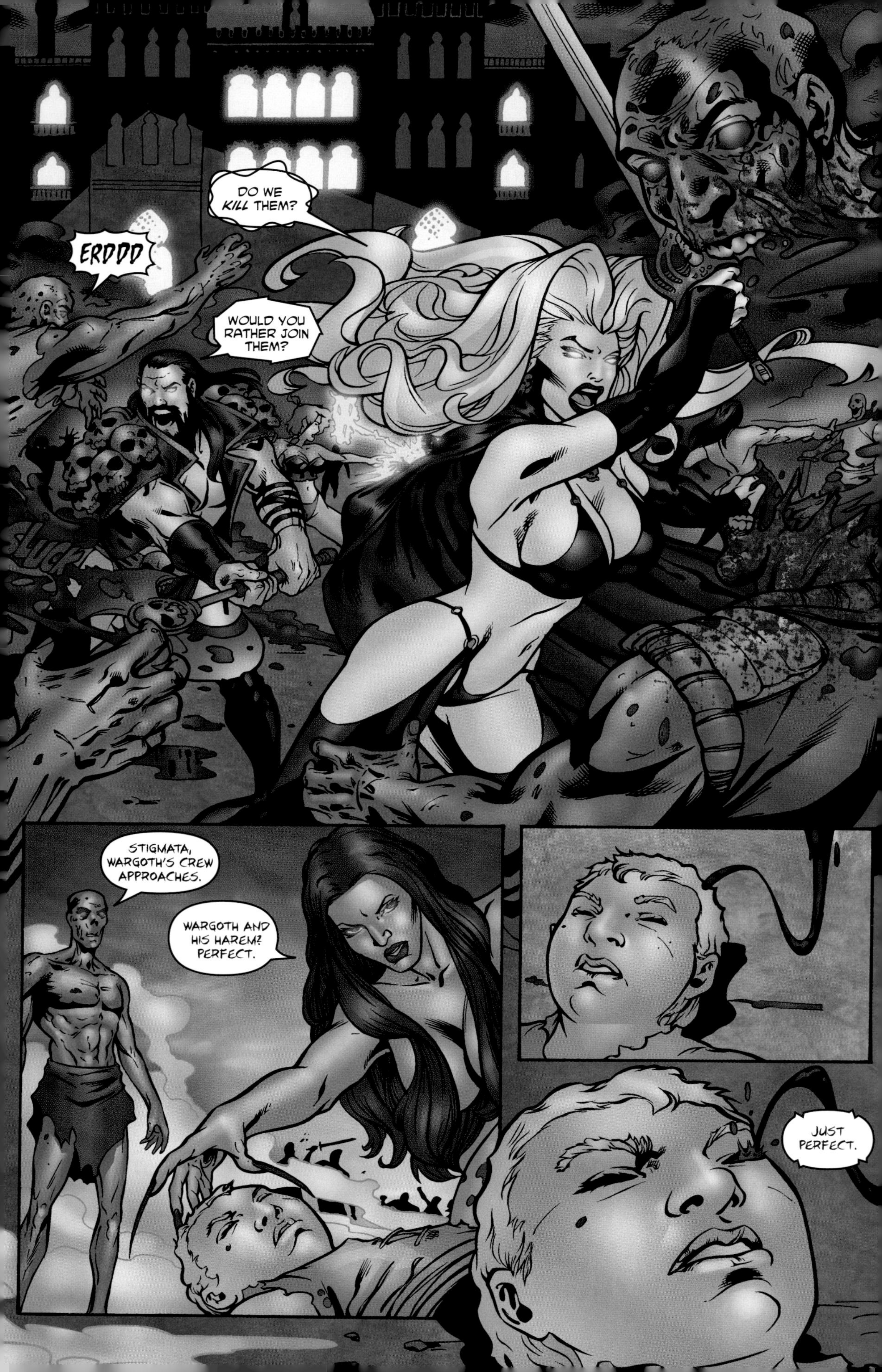
DO WE KILL THEM?
ERDDD
WOULD YOU RATHER JOIN THEM?
STIGMATA, WARGOTH'S CREW APPROACHES.
WARGOTH AND HIS HAREM? PERFECT.
JUST PERFECT.

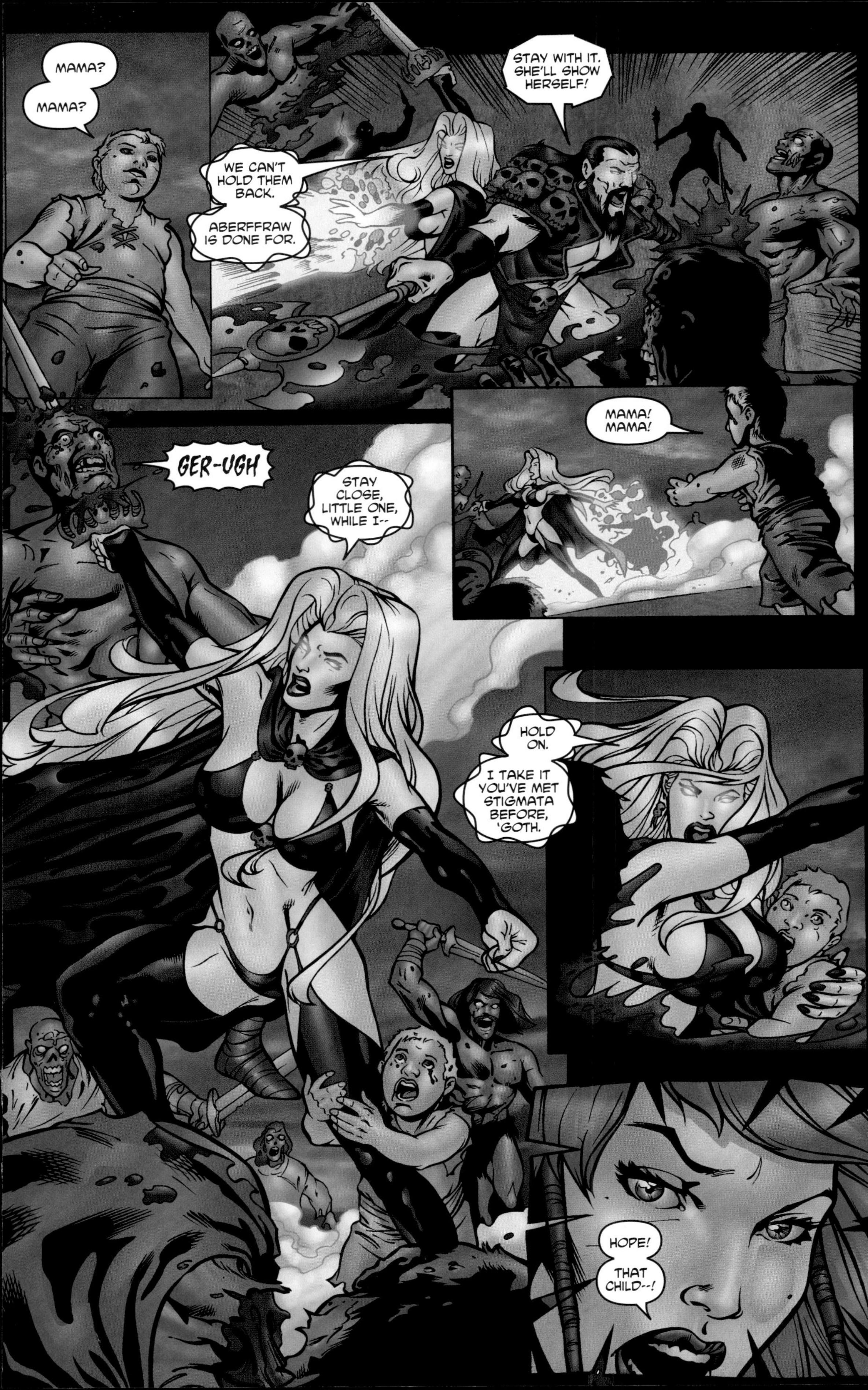
MAMA?
MAMA?
STAY WITH IT. SHE'LL SHOW HERSELF!
WE CAN'T HOLD THEM BACK.
ABERFFRAW IS DONE FOR.
MAMA! MAMA!
GER-UGH
STAY CLOSE, LITTLE ONE, WHILE I--
HOLD ON.
I TAKE IT YOU'VE MET STIGMATA BEFORE, 'GOTH.
HOPE!
THAT CHILD--!

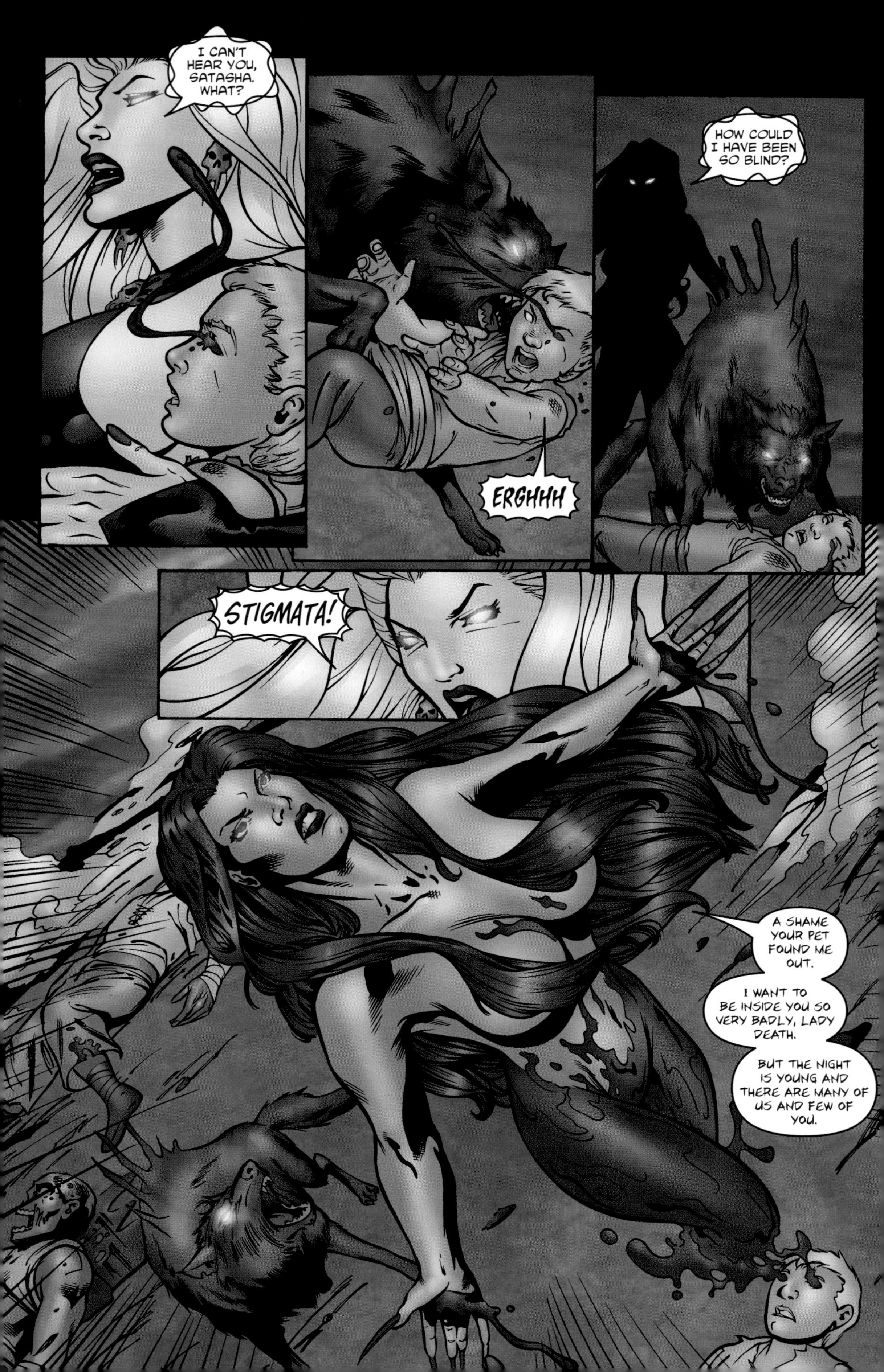
I CAN'T HEAR YOU, SATASHA. WHAT?
ERGHHH
HOW COULD I HAVE BEEN SO BLIND?
STIGMATA!
A SHAME YOUR PET FOUND ME OUT.
I WANT TO BE INSIDE YOU SO VERY BADLY, LADY DEATH.
BUT THE NIGHT IS YOUNG AND THERE ARE MANY OF US AND FEW OF YOU.

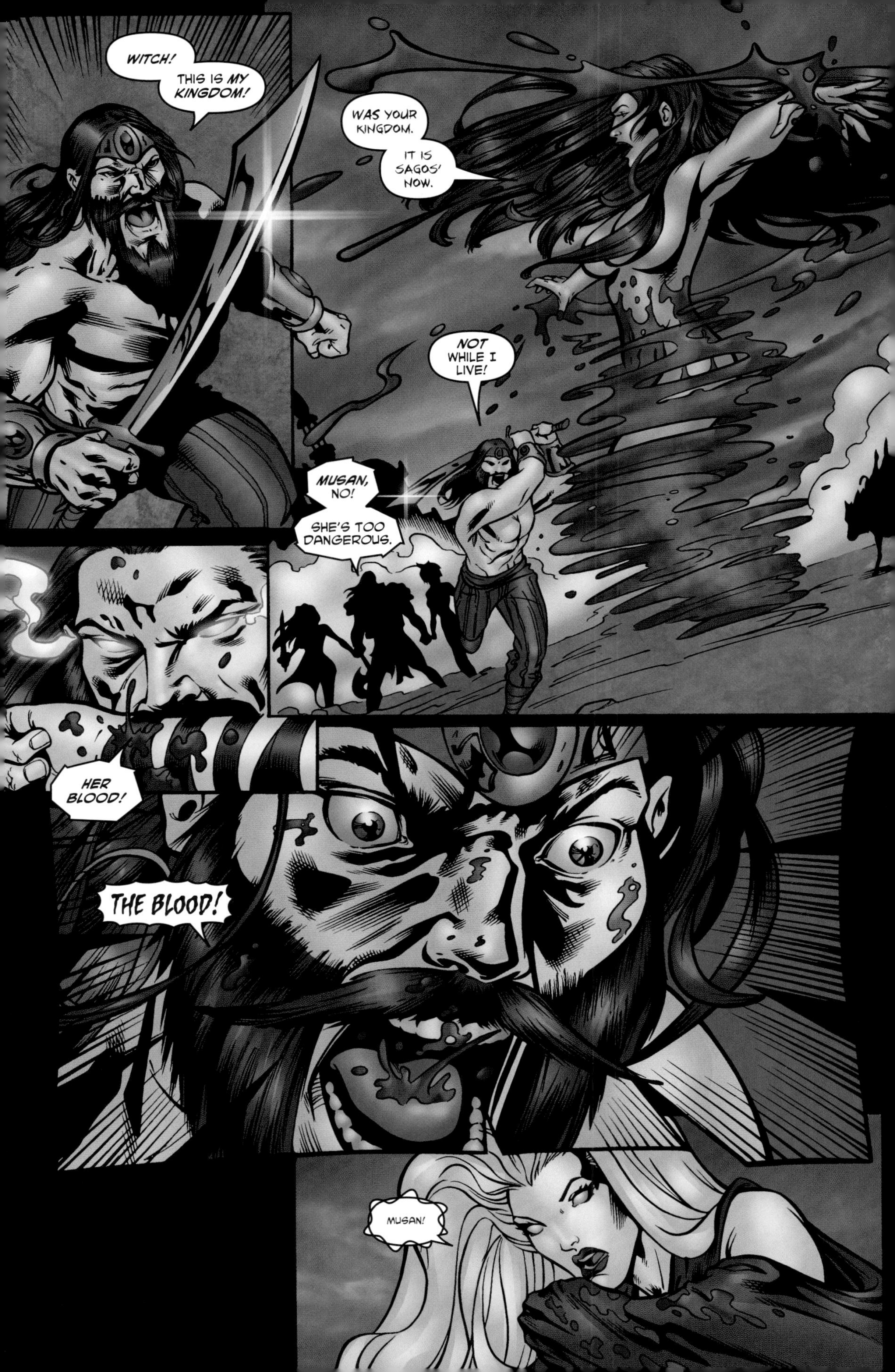
WITCH!
THIS IS MY KINGDOM!
WAS YOUR KINGDOM.
IT IS SAGOS' NOW.
NOT WHILE I LIVE!
MUSAN, NO!
SHE'S TOO DANGEROUS.
HER BLOOD!
THE BLOOD!
MUSAN!

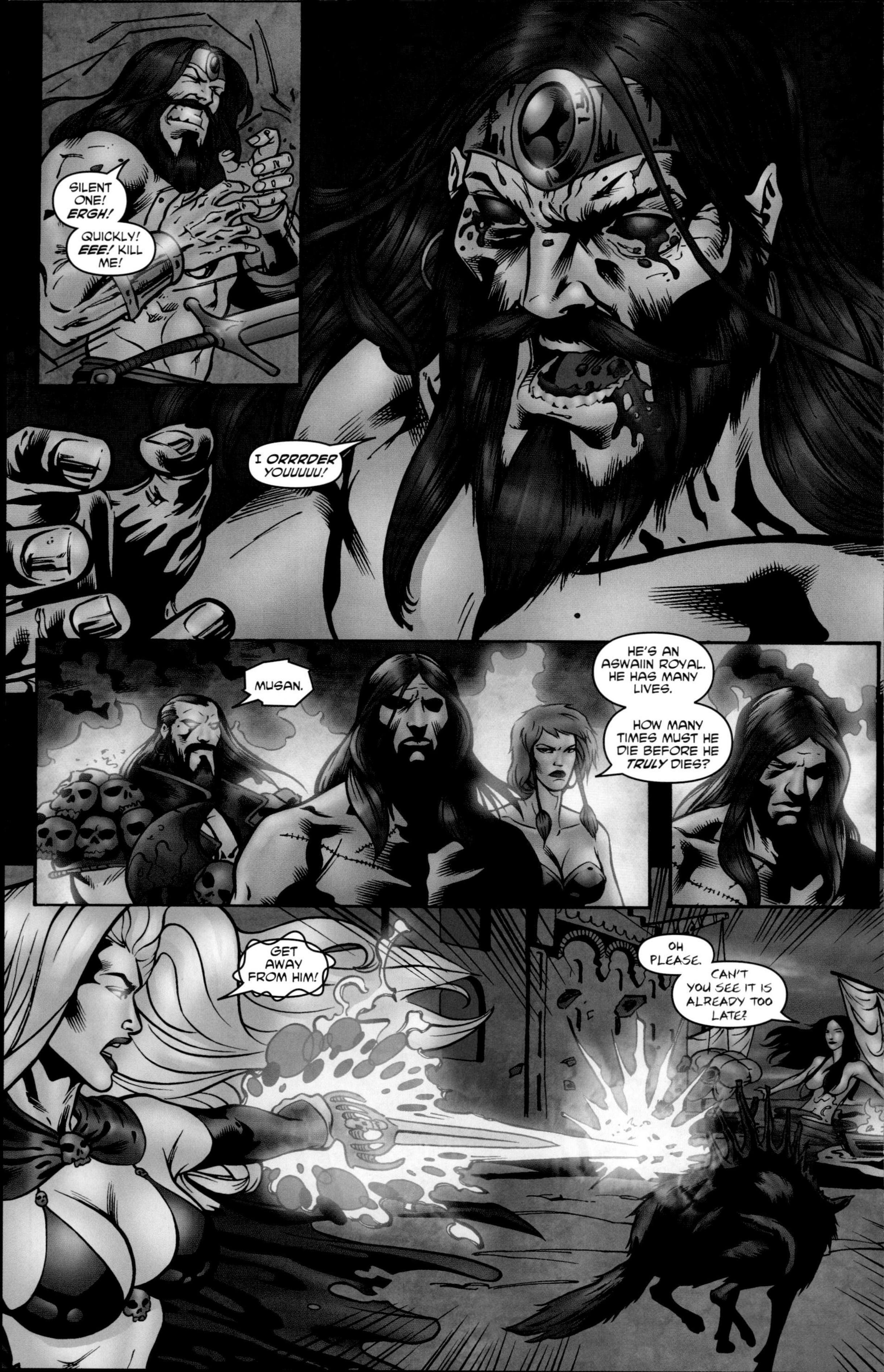
SILENT ONE! ERGH!
QUICKLY! EEE! KILL ME!
I ORRRDER YOUUUUU!
MUSAN.
HE'S AN ASWAIIN ROYAL. HE HAS MANY LIVES.
HOW MANY TIMES MUST HE DIE BEFORE HE TRULY DIES?
GET AWAY FROM HIM!
OH PLEASE.
CAN'T YOU SEE IT IS ALREADY TOO LATE?

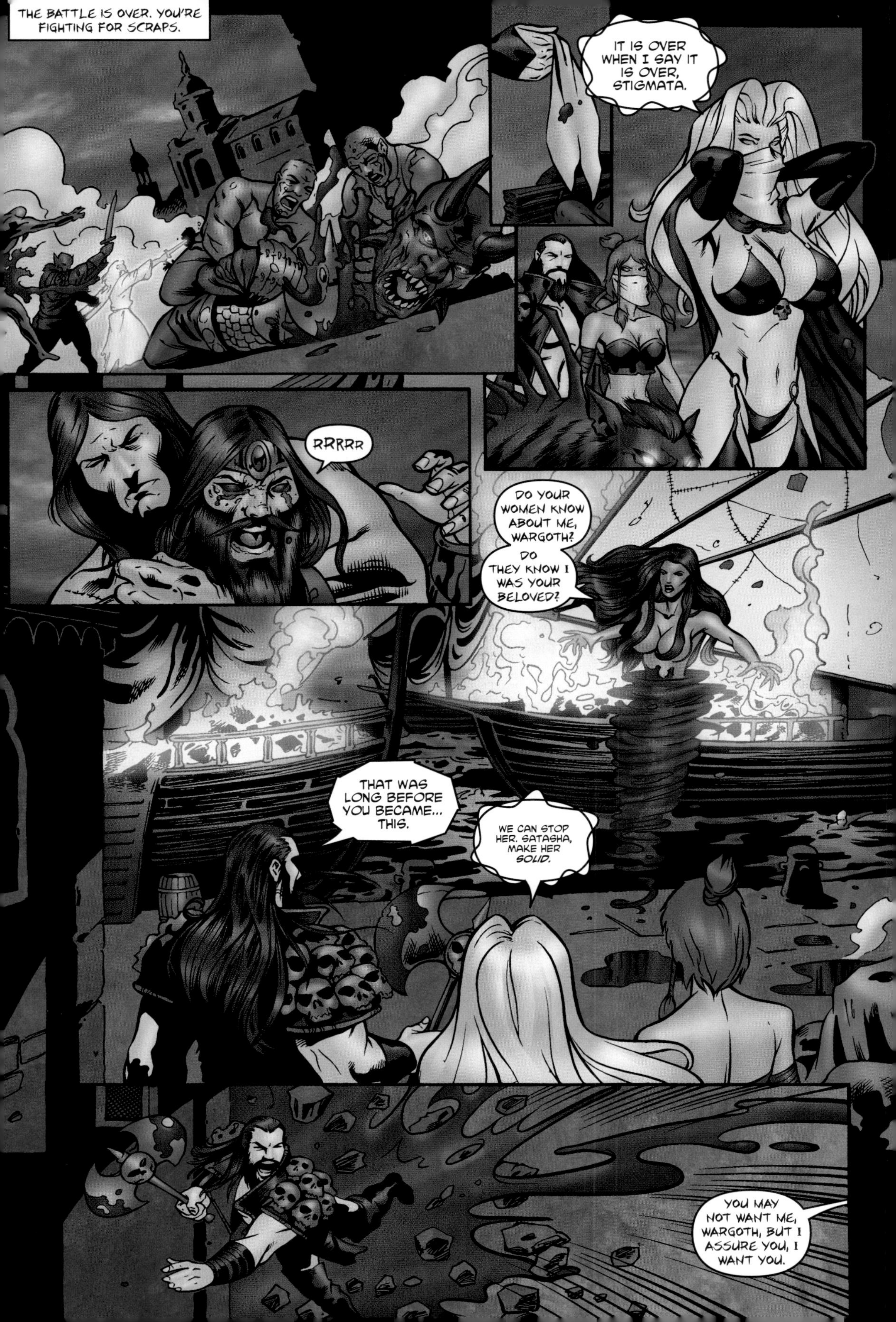
THE BATTLE IS OVER. YOU'RE FIGHTING FOR SCRAPS.
IT IS OVER WHEN I SAY IT IS OVER, STIGMATA.
RRRRR
DO YOUR WOMEN KNOW ABOUT ME, WARGOTH?
DO THEY KNOW I WAS YOUR BELOVED?
THAT WAS LONG BEFORE YOU BECAME... THIS.
WE CAN STOP HER. SATASHA, MAKE HER SOLID.
YOU MAY NOT WANT ME, WARGOTH, BUT I ASSURE YOU, I WANT YOU.

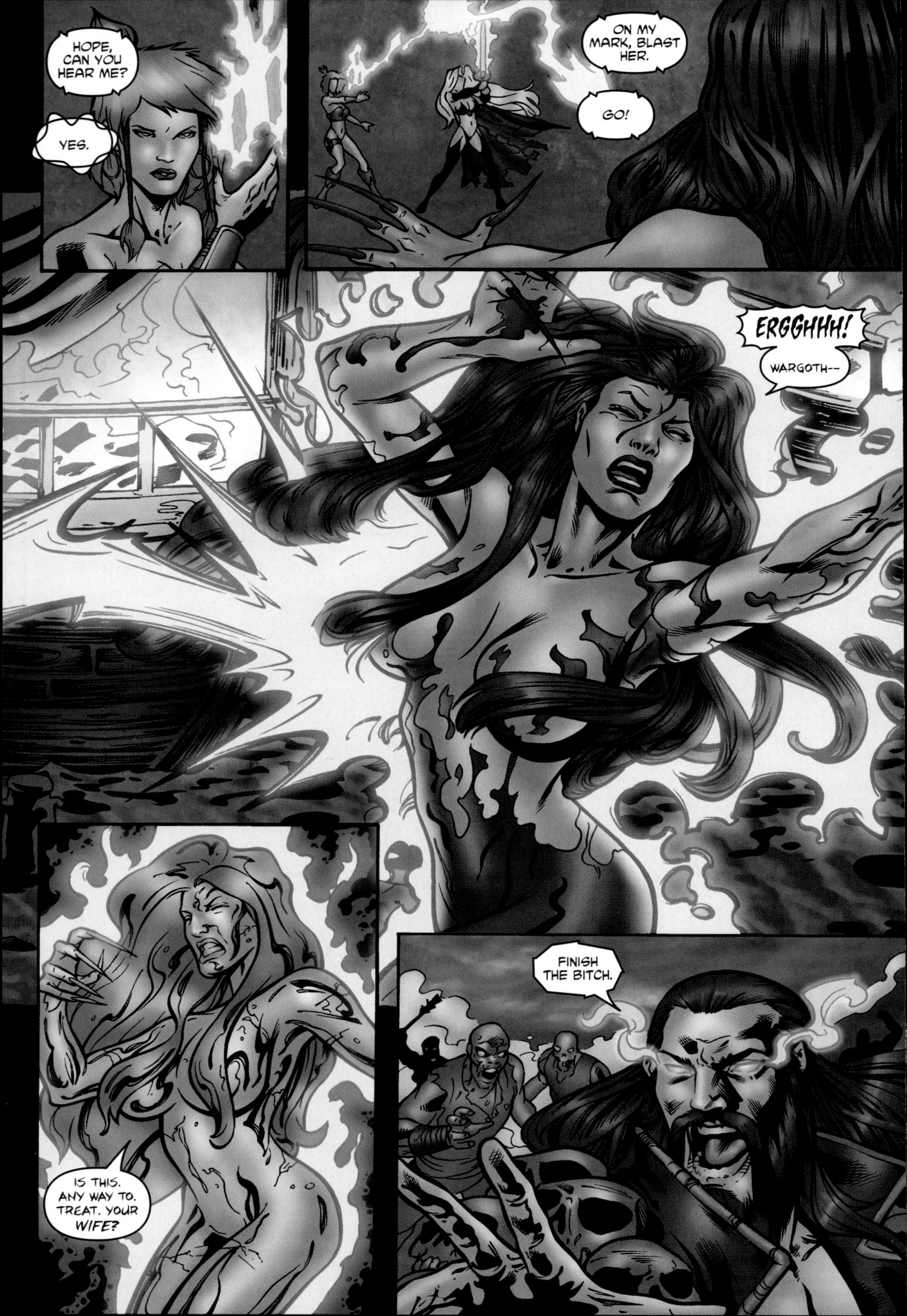
HOPE, CAN YOU HEAR ME?
YES.
ON MY MARK, BLAST HER.
GO!
ERGGHHH!
WARGOTH--
IS THIS. ANY WAY TO. TREAT. YOUR WIFE?
FINISH THE BITCH.

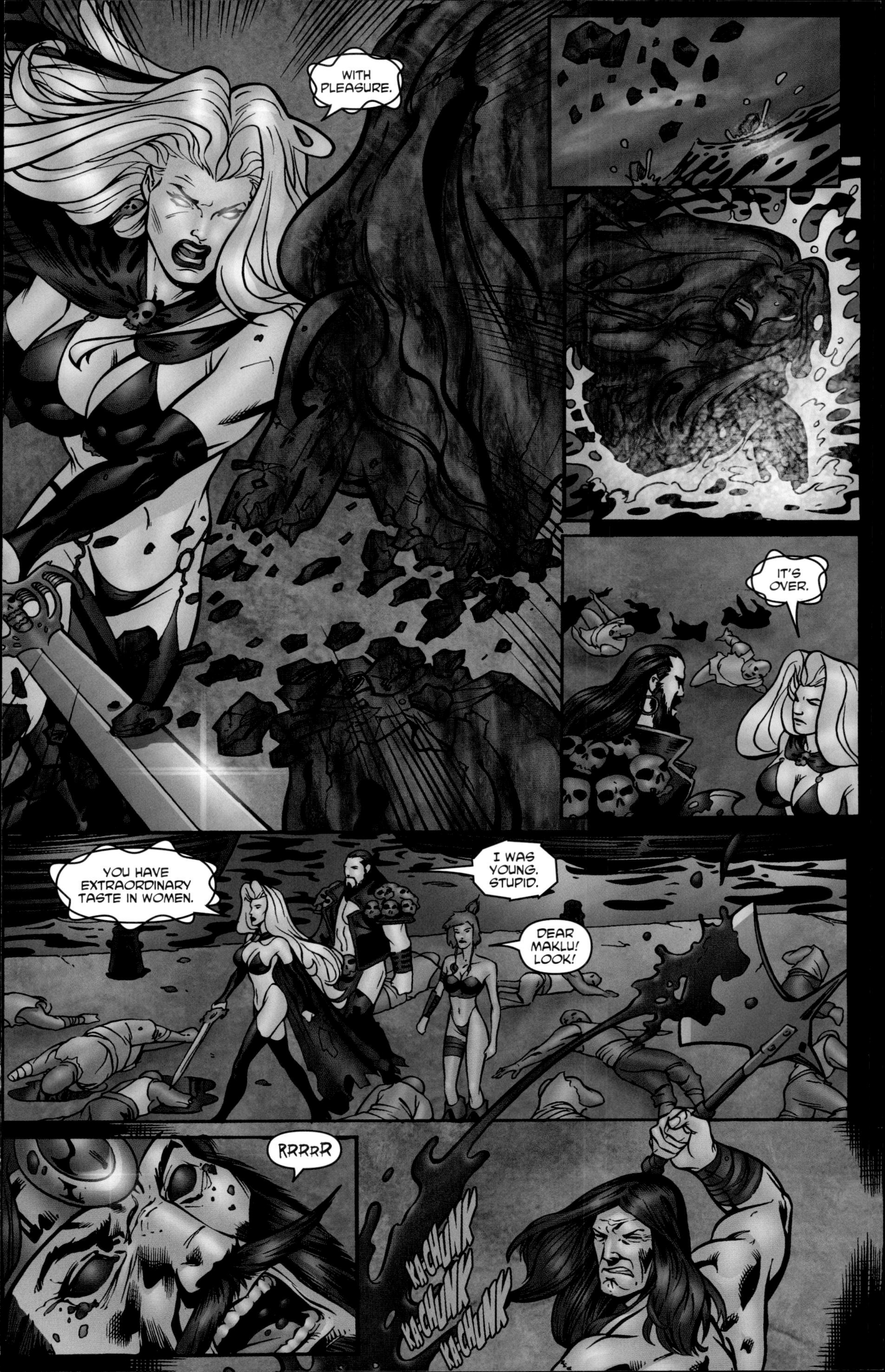
WITH PLEASURE.
IT'S OVER.
YOU HAVE EXTRAORDINARY TASTE IN WOMEN.
I WAS YOUNG. STUPID.
DEAR MAKLU! LOOK!
RRRRR
KA-CHUNK
KA-CHUNK
KA-CHUNK

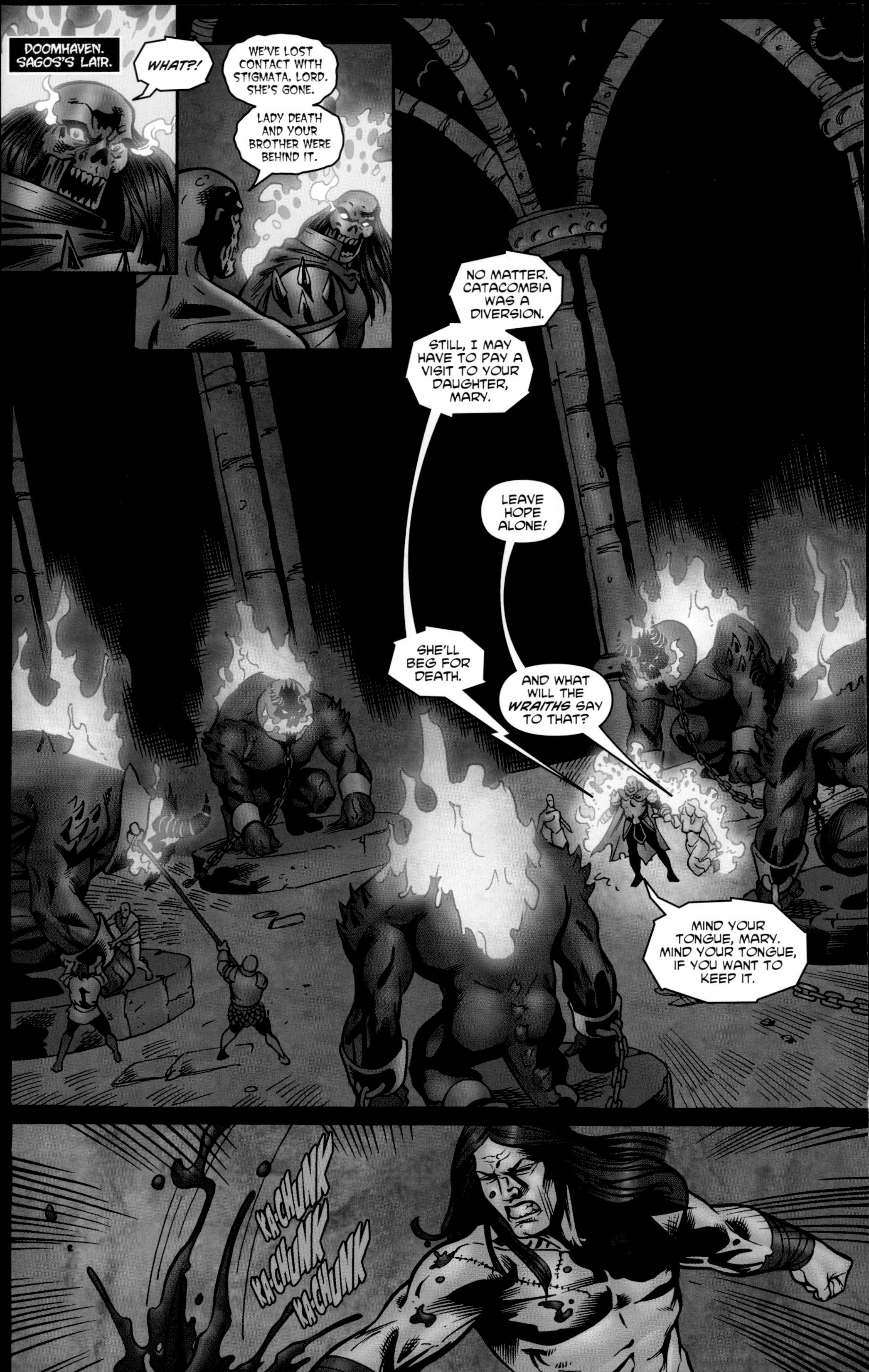
DOOMHAVEN. SAGOS'S LAIR.
WHAT?!
WE'VE LOST CONTACT WITH STIGMATA, LORD. SHE'S GONE.
LADY DEATH AND YOUR BROTHER WERE BEHIND IT.
NO MATTER. CATACOMBIA WAS A DIVERSION.
STILL, I MAY HAVE TO PAY A VISIT TO YOUR DAUGHTER, MARY.
LEAVE HOPE ALONE!
SHE'LL BEG FOR DEATH.
AND WHAT WILL THE *WRAITHS* SAY TO THAT?
MIND YOUR TONGUE, MARY. MIND YOUR TONGUE, IF YOU WANT TO KEEP IT.
KA-CHUNK
KA-CHUNK
KA-CHUNK

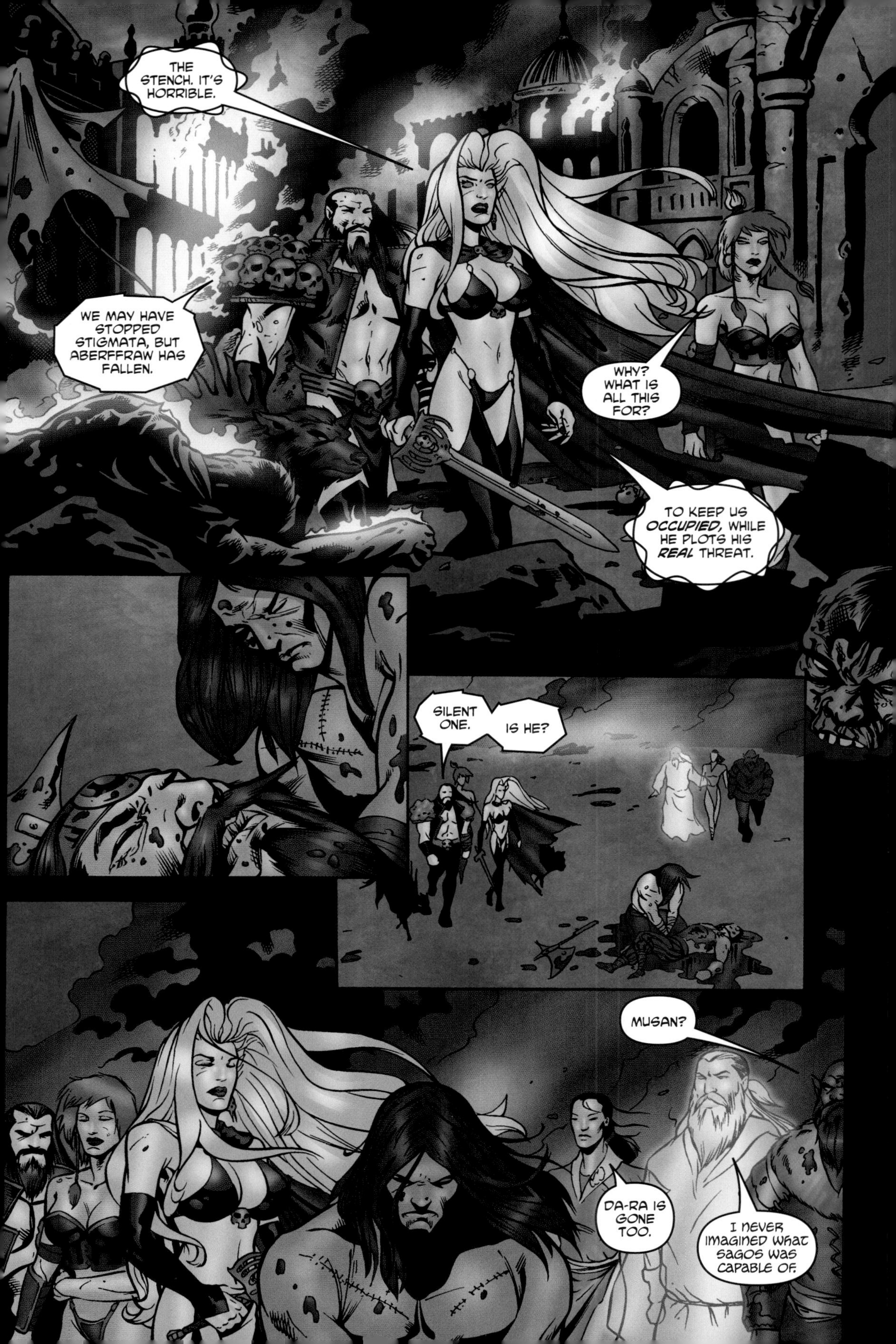
THE STENCH. IT'S HORRIBLE.
WE MAY HAVE STOPPED STIGMATA, BUT ABERFFRAW HAS FALLEN.
WHY? WHAT IS ALL THIS FOR?
TO KEEP US *OCCUPIED*, WHILE HE PLOTS HIS *REAL* THREAT.
SILENT ONE.
IS HE?
MUSAN?
DA-RA IS GONE TOO.
I NEVER IMAGINED WHAT SAGOS WAS CAPABLE OF.

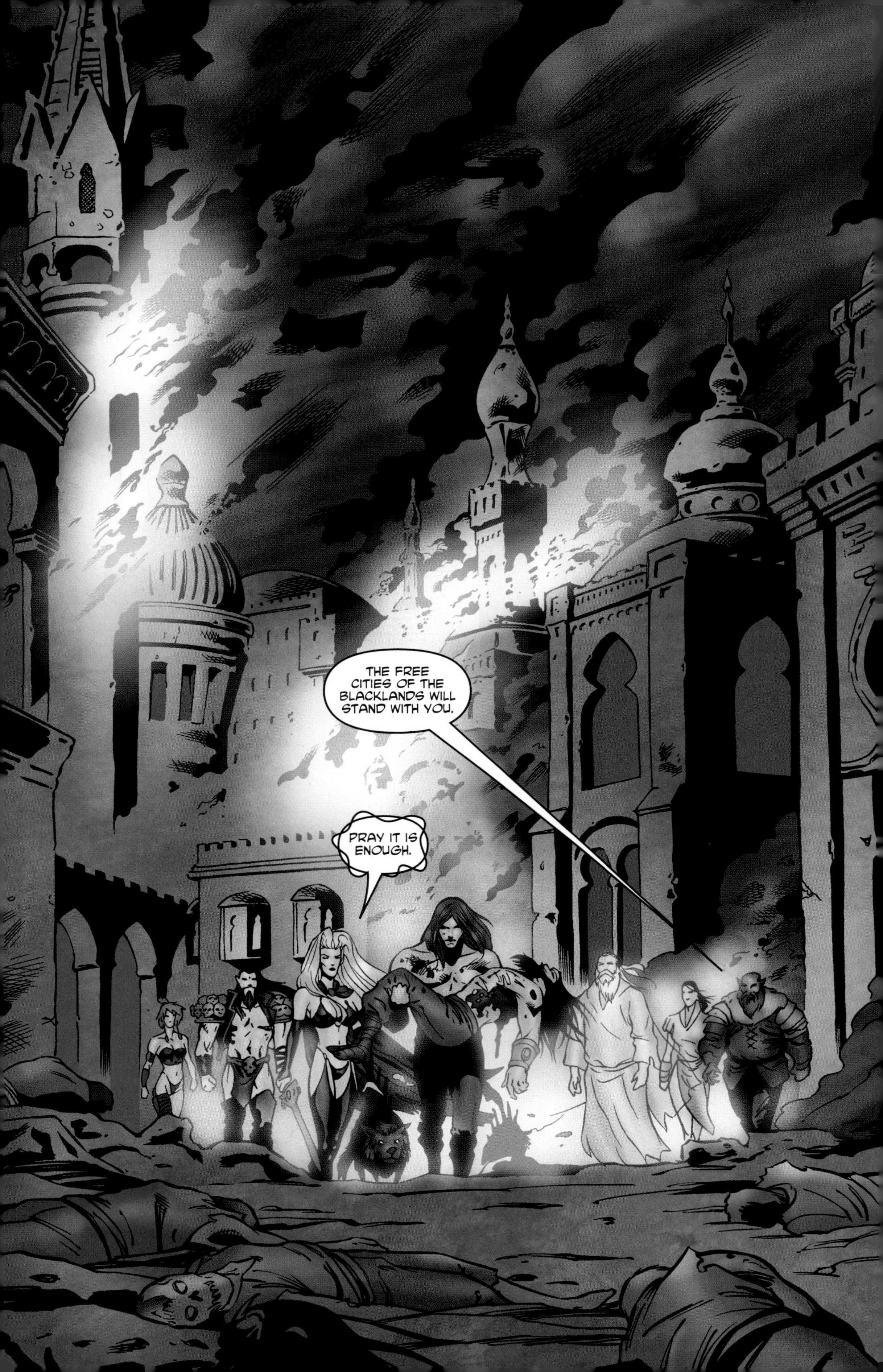
THE FREE CITIES OF THE BLACKLANDS WILL STAND WITH YOU.
PRAY IT IS ENOUGH.

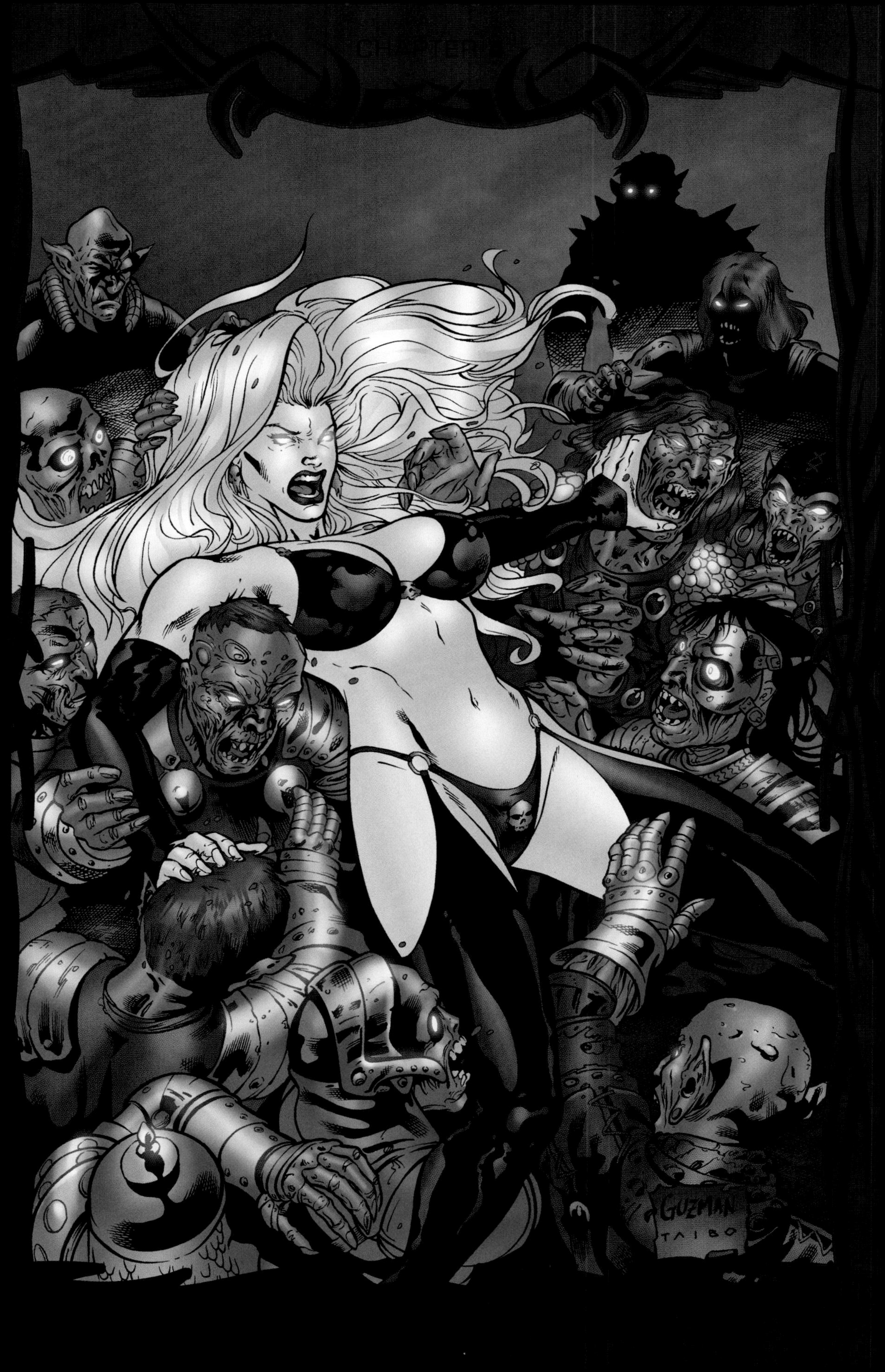
CHAPTER
GUZMAN
TAIBO

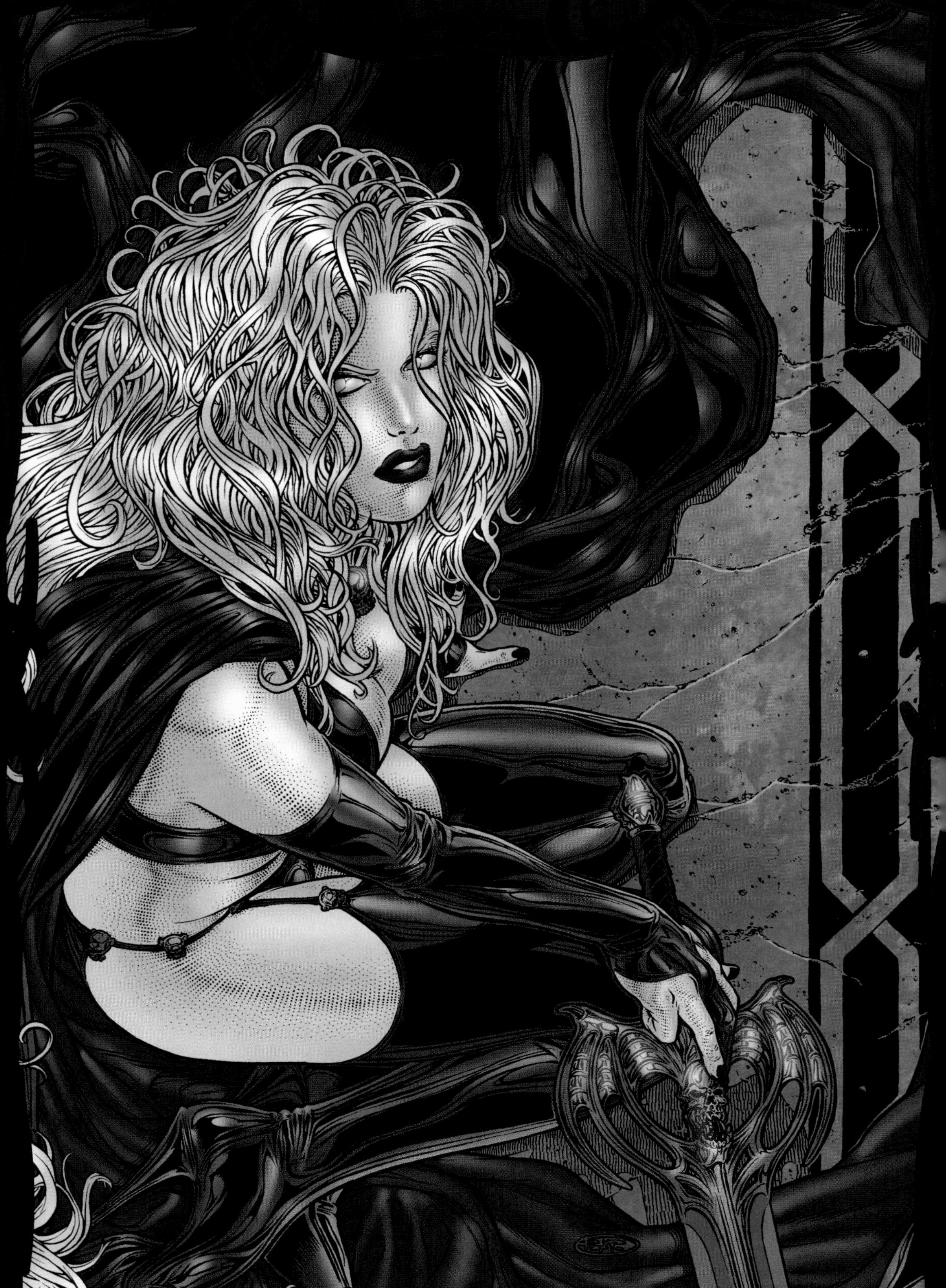

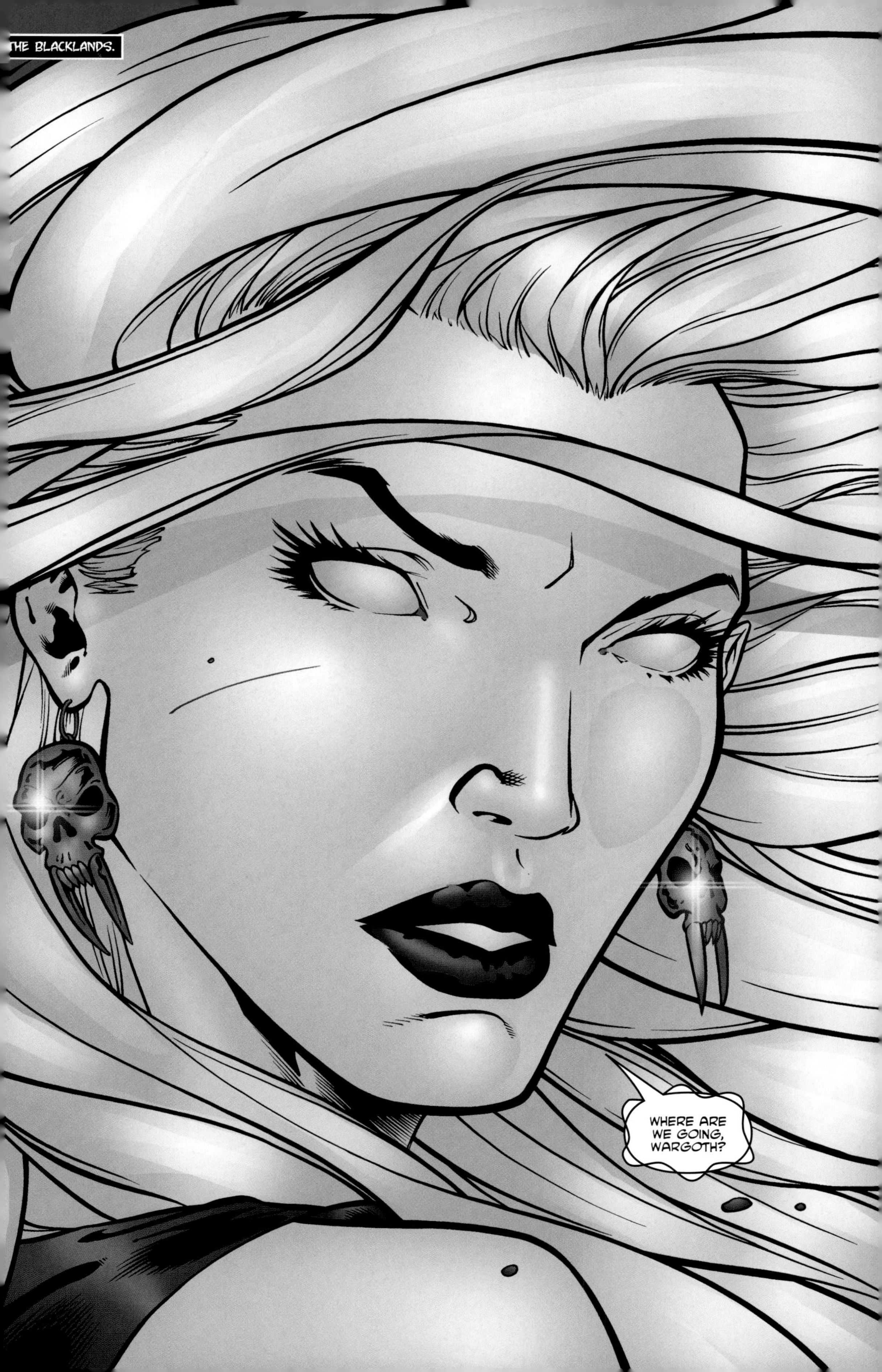
THE BLACKLANDS.
WHERE ARE WE GOING, WARGOTH?

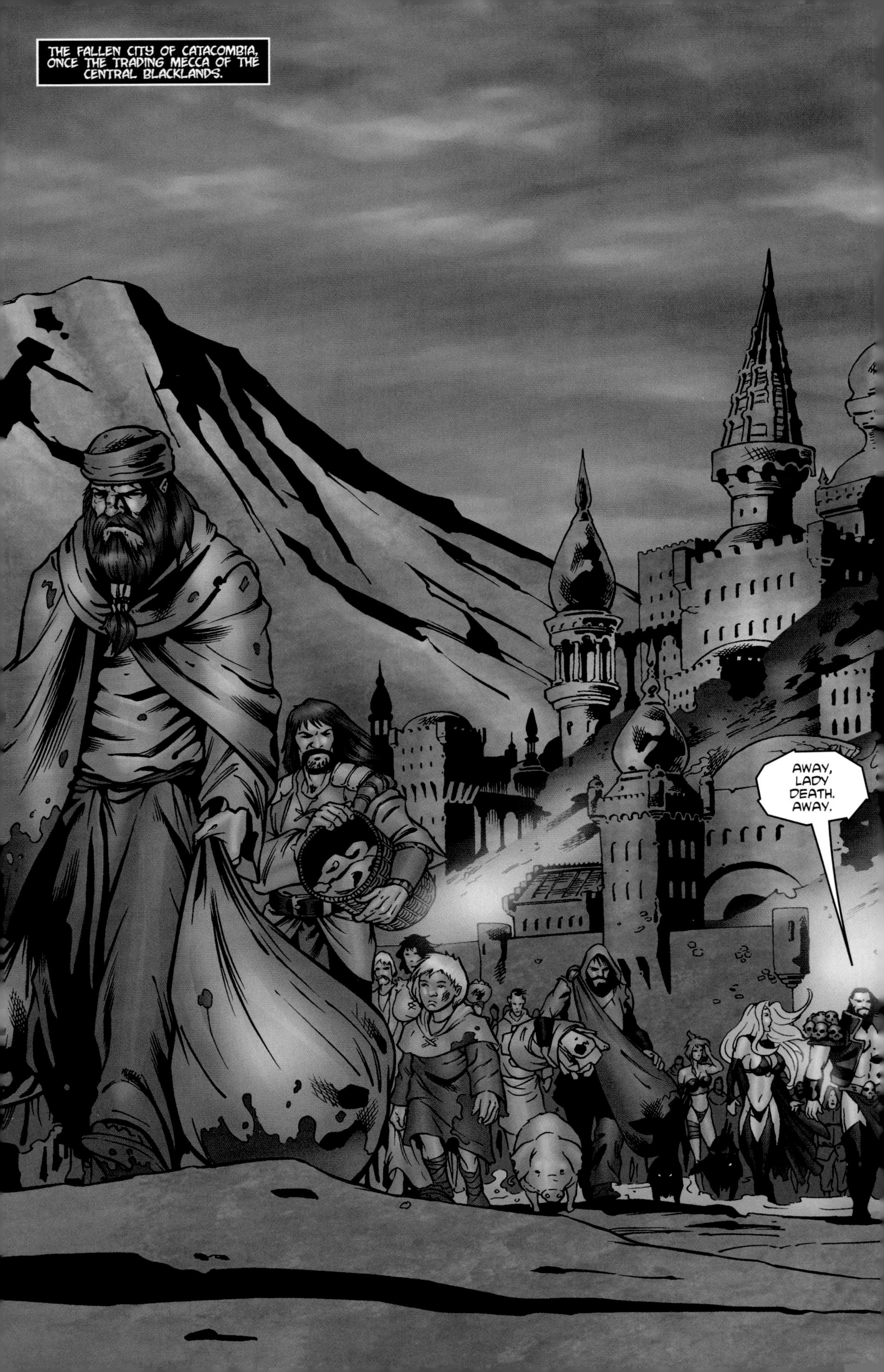
THE FALLEN CITY OF CATACOMBIA, ONCE THE TRADING MECCA OF THE CENTRAL BLACKLANDS.
AWAY, LADY DEATH. AWAY.

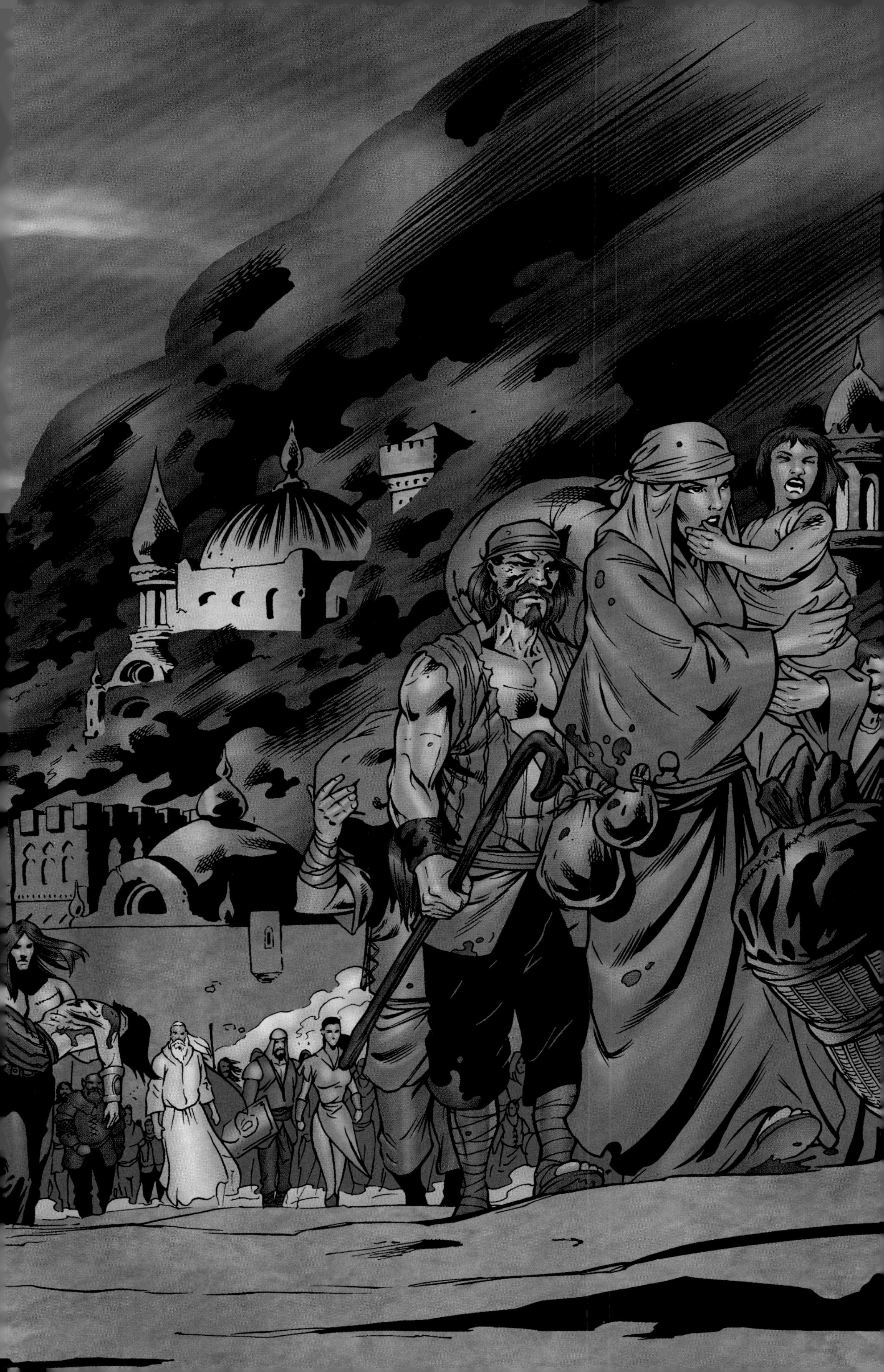

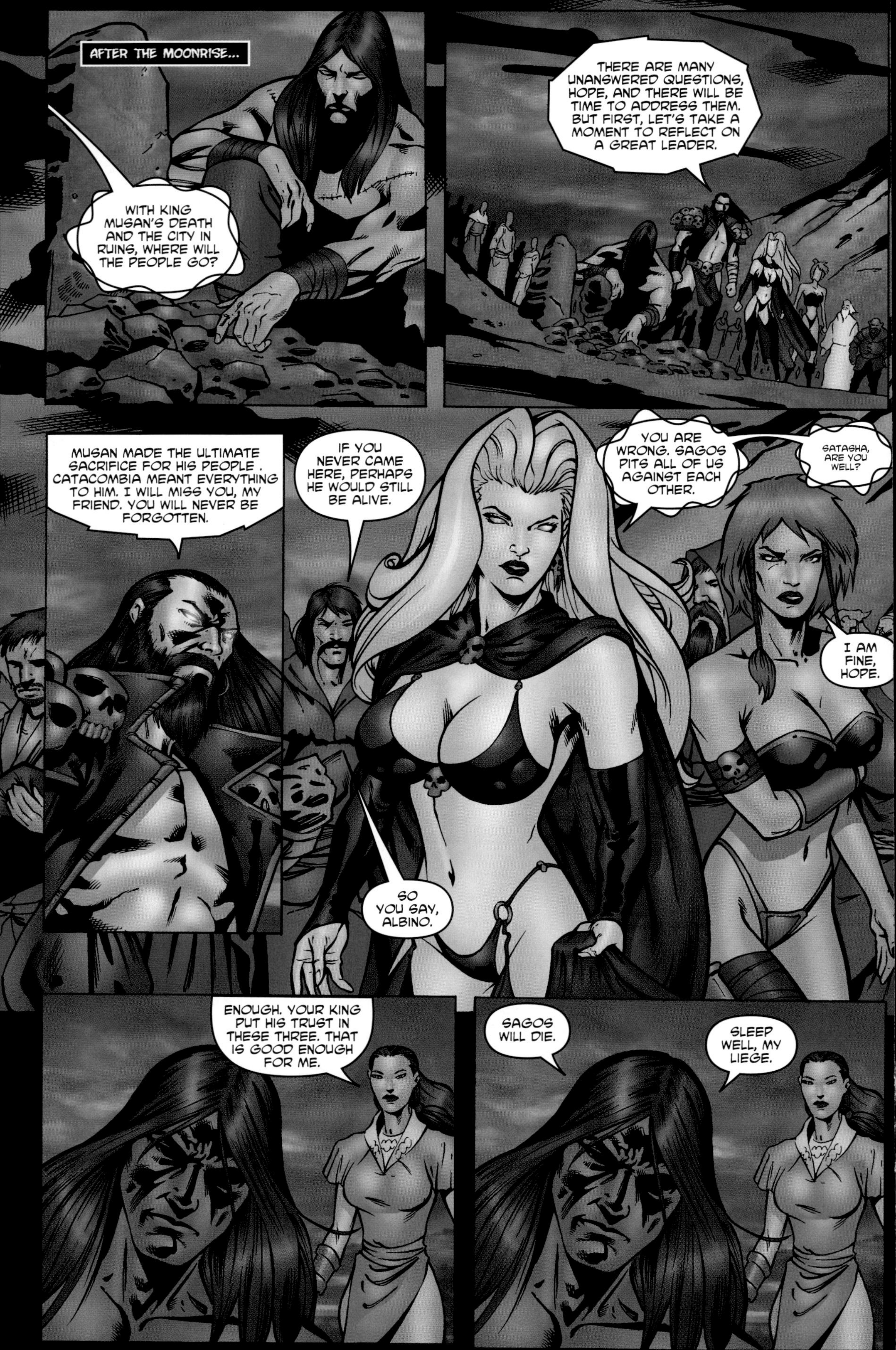
AFTER THE MOONRISE...
WITH KING MUSAN'S DEATH AND THE CITY IN RUINS, WHERE WILL THE PEOPLE GO?
THERE ARE MANY UNANSWERED QUESTIONS, HOPE, AND THERE WILL BE TIME TO ADDRESS THEM. BUT FIRST, LET'S TAKE A MOMENT TO REFLECT ON A GREAT LEADER.
MUSAN MADE THE ULTIMATE SACRIFICE FOR HIS PEOPLE . CATACOMBIA MEANT EVERYTHING TO HIM. I WILL MISS YOU, MY FRIEND. YOU WILL NEVER BE FORGOTTEN.
IF YOU NEVER CAME HERE, PERHAPS HE WOULD STILL BE ALIVE.
YOU ARE WRONG. SAGOS PITS ALL OF US AGAINST EACH OTHER.
SO YOU SAY, ALBINO.
SATASHA, ARE YOU WELL?
I AM FINE, HOPE.
ENOUGH. YOUR KING PUT HIS TRUST IN THESE THREE. THAT IS GOOD ENOUGH FOR ME.
SAGOS WILL DIE.
SLEEP WELL, MY LIEGE.

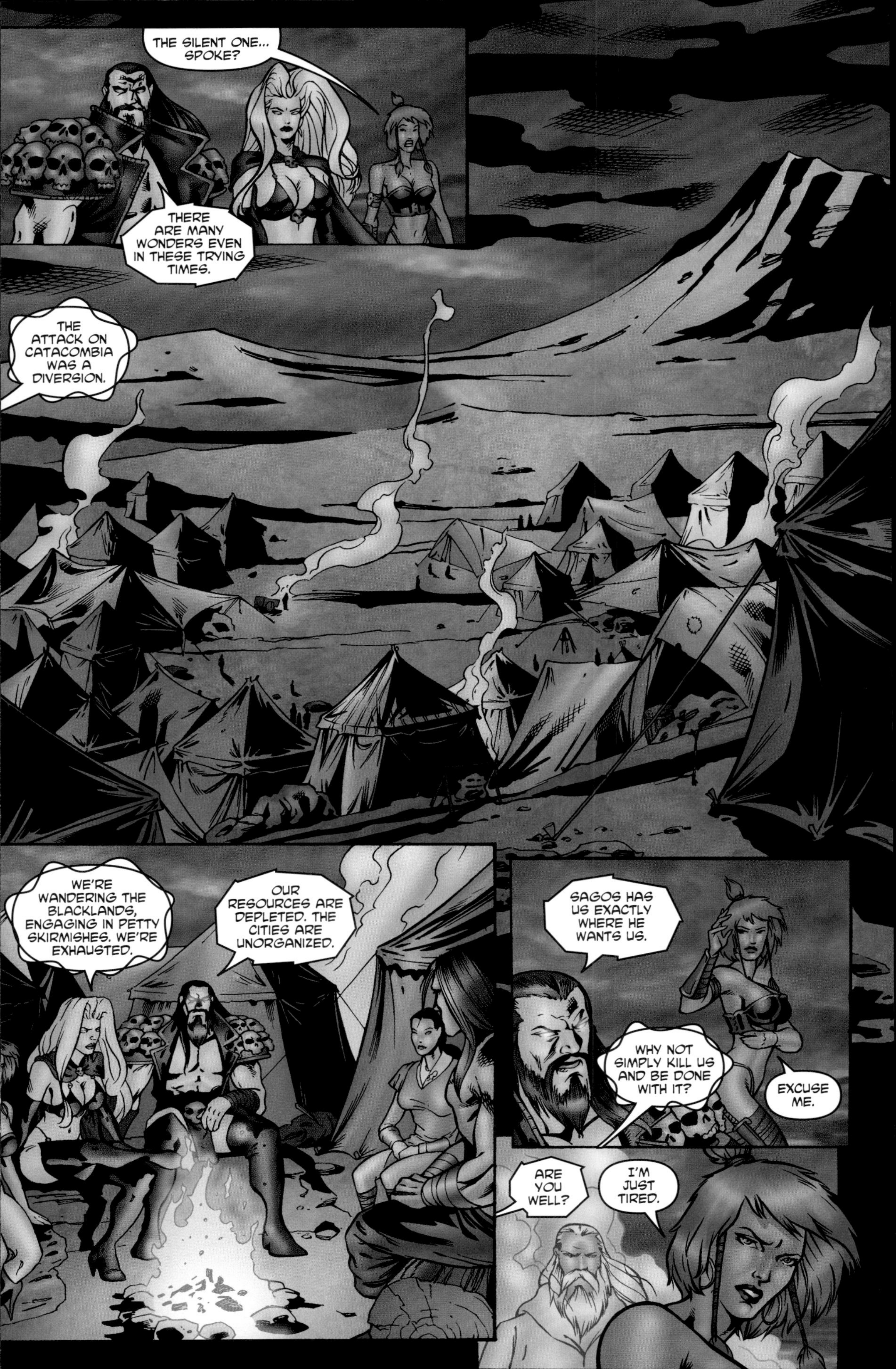
THE SILENT ONE... SPOKE?
THERE ARE MANY WONDERS EVEN IN THESE TRYING TIMES.
THE ATTACK ON CATACOMBIA WAS A DIVERSION.
WE'RE WANDERING THE BLACKLANDS, ENGAGING IN PETTY SKIRMISHES. WE'RE EXHAUSTED.
OUR RESOURCES ARE DEPLETED. THE CITIES ARE UNORGANIZED.
SAGOS HAS US EXACTLY WHERE HE WANTS US.
WHY NOT SIMPLY KILL US AND BE DONE WITH IT?
EXCUSE ME.
ARE YOU WELL?
I'M JUST TIRED.

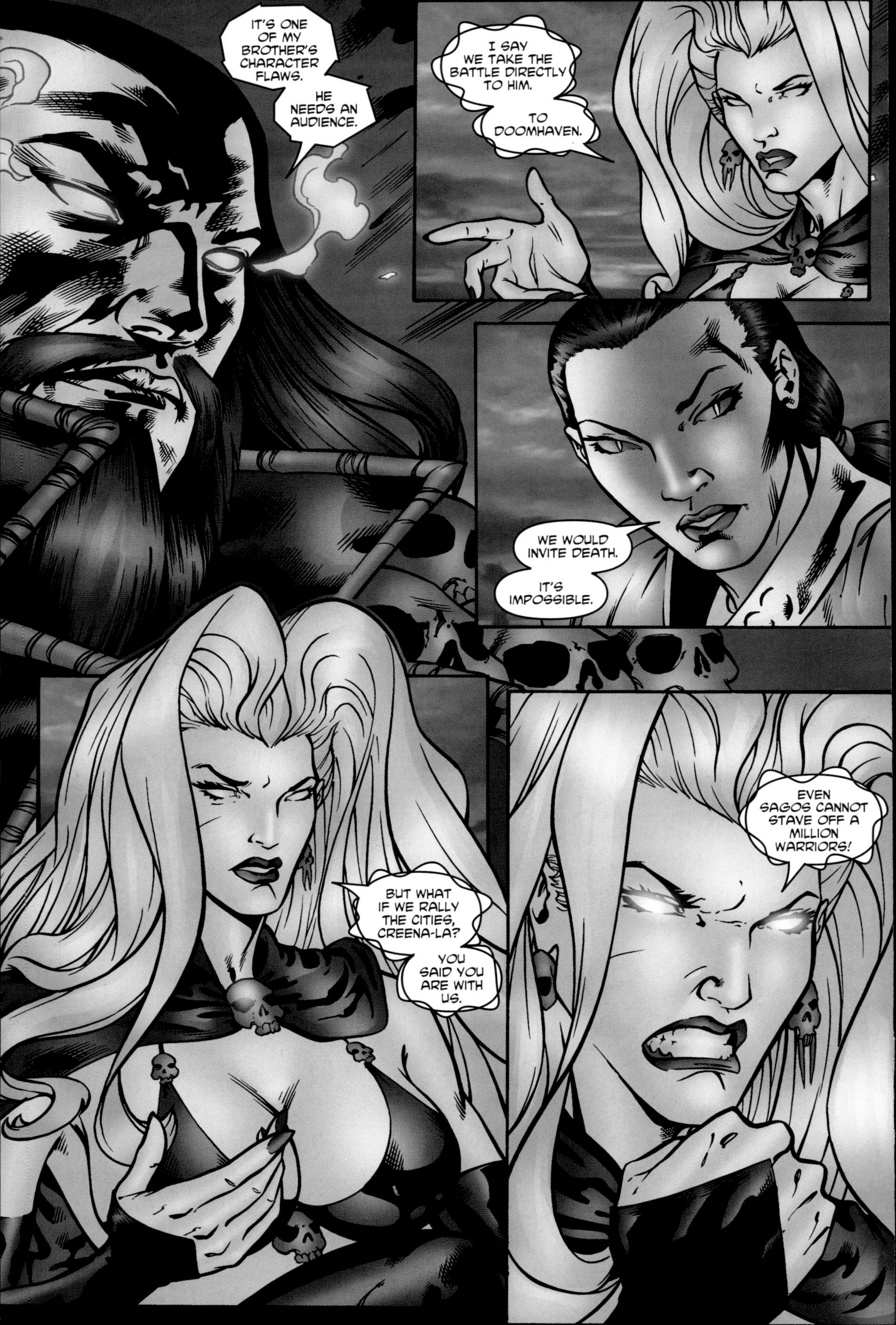
IT'S ONE OF MY BROTHER'S CHARACTER FLAWS.
HE NEEDS AN AUDIENCE.
I SAY WE TAKE THE BATTLE DIRECTLY TO HIM.
TO DOOMHAVEN.
WE WOULD INVITE DEATH.
IT'S IMPOSSIBLE.
BUT WHAT IF WE RALLY THE CITIES, CREENA-LA?
YOU SAID YOU ARE WITH US.
EVEN SAGOS CANNOT STAVE OFF A MILLION WARRIORS!

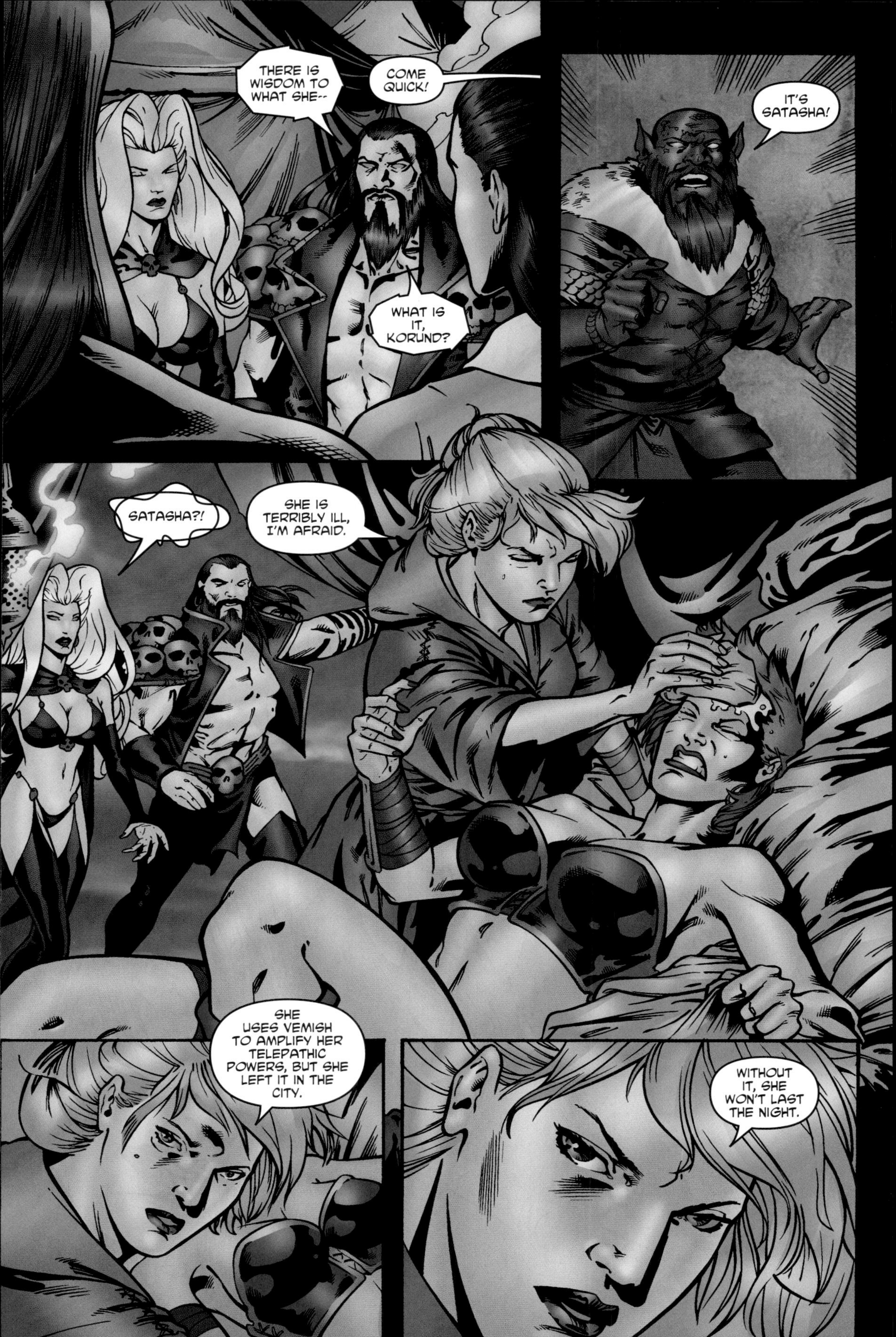
THERE IS WISDOM TO WHAT SHE--
COME QUICK!
WHAT IS IT, KORUND?
IT'S SATASHA!
SATASHA?!
SHE IS TERRIBLY ILL, I'M AFRAID.
SHE USES VEMISH TO AMPLIFY HER TELEPATHIC POWERS, BUT SHE LEFT IT IN THE CITY.
WITHOUT IT, SHE WON'T LAST THE NIGHT.

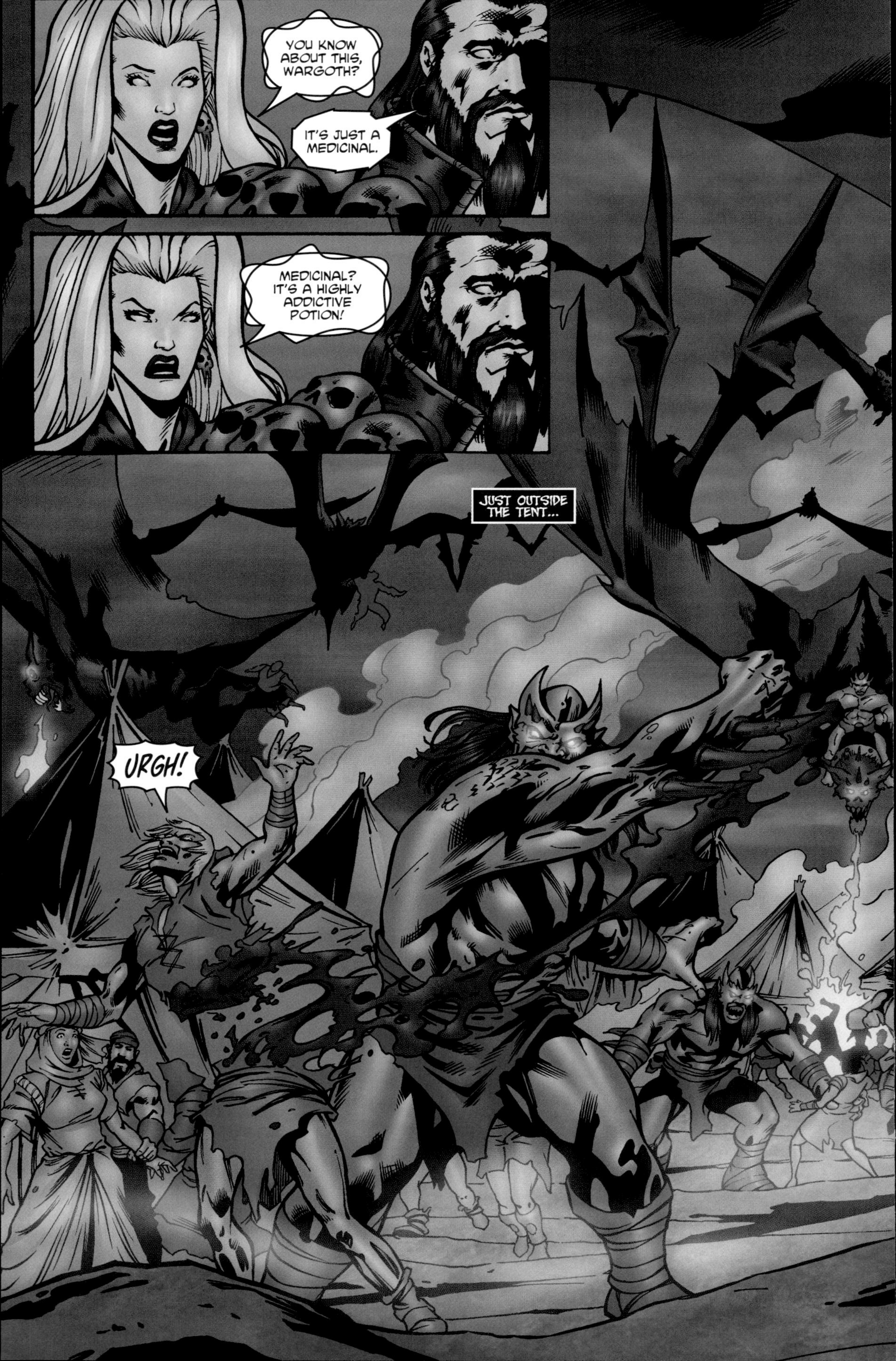
YOU KNOW ABOUT THIS, WARGOTH?
IT'S JUST A MEDICINAL.
MEDICINAL? IT'S A HIGHLY ADDICTIVE POTION!
JUST OUTSIDE THE TENT...
URGH!

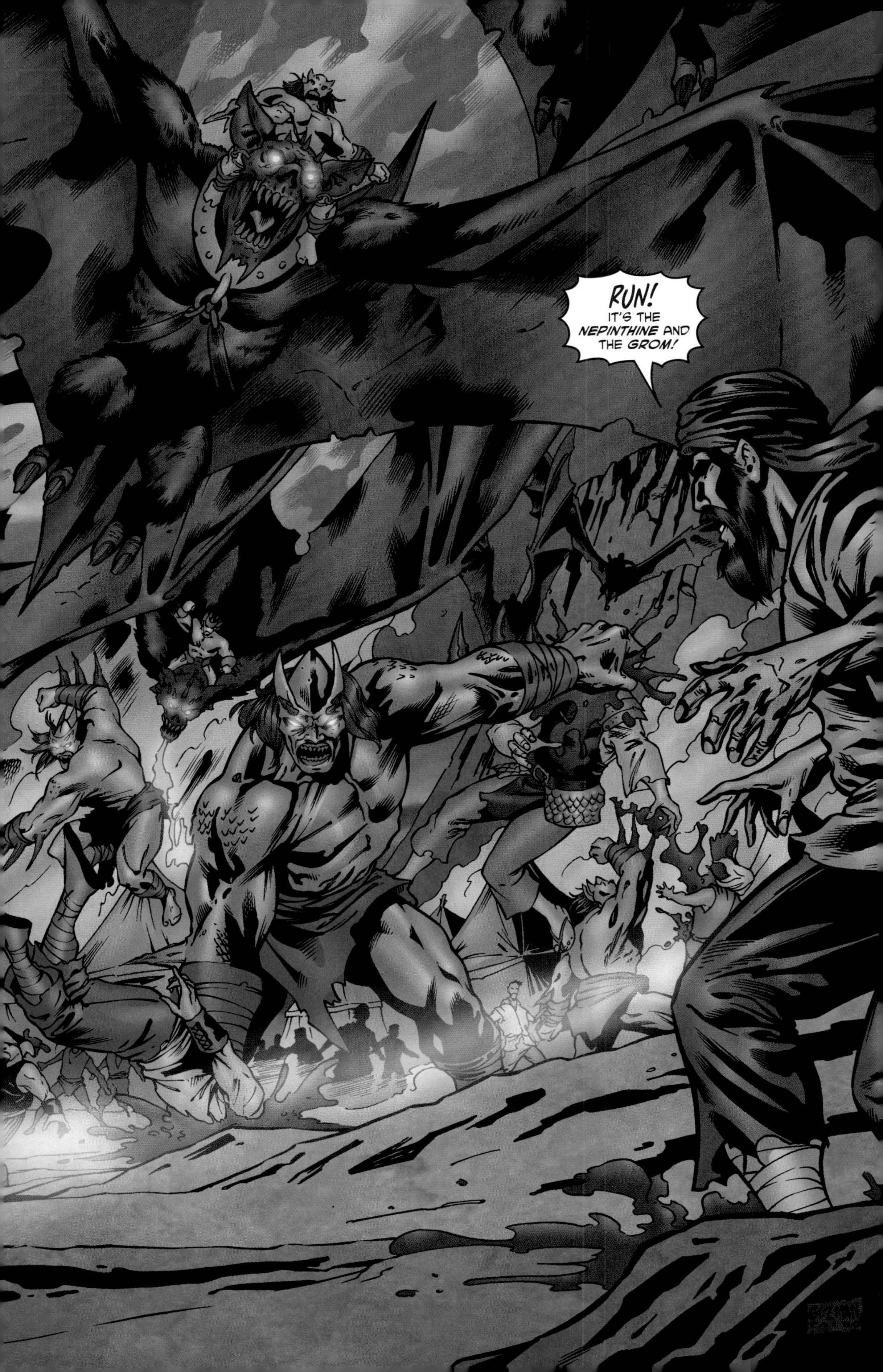
RUN! IT'S THE NEPINTHINE AND THE GROM!

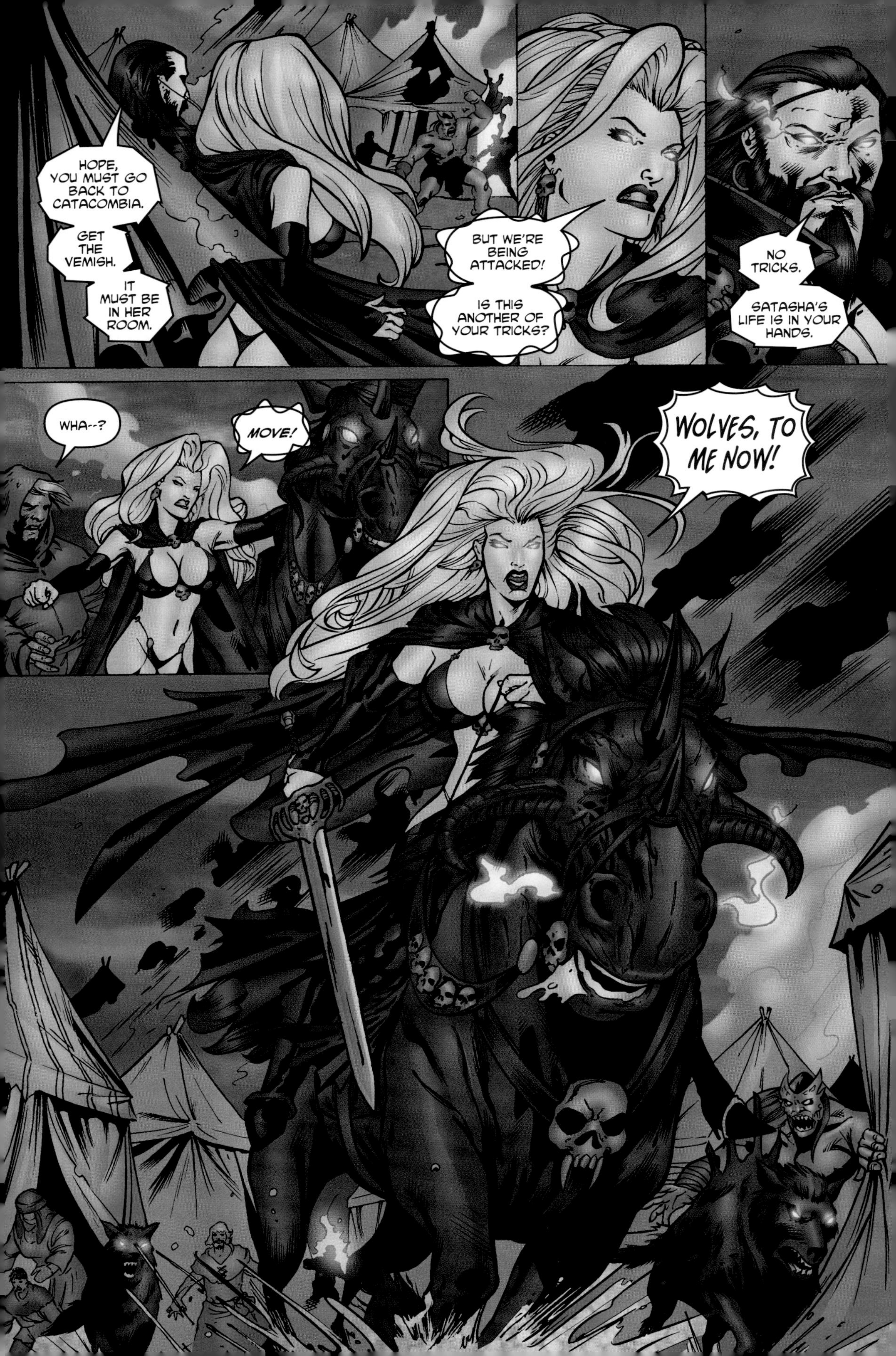
HOPE, YOU MUST GO BACK TO CATACOMBIA.
GET THE VEMISH.
IT MUST BE IN HER ROOM.
BUT WE'RE BEING ATTACKED!
IS THIS ANOTHER OF YOUR TRICKS?
NO TRICKS.
SATASHA'S LIFE IS IN YOUR HANDS.
WHA--?
MOVE!
WOLVES, TO ME NOW!

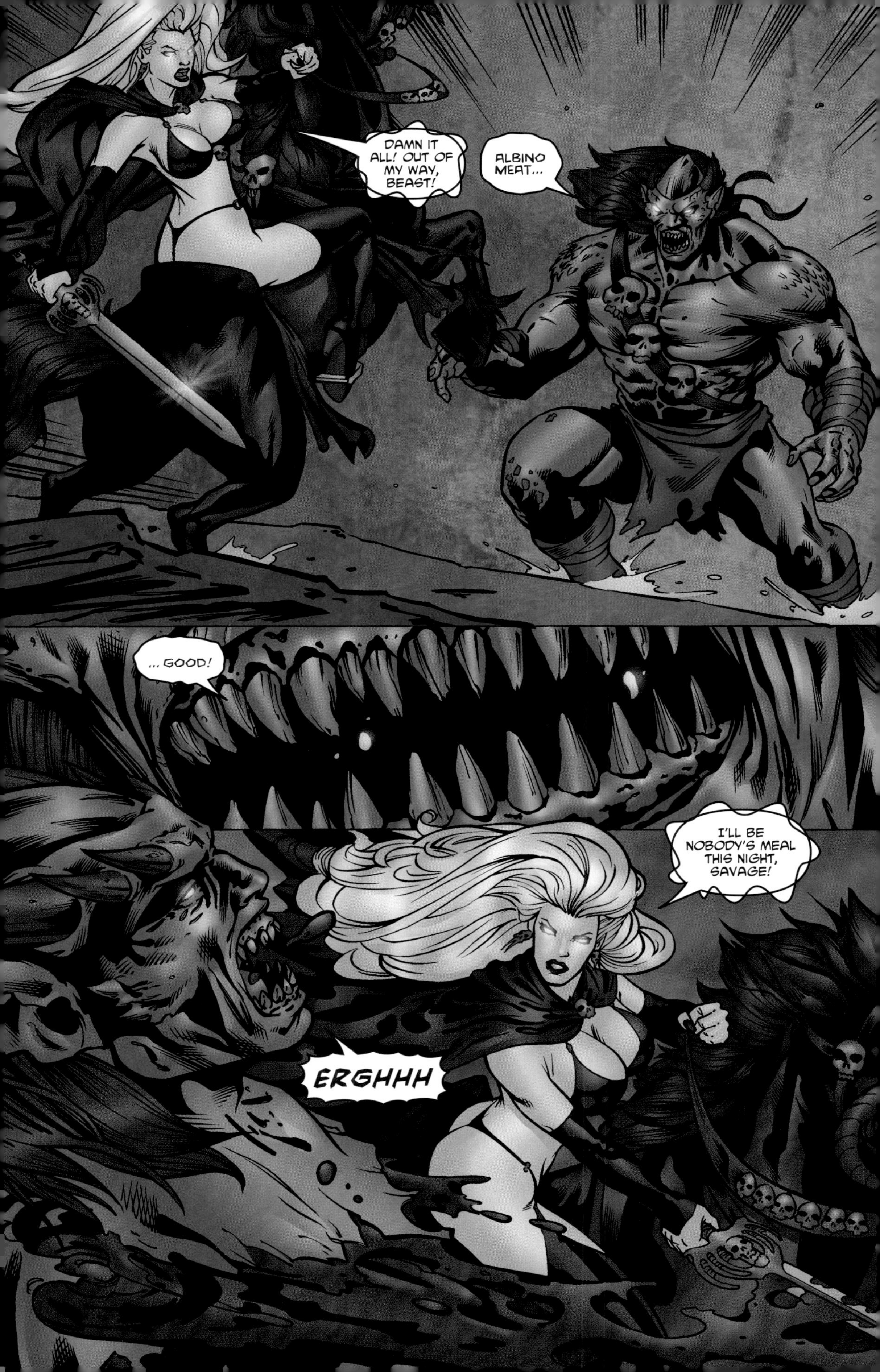
DAMN IT ALL! OUT OF MY WAY, BEAST!
ALBINO MEAT...
...GOOD!
I'LL BE NOBODY'S MEAL THIS NIGHT, SAVAGE!
ERGHHH

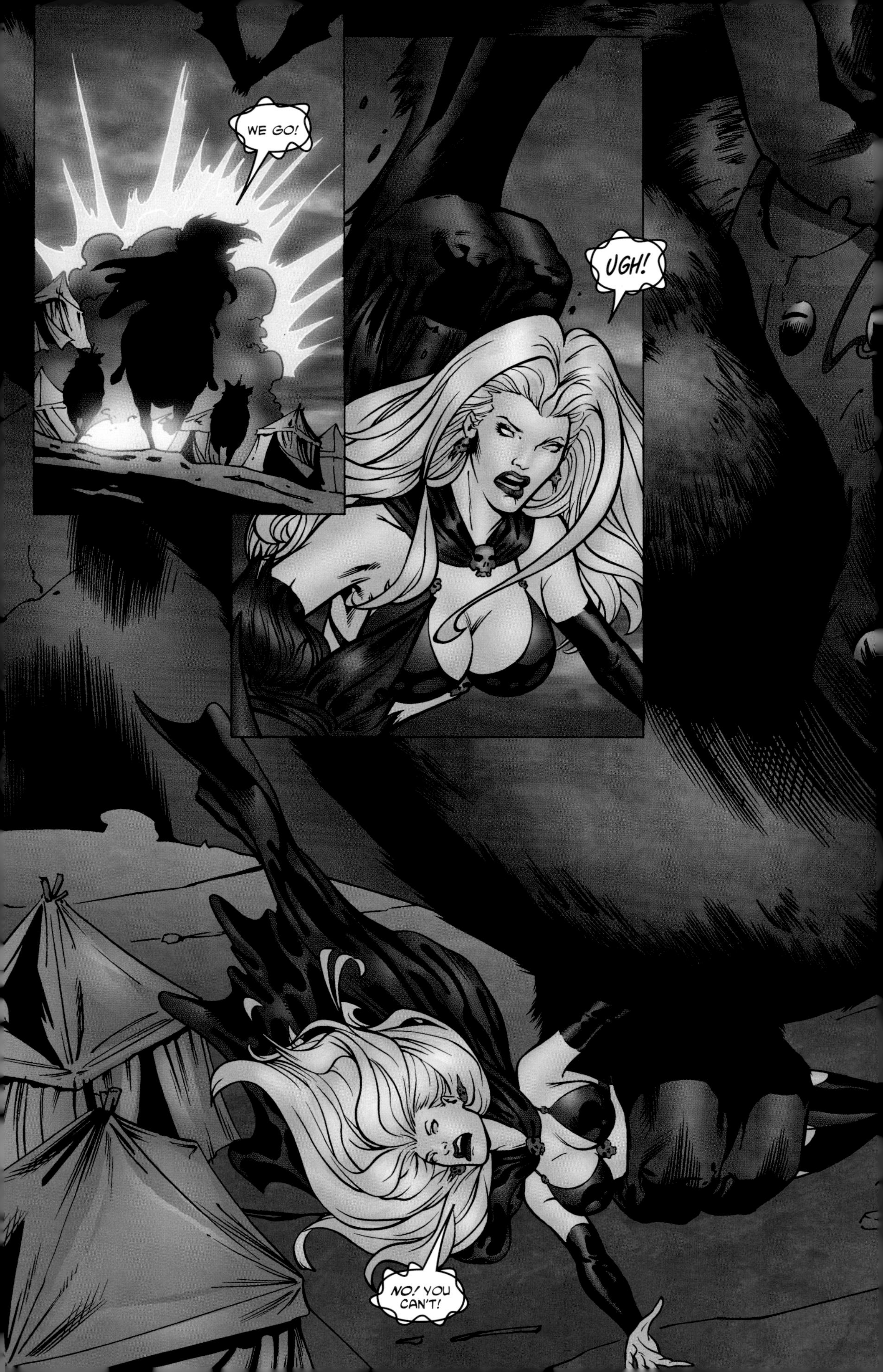
WE GO!
UGH!
NO! YOU CAN'T!

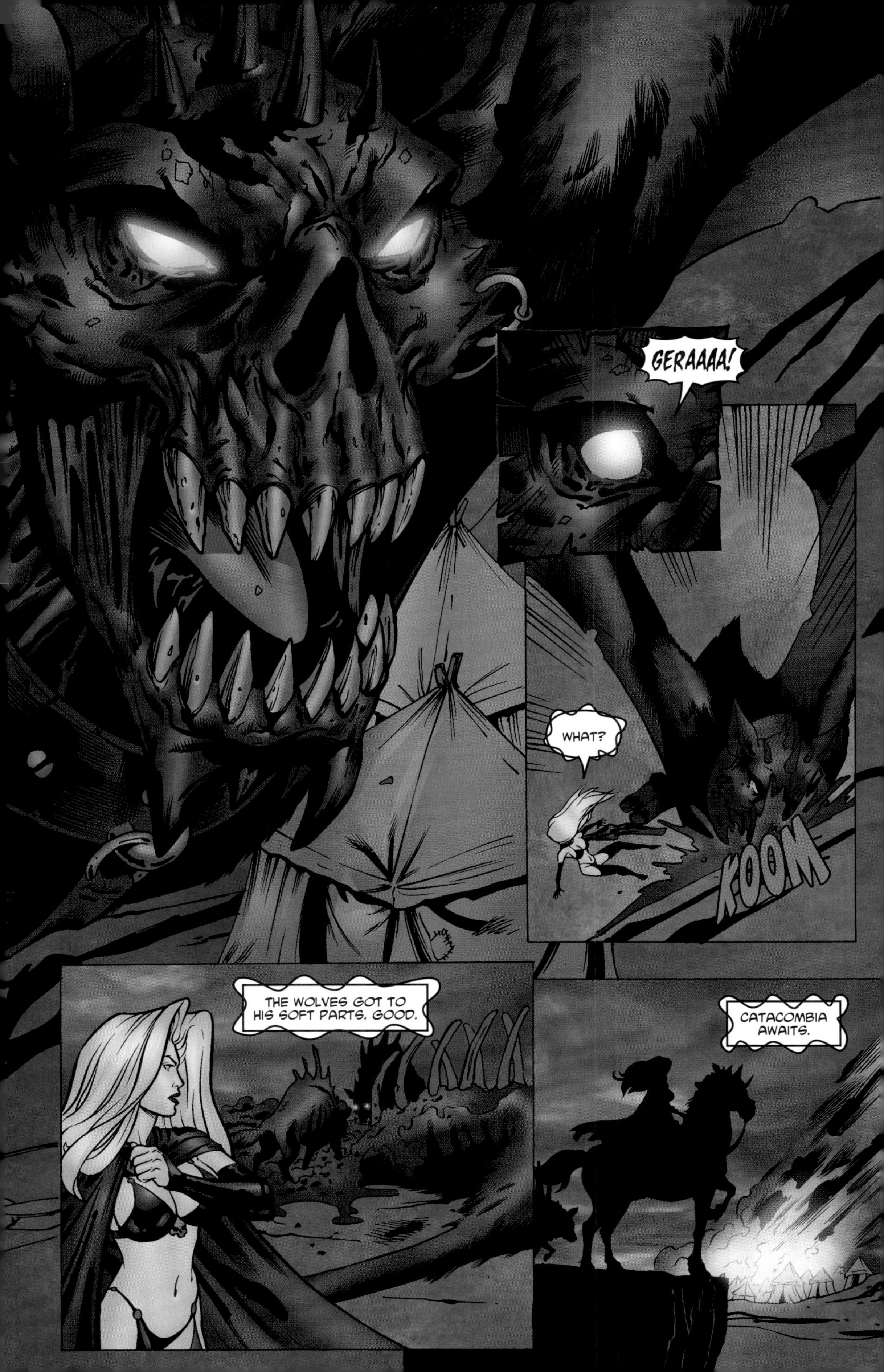
GERAAAA!
WHAT?
KOOM
THE WOLVES GOT TO HIS SOFT PARTS. GOOD.
CATACOMBIA AWAITS.

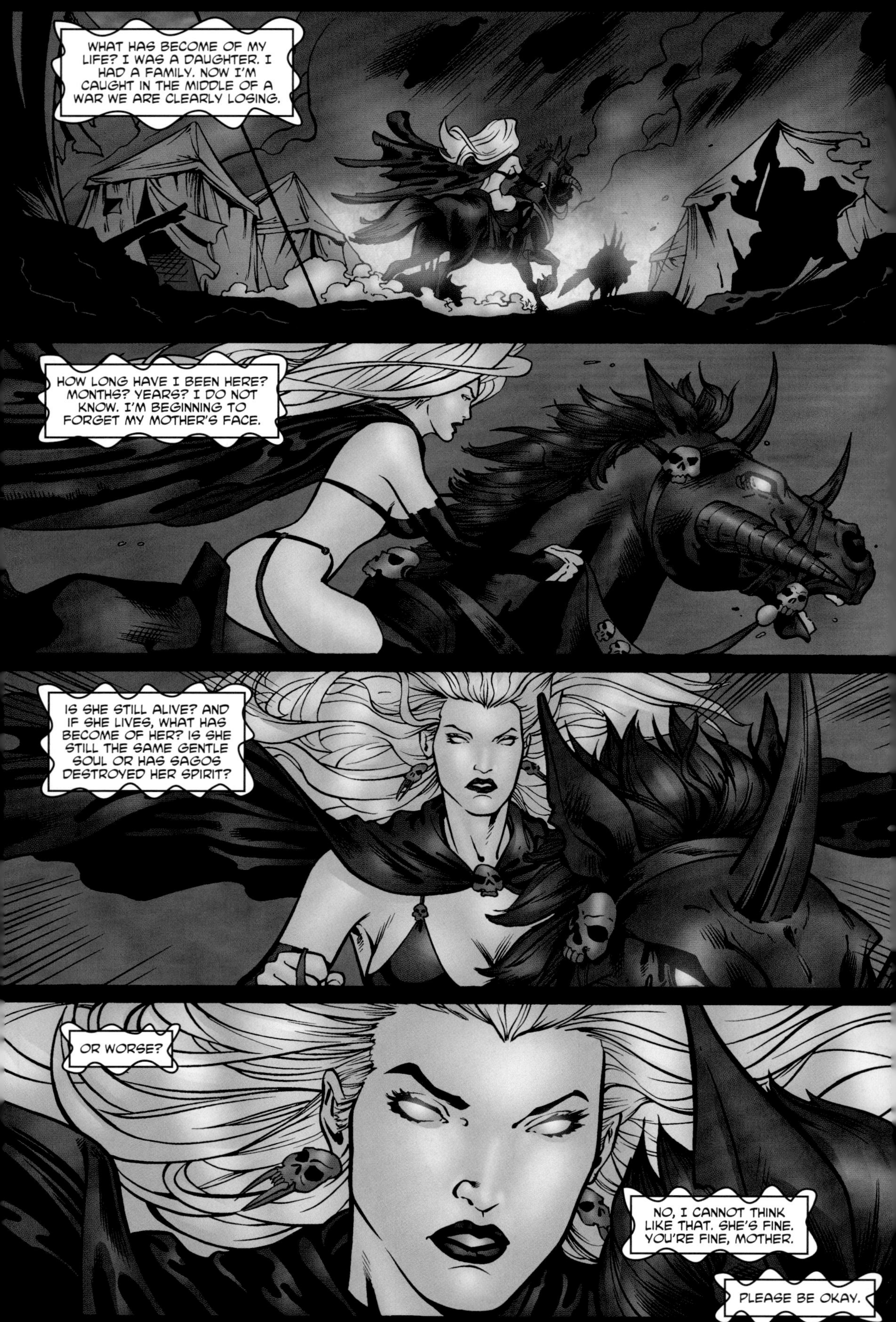
WHAT HAS BECOME OF MY LIFE? I WAS A DAUGHTER. I HAD A FAMILY. NOW I'M CAUGHT IN THE MIDDLE OF A WAR WE ARE CLEARLY LOSING.
HOW LONG HAVE I BEEN HERE? MONTHS? YEARS? I DO NOT KNOW. I'M BEGINNING TO FORGET MY MOTHER'S FACE.
IS SHE STILL ALIVE? AND IF SHE LIVES, WHAT HAS BECOME OF HER? IS SHE STILL THE SAME GENTLE SOUL OR HAS SAGOS DESTROYED HER SPIRIT?
OR WORSE?
NO, I CANNOT THINK LIKE THAT. SHE'S FINE. YOU'RE FINE, MOTHER.
PLEASE BE OKAY.

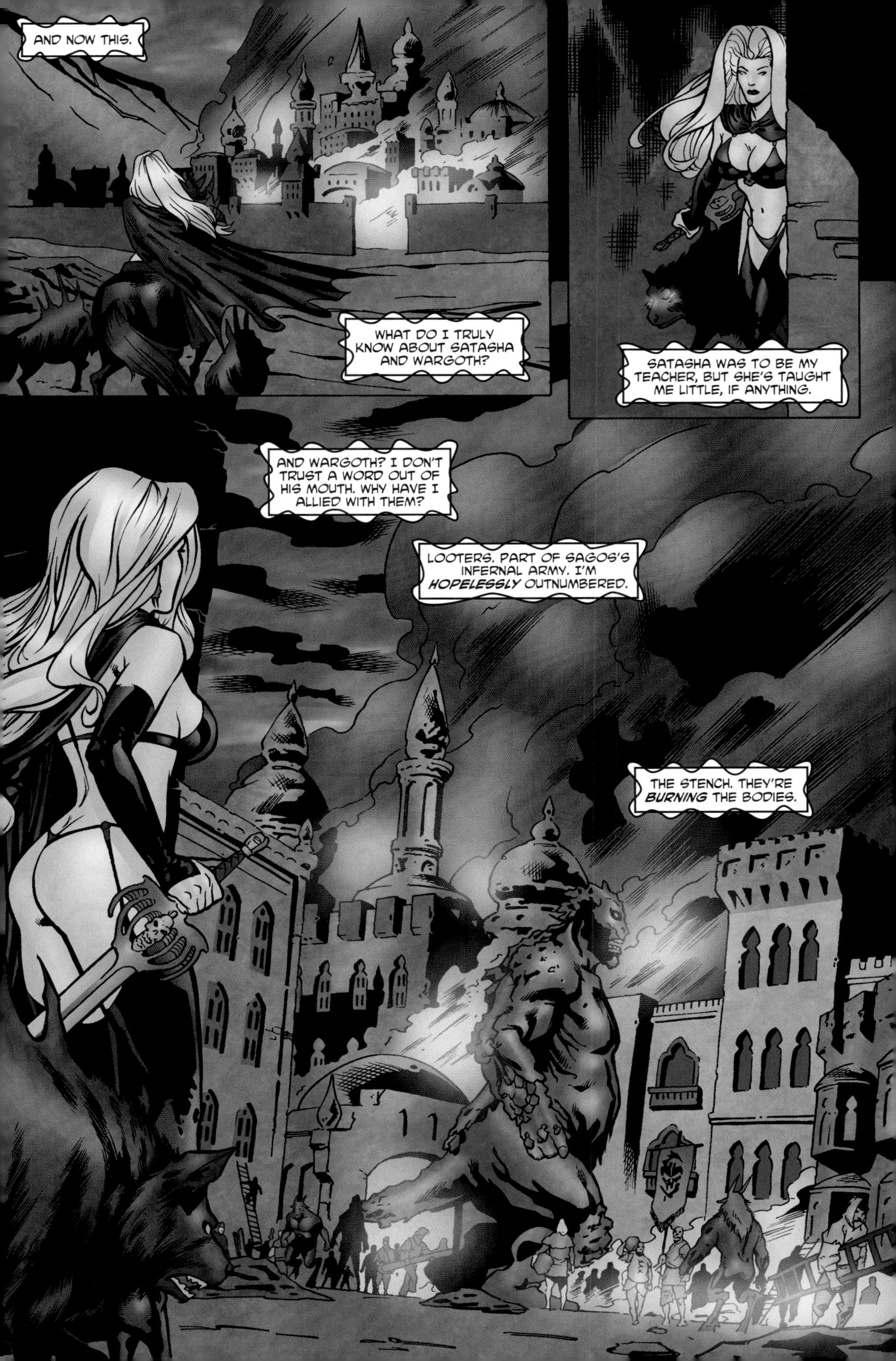
AND NOW THIS.
WHAT DO I TRULY KNOW ABOUT SATASHA AND WARGOTH?
SATASHA WAS TO BE MY TEACHER, BUT SHE'S TAUGHT ME LITTLE, IF ANYTHING.
AND WARGOTH? I DON'T TRUST A WORD OUT OF HIS MOUTH. WHY HAVE I ALLIED WITH THEM?
LOOTERS. PART OF SAGOS'S INFERNAL ARMY. I'M HOPELESSLY OUTNUMBERED.
THE STENCH. THEY'RE BURNING THE BODIES.

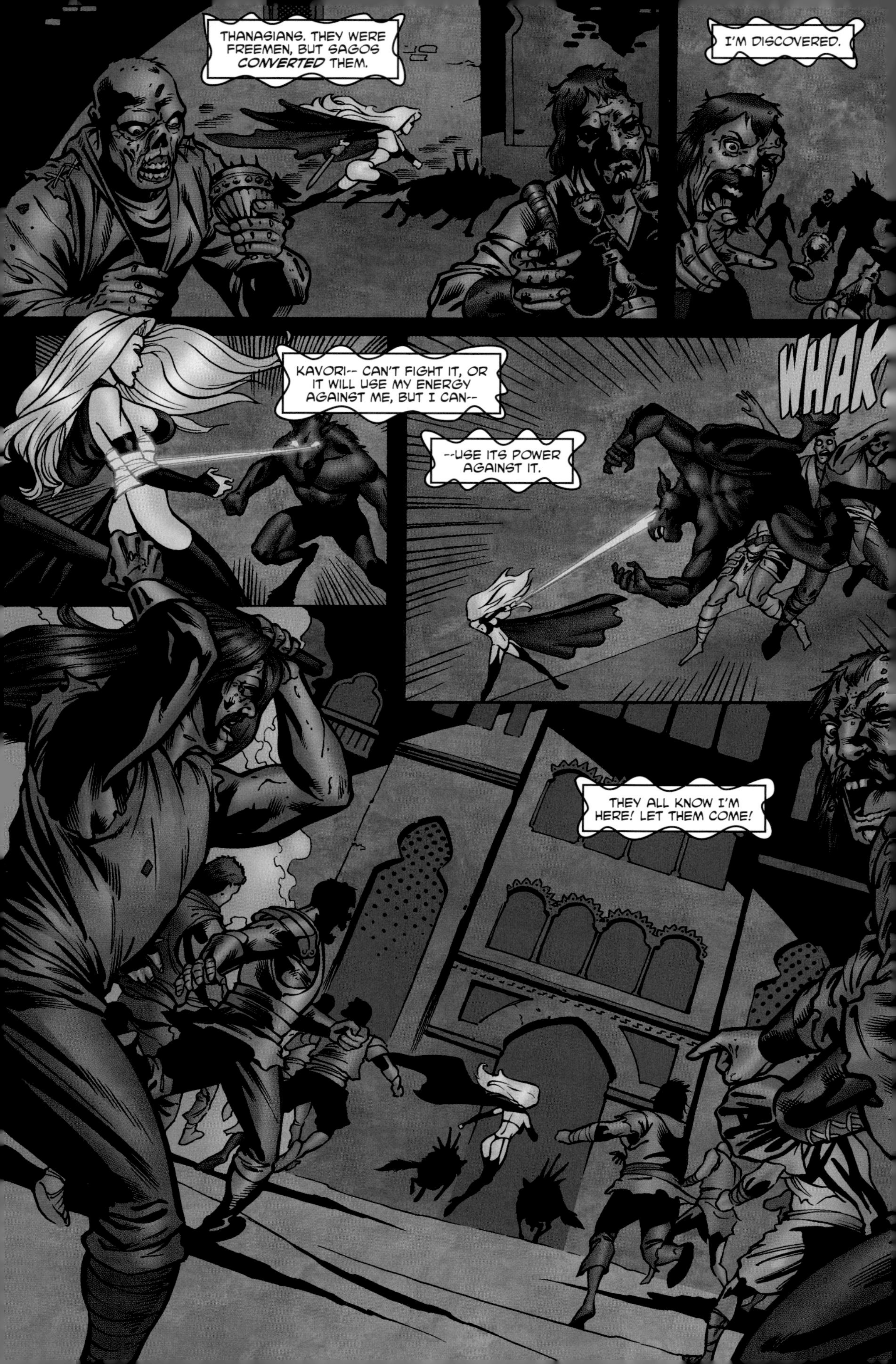
THANASIANS. THEY WERE FREEMEN, BUT SAGOS *CONVERTED* THEM.
I'M DISCOVERED.
KAVORI-- CAN'T FIGHT IT, OR IT WILL USE MY ENERGY AGAINST ME, BUT I CAN--
--USE ITS POWER AGAINST IT.
WHAK!
THEY ALL KNOW I'M HERE! LET THEM COME!

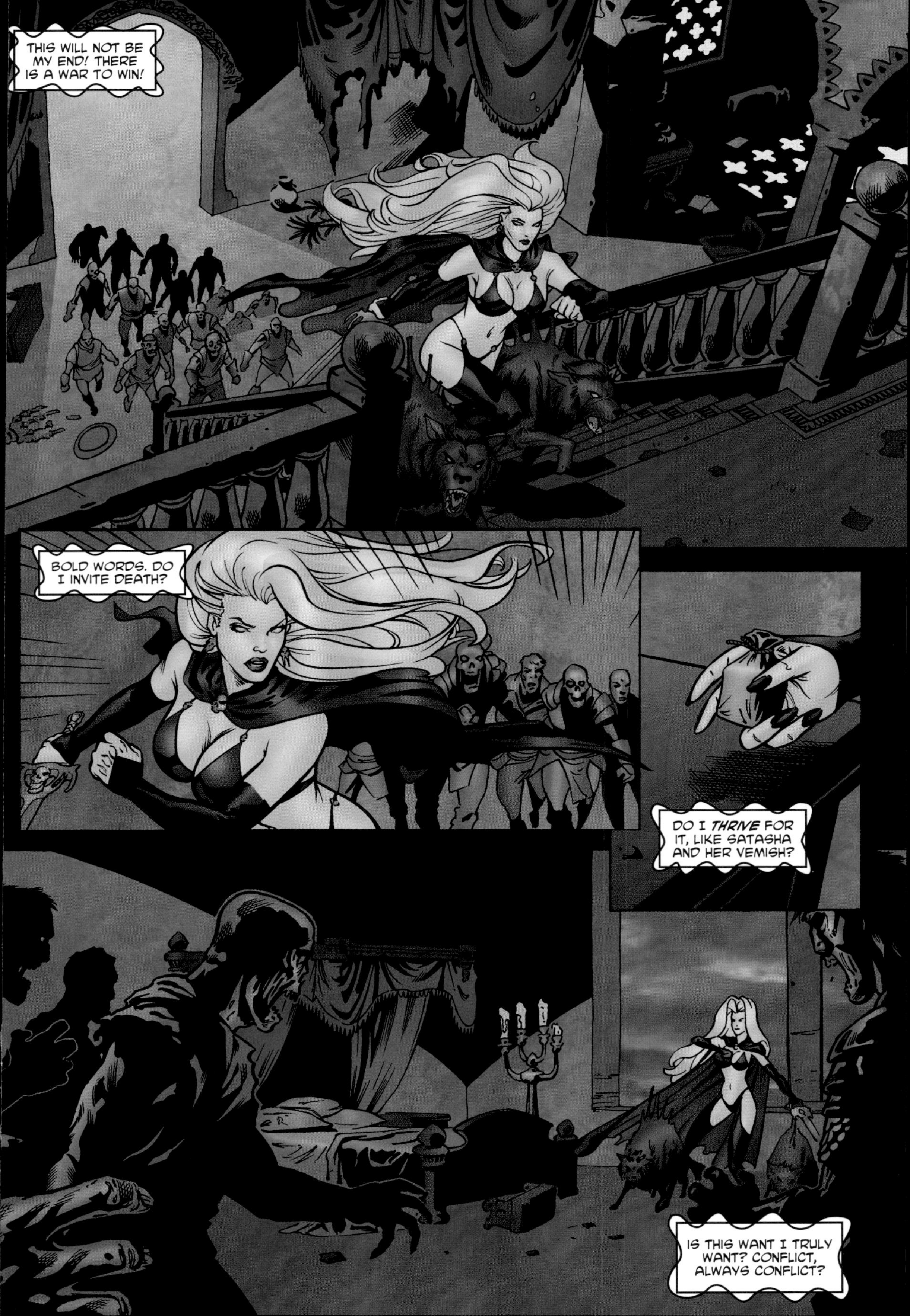
THIS WILL NOT BE MY END! THERE IS A WAR TO WIN!
BOLD WORDS. DO I INVITE DEATH?
DO I *THRIVE* FOR IT, LIKE SATASHA AND HER VEMISH?
IS THIS WANT I TRULY WANT? CONFLICT, ALWAYS CONFLICT?

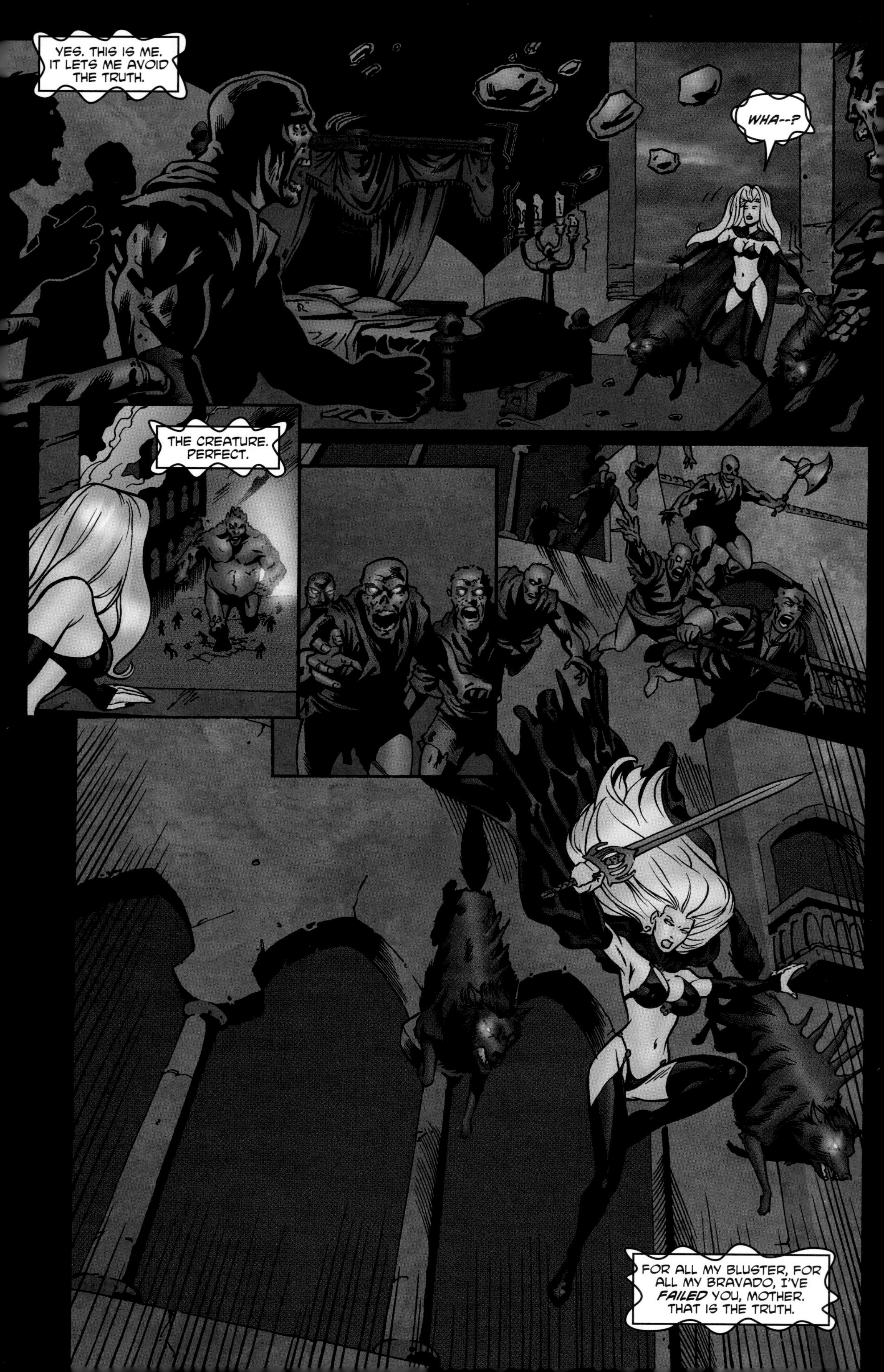
YES. THIS IS ME. IT LETS ME AVOID THE TRUTH.
WHA--?
THE CREATURE. PERFECT.
FOR ALL MY BLUSTER, FOR ALL MY BRAVADO, I'VE *FAILED* YOU, MOTHER. THAT IS THE TRUTH.

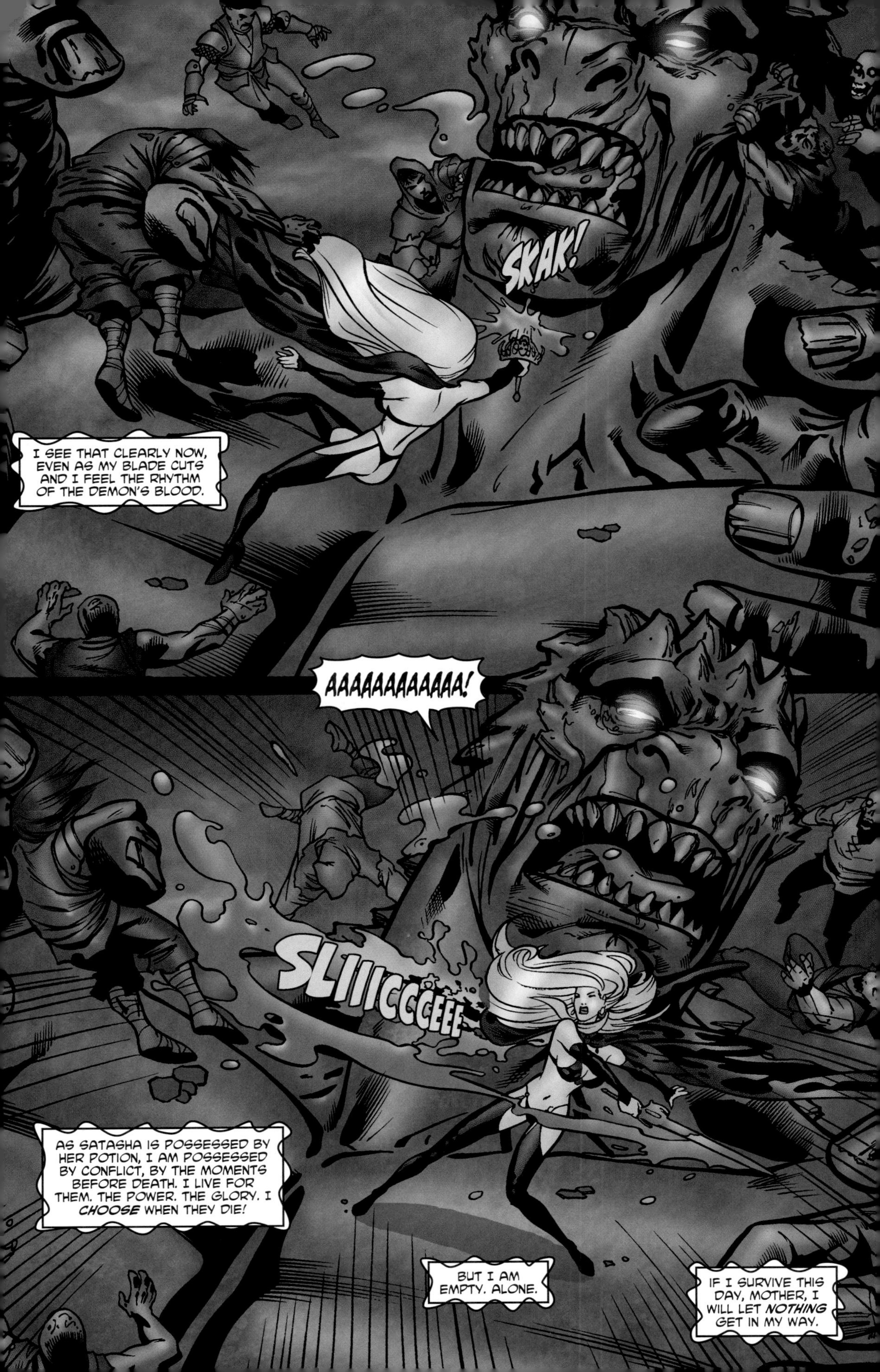
SKAK!
I SEE THAT CLEARLY NOW, EVEN AS MY BLADE CUTS AND I FEEL THE RHYTHM OF THE DEMON'S BLOOD.
AAAAAAAAAAAA!
SLIIICCCEEE
AS SATASHA IS POSSESSED BY HER POTION, I AM POSSESSED BY CONFLICT, BY THE MOMENTS BEFORE DEATH. I LIVE FOR THEM. THE POWER. THE GLORY. I *CHOOSE* WHEN THEY DIE!
BUT I AM EMPTY. ALONE.
IF I SURVIVE THIS DAY, MOTHER, I WILL LET *NOTHING* GET IN MY WAY.

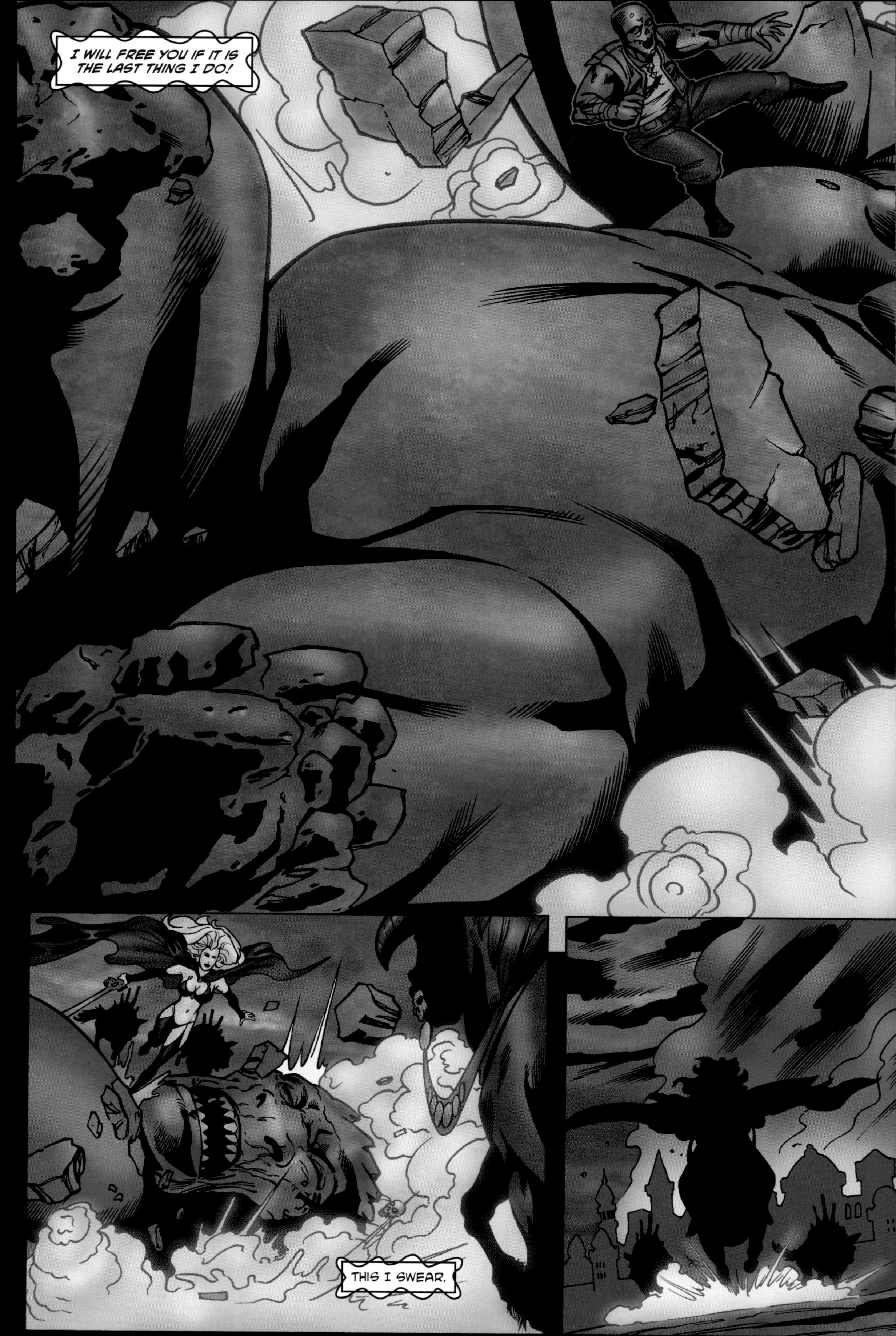
I WILL FREE YOU IF IT IS THE LAST THING I DO!
THIS I SWEAR.

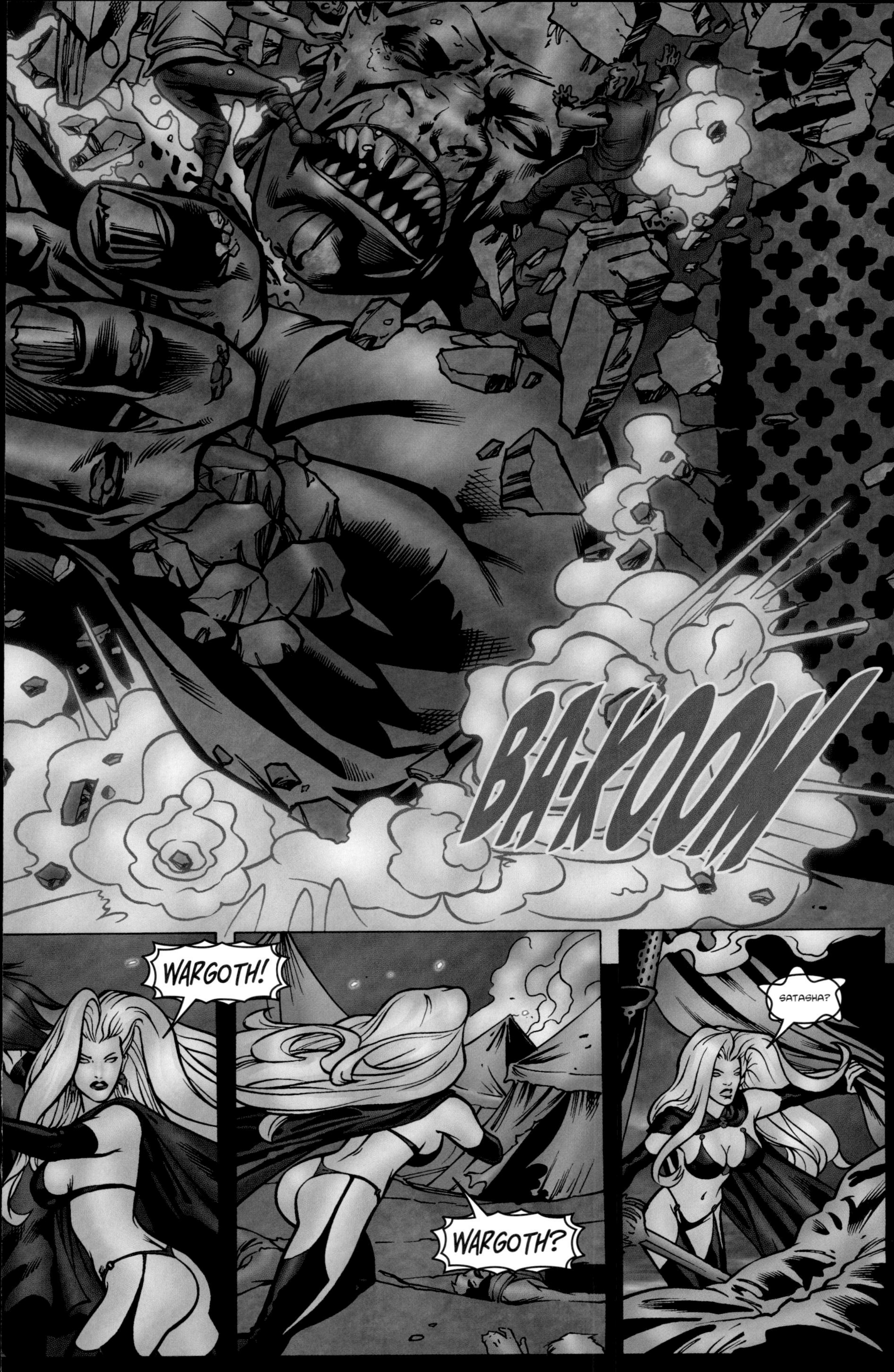
BA-KOOM
WARGOTH!
WARGOTH?
SATASHA?

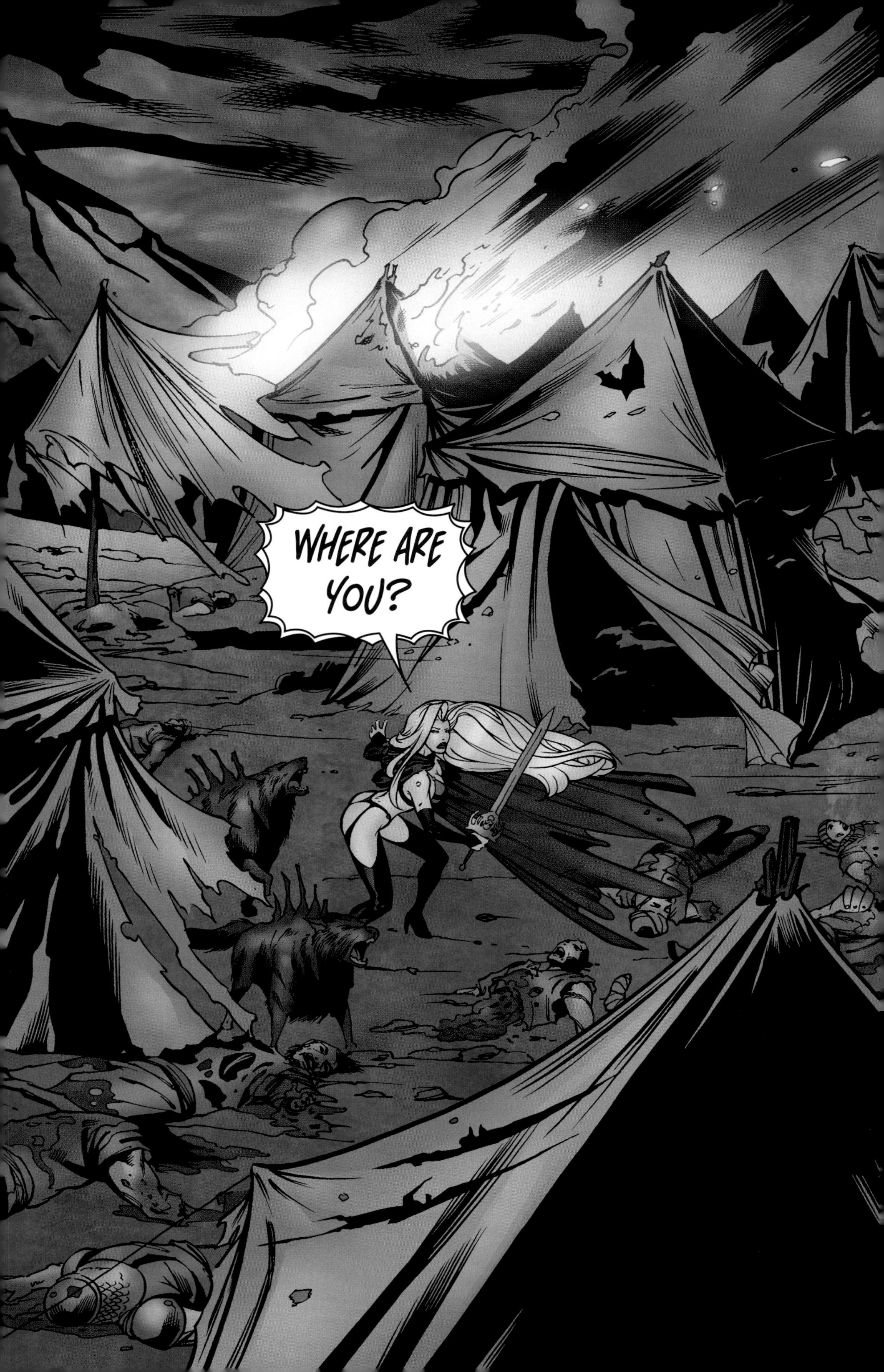
WHERE ARE YOU?

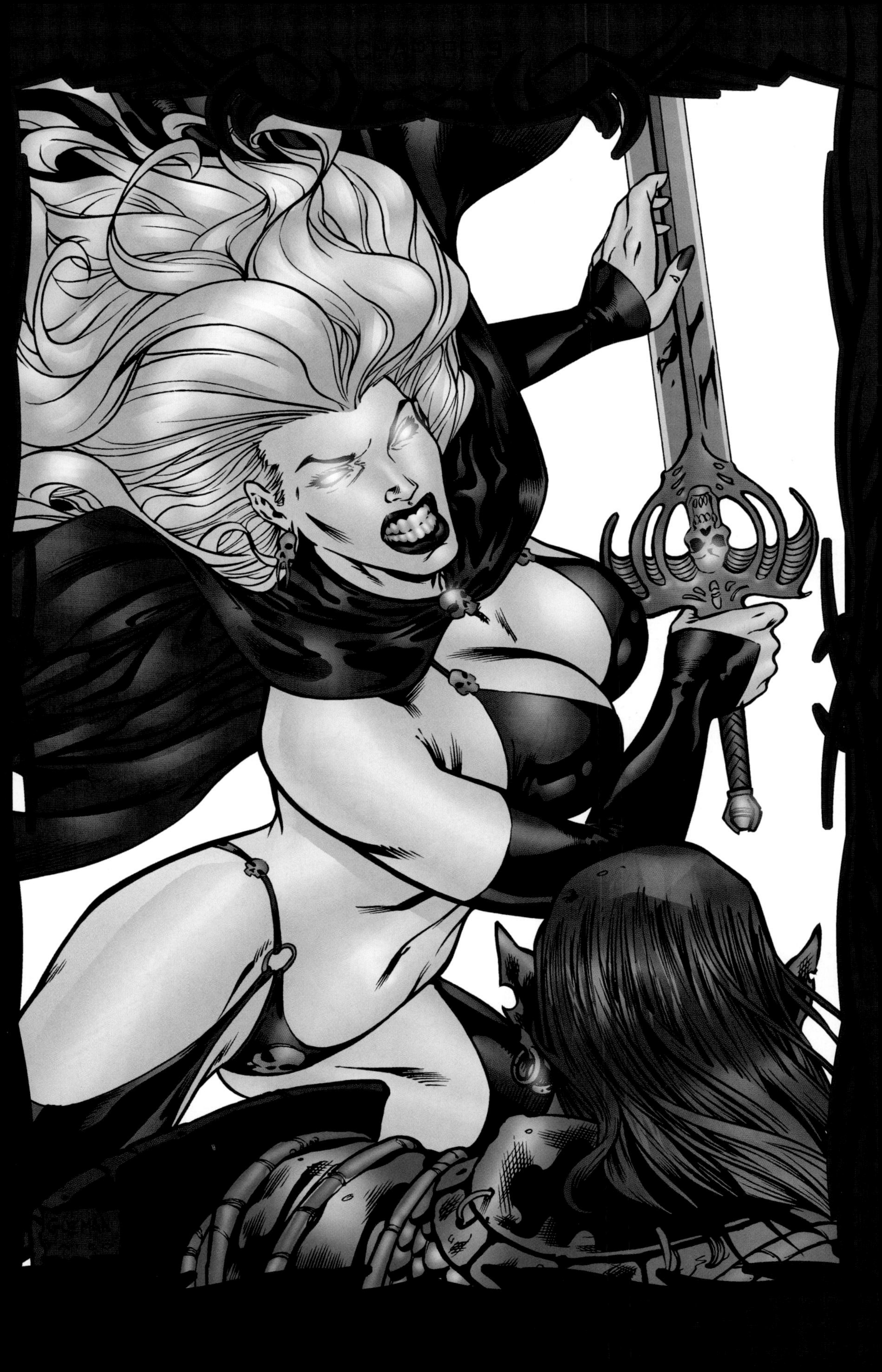

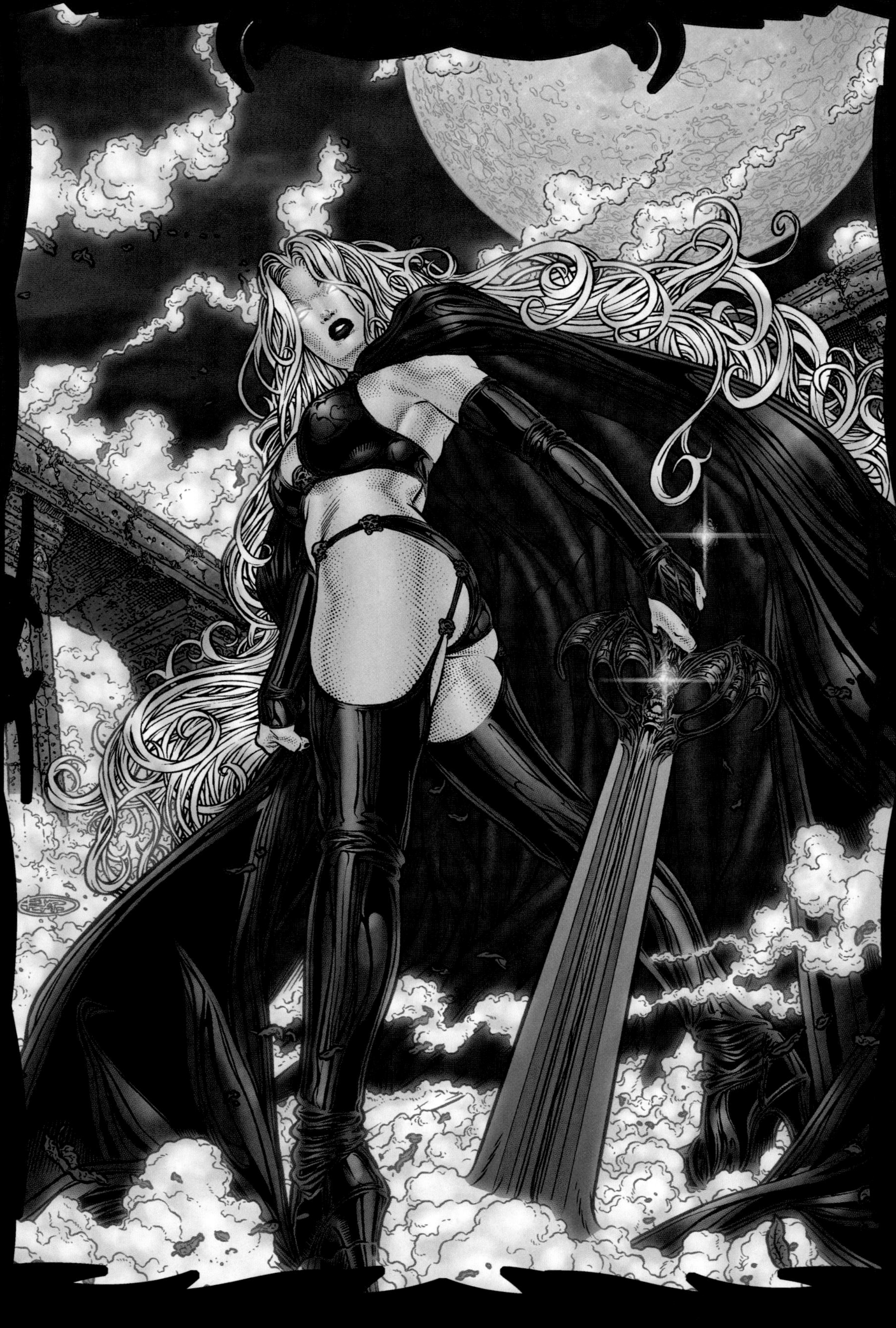

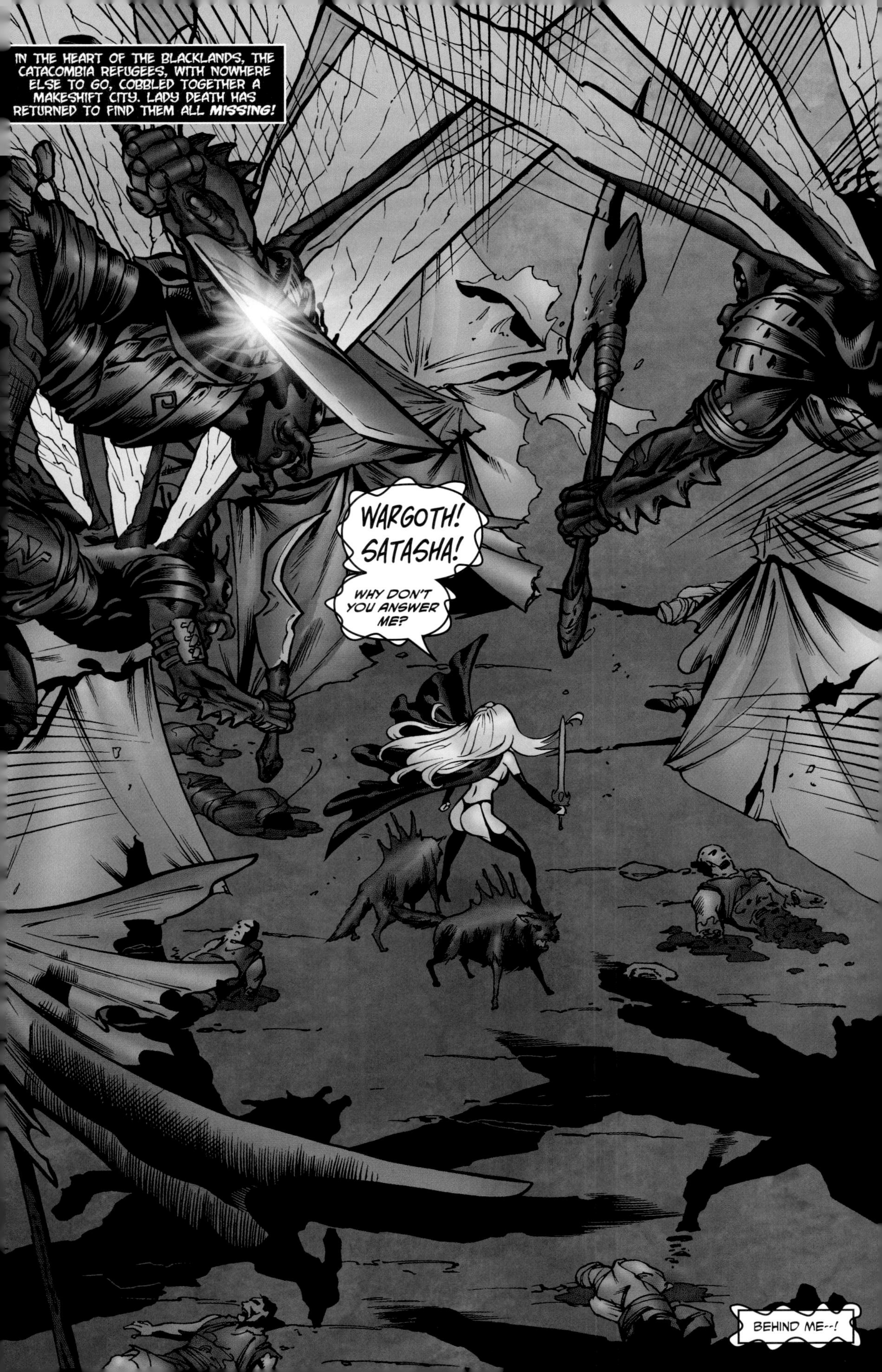
IN THE HEART OF THE BLACKLANDS, THE CATACOMBIA REFUGEES, WITH NOWHERE ELSE TO GO, COBBLED TOGETHER A MAKESHIFT CITY. LADY DEATH HAS RETURNED TO FIND THEM ALL *MISSING!*
WARGOTH! SATASHA!
WHY DON'T YOU ANSWER ME?
BEHIND ME--!

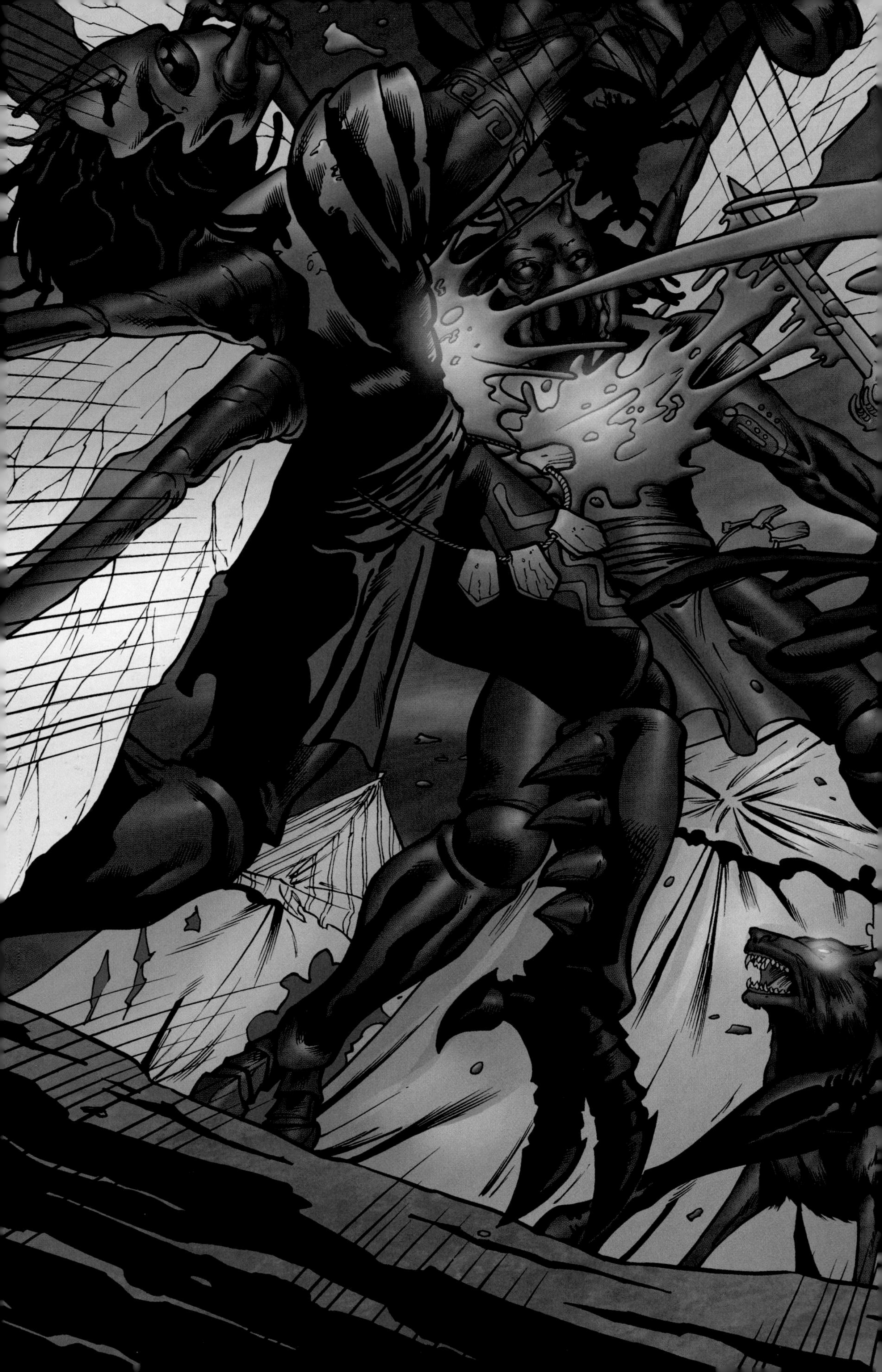

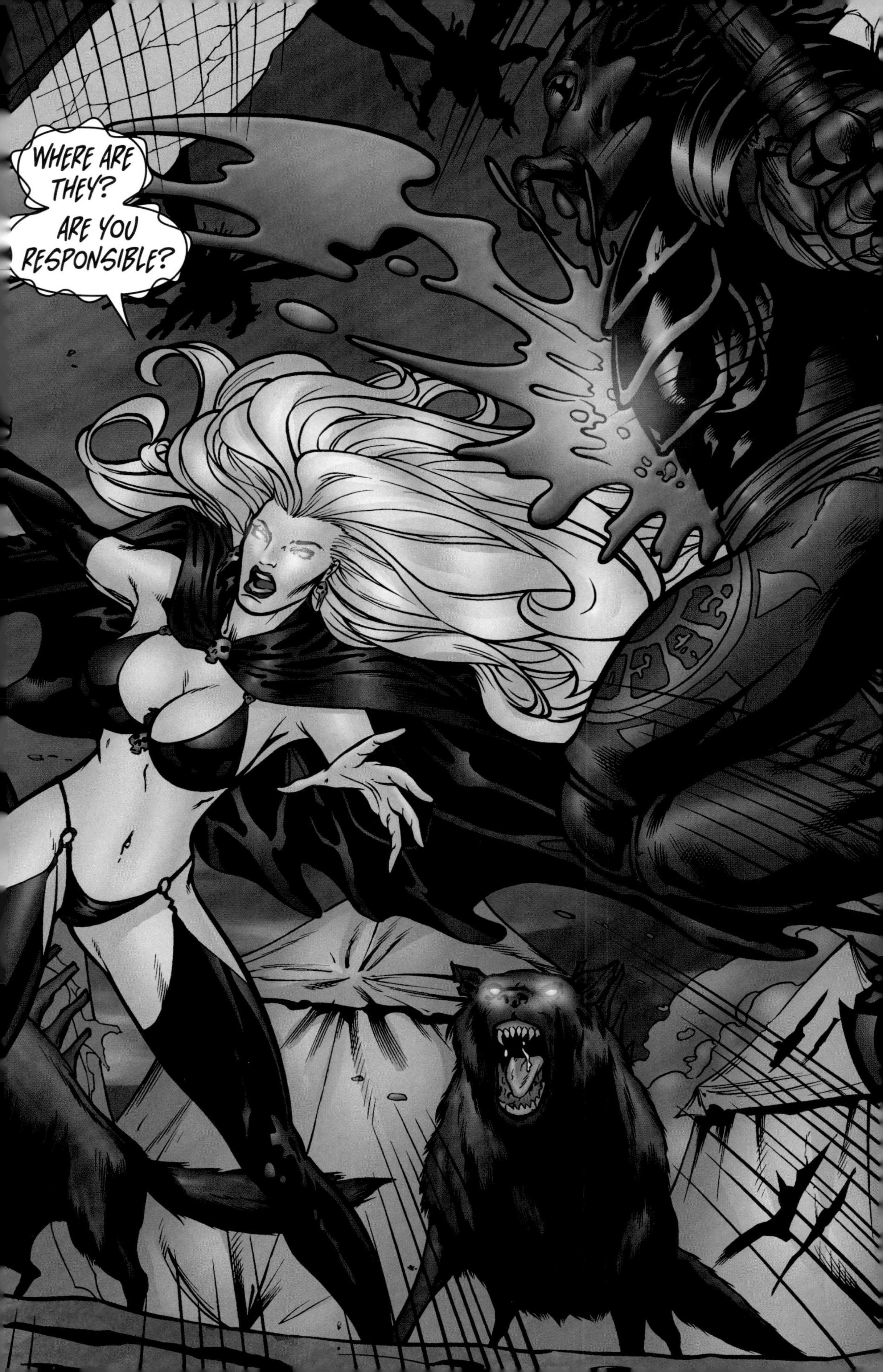
WHERE ARE THEY? ARE YOU RESPONSIBLE?

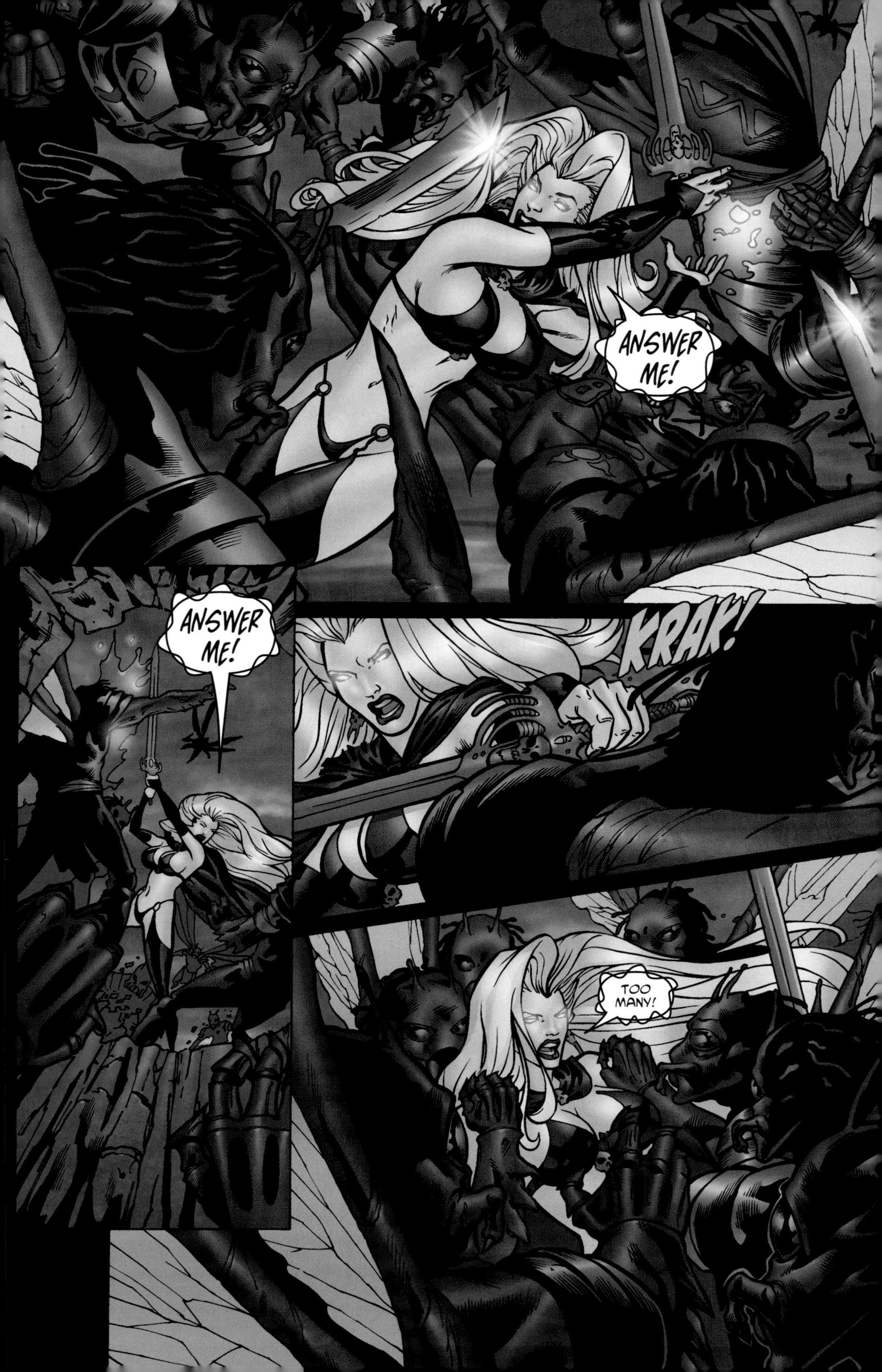
ANSWER ME!
ANSWER ME!
KRAK!
TOO MANY!

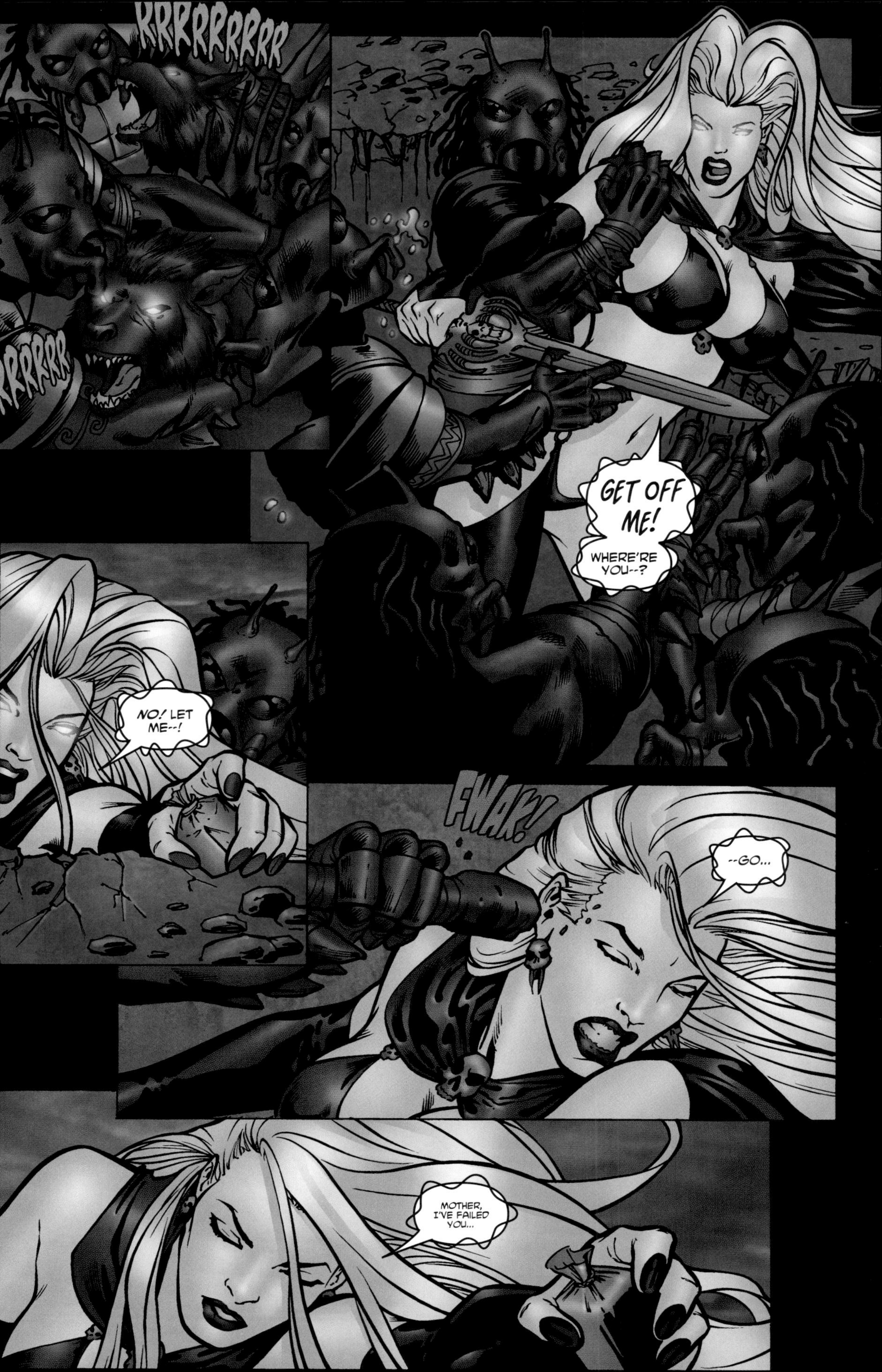
KRRRRRRRRR
RRRRRR
GET OFF ME!
WHERE'RE YOU--?
NO! LET ME--!
FWAK!
--GO...
MOTHER, I'VE FAILED YOU...

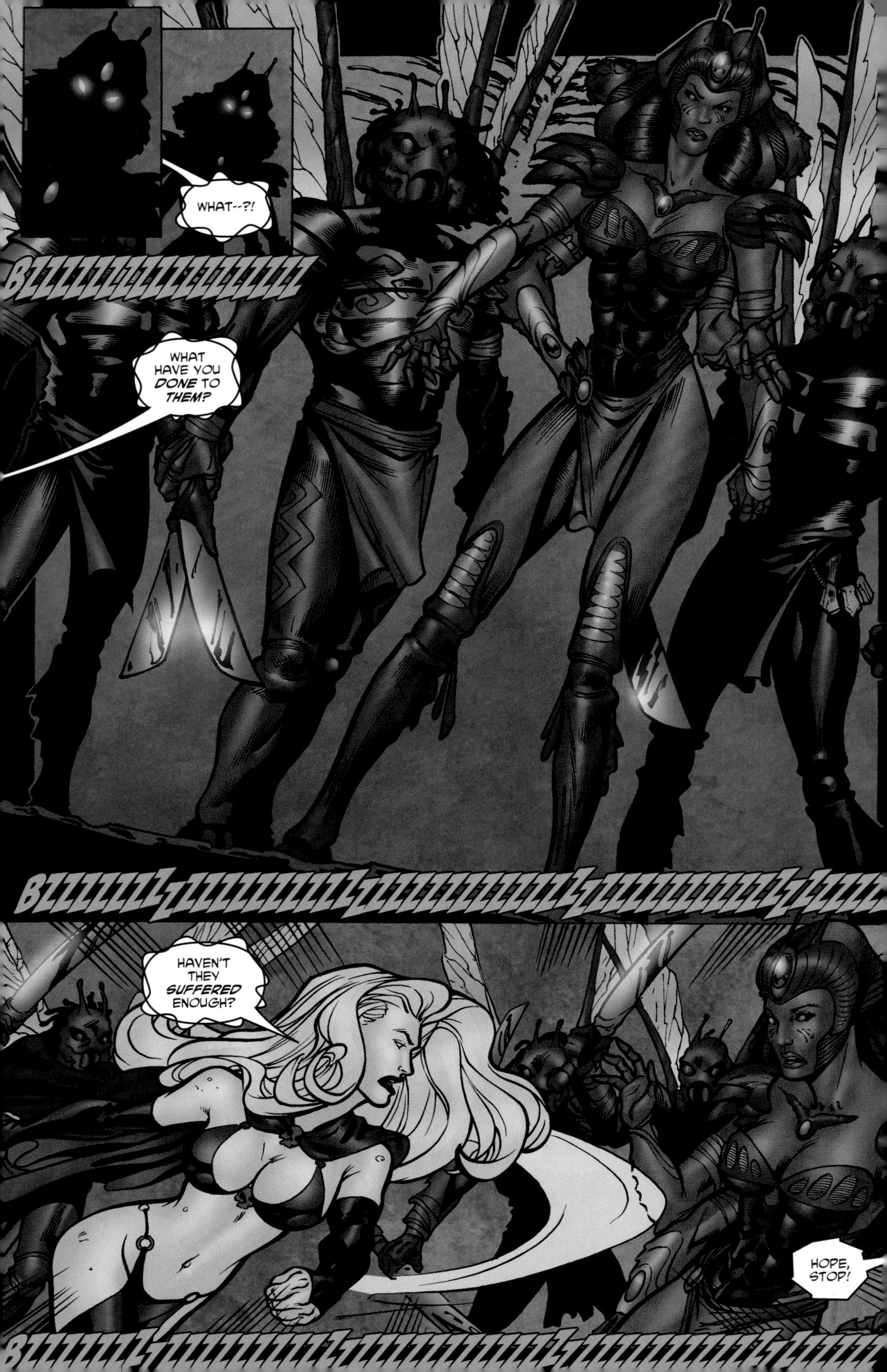
WHAT--?!
BZZZZZZZZZZZZZZZZZZZ
WHAT HAVE YOU *DONE* TO *THEM?*
BZZZZZZZZZZZZZZZZZZZZZZZZZZZZZZZZZZZZZZZZZZZZZZZZZZZZ
HAVEN'T THEY *SUFFERED* ENOUGH?
HOPE, STOP!
BZZZZZZZZZZZZZZZZZZZZZZZZZZZZZZZZZZZZZZZZZZZZZZZZZZZZ

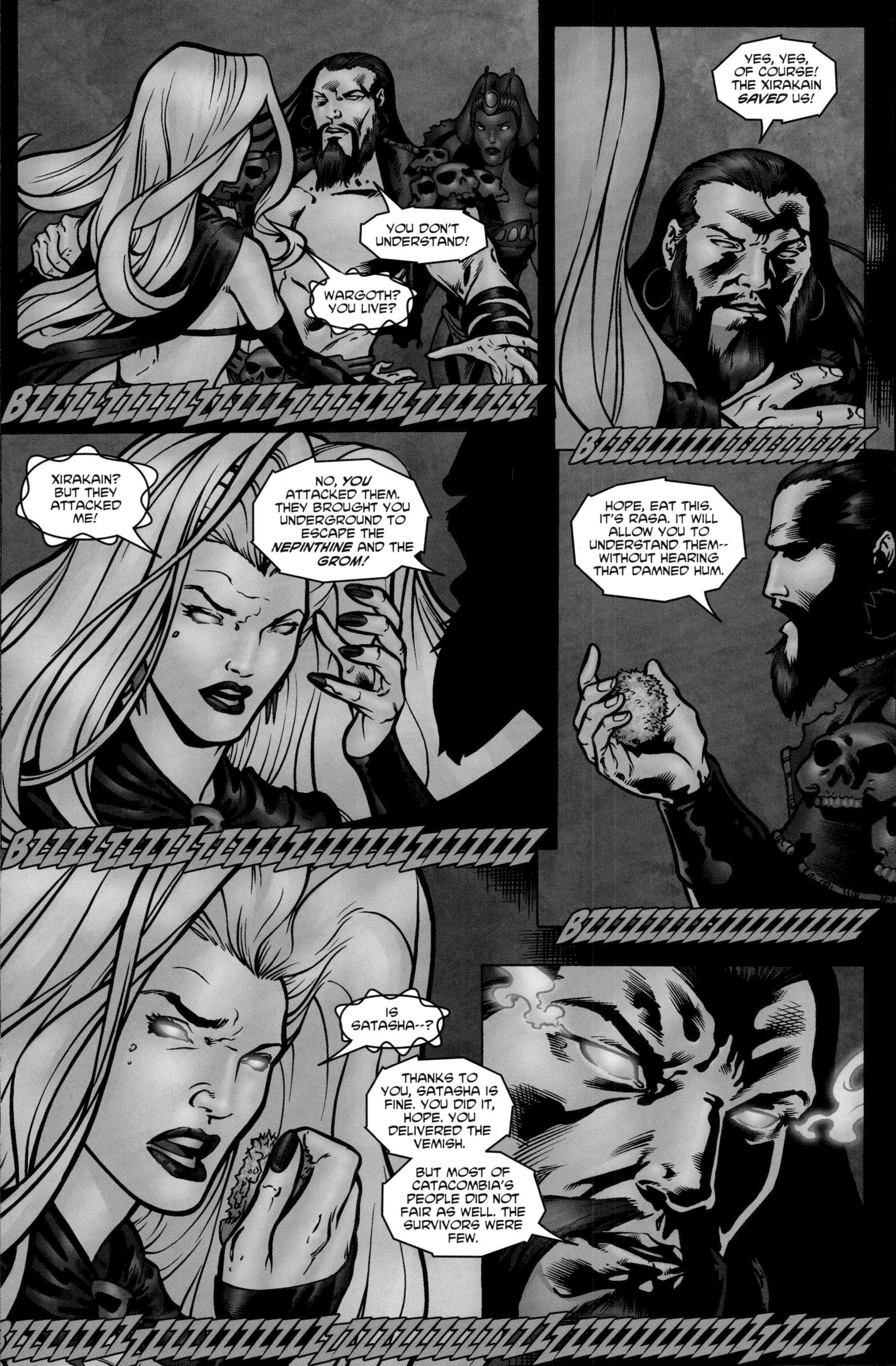
YOU DON'T UNDERSTAND!
WARGOTH? YOU LIVE?
BZZZZZZZZZZZZZZZZZZZZZZZZZZZZ
YES, YES, OF COURSE! THE XIRAKAIN *SAVED* US!
BZZZZZZZZZZZZZZZZZZZZ
XIRAKAIN? BUT THEY ATTACKED ME!
NO, *YOU* ATTACKED THEM. THEY BROUGHT YOU UNDERGROUND TO ESCAPE THE *NEPINTHINE* AND THE *GROM!*
BZZZZZZZZZZZZZZZZZZZZZZZZZZZZ
HOPE, EAT THIS. IT'S RASA. IT WILL ALLOW YOU TO UNDERSTAND THEM-- WITHOUT HEARING THAT DAMNED HUM.
BZZZZZZZZZZZZZZZZZZZ
IS SATASHA--?
THANKS TO YOU, SATASHA IS FINE. YOU DID IT, HOPE. YOU DELIVERED THE VEMISH.
BUT MOST OF CATACOMBIA'S PEOPLE DID NOT FAIR AS WELL. THE SURVIVORS WERE FEW.
BZZZZZZZZZZZZZZZZZZZZZZZZZZZZZZZZZZZZZZZZZZZZZZZZZZZ

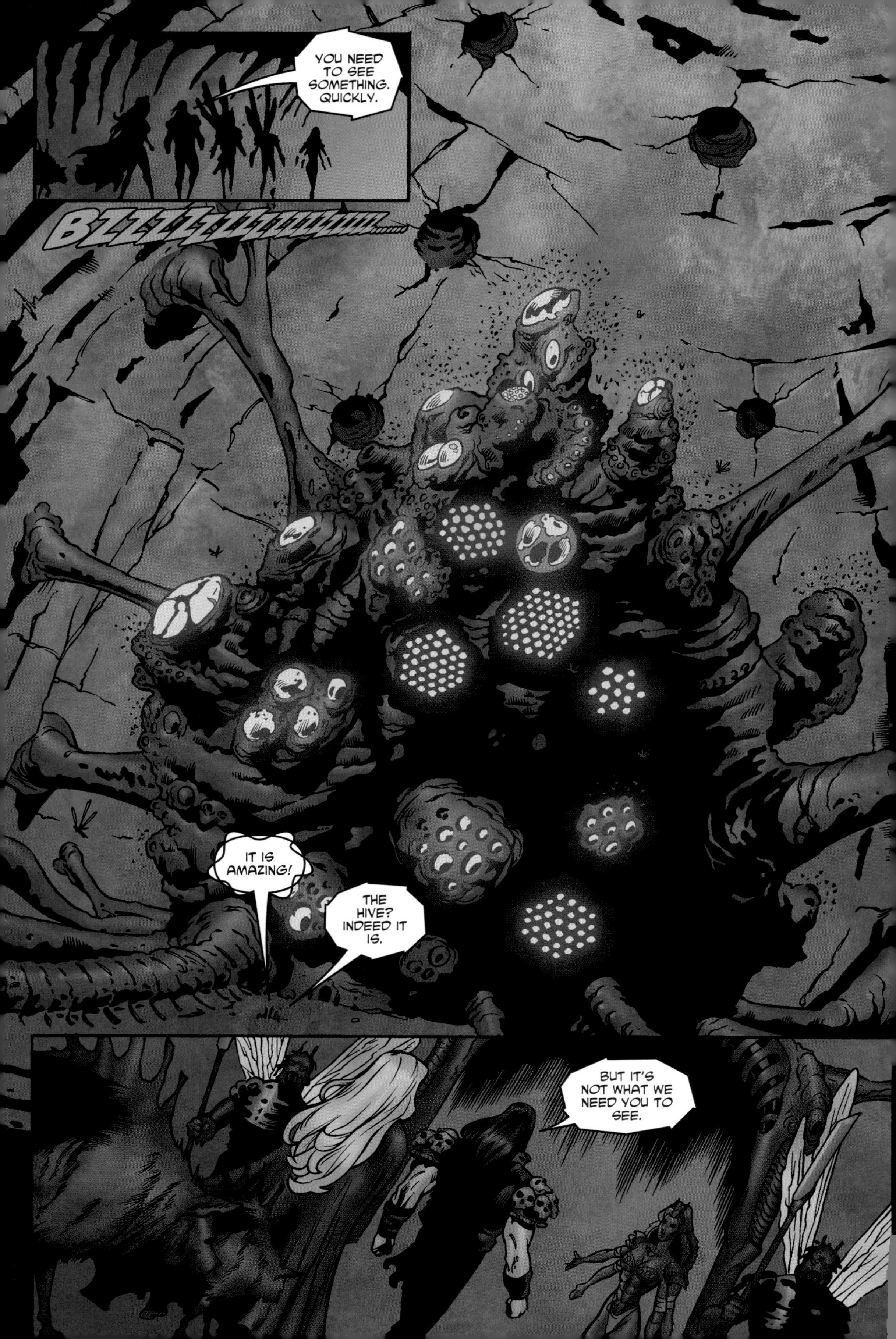
YOU NEED TO SEE SOMETHING. QUICKLY.
BZZZZZZZZZZZZZ.......
IT IS AMAZING!
THE HIVE? INDEED IT IS.
BUT IT'S NOT WHAT WE NEED YOU TO SEE.

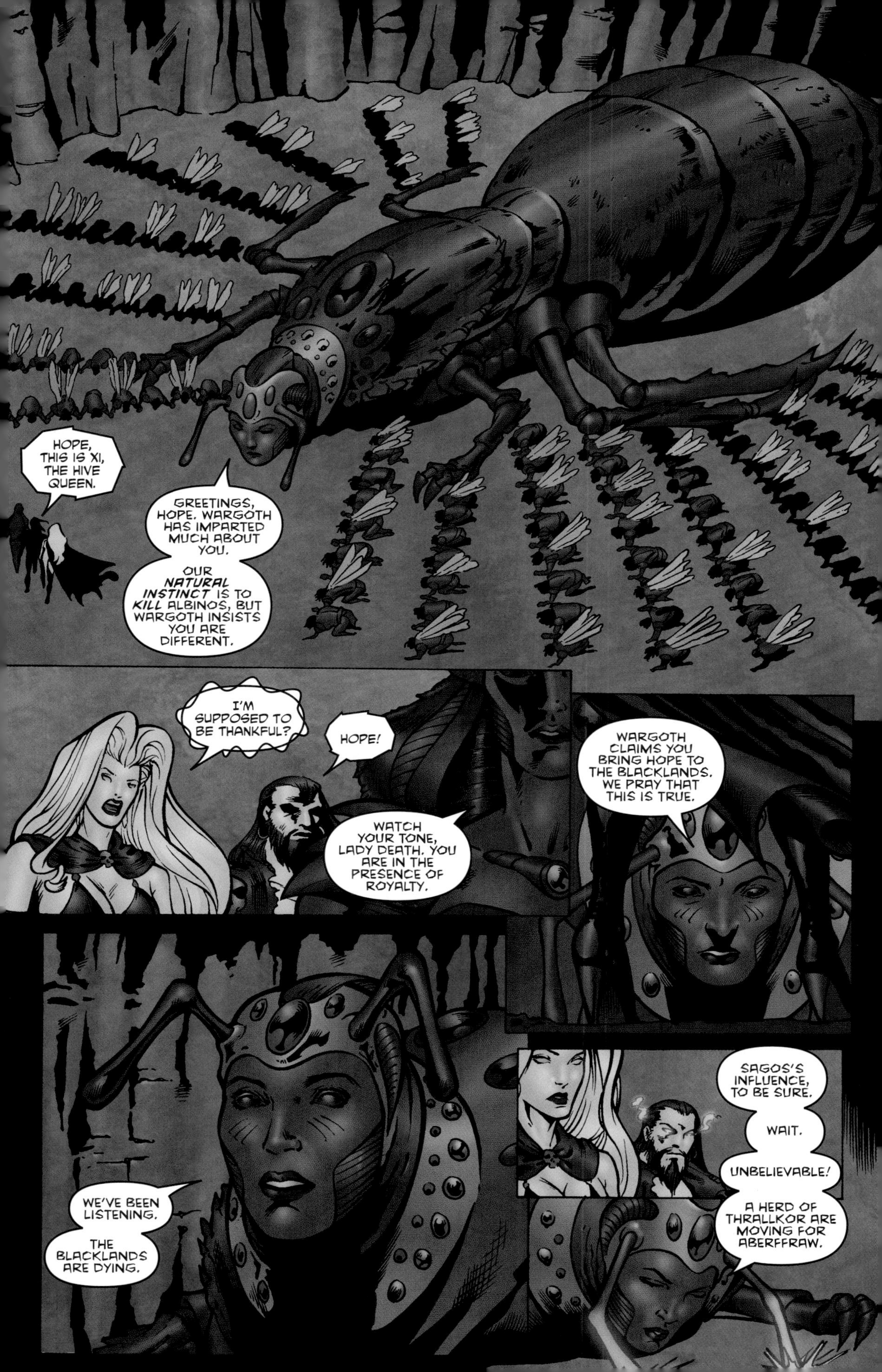
HOPE, THIS IS XI, THE HIVE QUEEN.
GREETINGS, HOPE. WARGOTH HAS IMPARTED MUCH ABOUT YOU.
OUR NATURAL INSTINCT IS TO KILL ALBINOS, BUT WARGOTH INSISTS YOU ARE DIFFERENT.
I'M SUPPOSED TO BE THANKFUL?
HOPE!
WATCH YOUR TONE, LADY DEATH. YOU ARE IN THE PRESENCE OF ROYALTY.
WARGOTH CLAIMS YOU BRING HOPE TO THE BLACKLANDS. WE PRAY THAT THIS IS TRUE.
WE'VE BEEN LISTENING.
THE BLACKLANDS ARE DYING.
SAGOS'S INFLUENCE, TO BE SURE.
WAIT.
UNBELIEVABLE!
A HERD OF THRALLKOR ARE MOVING FOR ABERFFRAW.

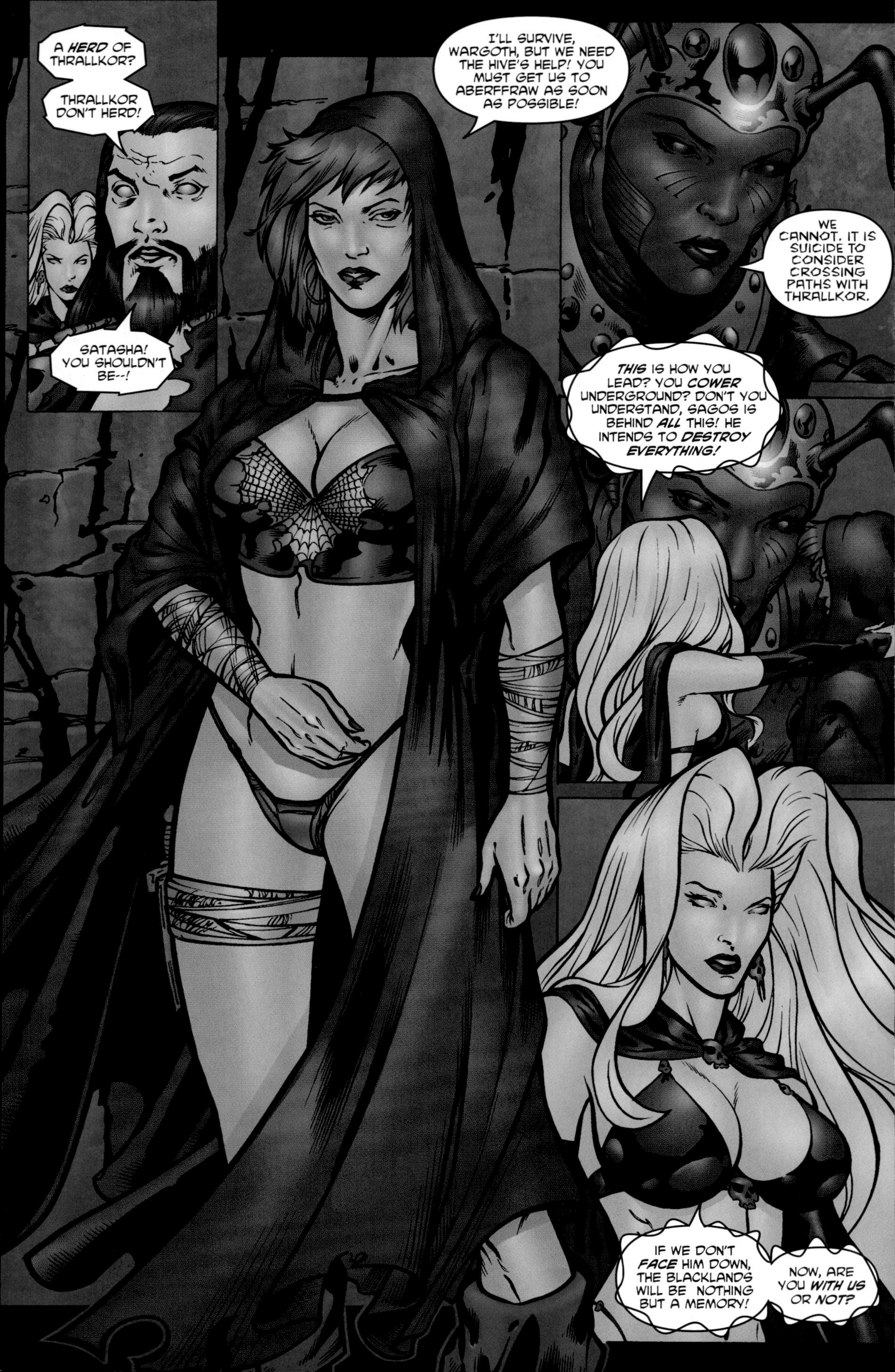
A HERD OF THRALLKOR?
THRALLKOR DON'T HERD!
SATASHA! YOU SHOULDN'T BE--!
I'LL SURVIVE, WARGOTH, BUT WE NEED THE HIVE'S HELP! YOU MUST GET US TO ABERFFRAW AS SOON AS POSSIBLE!
WE CANNOT. IT IS SUICIDE TO CONSIDER CROSSING PATHS WITH THRALLKOR.
THIS IS HOW YOU LEAD? YOU COWER UNDERGROUND? DON'T YOU UNDERSTAND, SAGOS IS BEHIND ALL THIS! HE INTENDS TO DESTROY EVERYTHING!
IF WE DON'T FACE HIM DOWN, THE BLACKLANDS WILL BE NOTHING BUT A MEMORY!
NOW, ARE YOU WITH US OR NOT?

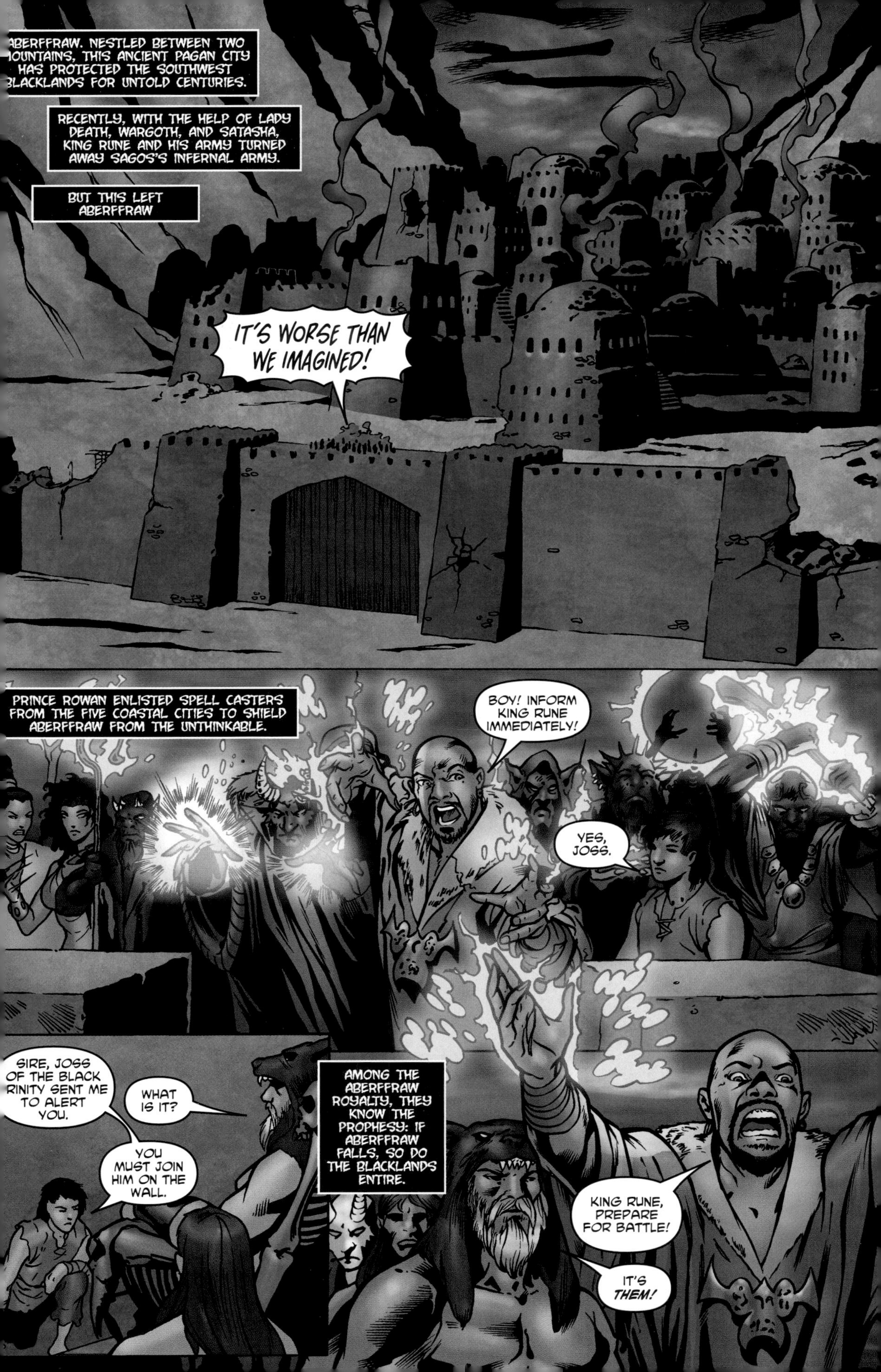
ABERFFRAW. NESTLED BETWEEN TWO MOUNTAINS, THIS ANCIENT PAGAN CITY HAS PROTECTED THE SOUTHWEST BLACKLANDS FOR UNTOLD CENTURIES.
RECENTLY, WITH THE HELP OF LADY DEATH, WARGOTH, AND SATASHA, KING RUNE AND HIS ARMY TURNED AWAY SAGOS'S INFERNAL ARMY.
BUT THIS LEFT ABERFFRAW
IT'S WORSE THAN WE IMAGINED!
PRINCE ROWAN ENLISTED SPELL CASTERS FROM THE FIVE COASTAL CITIES TO SHIELD ABERFFRAW FROM THE UNTHINKABLE.
BOY! INFORM KING RUNE IMMEDIATELY!
YES, JOSS.
SIRE, JOSS OF THE BLACK RINITY SENT ME TO ALERT YOU.
WHAT IS IT?
YOU MUST JOIN HIM ON THE WALL.
AMONG THE ABERFFRAW ROYALTY, THEY KNOW THE PROPHESY: IF ABERFFRAW FALLS, SO DO THE BLACKLANDS ENTIRE.
KING RUNE, PREPARE FOR BATTLE!
IT'S THEM!

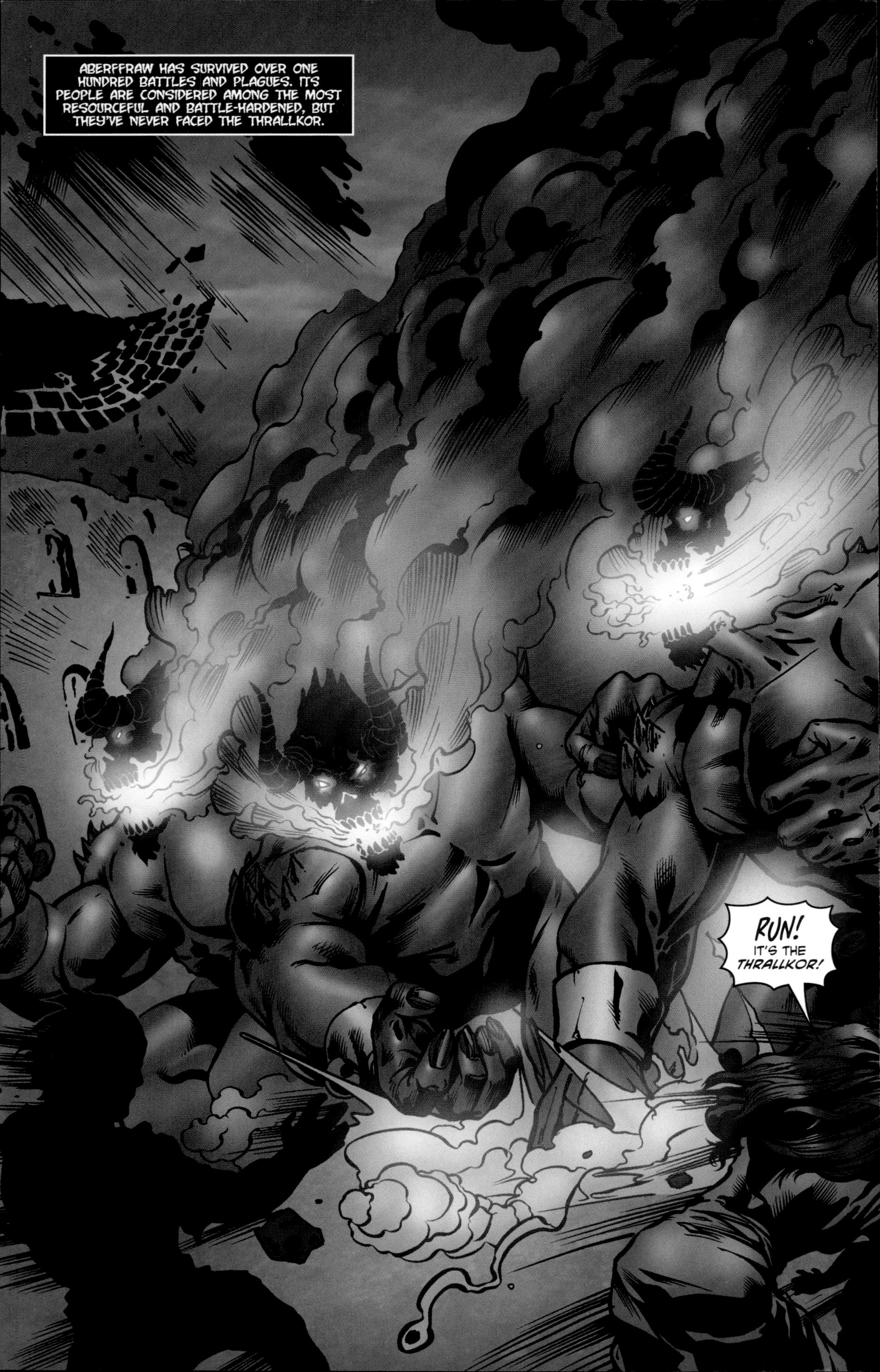
ABERFFRAW HAS SURVIVED OVER ONE HUNDRED BATTLES AND PLAGUES. ITS PEOPLE ARE CONSIDERED AMONG THE MOST RESOURCEFUL AND BATTLE-HARDENED, BUT THEY'VE NEVER FACED THE THRALLKOR.
RUN! IT'S THE *THRALLKOR!*

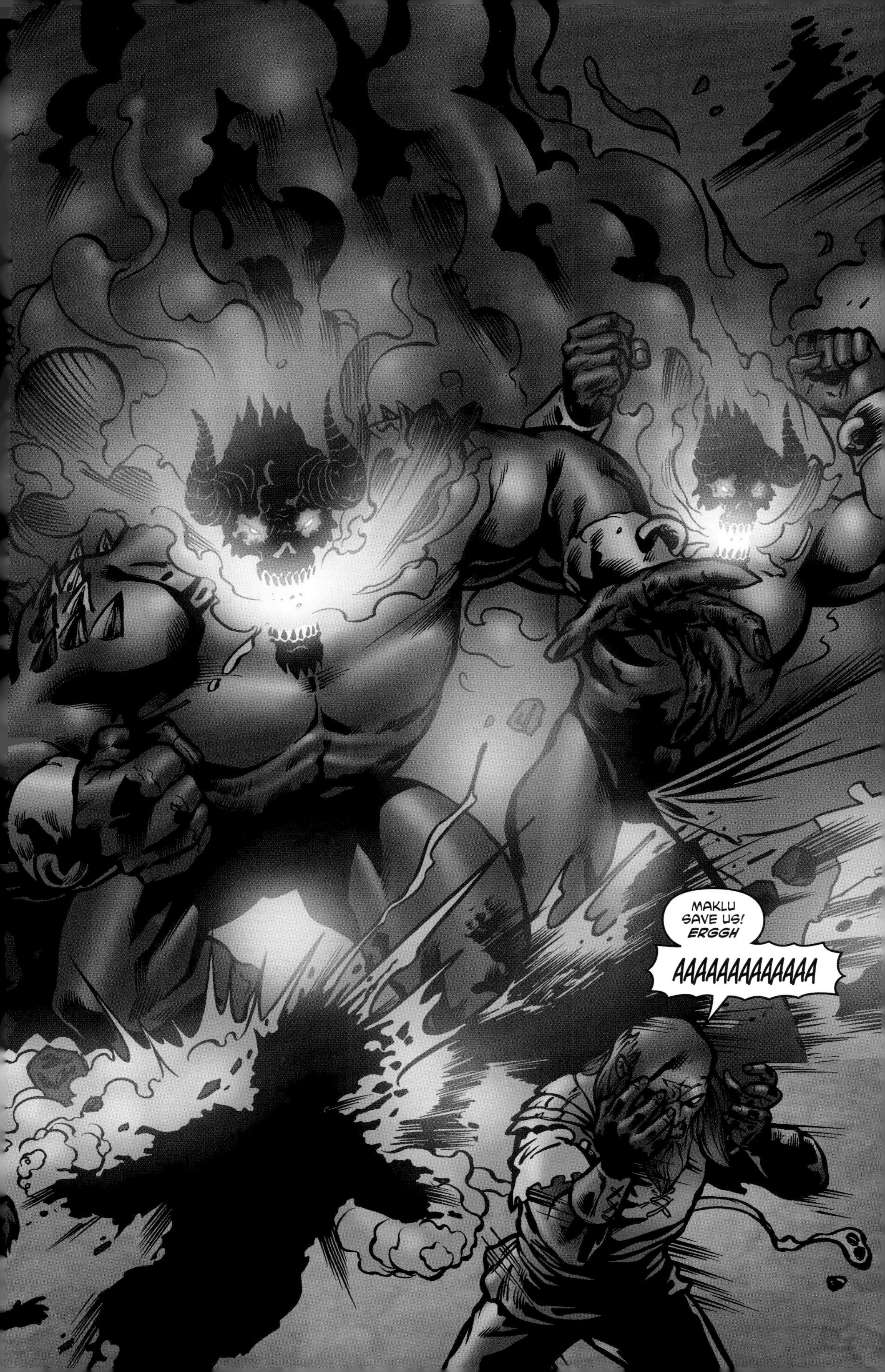
MAKLU SAVE US! ERGGH
AAAAAAAAAAAAA

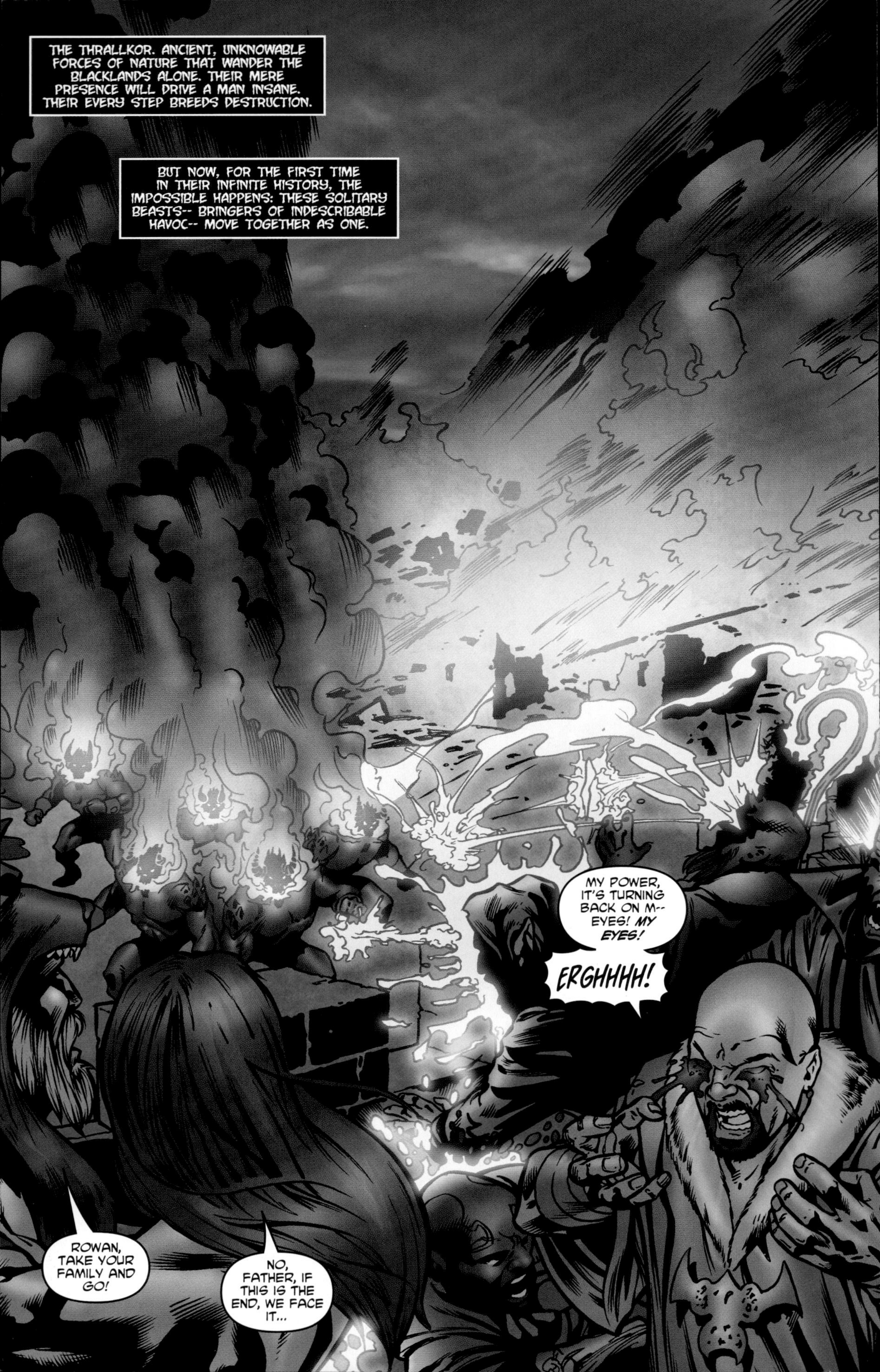
THE THRALLKOR. ANCIENT, UNKNOWABLE FORCES OF NATURE THAT WANDER THE BLACKLANDS ALONE. THEIR MERE PRESENCE WILL DRIVE A MAN INSANE. THEIR EVERY STEP BREEDS DESTRUCTION.
BUT NOW, FOR THE FIRST TIME IN THEIR INFINITE HISTORY, THE IMPOSSIBLE HAPPENS: THESE SOLITARY BEASTS-- BRINGERS OF INDESCRIBABLE HAVOC-- MOVE TOGETHER AS ONE.
MY POWER, IT'S TURNING BACK ON M-- EYES! MY EYES!
ERGHHHH!
ROWAN, TAKE YOUR FAMILY AND GO!
NO, FATHER, IF THIS IS THE END, WE FACE IT...

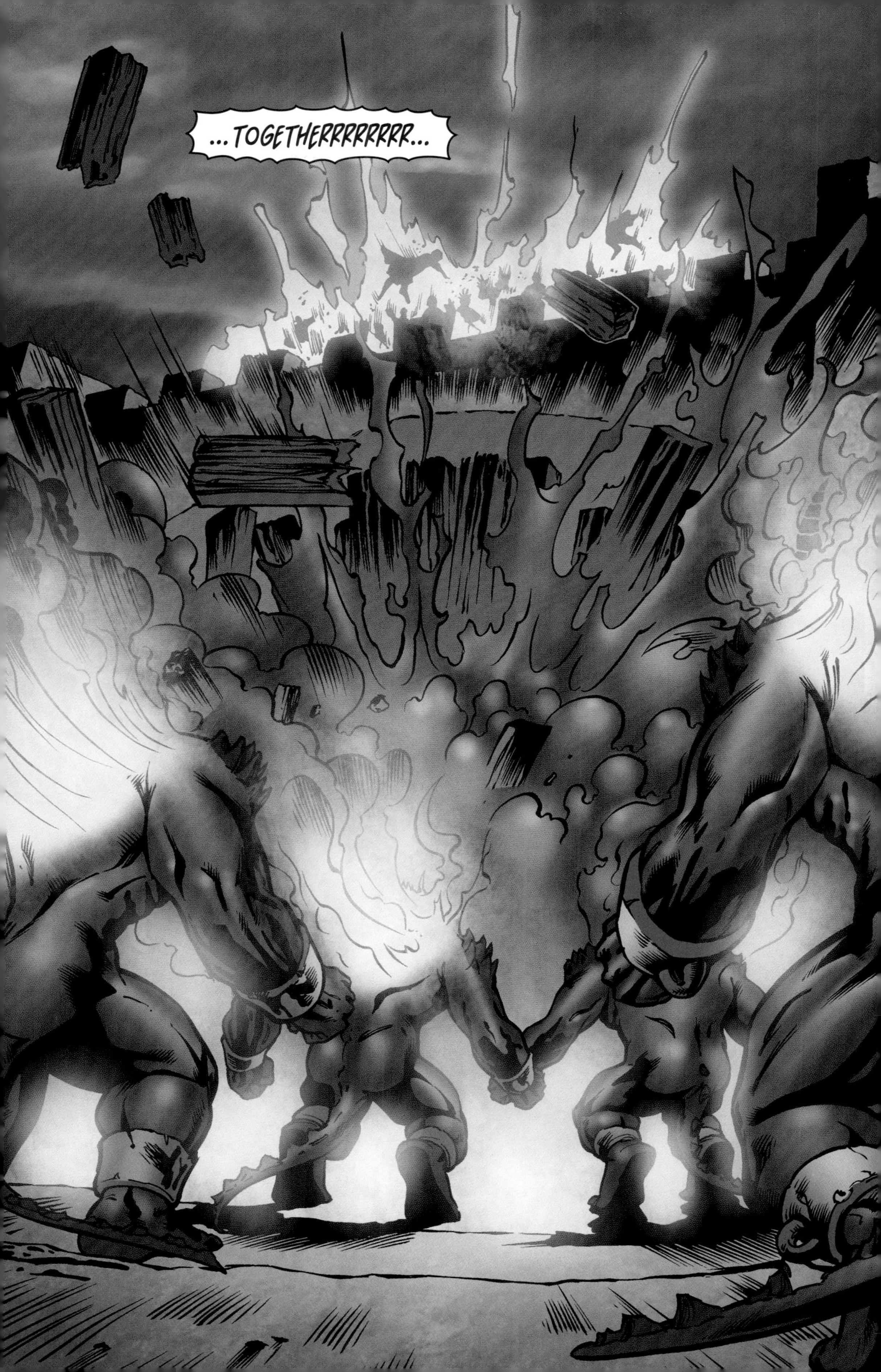
...TOGETHERRRRRRR...

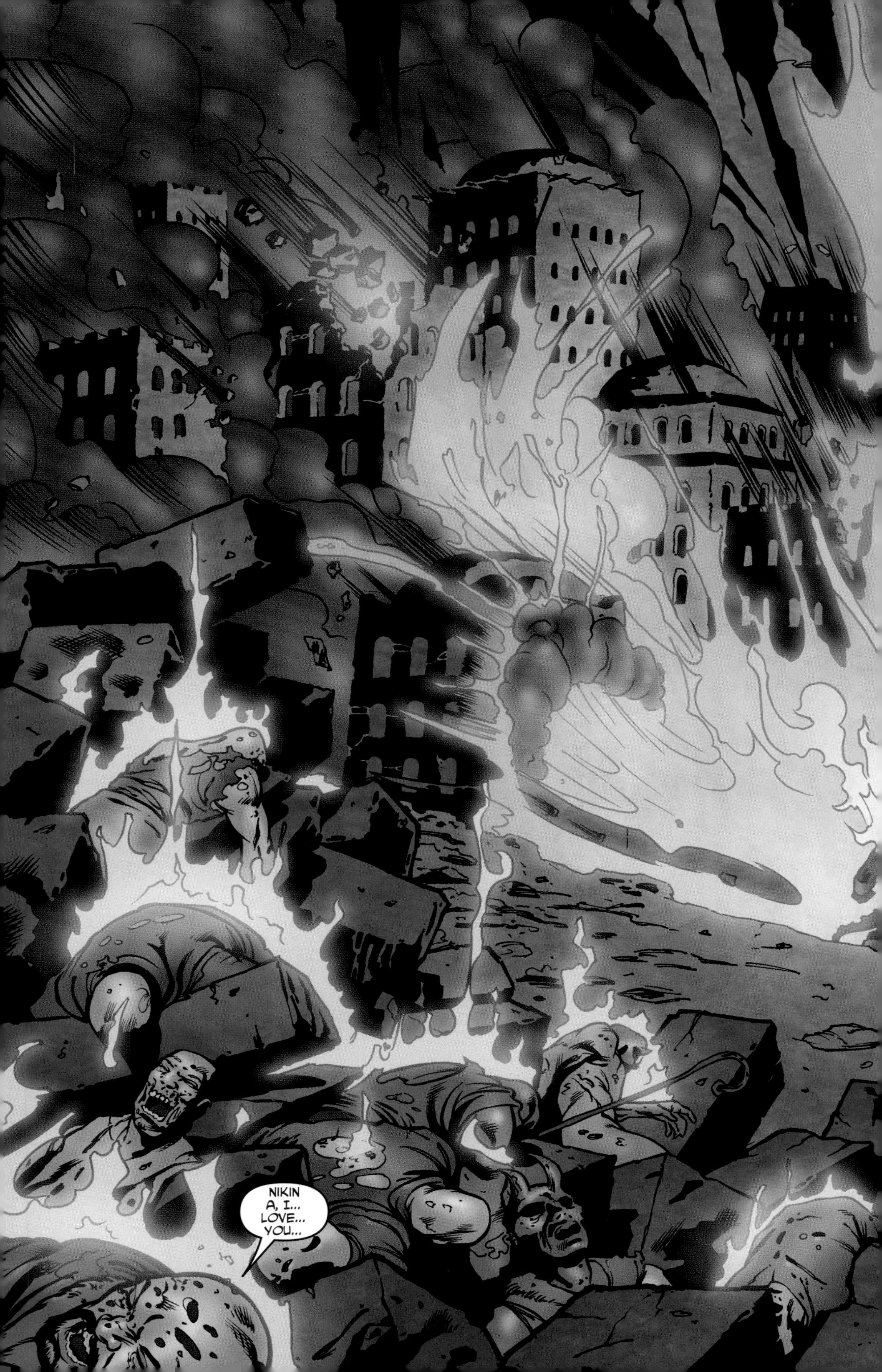
NIKIN A, I... LOVE... YOU...

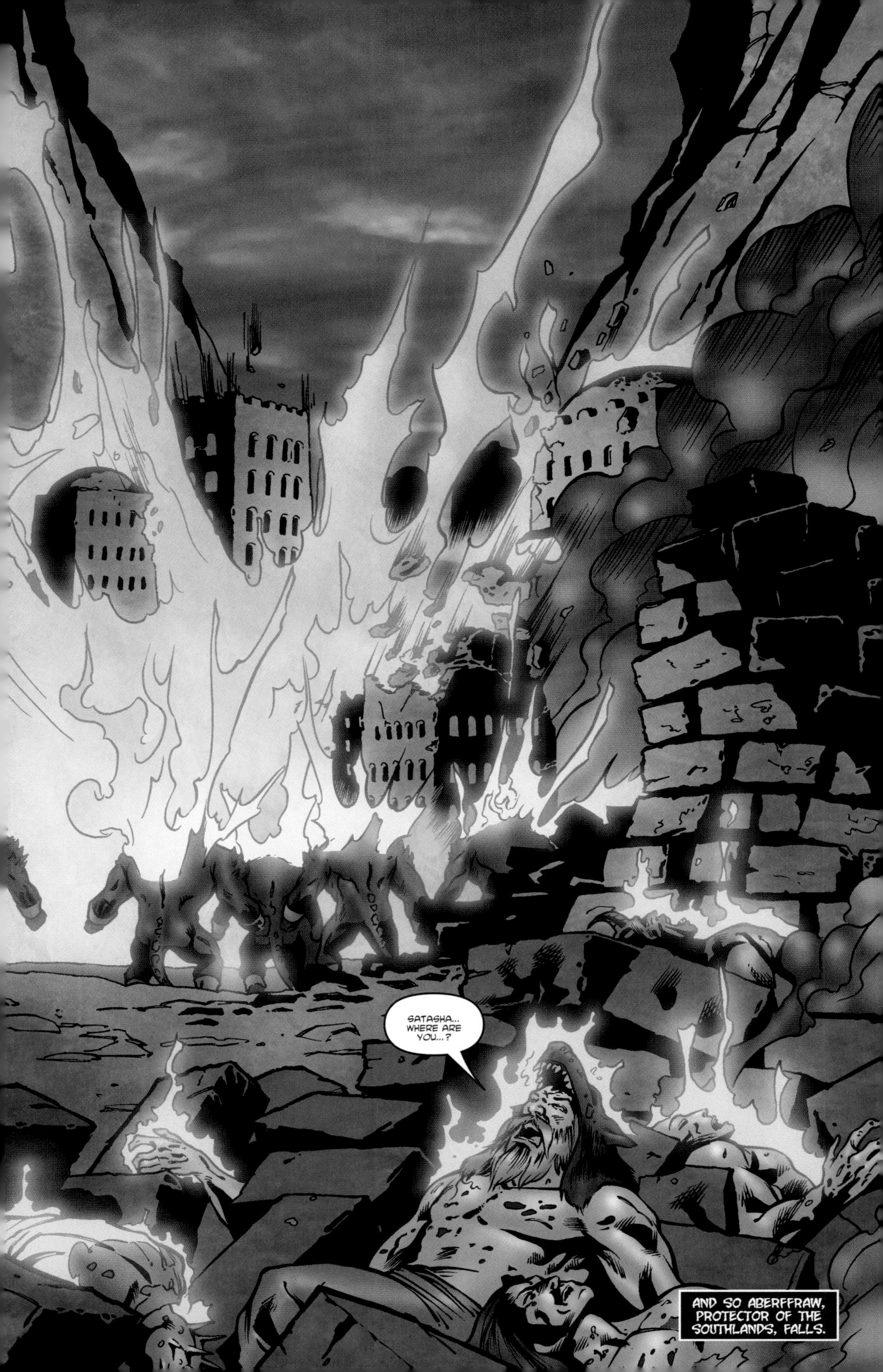
SATASHA... WHERE ARE YOU...?
AND SO ABERFFRAW, PROTECTOR OF THE SOUTHLANDS, FALLS.

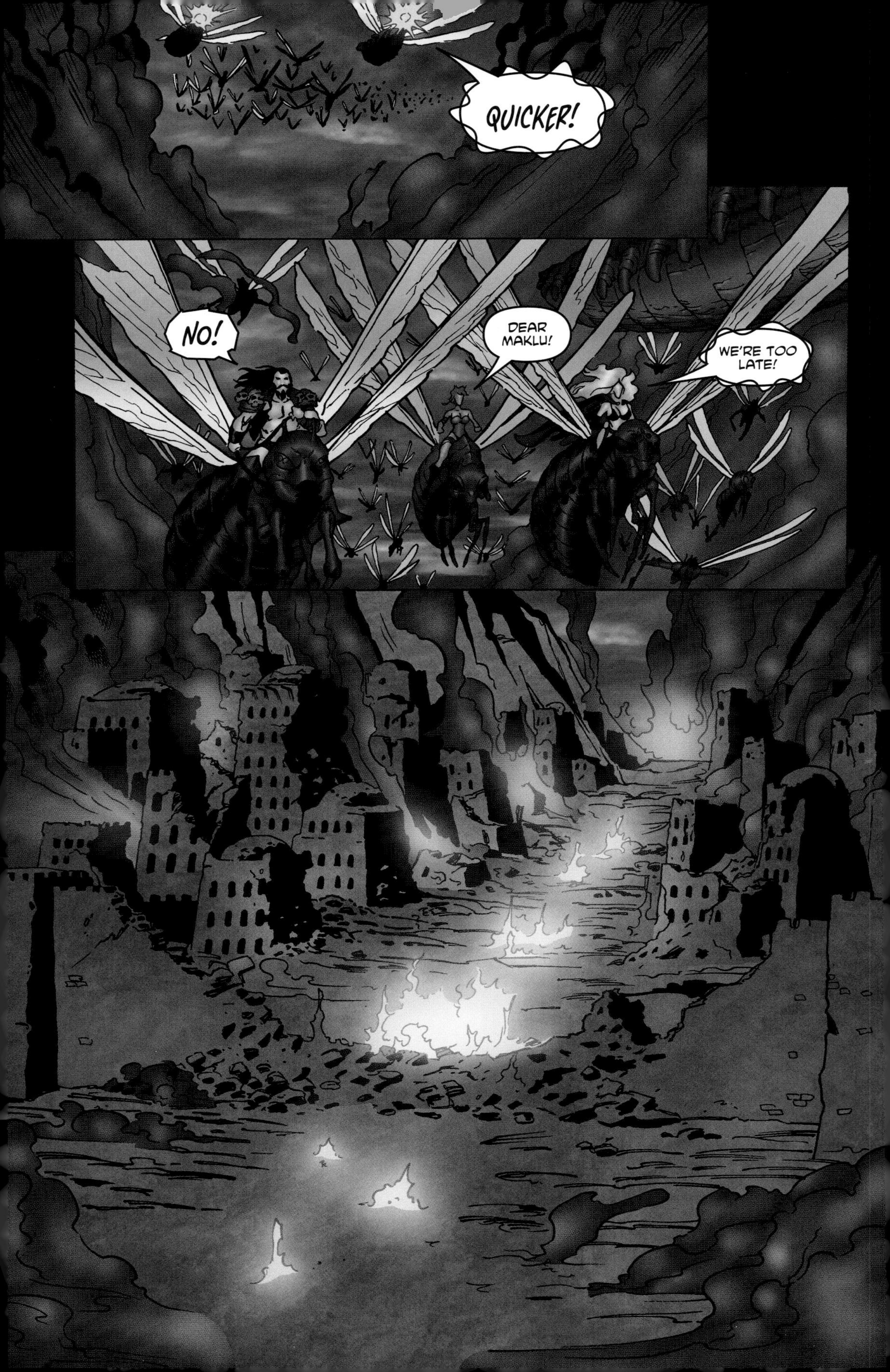
QUICKER!
NO!
DEAR MAKLU!
WE'RE TOO LATE!

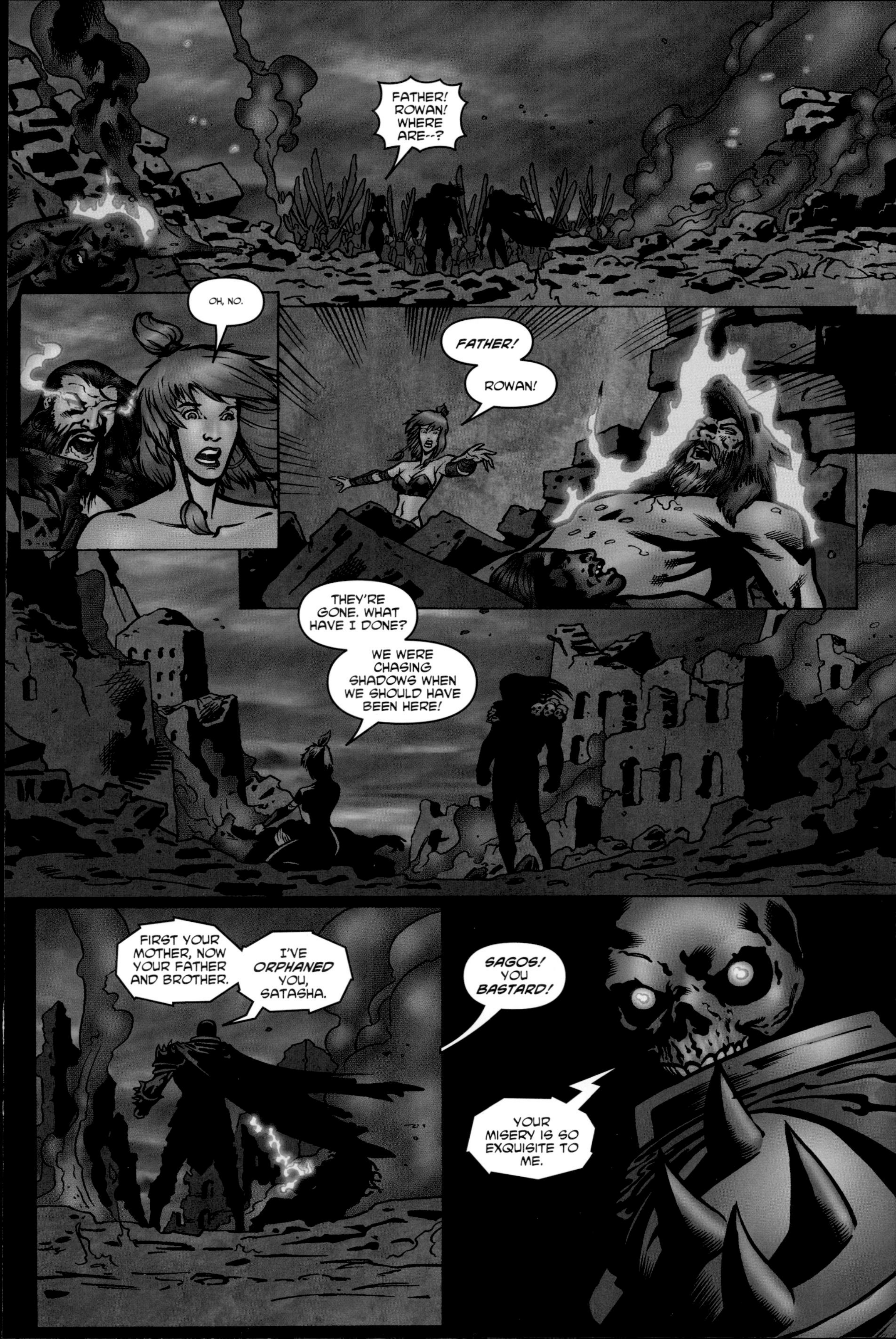
FATHER! ROWAN! WHERE ARE--?
OH, NO.
FATHER!
ROWAN!
THEY'RE GONE. WHAT HAVE I DONE?
WE WERE CHASING SHADOWS WHEN WE SHOULD HAVE BEEN HERE!
FIRST YOUR MOTHER, NOW YOUR FATHER AND BROTHER.
I'VE ORPHANED YOU, SATASHA.
SAGOS! YOU BASTARD!
YOUR MISERY IS SO EXQUISITE TO ME.

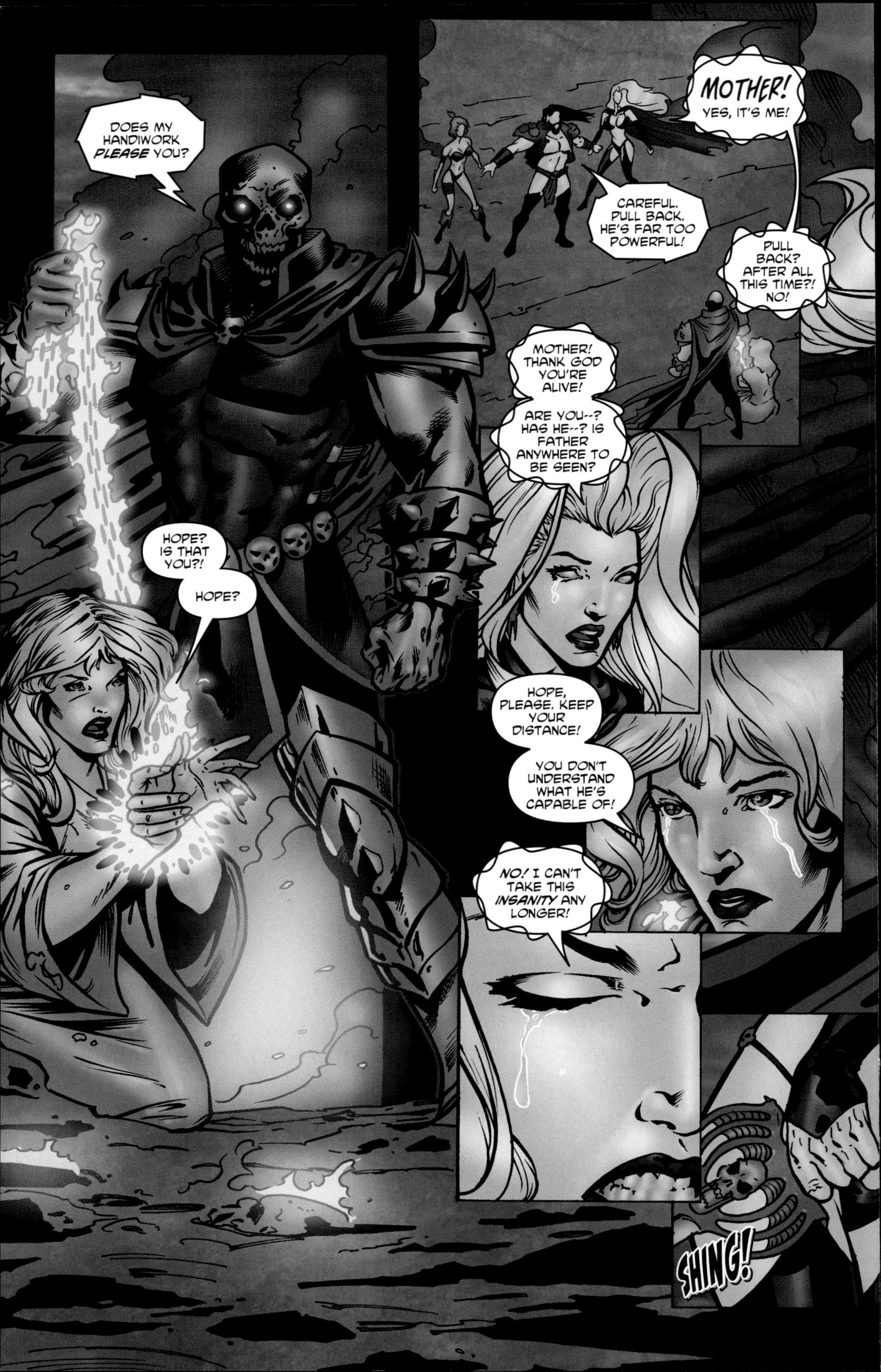

DOES MY HANDIWORK *PLEASE* YOU?
MOTHER! YES, IT'S ME!
CAREFUL. PULL BACK. HE'S FAR TOO POWERFUL!
PULL BACK? AFTER ALL THIS TIME?! NO!
HOPE? IS THAT YOU?!
HOPE?
MOTHER! THANK GOD YOU'RE ALIVE!
ARE YOU--? HAS HE--? IS FATHER ANYWHERE TO BE SEEN?
HOPE, PLEASE. KEEP YOUR DISTANCE!
YOU DON'T UNDERSTAND WHAT HE'S CAPABLE OF!
NO! I CAN'T TAKE THIS *INSANITY* ANY LONGER!
SHING!

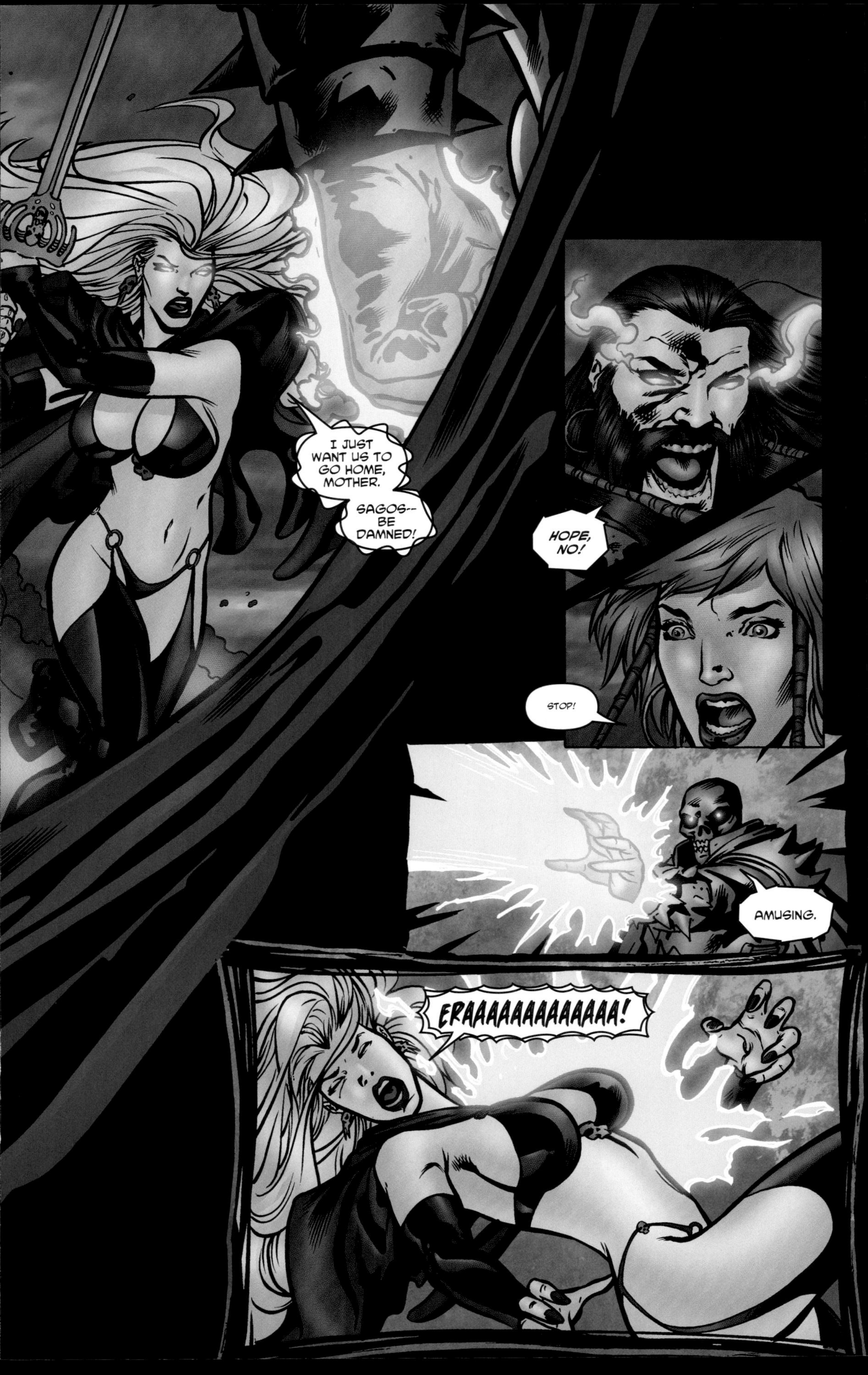
I JUST WANT US TO GO HOME, MOTHER.
SAGOS-- BE DAMNED!
HOPE, NO!
STOP!
AMUSING.
ERAAAAAAAAAAAAA!

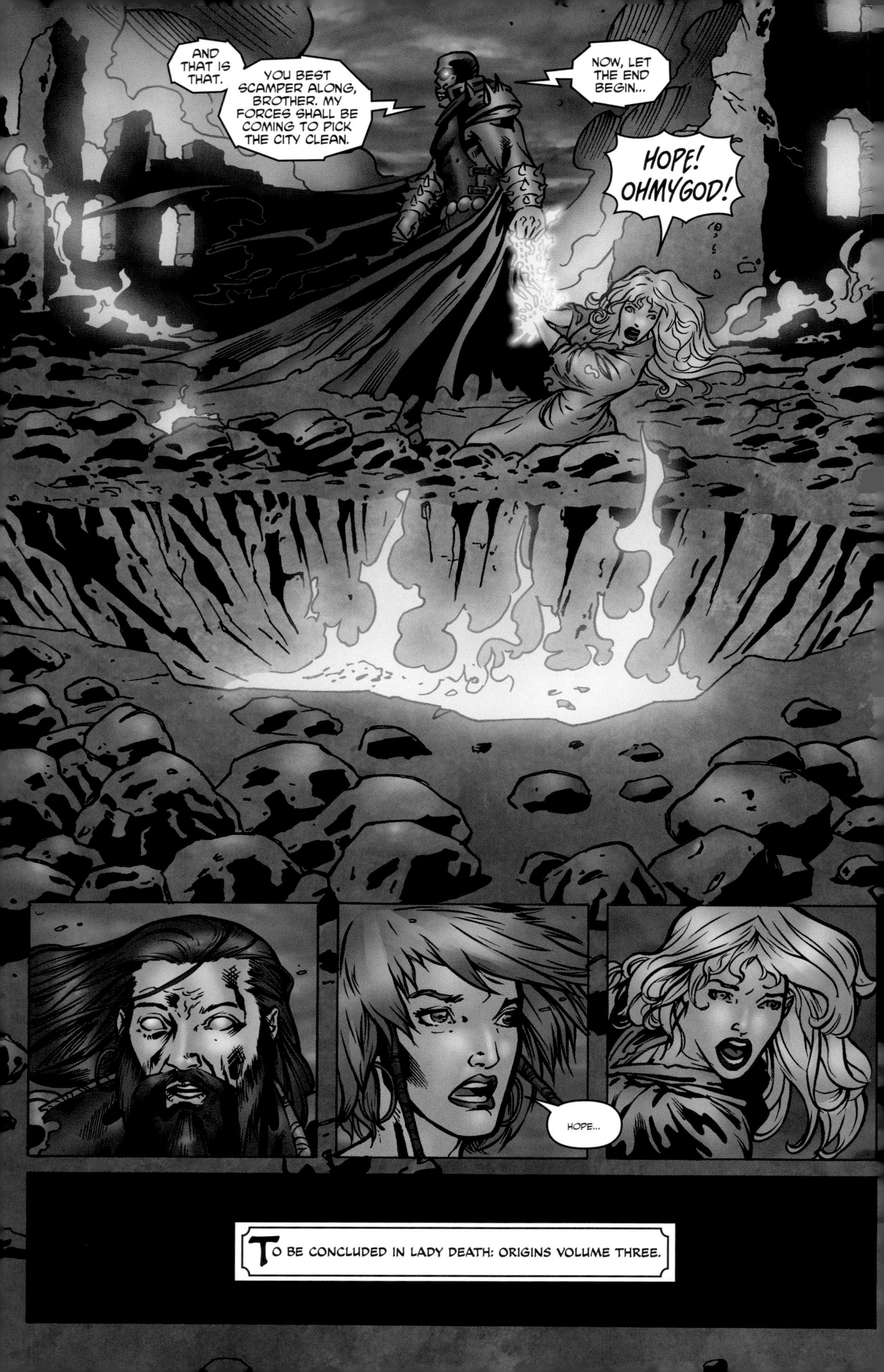
AND THAT IS THAT.
YOU BEST SCAMPER ALONG, BROTHER. MY FORCES SHALL BE COMING TO PICK THE CITY CLEAN.
NOW, LET THE END BEGIN...
HOPE! OHMYGOD!
HOPE...
TO BE CONCLUDED IN LADY DEATH: ORIGINS VOLUME THREE.

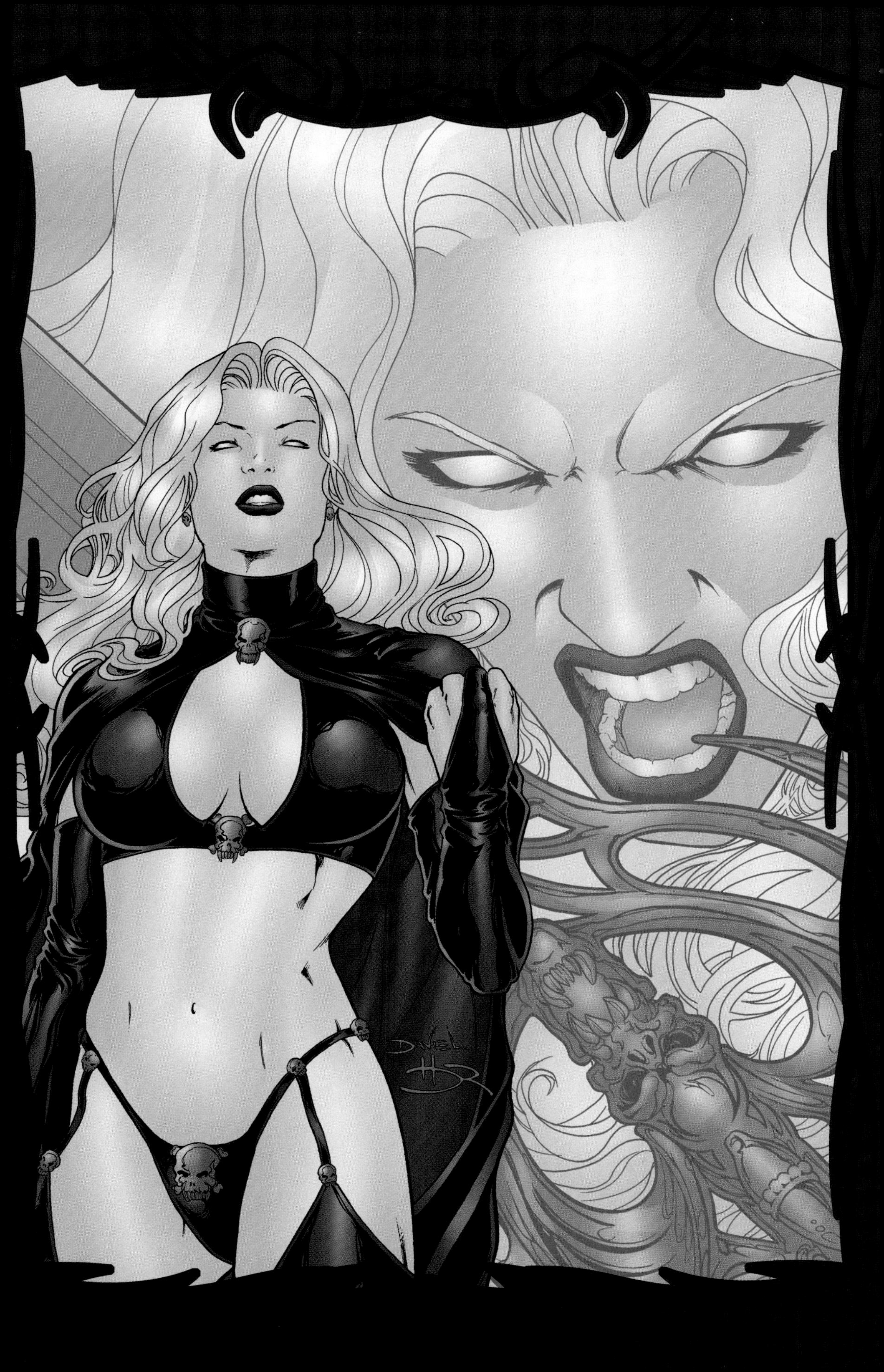

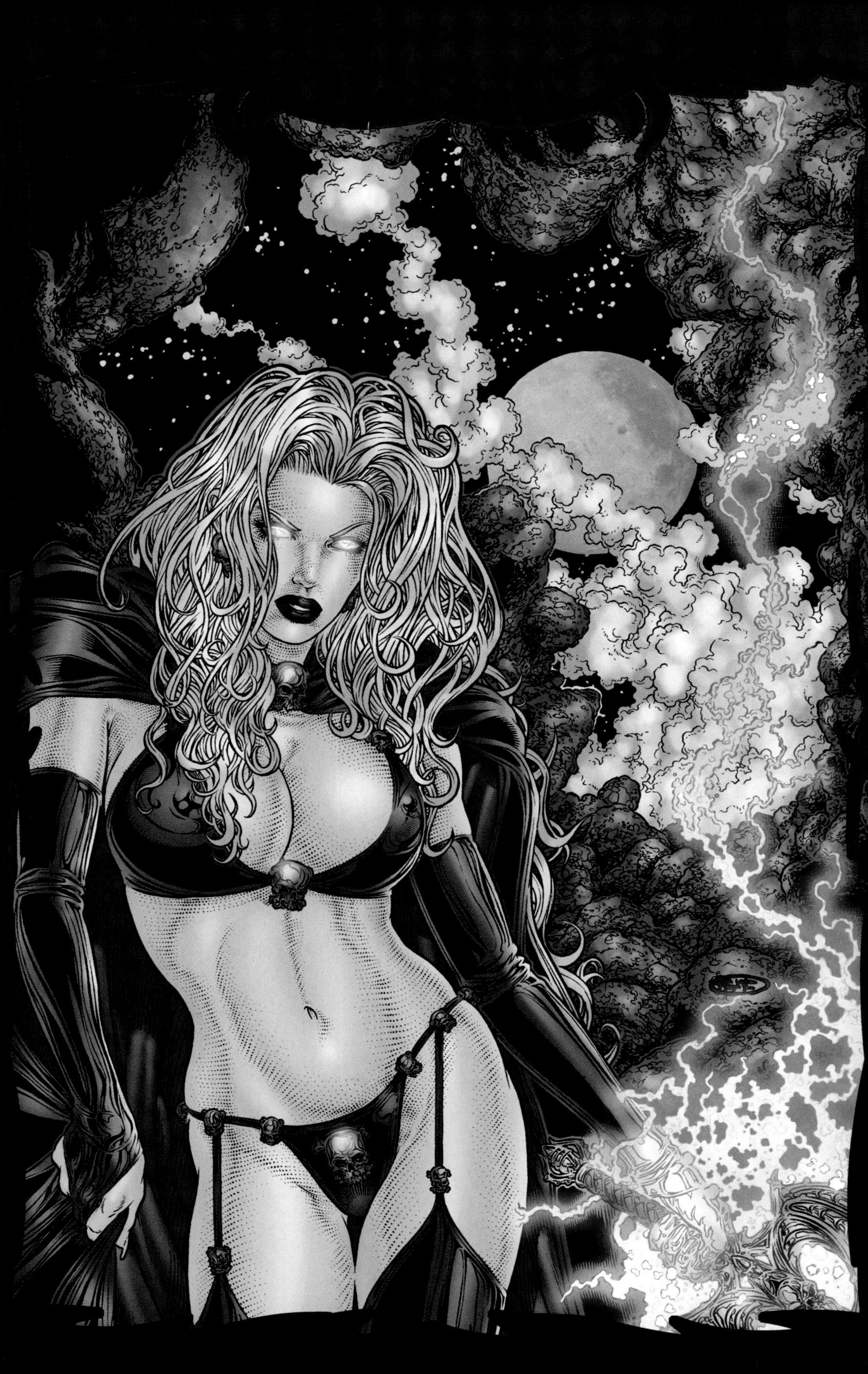

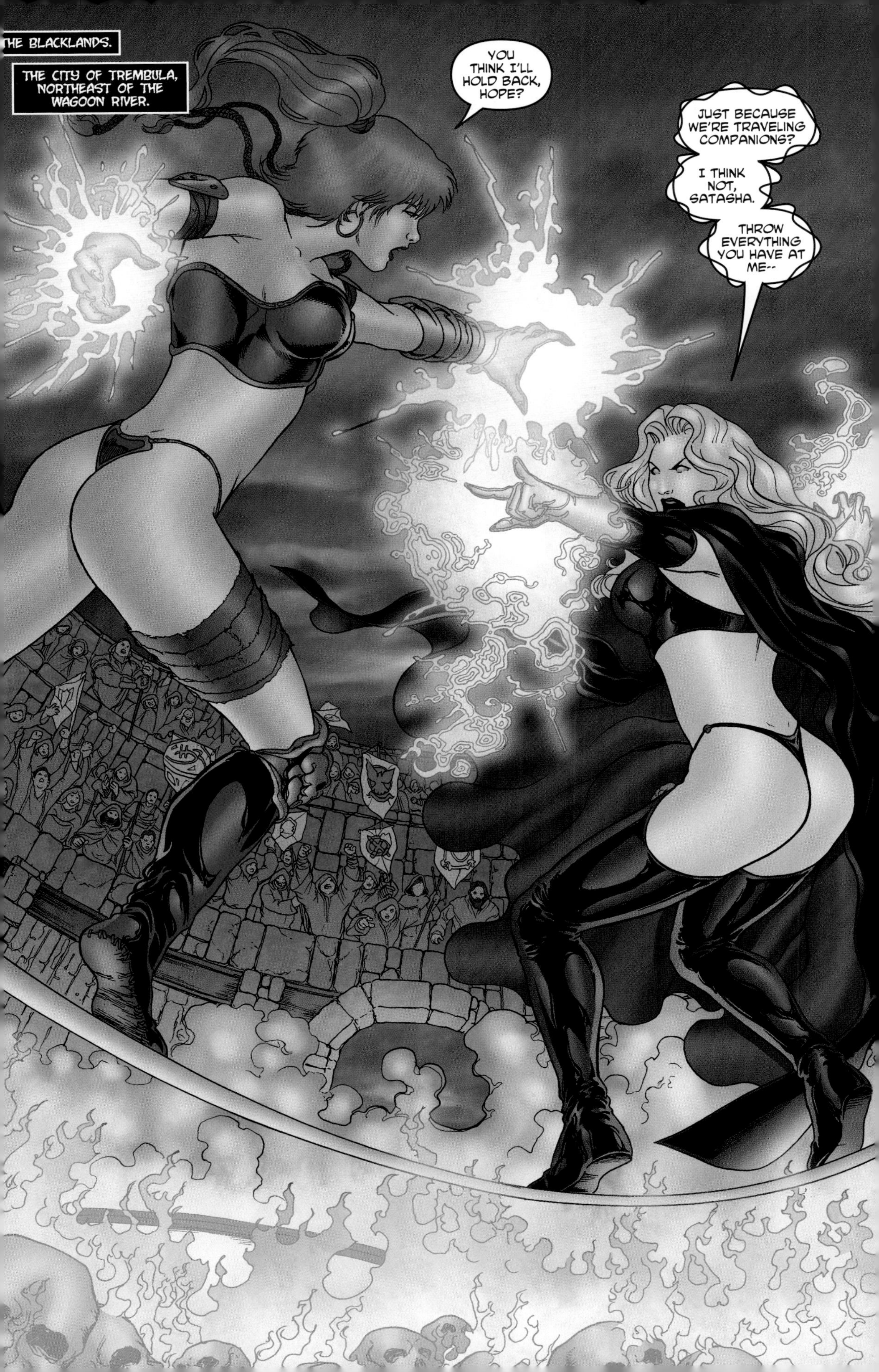

THE BLACKLANDS.
THE CITY OF TREMBULA, NORTHEAST OF THE WAGOON RIVER.
YOU THINK I'LL HOLD BACK, HOPE?
JUST BECAUSE WE'RE TRAVELING COMPANIONS?
I THINK NOT, SATASHA.
THROW EVERYTHING YOU HAVE AT ME--

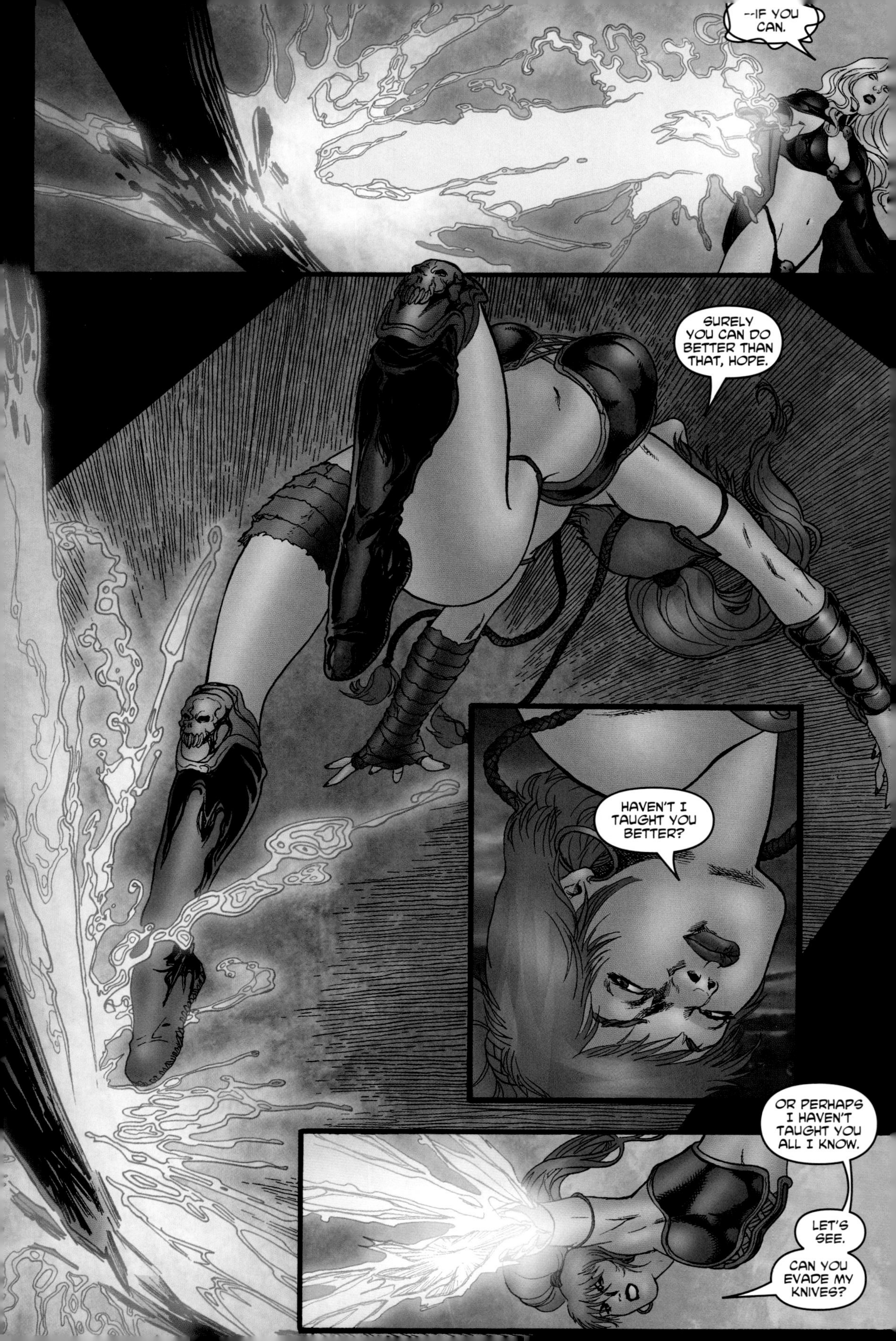
--IF YOU CAN.
SURELY YOU CAN DO BETTER THAN THAT, HOPE.
HAVEN'T I TAUGHT YOU BETTER?
OR PERHAPS I HAVEN'T TAUGHT YOU ALL I KNOW.
LET'S SEE.
CAN YOU EVADE MY KNIVES?

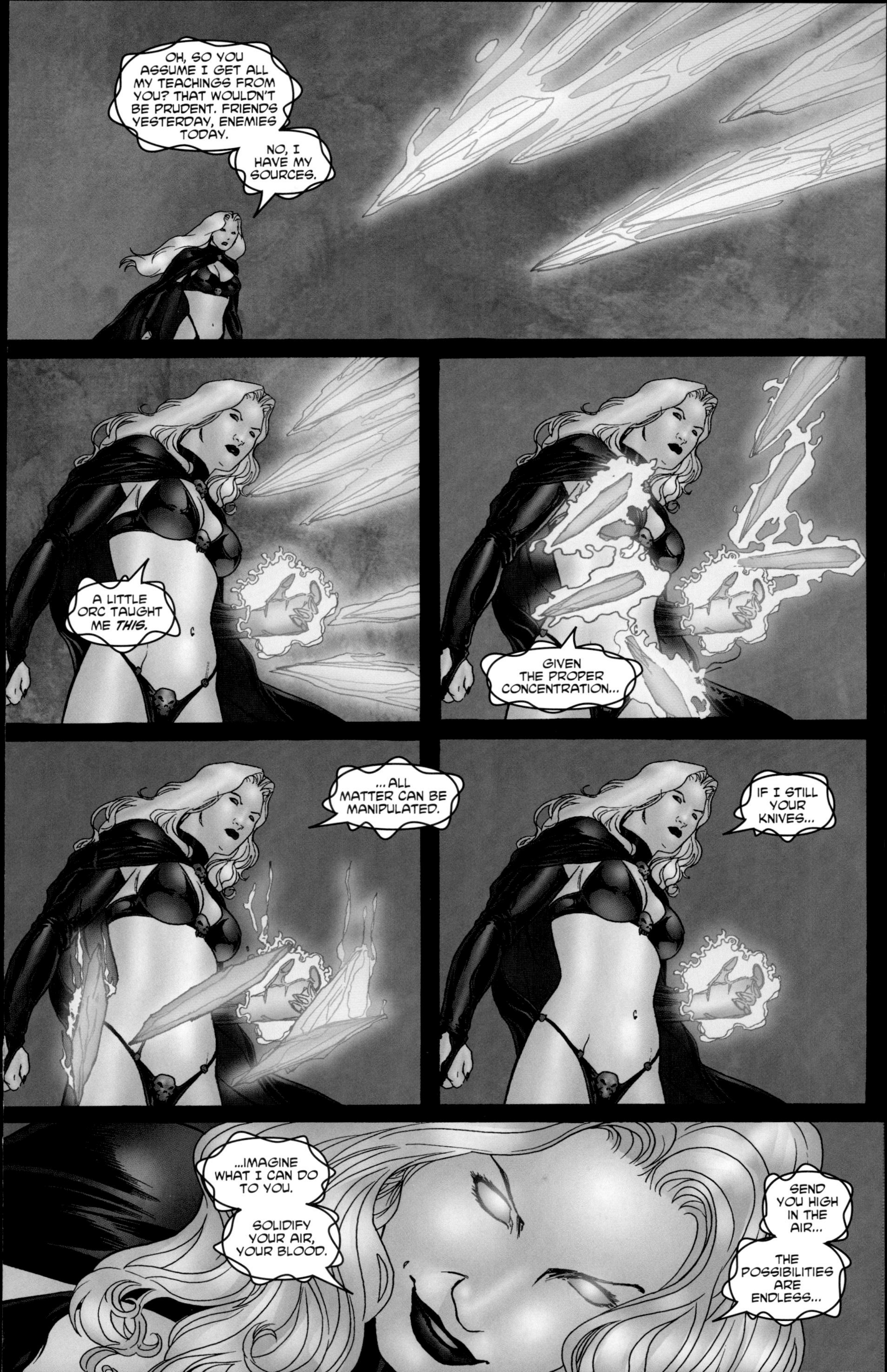
OH, SO YOU ASSUME I GET ALL MY TEACHINGS FROM YOU? THAT WOULDN'T BE PRUDENT. FRIENDS YESTERDAY, ENEMIES TODAY.
NO, I HAVE MY SOURCES.
A LITTLE ORC TAUGHT ME *THIS*.
GIVEN THE PROPER CONCENTRATION...
...ALL MATTER CAN BE MANIPULATED.
IF I STILL YOUR KNIVES...
...IMAGINE WHAT I CAN DO TO YOU.
SOLIDIFY YOUR AIR, YOUR BLOOD.
SEND YOU HIGH IN THE AIR...
THE POSSIBILITIES ARE ENDLESS...

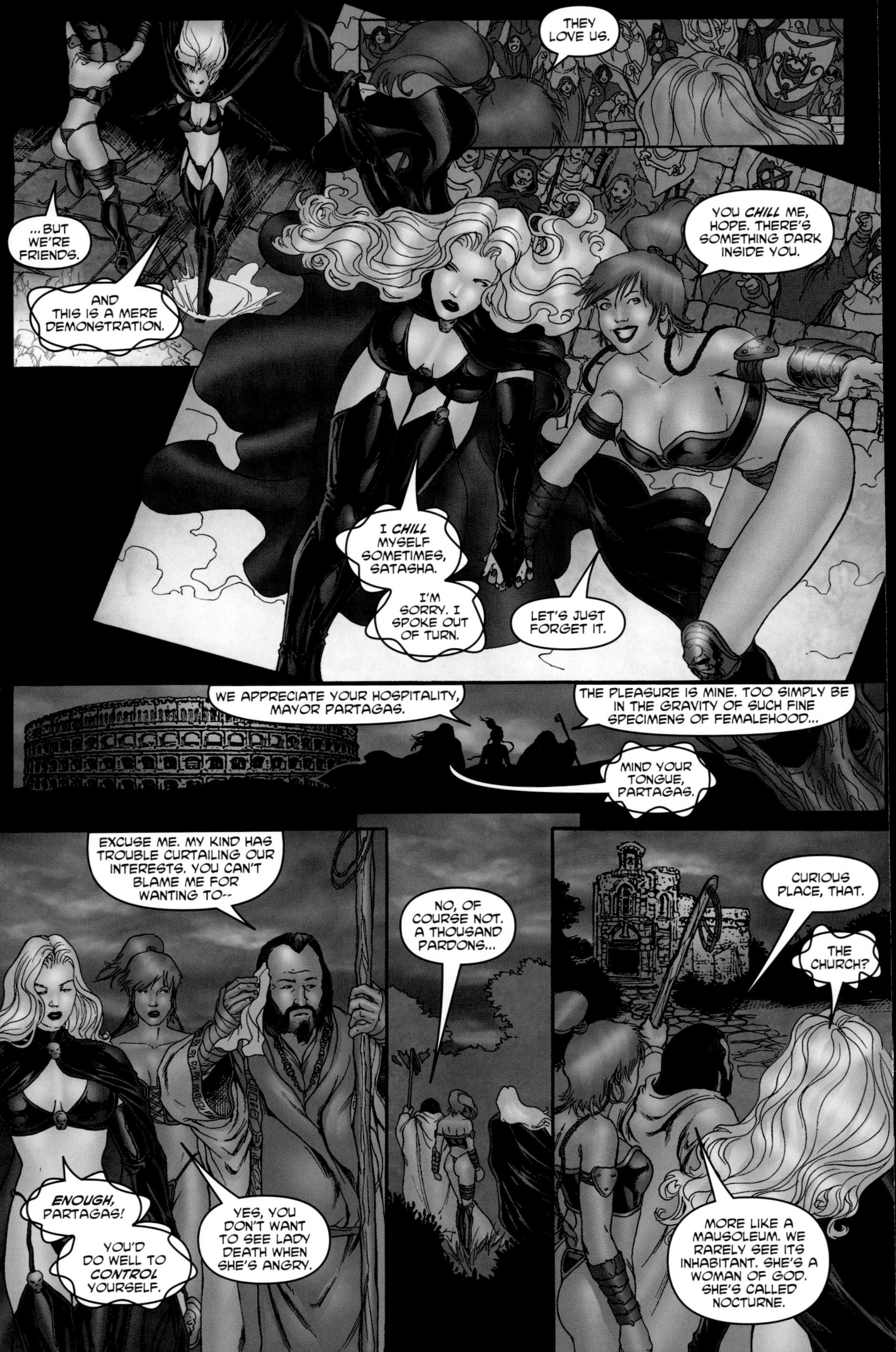
...BUT WE'RE FRIENDS.
AND THIS IS A MERE DEMONSTRATION.
THEY LOVE US.
YOU CHILL ME, HOPE. THERE'S SOMETHING DARK INSIDE YOU.
I CHILL MYSELF SOMETIMES, SATASHA.
I'M SORRY. I SPOKE OUT OF TURN.
LET'S JUST FORGET IT.
WE APPRECIATE YOUR HOSPITALITY, MAYOR PARTAGAS.
THE PLEASURE IS MINE. TOO SIMPLY BE IN THE GRAVITY OF SUCH FINE SPECIMENS OF FEMALEHOOD...
MIND YOUR TONGUE, PARTAGAS.
EXCUSE ME. MY KIND HAS TROUBLE CURTAILING OUR INTERESTS. YOU CAN'T BLAME ME FOR WANTING TO--
ENOUGH, PARTAGAS!
YOU'D DO WELL TO CONTROL YOURSELF.
YES, YOU DON'T WANT TO SEE LADY DEATH WHEN SHE'S ANGRY.
NO, OF COURSE NOT. A THOUSAND PARDONS...
CURIOUS PLACE, THAT.
THE CHURCH?
MORE LIKE A MAUSOLEUM. WE RARELY SEE ITS INHABITANT. SHE'S A WOMAN OF GOD. SHE'S CALLED NOCTURNE.

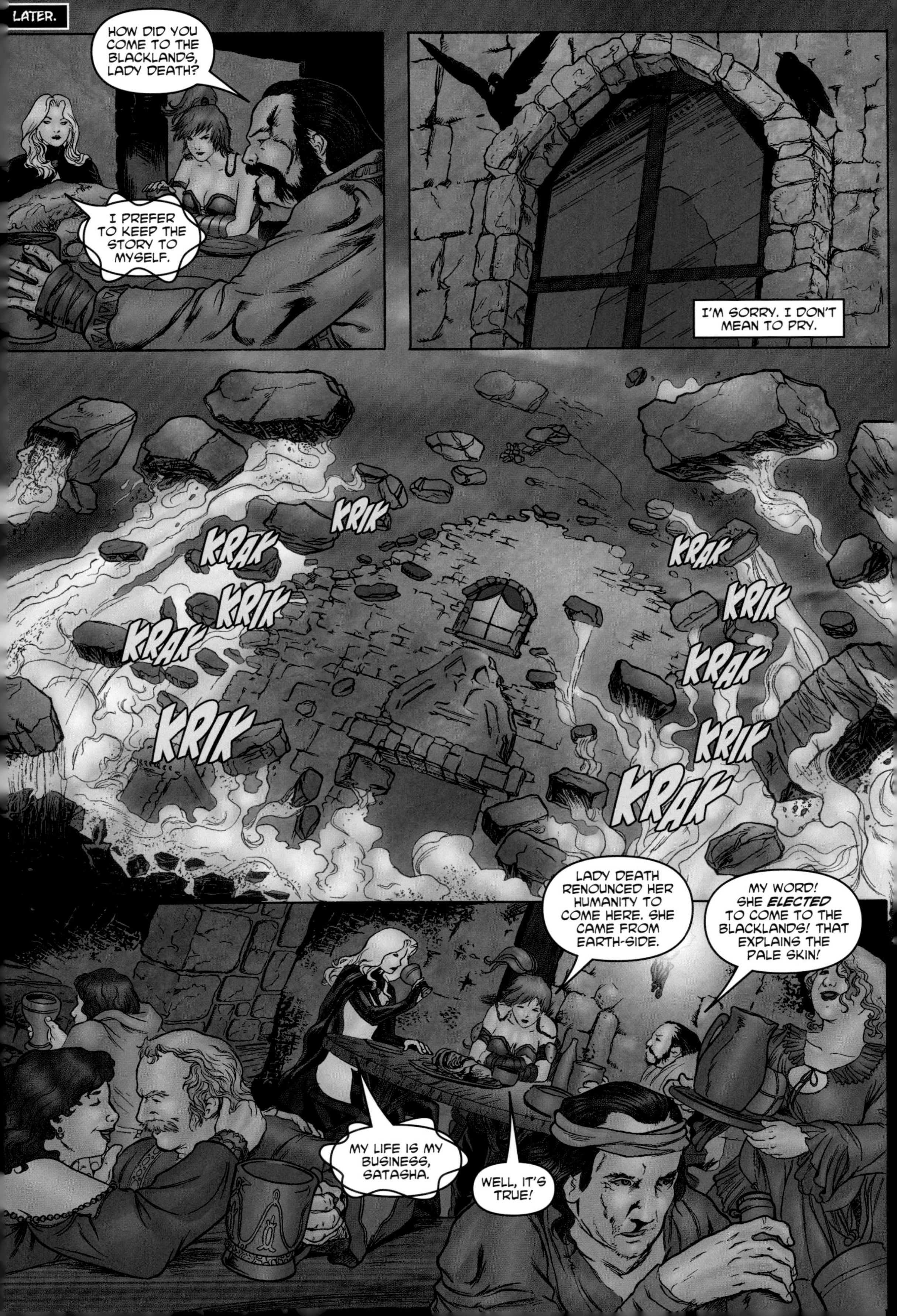
LATER.
HOW DID YOU COME TO THE BLACKLANDS, LADY DEATH?
I PREFER TO KEEP THE STORY TO MYSELF.
I'M SORRY. I DON'T MEAN TO PRY.
KRIK
KRAK
KRIK
KRAK
KRIK
KRAK
KRIK
KRAK
KRIK
KRAK
LADY DEATH RENOUNCED HER HUMANITY TO COME HERE. SHE CAME FROM EARTH-SIDE.
MY WORD! SHE *ELECTED* TO COME TO THE BLACKLANDS! THAT EXPLAINS THE PALE SKIN!
MY LIFE IS MY BUSINESS, SATASHA.
WELL, IT'S TRUE!

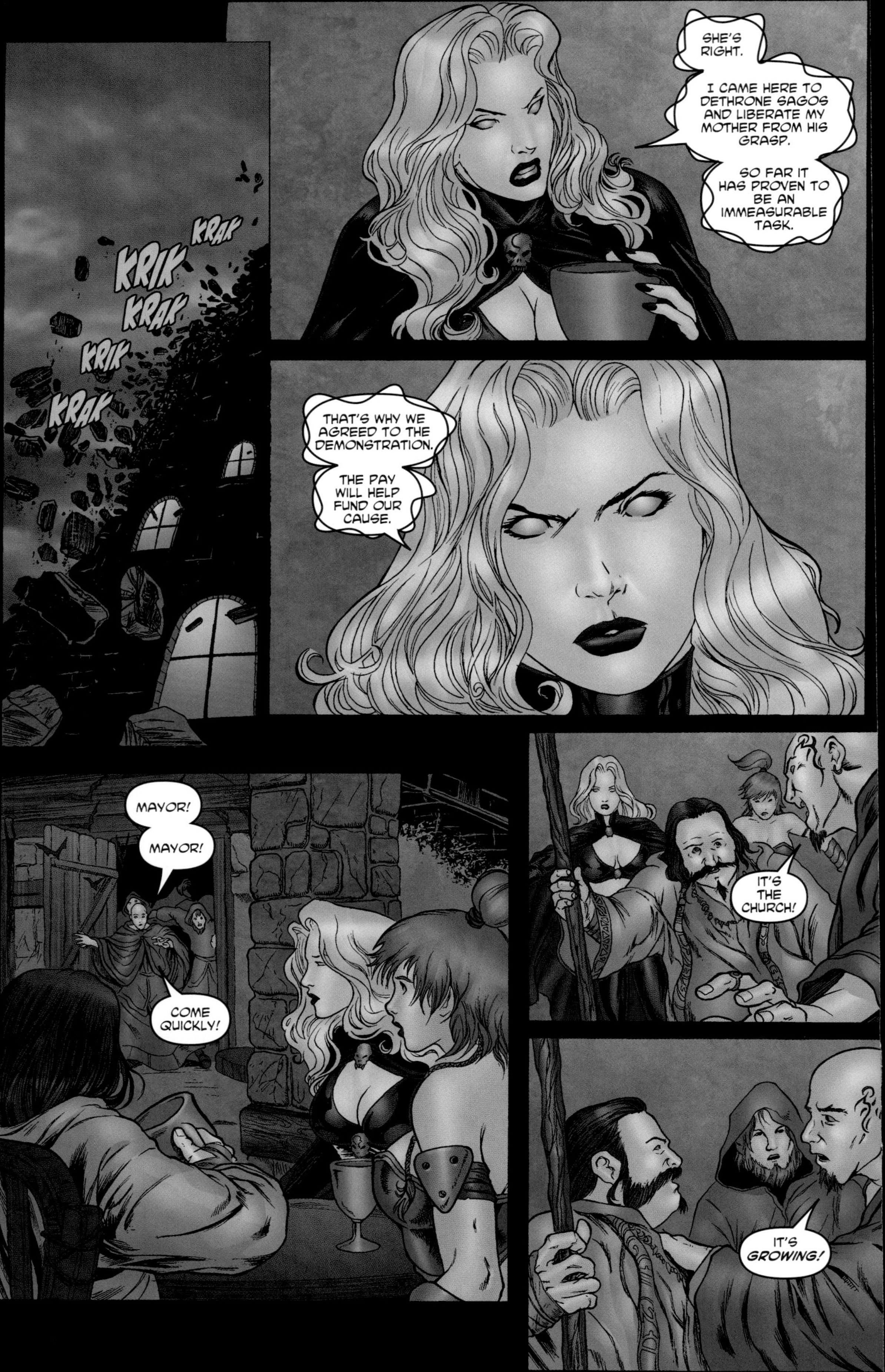
KRAK
KRIK
KRAK
KRIK
KRAK
SHE'S RIGHT.
I CAME HERE TO DETHRONE SAGOS AND LIBERATE MY MOTHER FROM HIS GRASP.
SO FAR IT HAS PROVEN TO BE AN IMMEASURABLE TASK.
THAT'S WHY WE AGREED TO THE DEMONSTRATION.
THE PAY WILL HELP FUND OUR CAUSE.
MAYOR!
MAYOR!
COME QUICKLY!
IT'S THE CHURCH!
IT'S GROWING!

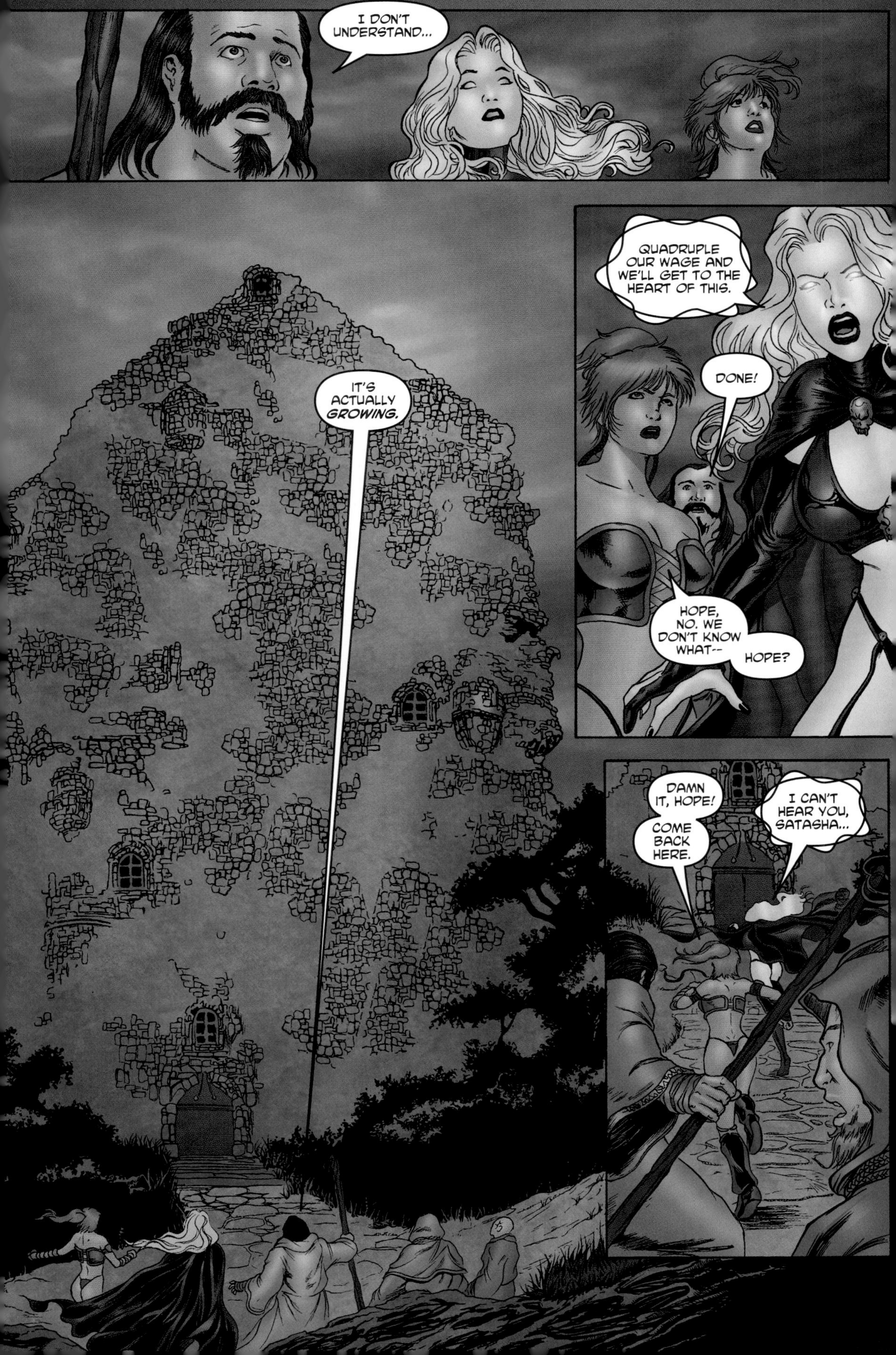
I DON'T UNDERSTAND...
IT'S ACTUALLY GROWING.
QUADRUPLE OUR WAGE AND WE'LL GET TO THE HEART OF THIS.
DONE!
HOPE, NO. WE DON'T KNOW WHAT--
HOPE?
DAMN IT, HOPE!
COME BACK HERE.
I CAN'T HEAR YOU, SATASHA...

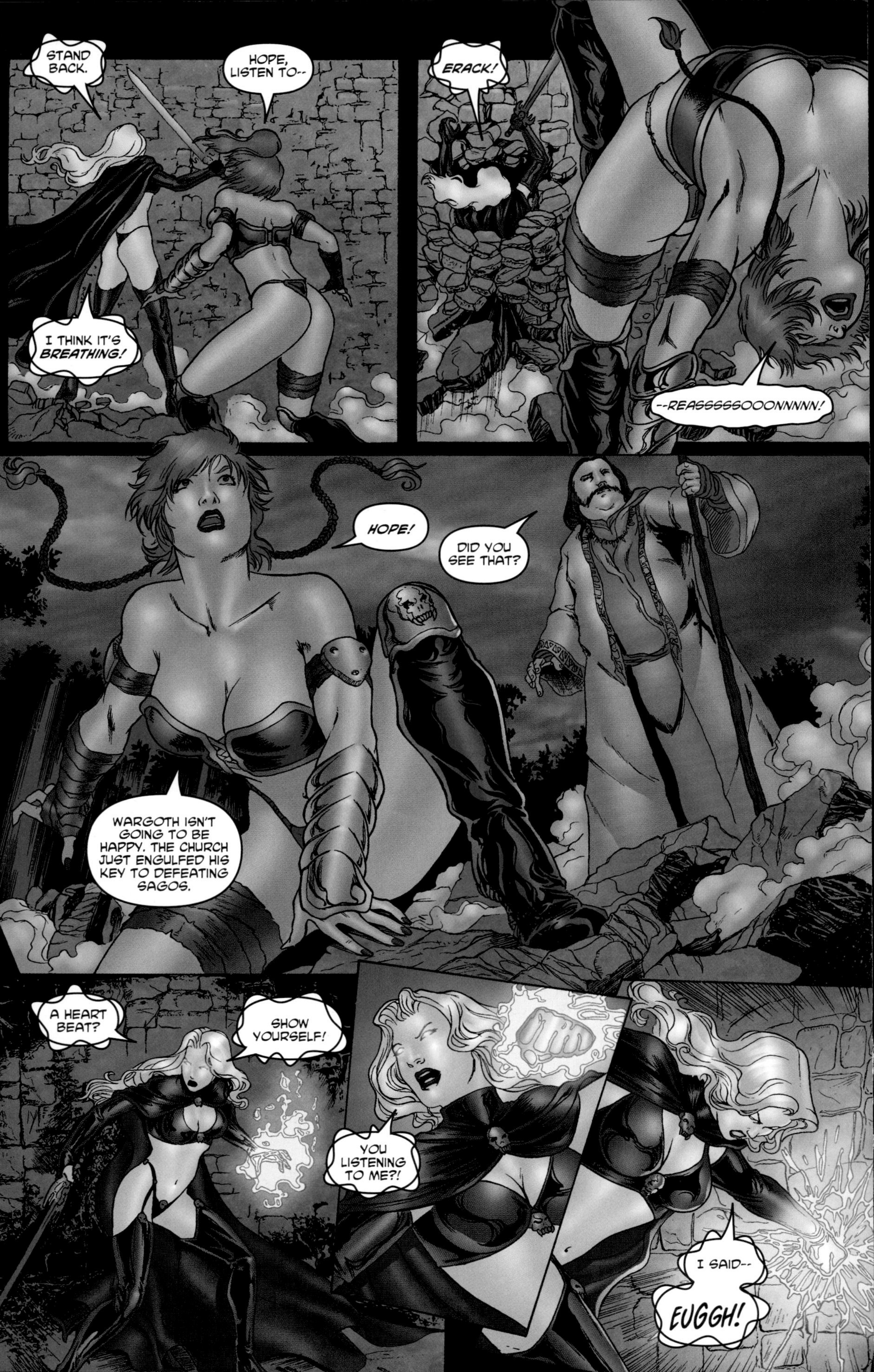

STAND BACK.
HOPE, LISTEN TO--
I THINK IT'S *BREATHING!*
ERACK!
--REASSSSSOOONNNNN!
HOPE!
DID YOU SEE THAT?
WARGOTH ISN'T GOING TO BE HAPPY. THE CHURCH JUST ENGULFED HIS KEY TO DEFEATING SAGOS.
A HEART BEAT?
SHOW YOURSELF!
YOU LISTENING TO ME?!
I SAID--
EUGGH!

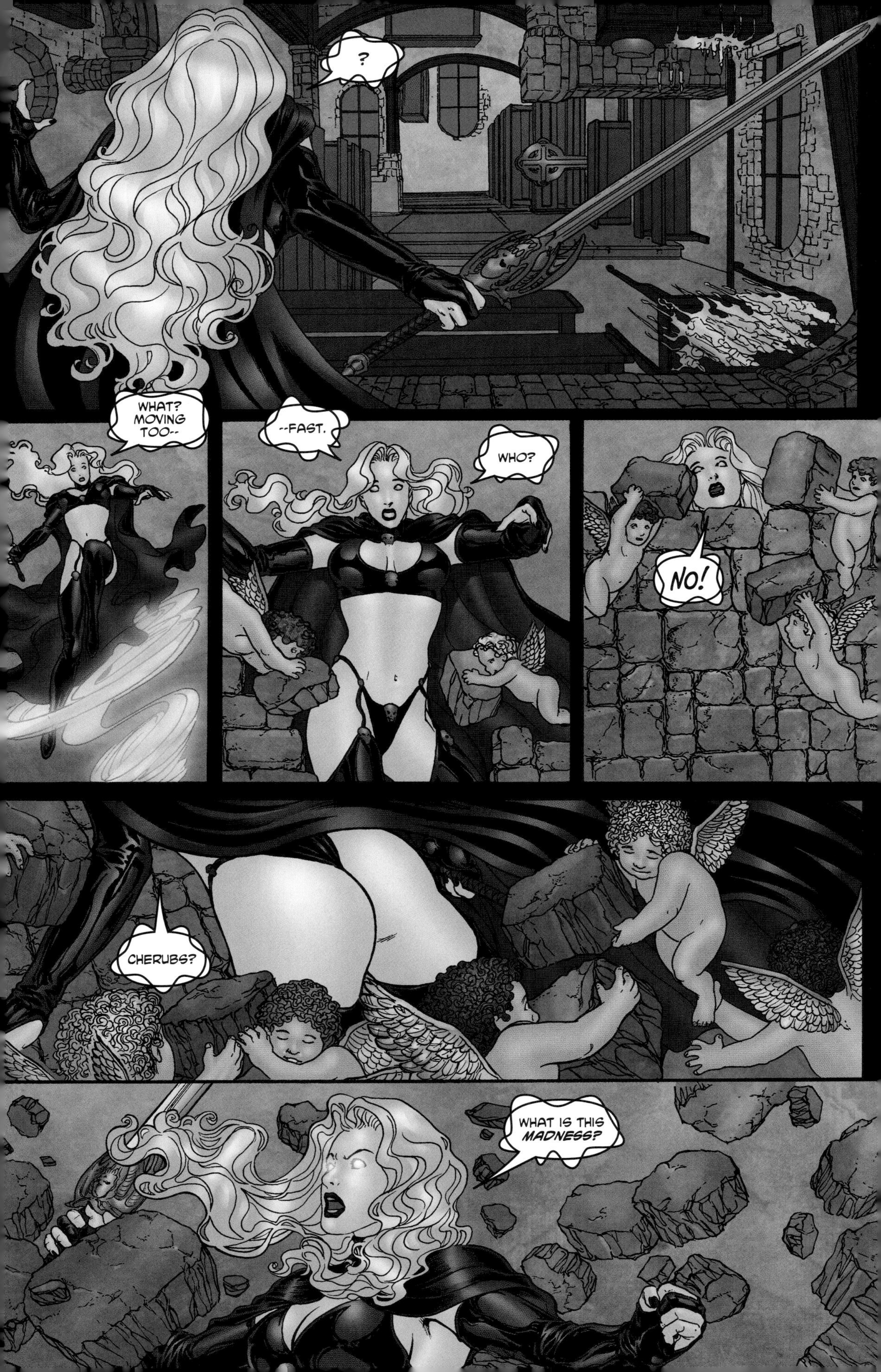
?
WHAT? MOVING TOO--
--FAST.
WHO?
NO!
CHERUBS?
WHAT IS THIS *MADNESS?*

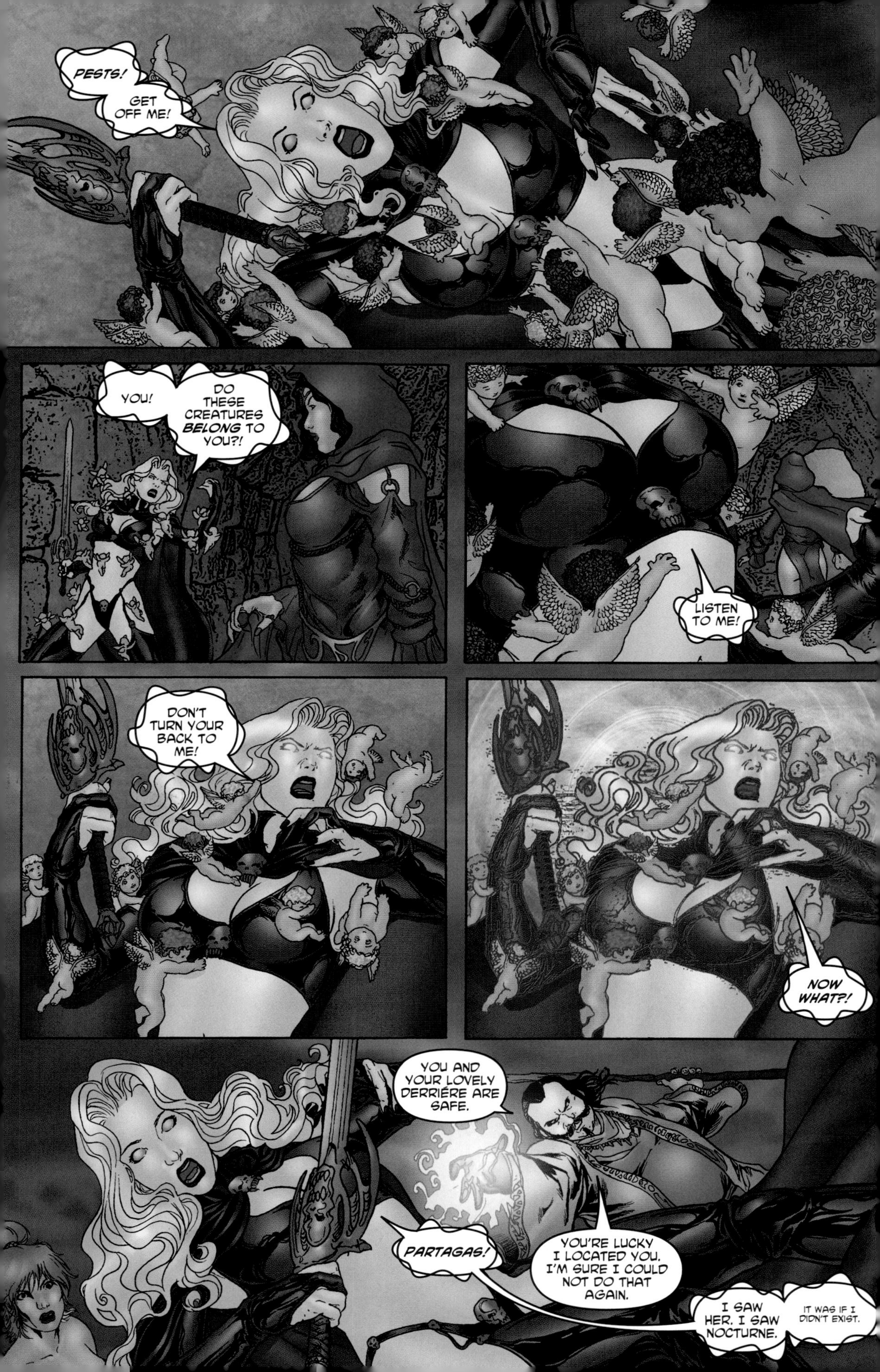
PESTS!
GET OFF ME!
YOU!
DO THESE CREATURES *BELONG* TO YOU?!
LISTEN TO ME!
DON'T TURN YOUR BACK TO ME!
NOW WHAT?!
YOU AND YOUR LOVELY DERRIÉRE ARE SAFE.
PARTAGAS!
YOU'RE LUCKY I LOCATED YOU. I'M SURE I COULD NOT DO THAT AGAIN.
I SAW HER. I SAW NOCTURNE.
IT WAS IF I DIDN'T EXIST.

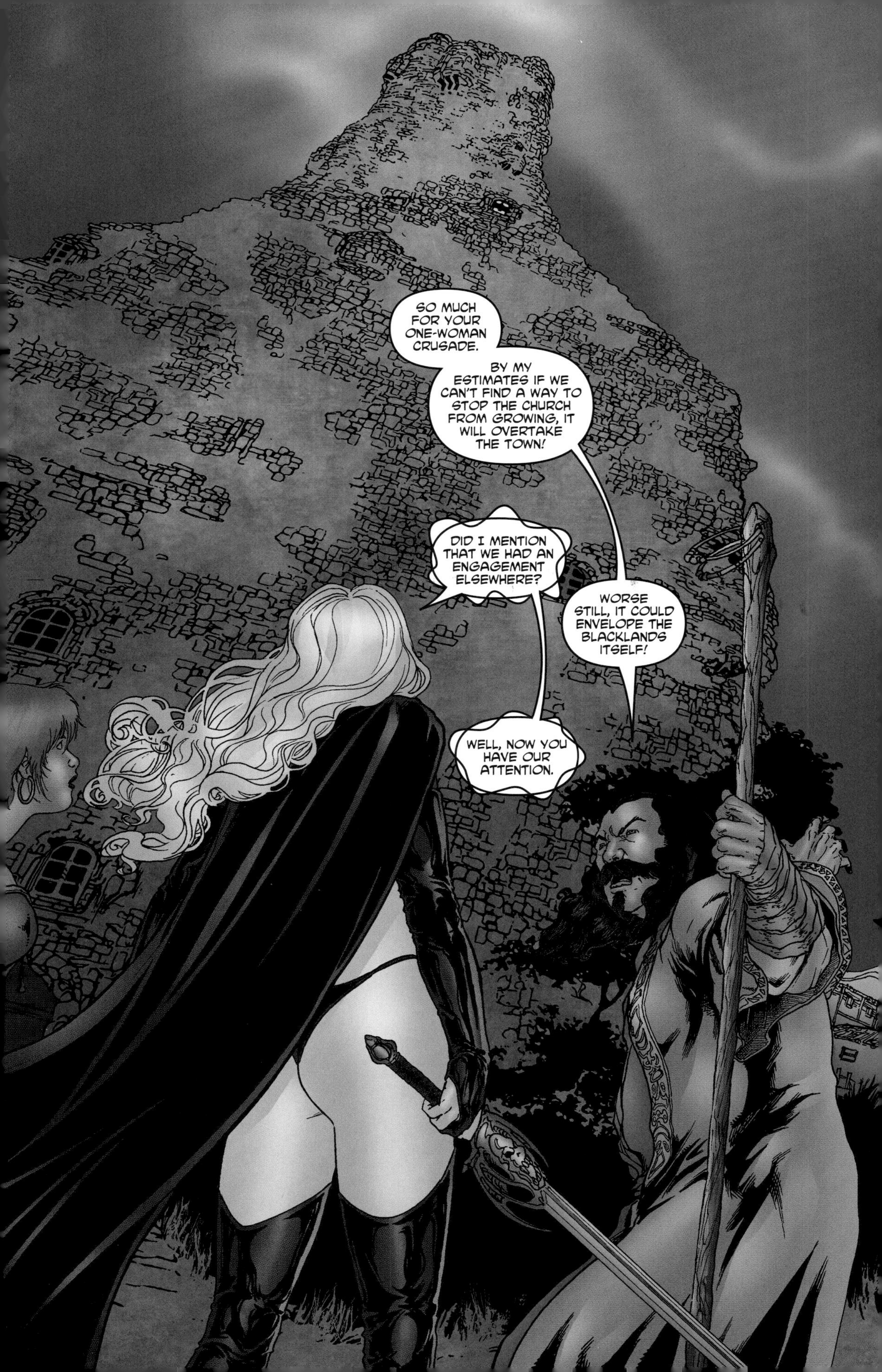
SO MUCH FOR YOUR ONE-WOMAN CRUSADE.
BY MY ESTIMATES IF WE CAN'T FIND A WAY TO STOP THE CHURCH FROM GROWING, IT WILL OVERTAKE THE TOWN!
DID I MENTION THAT WE HAD AN ENGAGEMENT ELSEWHERE?
WORSE STILL, IT COULD ENVELOPE THE BLACKLANDS ITSELF!
WELL, NOW YOU HAVE OUR ATTENTION.

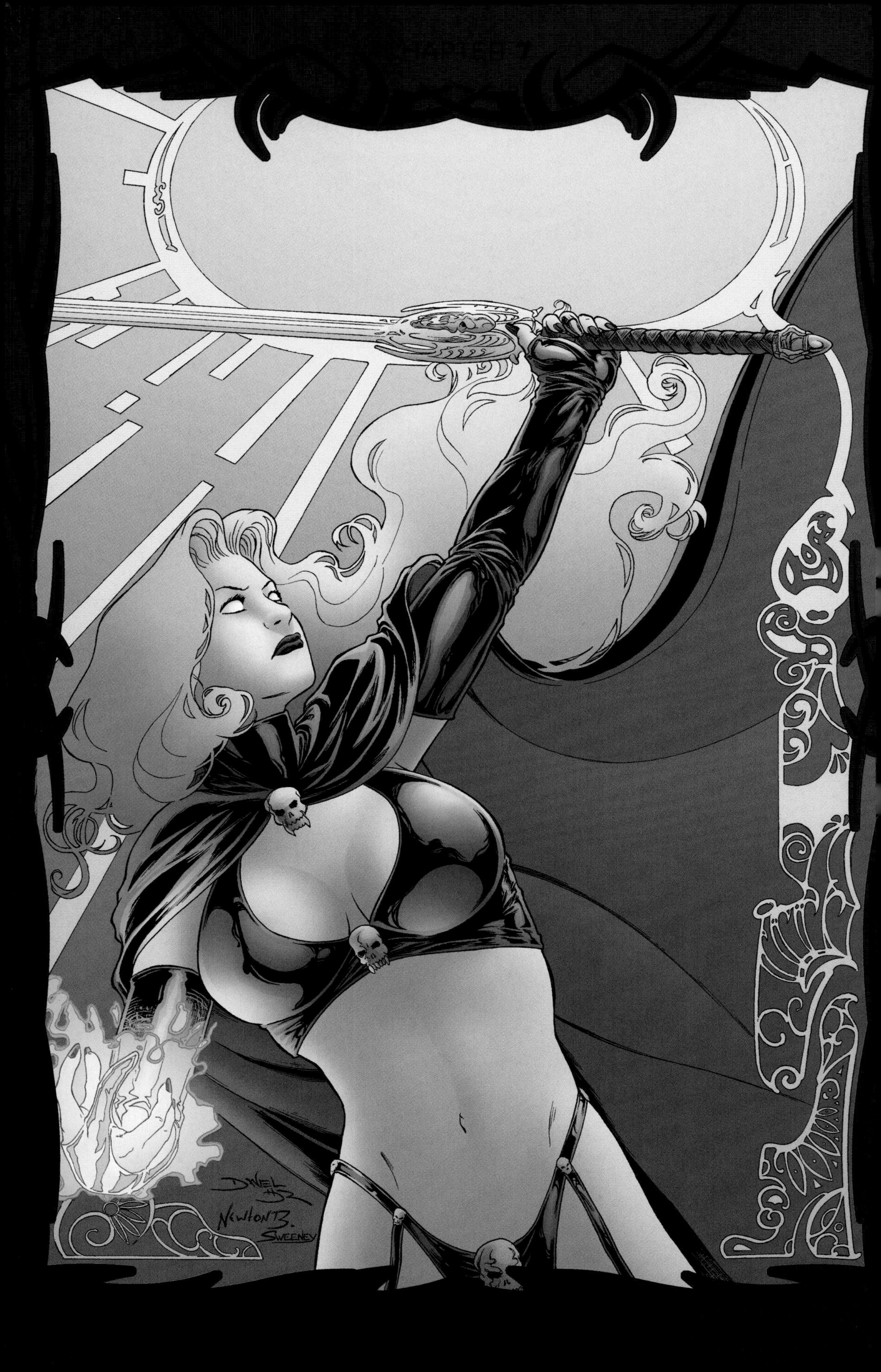
NEWTON B. SWEENEY

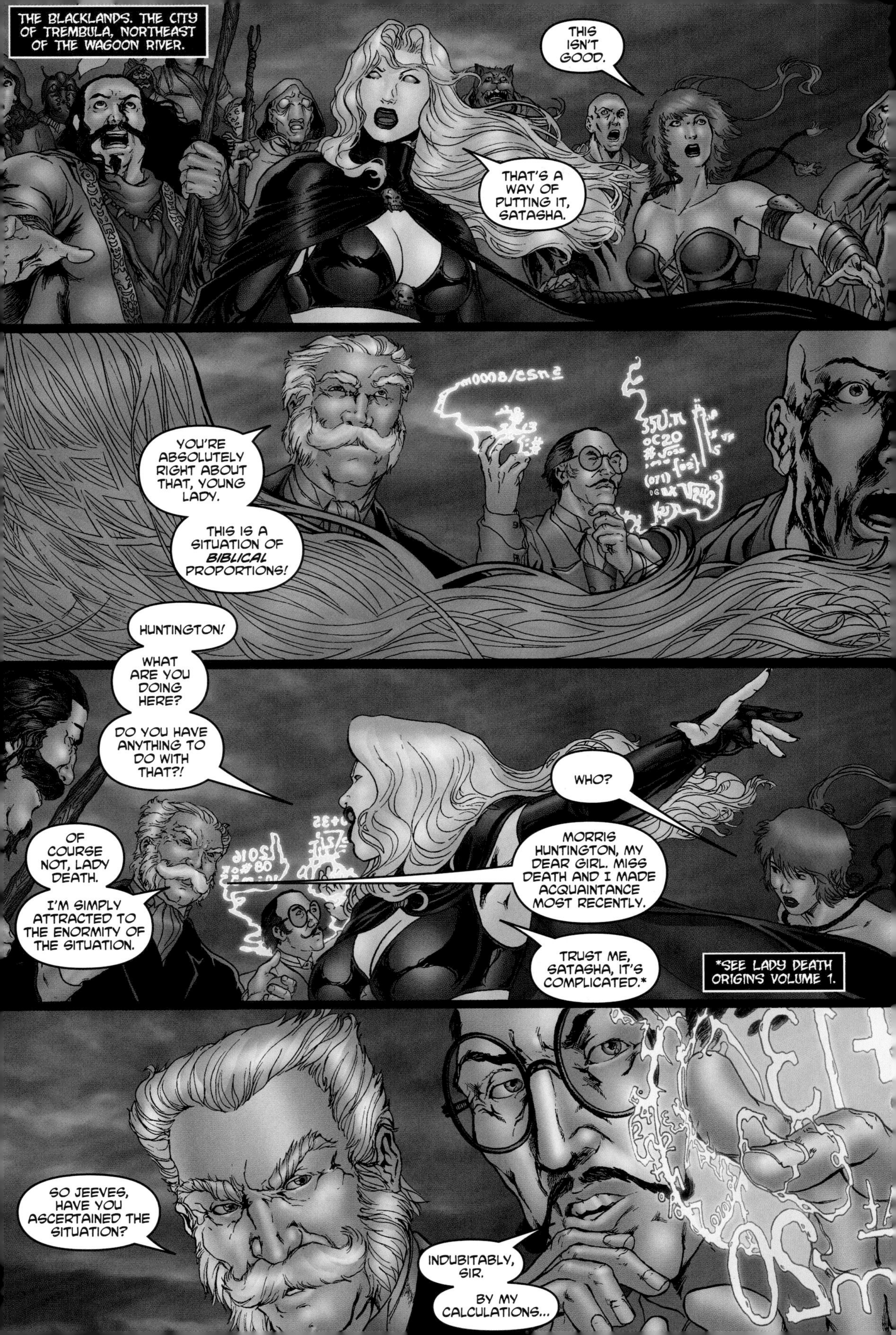
THE BLACKLANDS. THE CITY OF TREMBULA, NORTHEAST OF THE WAGOON RIVER.
THIS ISN'T GOOD.
THAT'S A WAY OF PUTTING IT, SATASHA.
YOU'RE ABSOLUTELY RIGHT ABOUT THAT, YOUNG LADY.
THIS IS A SITUATION OF *BIBLICAL* PROPORTIONS!
HUNTINGTON!
WHAT ARE YOU DOING HERE?
DO YOU HAVE ANYTHING TO DO WITH THAT?!
WHO?
OF COURSE NOT, LADY DEATH.
I'M SIMPLY ATTRACTED TO THE ENORMITY OF THE SITUATION.
MORRIS HUNTINGTON, MY DEAR GIRL. MISS DEATH AND I MADE ACQUAINTANCE MOST RECENTLY.
TRUST ME, SATASHA, IT'S COMPLICATED.*
*SEE LADY DEATH ORIGINS VOLUME 1.
SO JEEVES, HAVE YOU ASCERTAINED THE SITUATION?
INDUBITABLY, SIR.
BY MY CALCULATIONS...

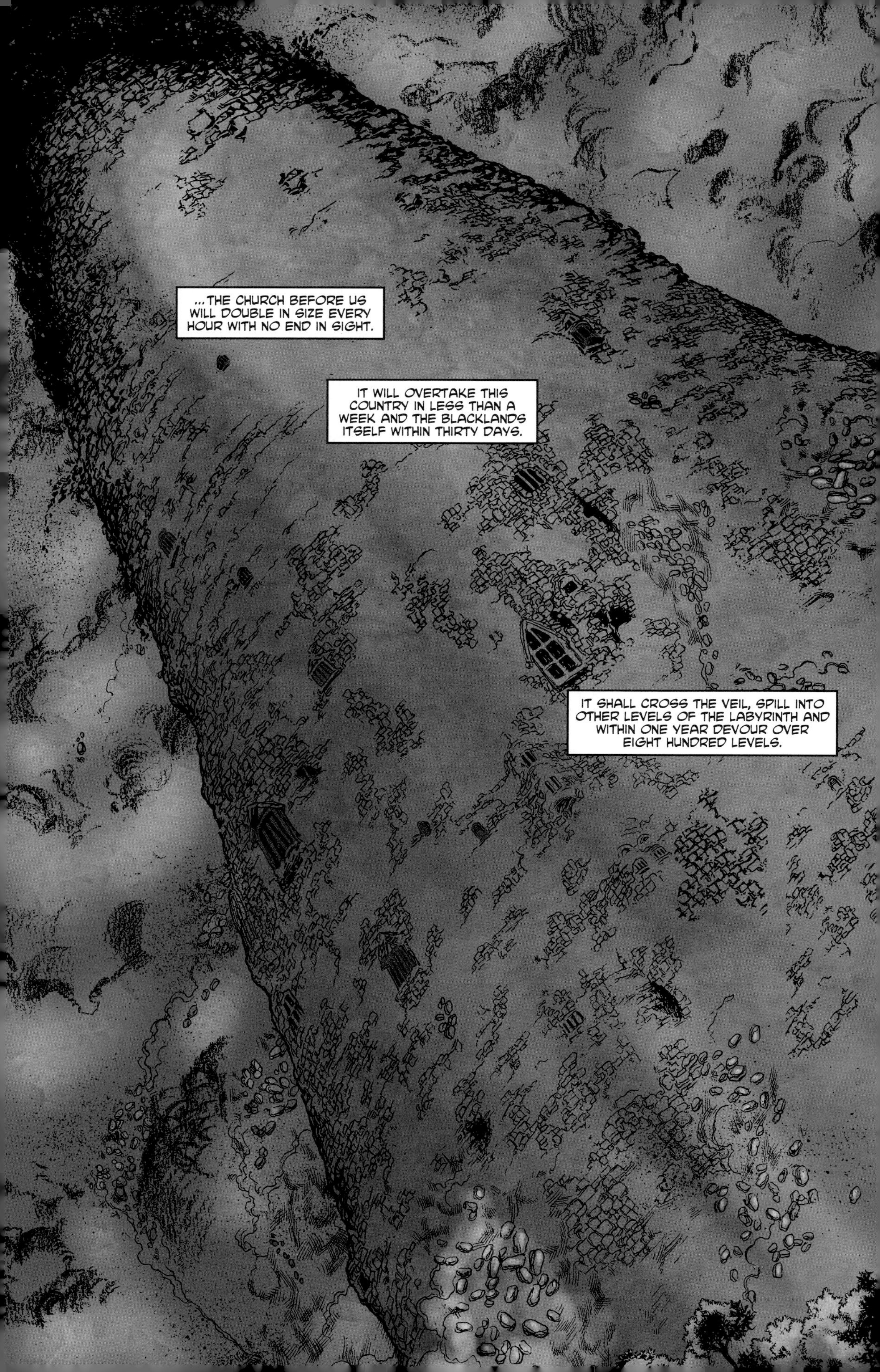
...THE CHURCH BEFORE US WILL DOUBLE IN SIZE EVERY HOUR WITH NO END IN SIGHT.
IT WILL OVERTAKE THIS COUNTRY IN LESS THAN A WEEK AND THE BLACKLANDS ITSELF WITHIN THIRTY DAYS.
IT SHALL CROSS THE VEIL, SPILL INTO OTHER LEVELS OF THE LABYRINTH AND WITHIN ONE YEAR DEVOUR OVER EIGHT HUNDRED LEVELS.

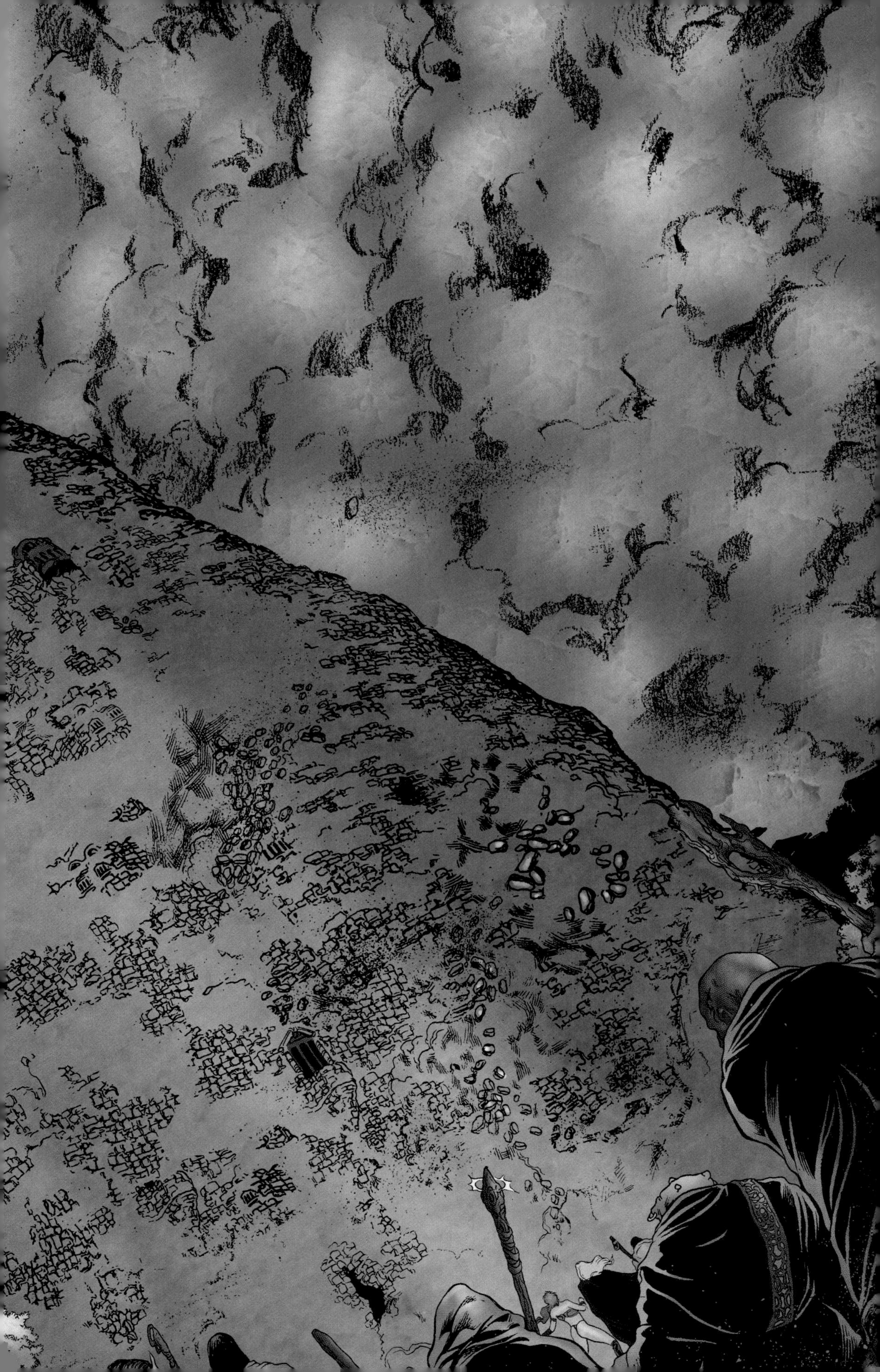

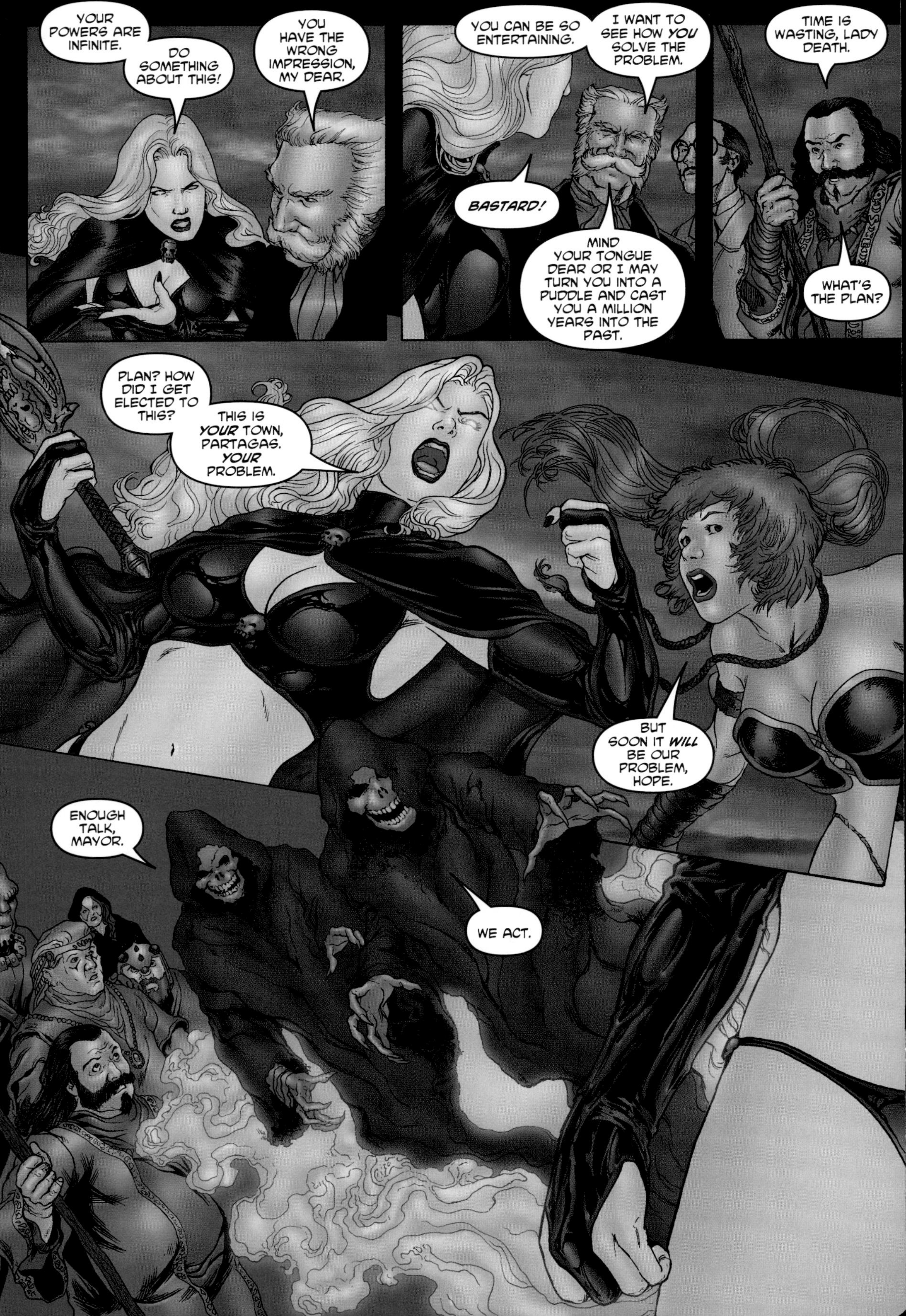
YOUR POWERS ARE INFINITE.
DO SOMETHING ABOUT THIS!
YOU HAVE THE WRONG IMPRESSION, MY DEAR.
YOU CAN BE SO ENTERTAINING.
I WANT TO SEE HOW *YOU* SOLVE THE PROBLEM.
BASTARD!
MIND YOUR TONGUE DEAR OR I MAY TURN YOU INTO A PUDDLE AND CAST YOU A MILLION YEARS INTO THE PAST.
TIME IS WASTING, LADY DEATH.
WHAT'S THE PLAN?
PLAN? HOW DID I GET ELECTED TO THIS?
THIS IS *YOUR* TOWN, PARTAGAS. *YOUR* PROBLEM.
BUT SOON IT *WILL* BE OUR PROBLEM, HOPE.
ENOUGH TALK, MAYOR.
WE ACT.

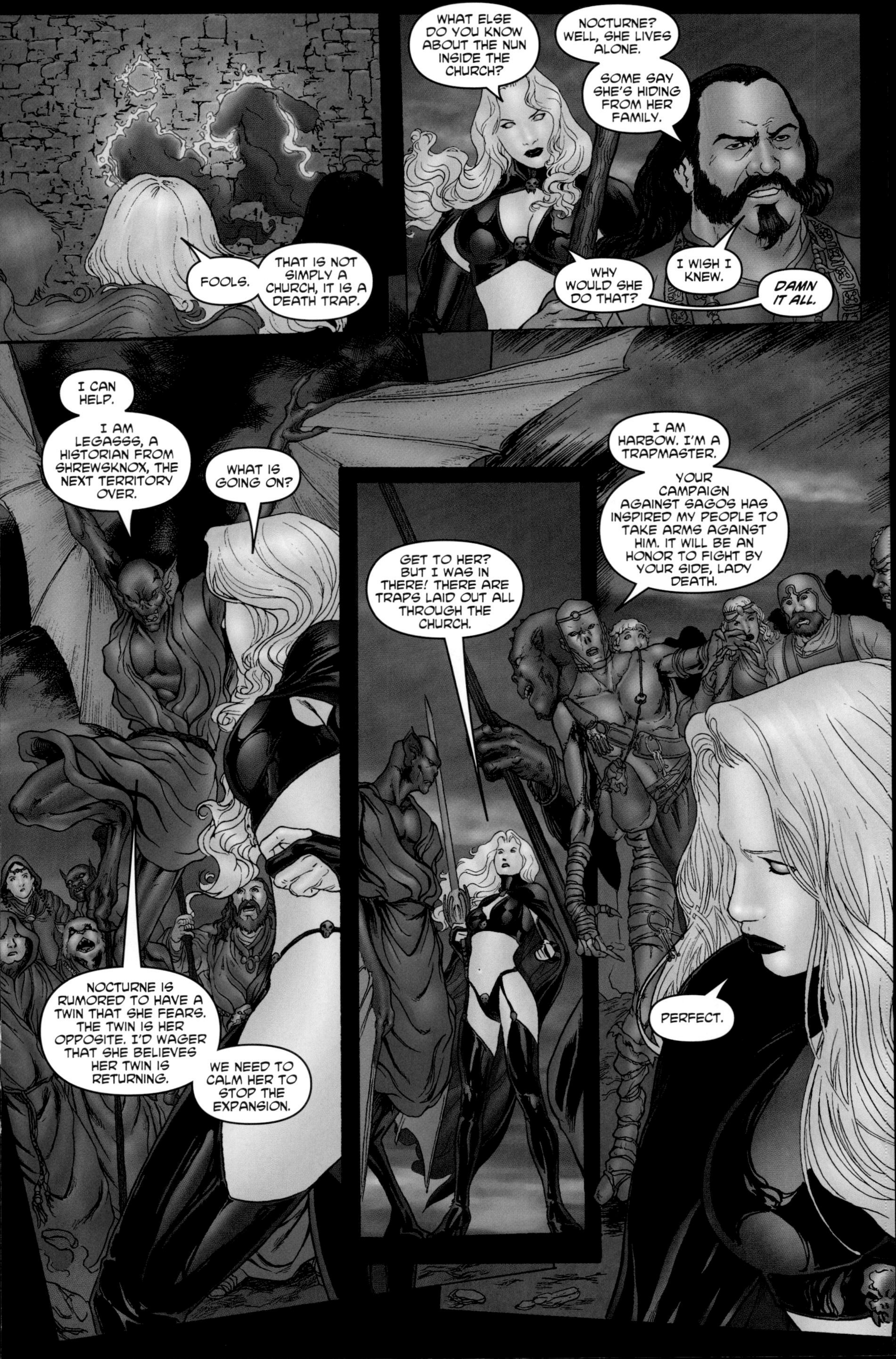
FOOLS.
THAT IS NOT SIMPLY A CHURCH, IT IS A DEATH TRAP.
WHAT ELSE DO YOU KNOW ABOUT THE NUN INSIDE THE CHURCH?
NOCTURNE? WELL, SHE LIVES ALONE.
SOME SAY SHE'S HIDING FROM HER FAMILY.
WHY WOULD SHE DO THAT?
I WISH I KNEW.
DAMN IT ALL.
I CAN HELP.
I AM LEGASSS, A HISTORIAN FROM SHREWSKNOX, THE NEXT TERRITORY OVER.
WHAT IS GOING ON?
NOCTURNE IS RUMORED TO HAVE A TWIN THAT SHE FEARS. THE TWIN IS HER OPPOSITE. I'D WAGER THAT SHE BELIEVES HER TWIN IS RETURNING.
WE NEED TO CALM HER TO STOP THE EXPANSION.
GET TO HER? BUT I WAS IN THERE! THERE ARE TRAPS LAID OUT ALL THROUGH THE CHURCH.
I AM HARBOW. I'M A TRAPMASTER.
YOUR CAMPAIGN AGAINST SAGOS HAS INSPIRED MY PEOPLE TO TAKE ARMS AGAINST HIM. IT WILL BE AN HONOR TO FIGHT BY YOUR SIDE, LADY DEATH.
PERFECT.

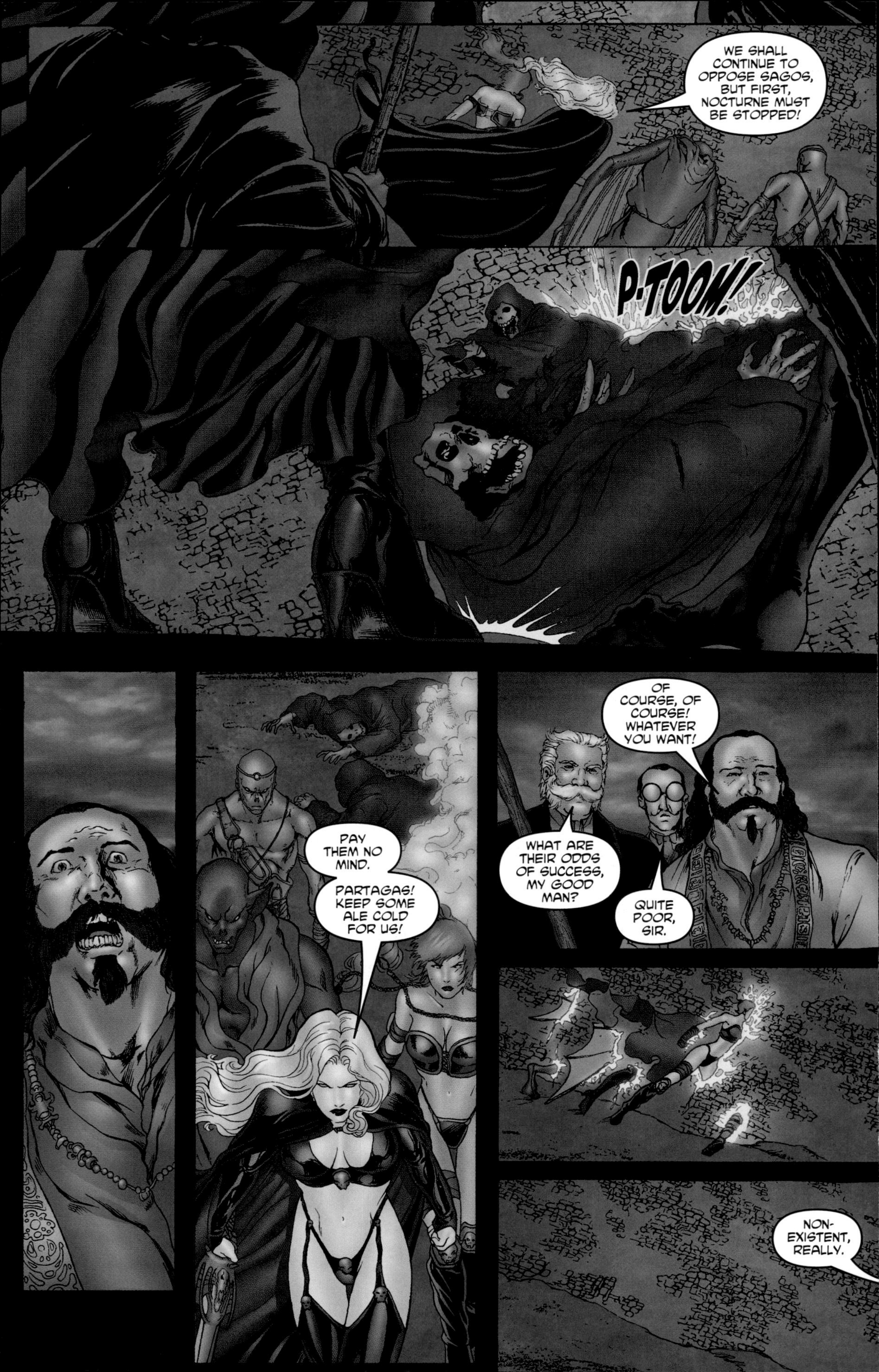
WE SHALL CONTINUE TO OPPOSE SAGOS, BUT FIRST, NOCTURNE MUST BE STOPPED!
P-TOOM!
PAY THEM NO MIND.
PARTAGAS! KEEP SOME ALE COLD FOR US!
OF COURSE, OF COURSE! WHATEVER YOU WANT!
WHAT ARE THEIR ODDS OF SUCCESS, MY GOOD MAN?
QUITE POOR, SIR.
NON-EXISTENT, REALLY.

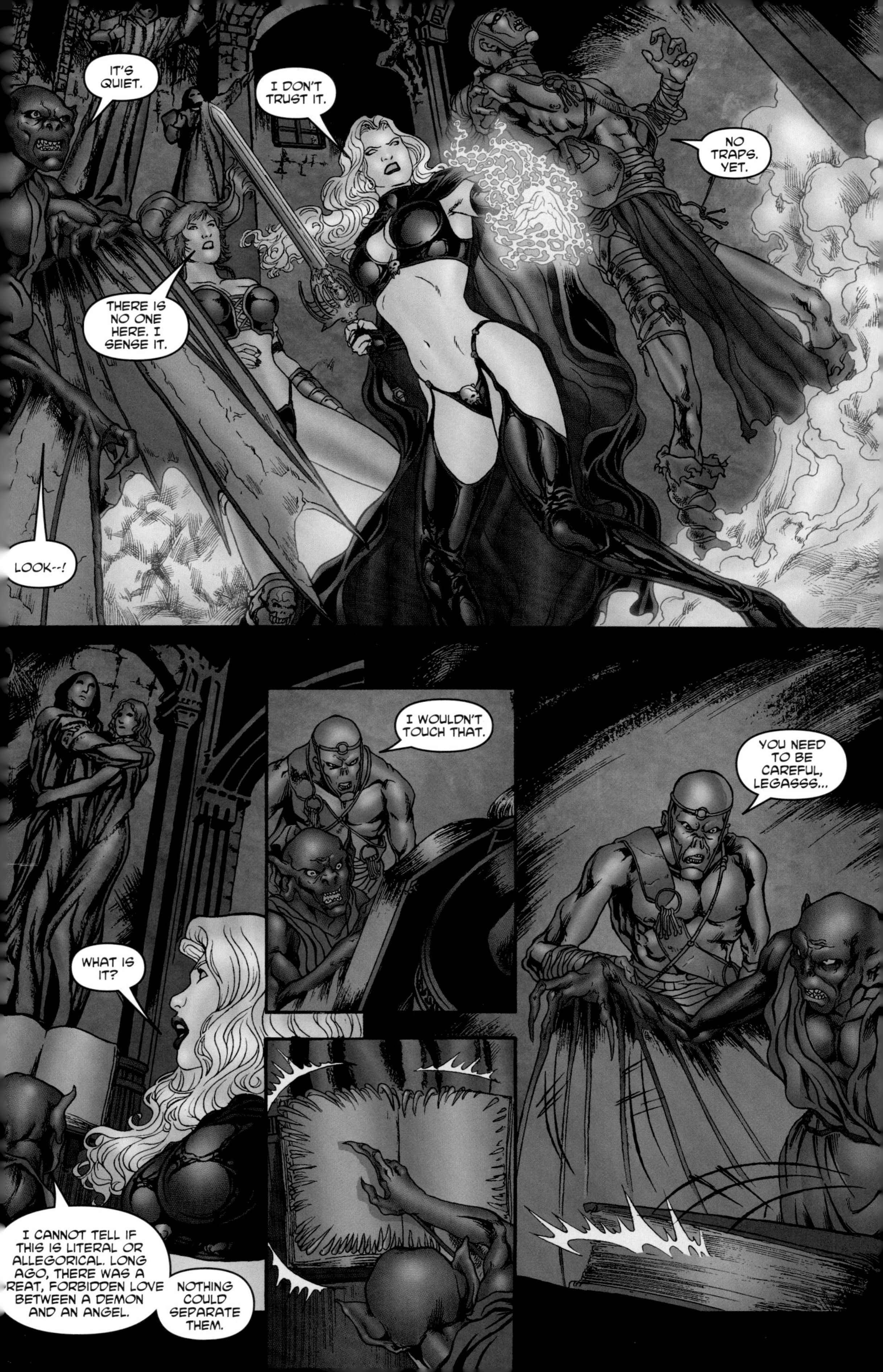
IT'S QUIET.
I DON'T TRUST IT.
NO TRAPS. YET.
THERE IS NO ONE HERE. I SENSE IT.
LOOK--!
I WOULDN'T TOUCH THAT.
YOU NEED TO BE CAREFUL, LEGASSS...
WHAT IS IT?
I CANNOT TELL IF THIS IS LITERAL OR ALLEGORICAL. LONG AGO, THERE WAS A REAT, FORBIDDEN LOVE BETWEEN A DEMON AND AN ANGEL.
NOTHING COULD SEPARATE THEM.

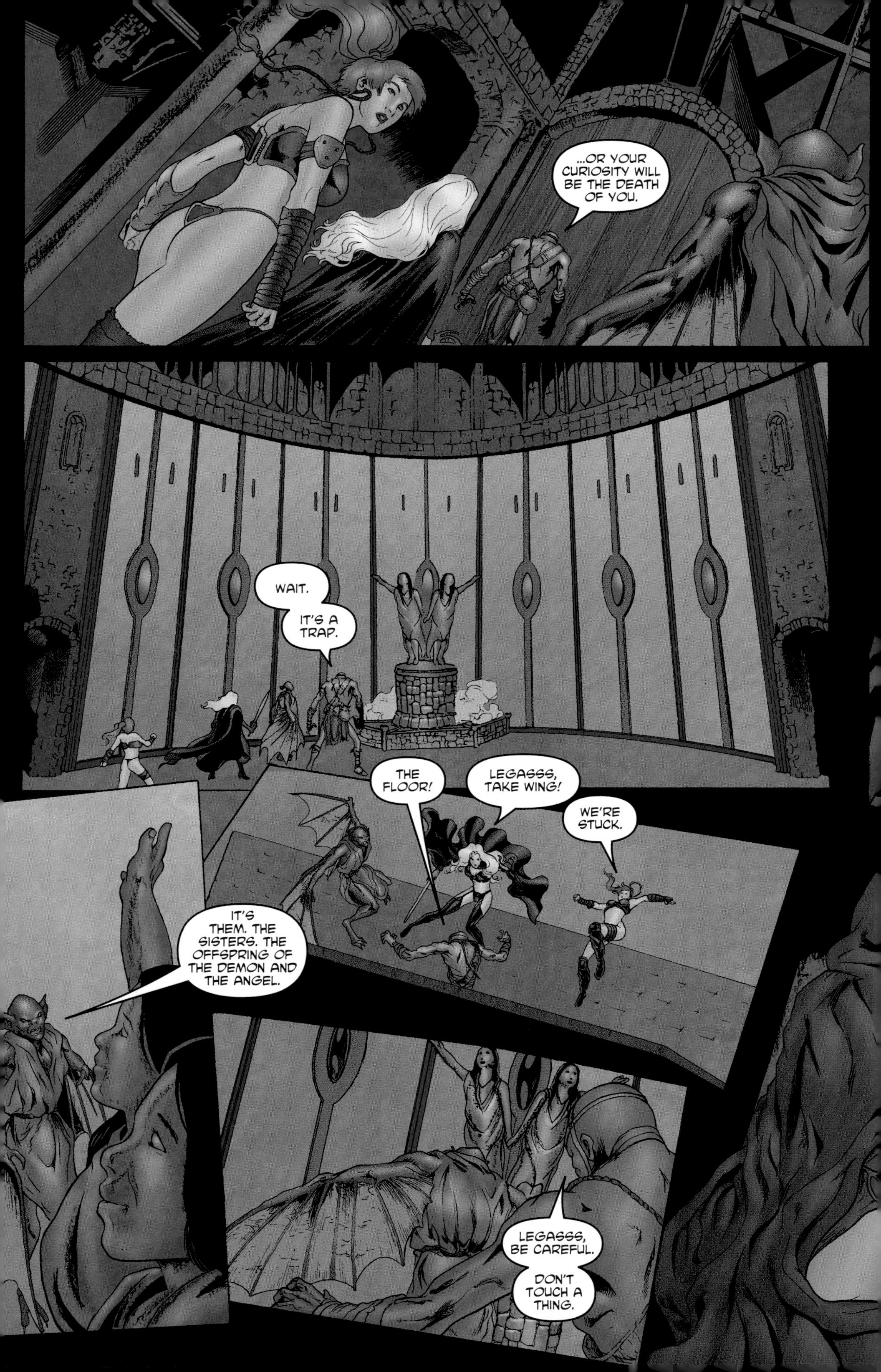
...OR YOUR CURIOSITY WILL BE THE DEATH OF YOU.
WAIT.
IT'S A TRAP.
THE FLOOR!
LEGASSS, TAKE WING!
WE'RE STUCK.
IT'S THEM. THE SISTERS. THE OFFSPRING OF THE DEMON AND THE ANGEL.
LEGASSS, BE CAREFUL.
DON'T TOUCH A THING.

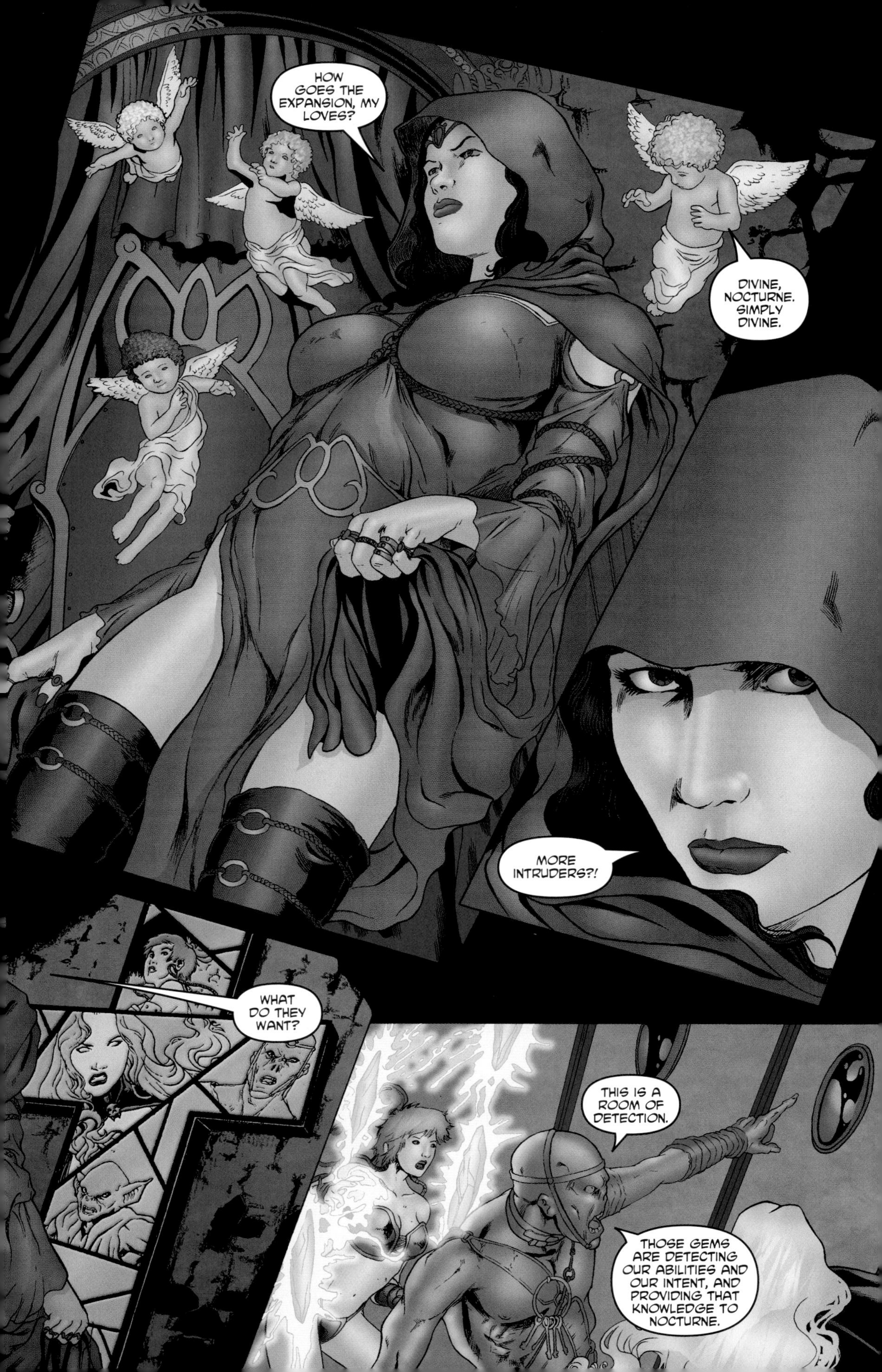
HOW GOES THE EXPANSION, MY LOVES?
DIVINE, NOCTURNE. SIMPLY DIVINE.
MORE INTRUDERS?!
WHAT DO THEY WANT?
THIS IS A ROOM OF DETECTION.
THOSE GEMS ARE DETECTING OUR ABILITIES AND OUR INTENT, AND PROVIDING THAT KNOWLEDGE TO NOCTURNE.

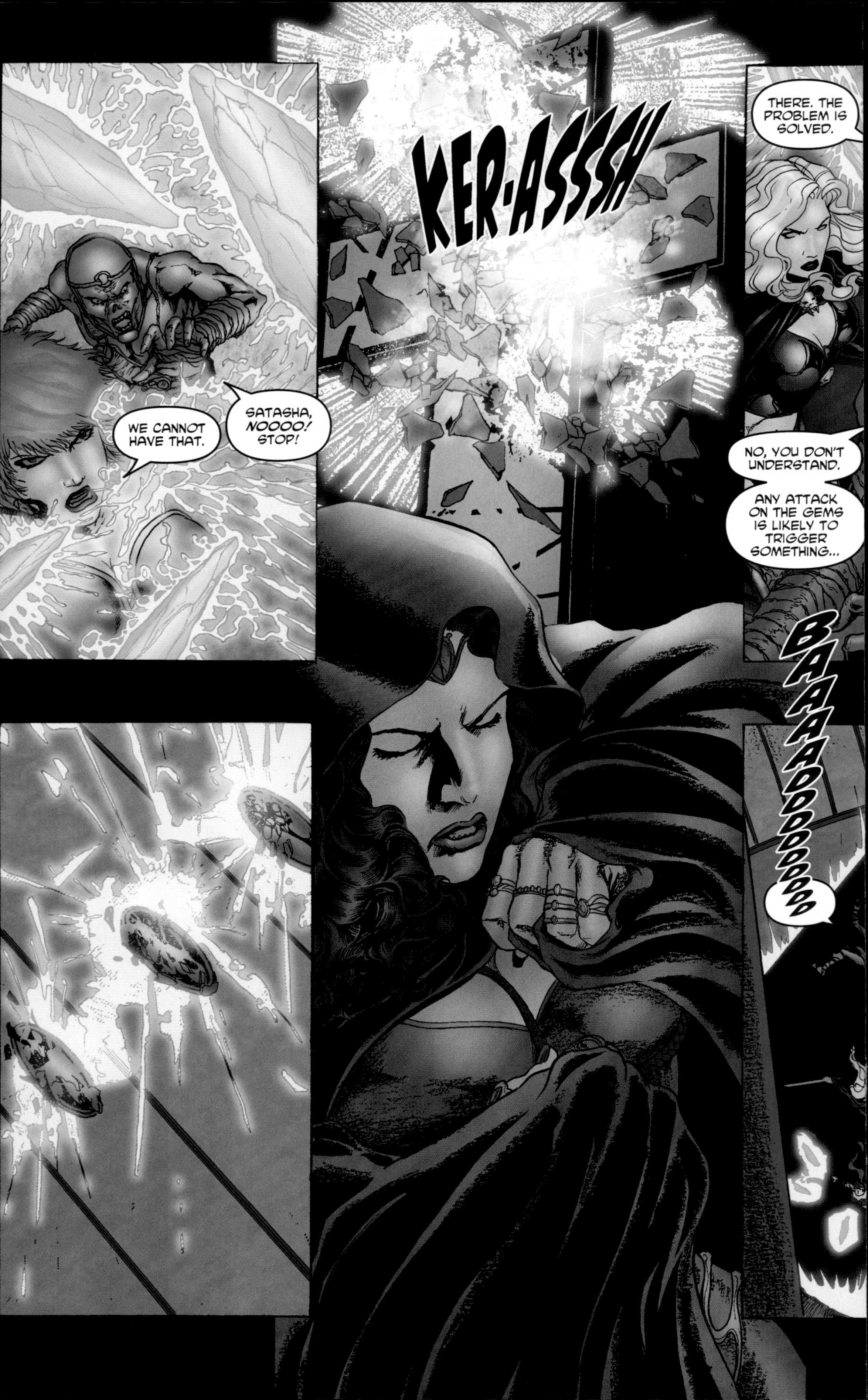

SATASHA, NOOOO! STOP!
WE CANNOT HAVE THAT.
KER-ASSSH
THERE. THE PROBLEM IS SOLVED.
NO, YOU DON'T UNDERSTAND.
ANY ATTACK ON THE GEMS IS LIKELY TO TRIGGER SOMETHING...
BAAAAAOOOOOOOO

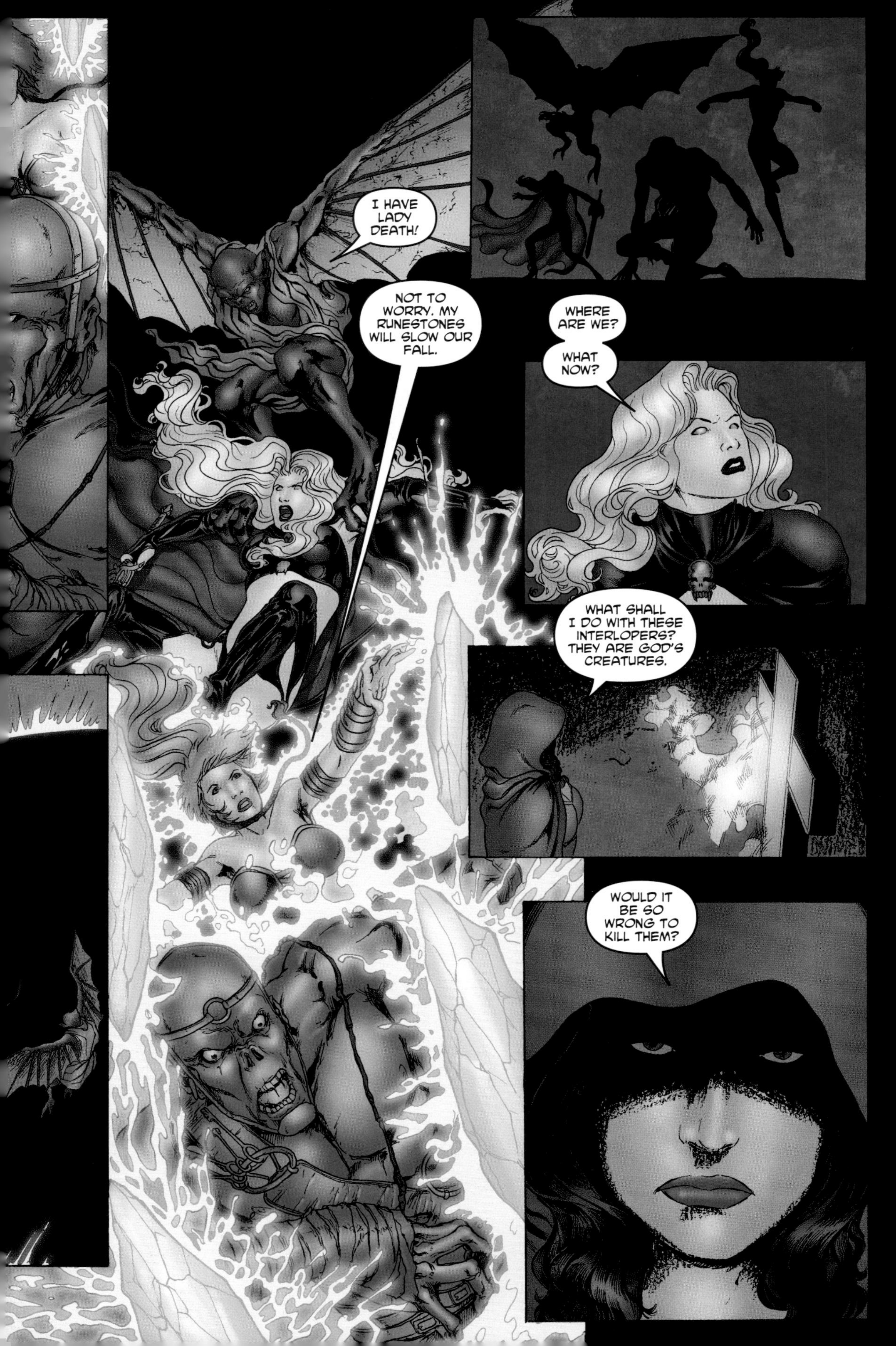
I HAVE LADY DEATH!
NOT TO WORRY. MY RUNESTONES WILL SLOW OUR FALL.
WHERE ARE WE?
WHAT NOW?
WHAT SHALL I DO WITH THESE INTERLOPERS? THEY ARE GOD'S CREATURES.
WOULD IT BE SO WRONG TO KILL THEM?

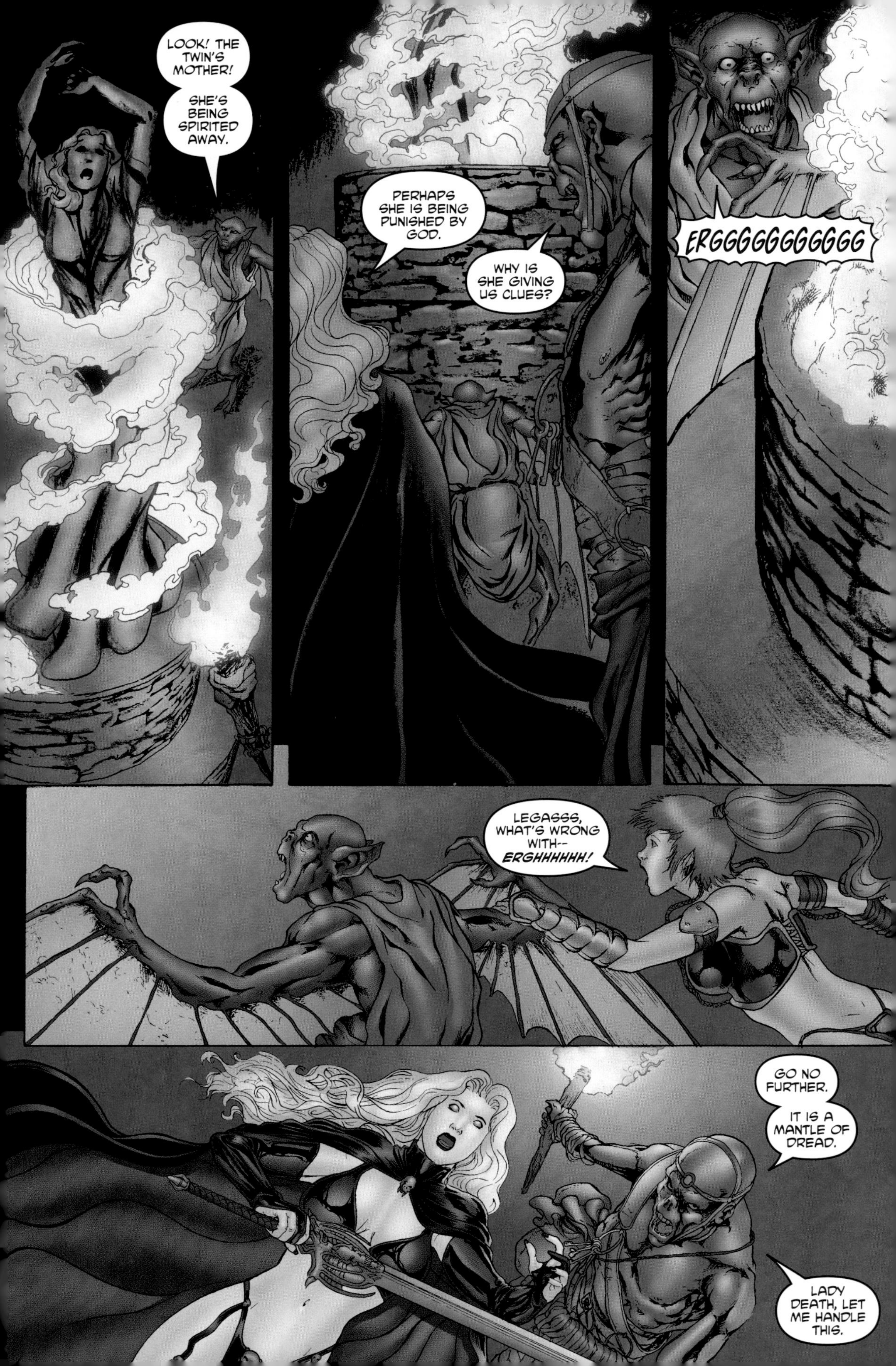
LOOK! THE TWIN'S MOTHER!
SHE'S BEING SPIRITED AWAY.
PERHAPS SHE IS BEING PUNISHED BY GOD.
WHY IS SHE GIVING US CLUES?
ERGGGGGGGGGGG
LEGASSS, WHAT'S WRONG WITH-- ERGHHHHHH!
GO NO FURTHER.
IT IS A MANTLE OF DREAD.
LADY DEATH, LET ME HANDLE THIS.

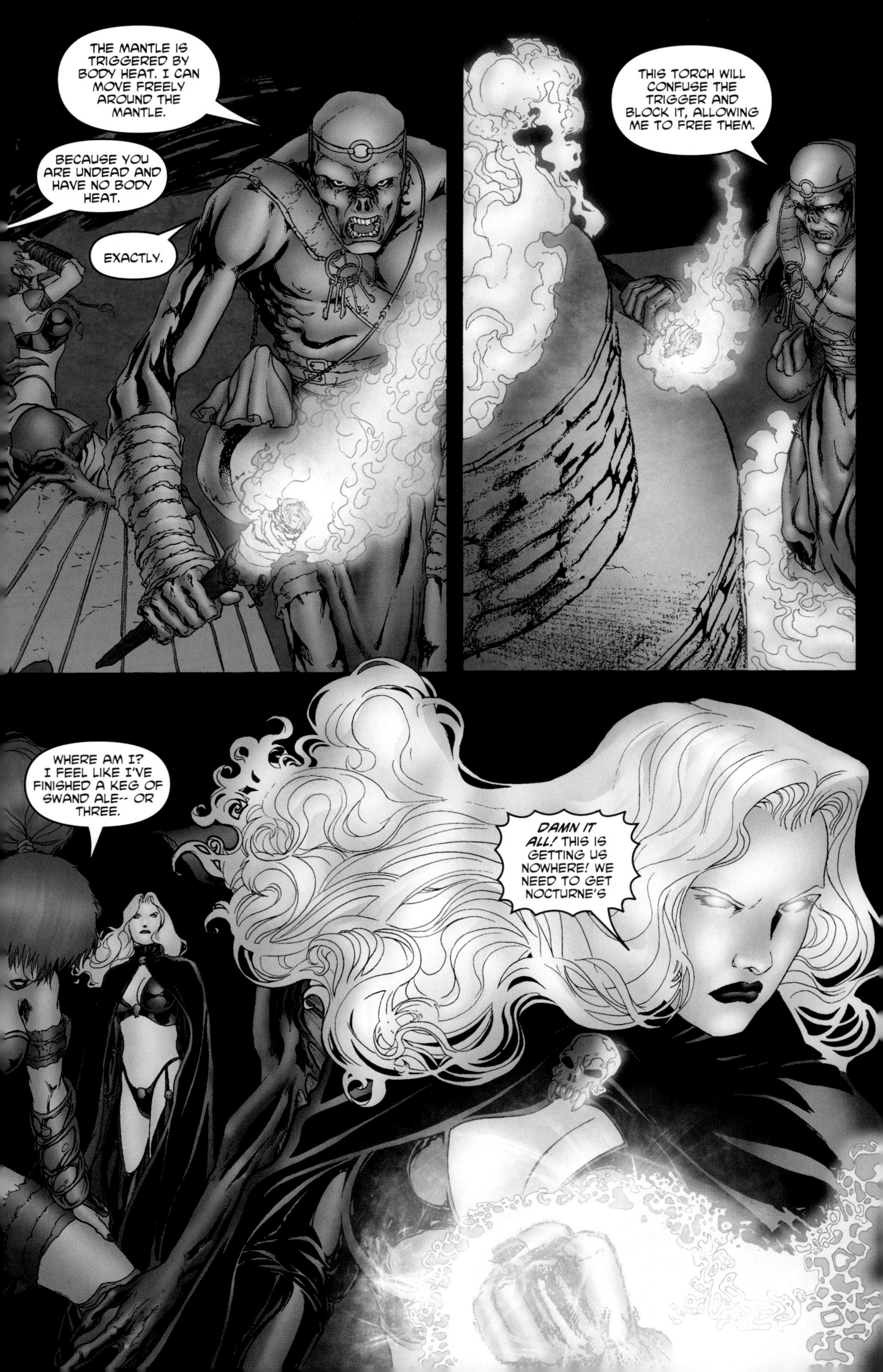
THE MANTLE IS TRIGGERED BY BODY HEAT. I CAN MOVE FREELY AROUND THE MANTLE.
BECAUSE YOU ARE UNDEAD AND HAVE NO BODY HEAT.
EXACTLY.
THIS TORCH WILL CONFUSE THE TRIGGER AND BLOCK IT, ALLOWING ME TO FREE THEM.
WHERE AM I? I FEEL LIKE I'VE FINISHED A KEG OF SWAND ALE-- OR THREE.
DAMN IT ALL! THIS IS GETTING US NOWHERE! WE NEED TO GET NOCTURNE'S

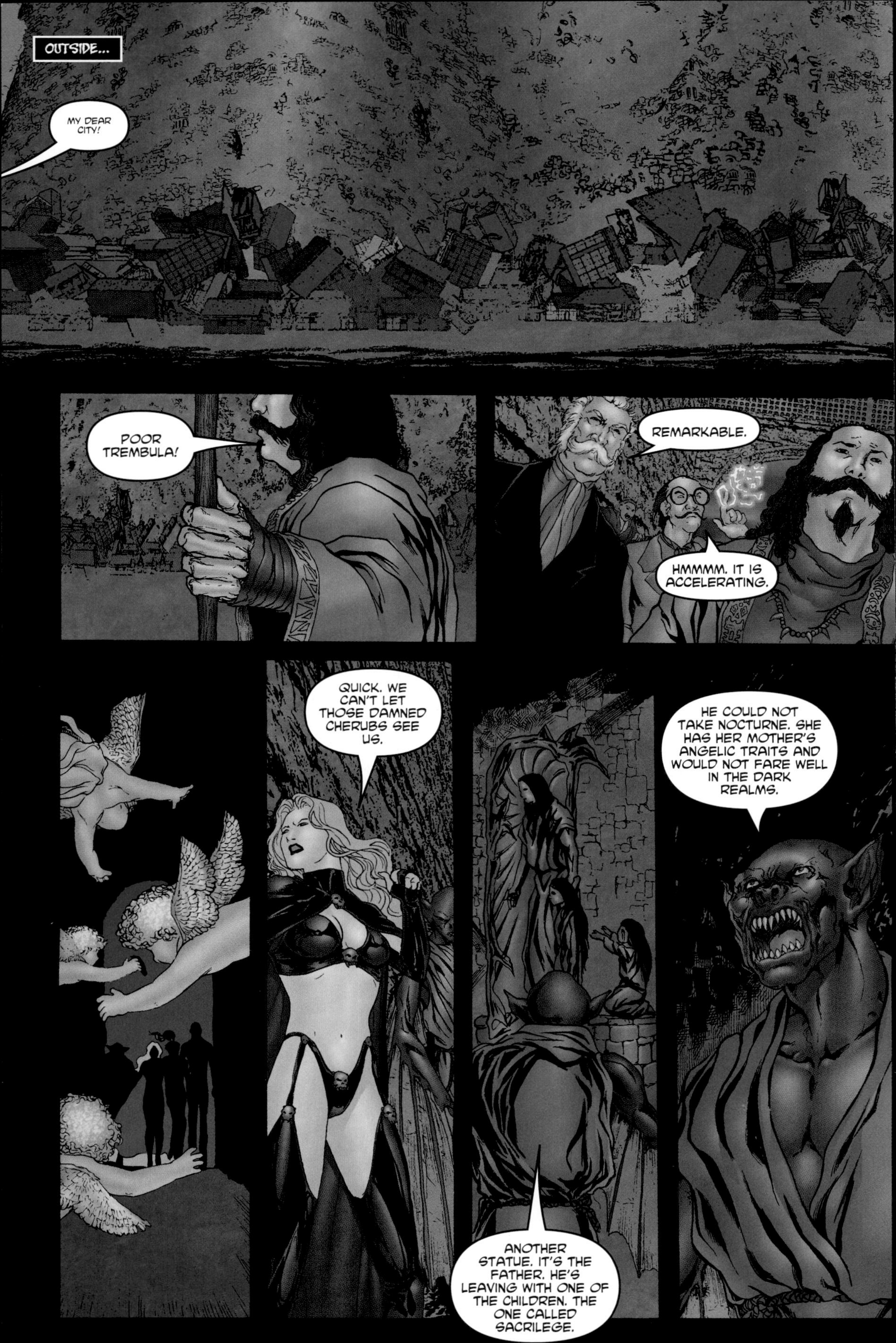
OUTSIDE...
MY DEAR CITY!
POOR TREMBULA!
REMARKABLE.
HMMMM. IT IS ACCELERATING.
QUICK. WE CAN'T LET THOSE DAMNED CHERUBS SEE US.
ANOTHER STATUE. IT'S THE FATHER. HE'S LEAVING WITH ONE OF THE CHILDREN. THE ONE CALLED SACRILEGE.
HE COULD NOT TAKE NOCTURNE. SHE HAS HER MOTHER'S ANGELIC TRAITS AND WOULD NOT FARE WELL IN THE DARK REALMS.

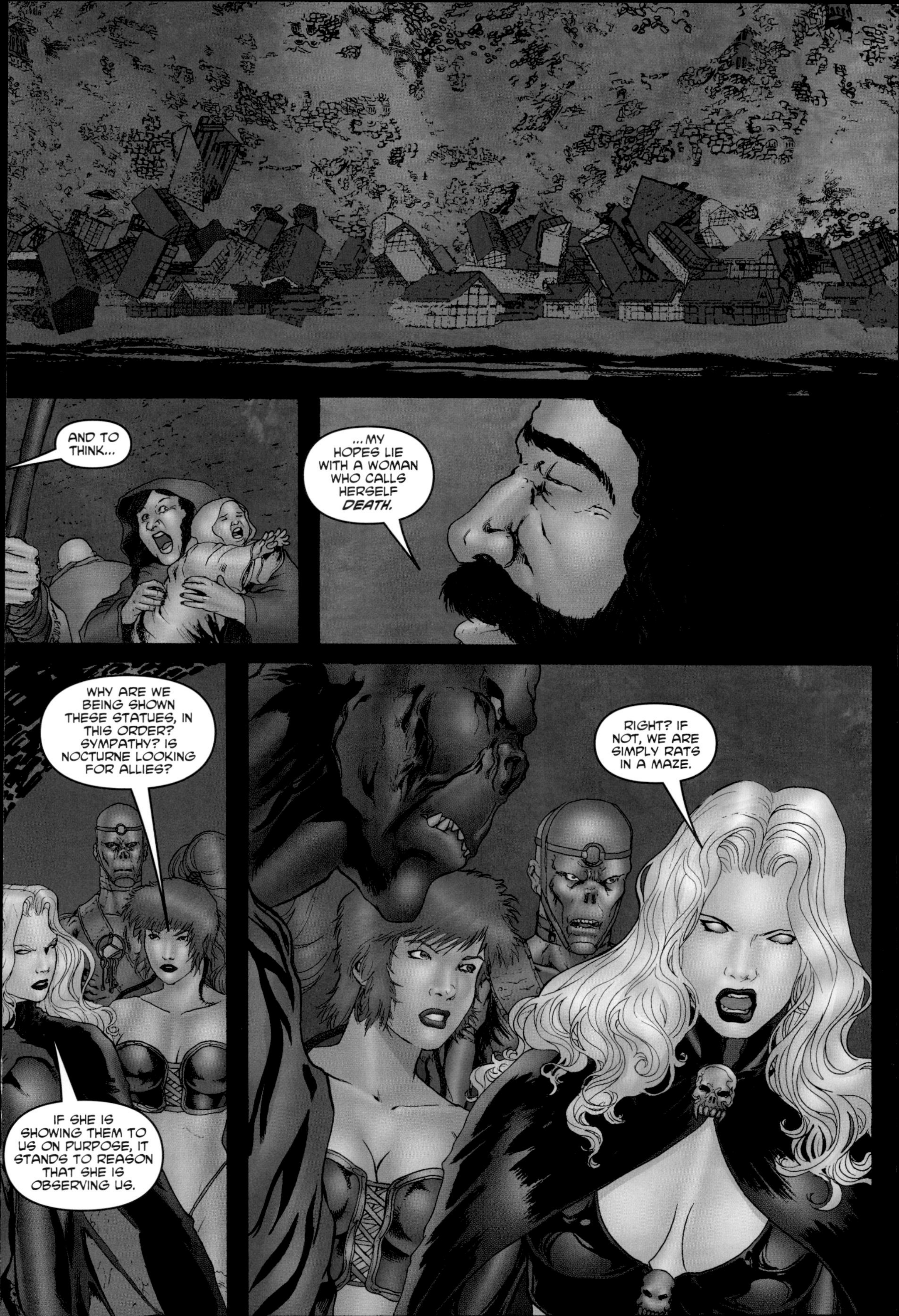
AND TO THINK...
...MY HOPES LIE WITH A WOMAN WHO CALLS HERSELF *DEATH.*
WHY ARE WE BEING SHOWN THESE STATUES, IN THIS ORDER? SYMPATHY? IS NOCTURNE LOOKING FOR ALLIES?
IF SHE IS SHOWING THEM TO US ON PURPOSE, IT STANDS TO REASON THAT SHE IS OBSERVING US.
RIGHT? IF NOT, WE ARE SIMPLY RATS IN A MAZE.

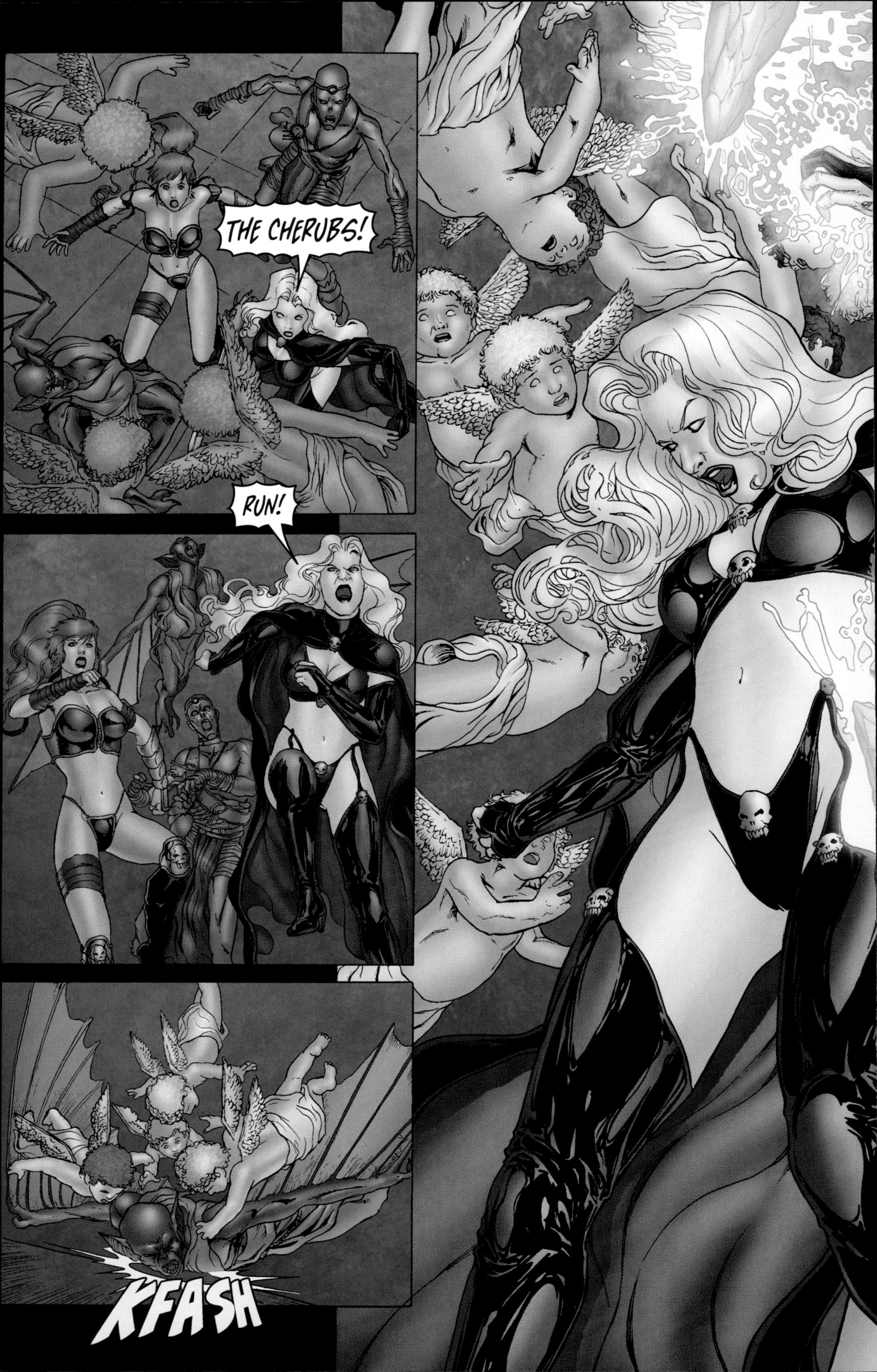
THE CHERUBS!
RUN!
KFASH

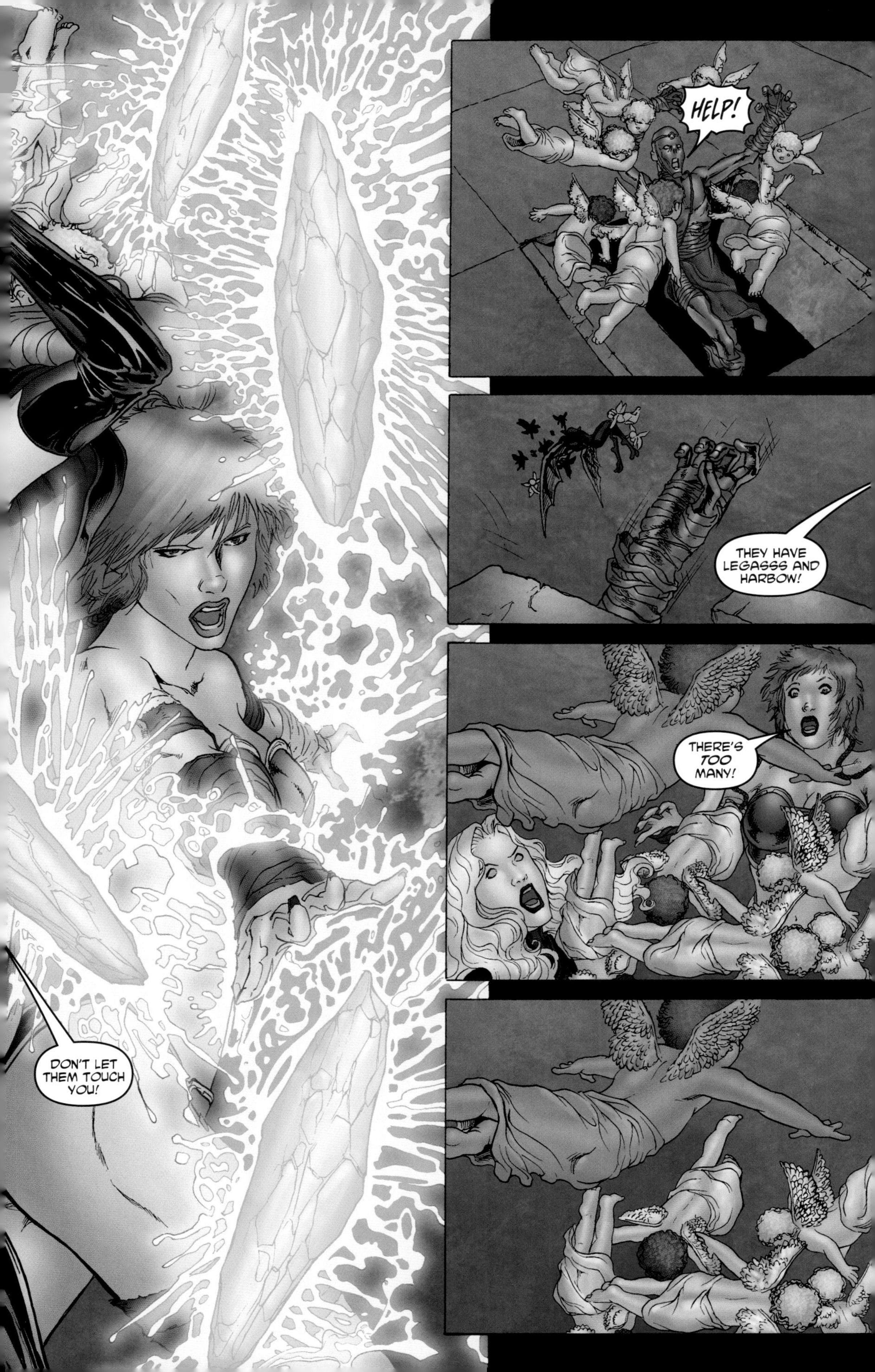
HELP!
THEY HAVE LEGASSS AND HARBOW!
THERE'S TOO MANY!
DON'T LET THEM TOUCH YOU!

GOOD WORK, SATASHA.

DON'T THANK ME YET. THE ILLUSION WILL ONLY LAST FOR SO LONG...

WE HAVE TO SAVE LEGASSS AND HARBOW.

NO. WE MUST FIND NOCTURNE AND STOP THE EXPANSION.

WHAT?!

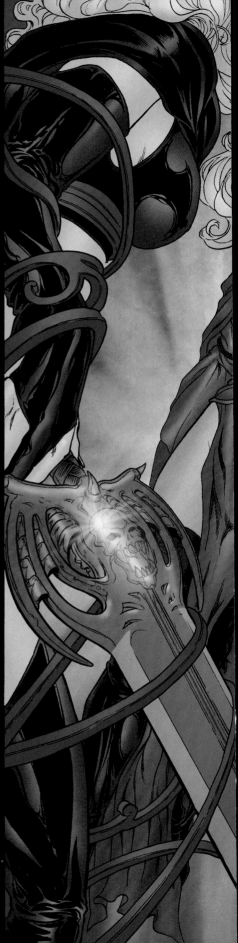

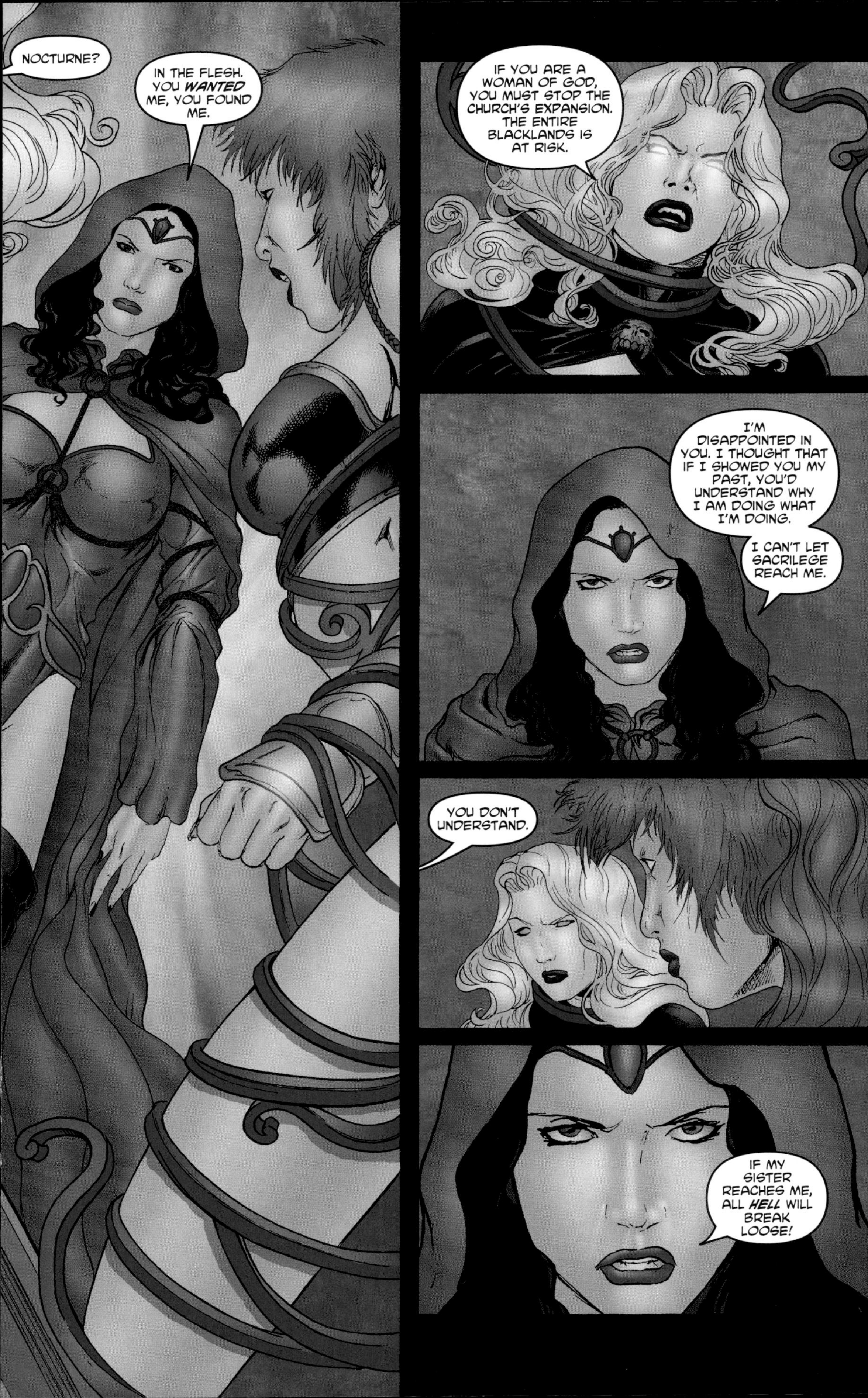
NOCTURNE?
IN THE FLESH. YOU WANTED ME, YOU FOUND ME.
IF YOU ARE A WOMAN OF GOD, YOU MUST STOP THE CHURCH'S EXPANSION. THE ENTIRE BLACKLANDS IS AT RISK.
I'M DISAPPOINTED IN YOU. I THOUGHT THAT IF I SHOWED YOU MY PAST, YOU'D UNDERSTAND WHY I AM DOING WHAT I'M DOING.
I CAN'T LET SACRILEGE REACH ME.
YOU DON'T UNDERSTAND.
IF MY SISTER REACHES ME, ALL HELL WILL BREAK LOOSE!

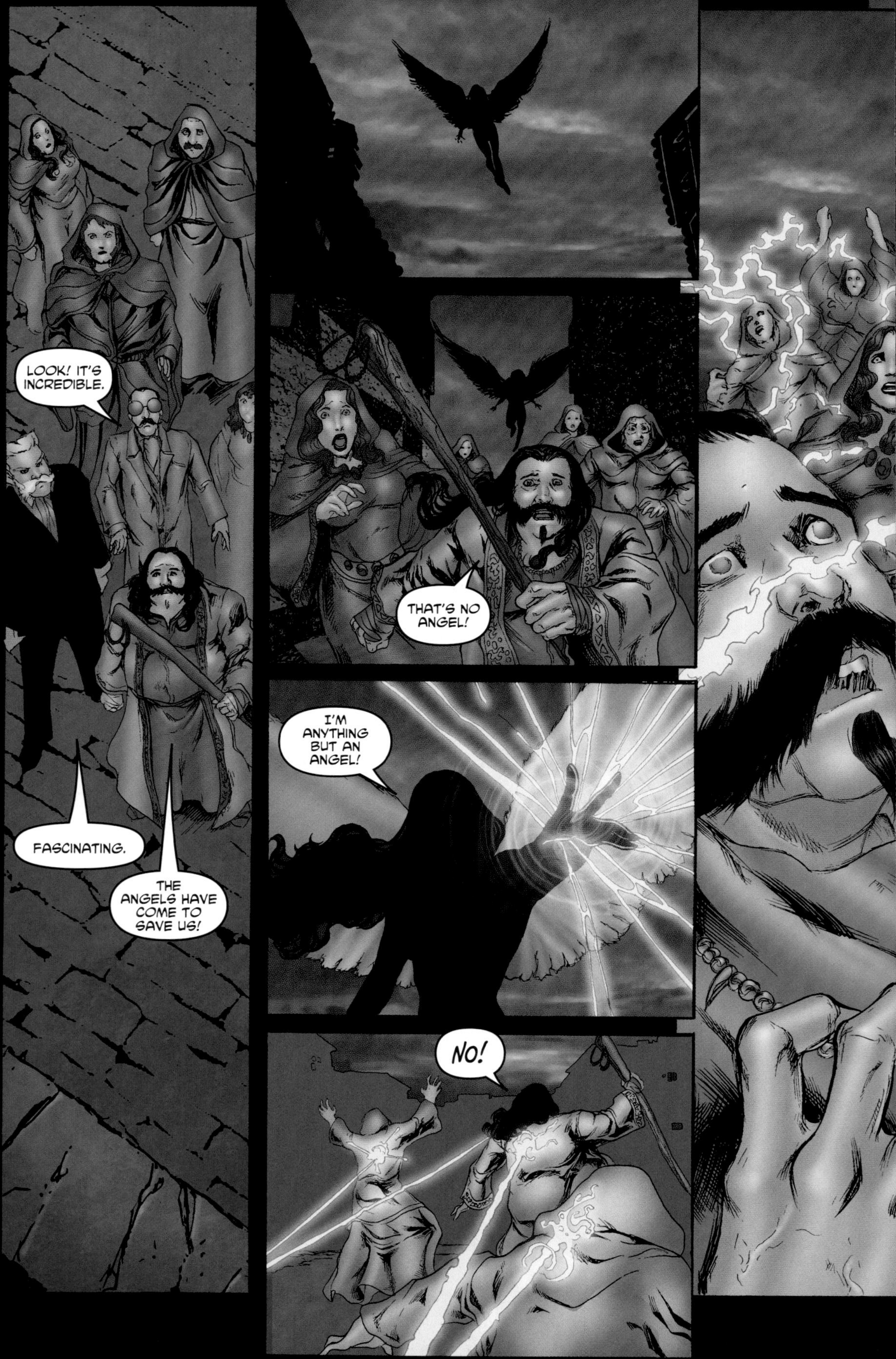

LOOK! IT'S INCREDIBLE.
FASCINATING.
THE ANGELS HAVE COME TO SAVE US!
THAT'S NO ANGEL!
I'M ANYTHING BUT AN ANGEL!
NO!

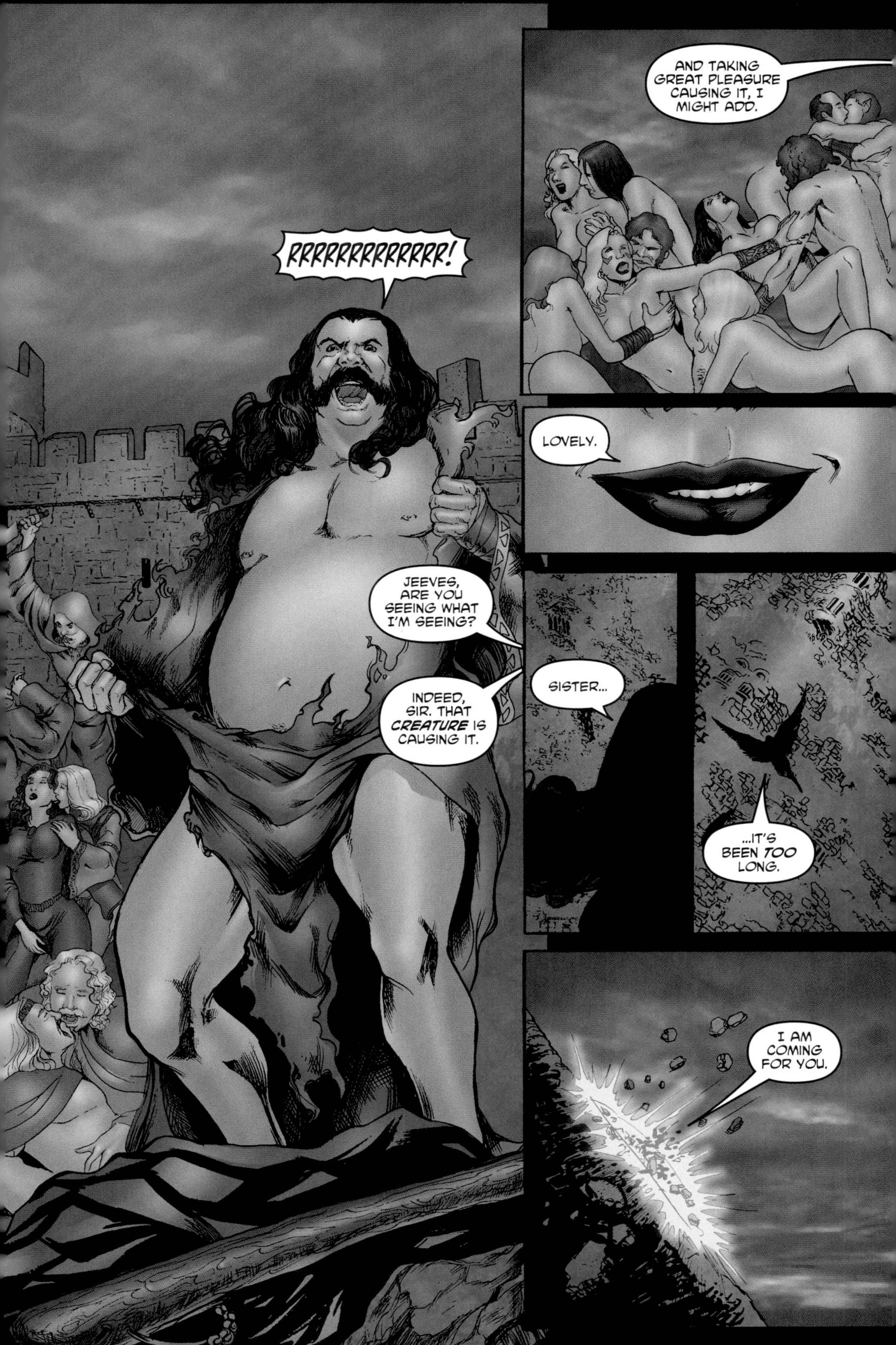
RRRRRRRRRRRRR!
JEEVES, ARE YOU SEEING WHAT I'M SEEING?
INDEED, SIR. THAT *CREATURE* IS CAUSING IT.
AND TAKING GREAT PLEASURE CAUSING IT, I MIGHT ADD.
LOVELY.
SISTER...
...IT'S BEEN *TOO* LONG.
I AM COMING FOR YOU.

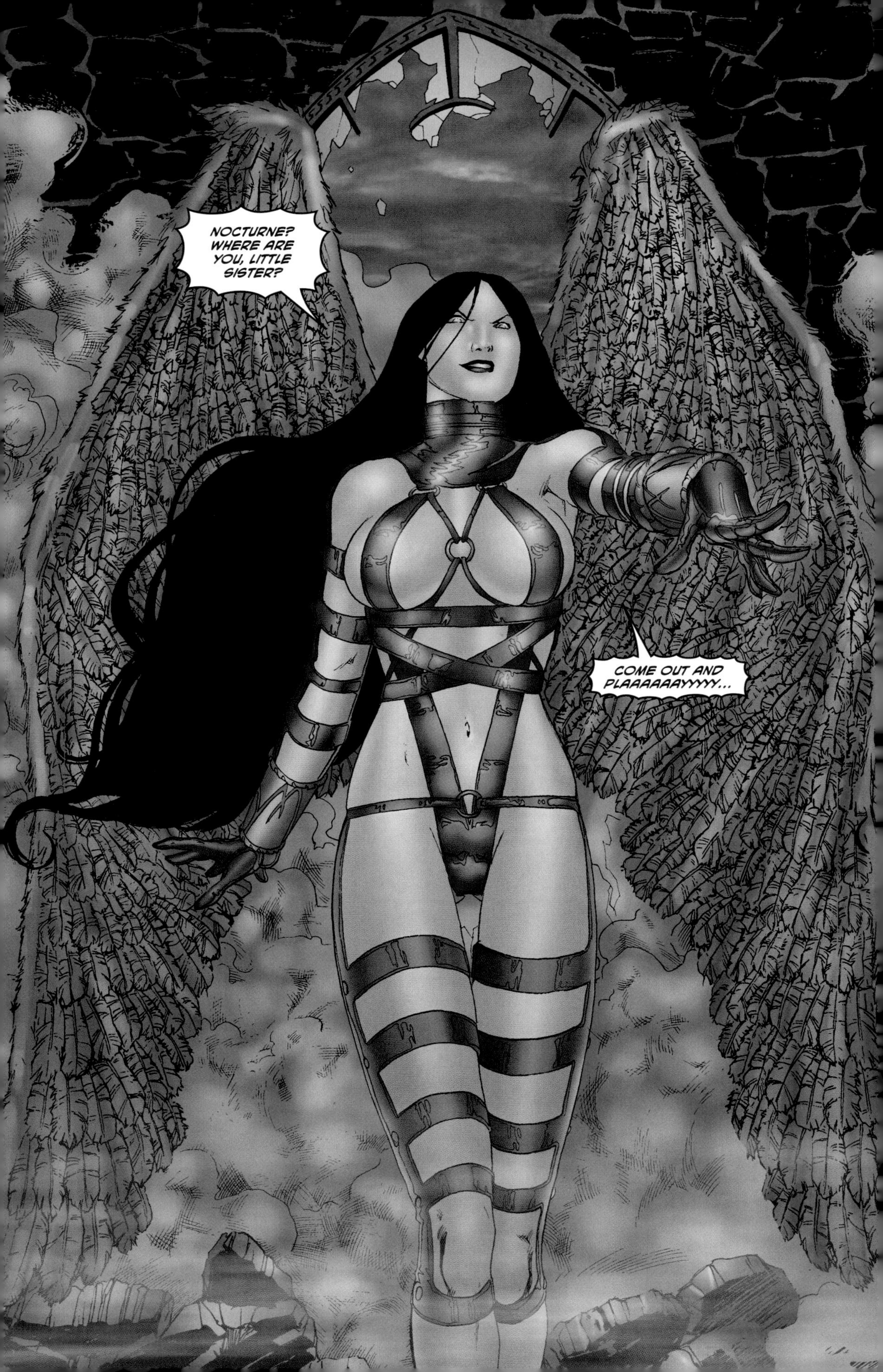
NOCTURNE? WHERE ARE YOU, LITTLE SISTER?
COME OUT AND PLAAAAAAYYYYY...

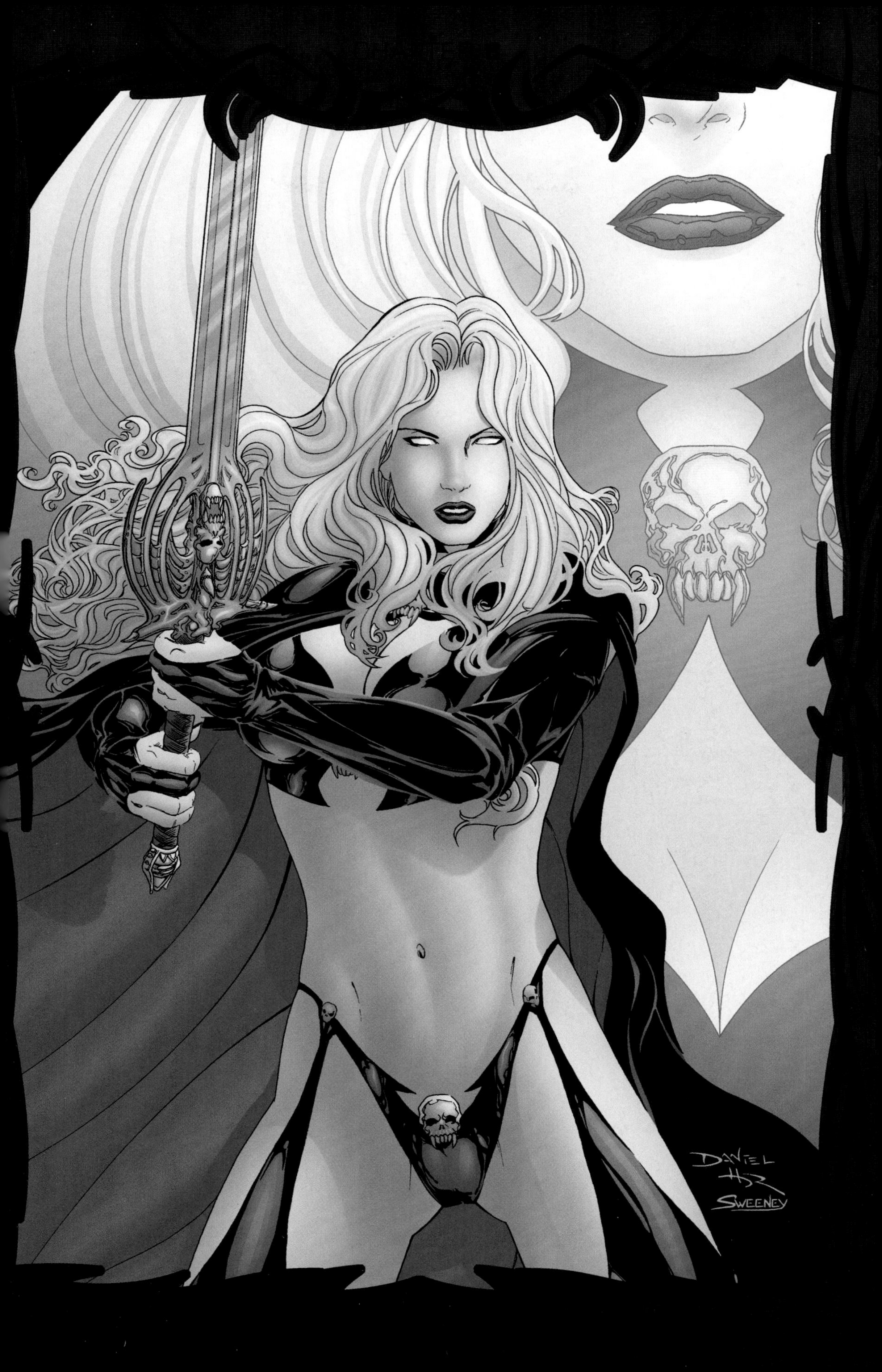
DANIEL
SWEENEY

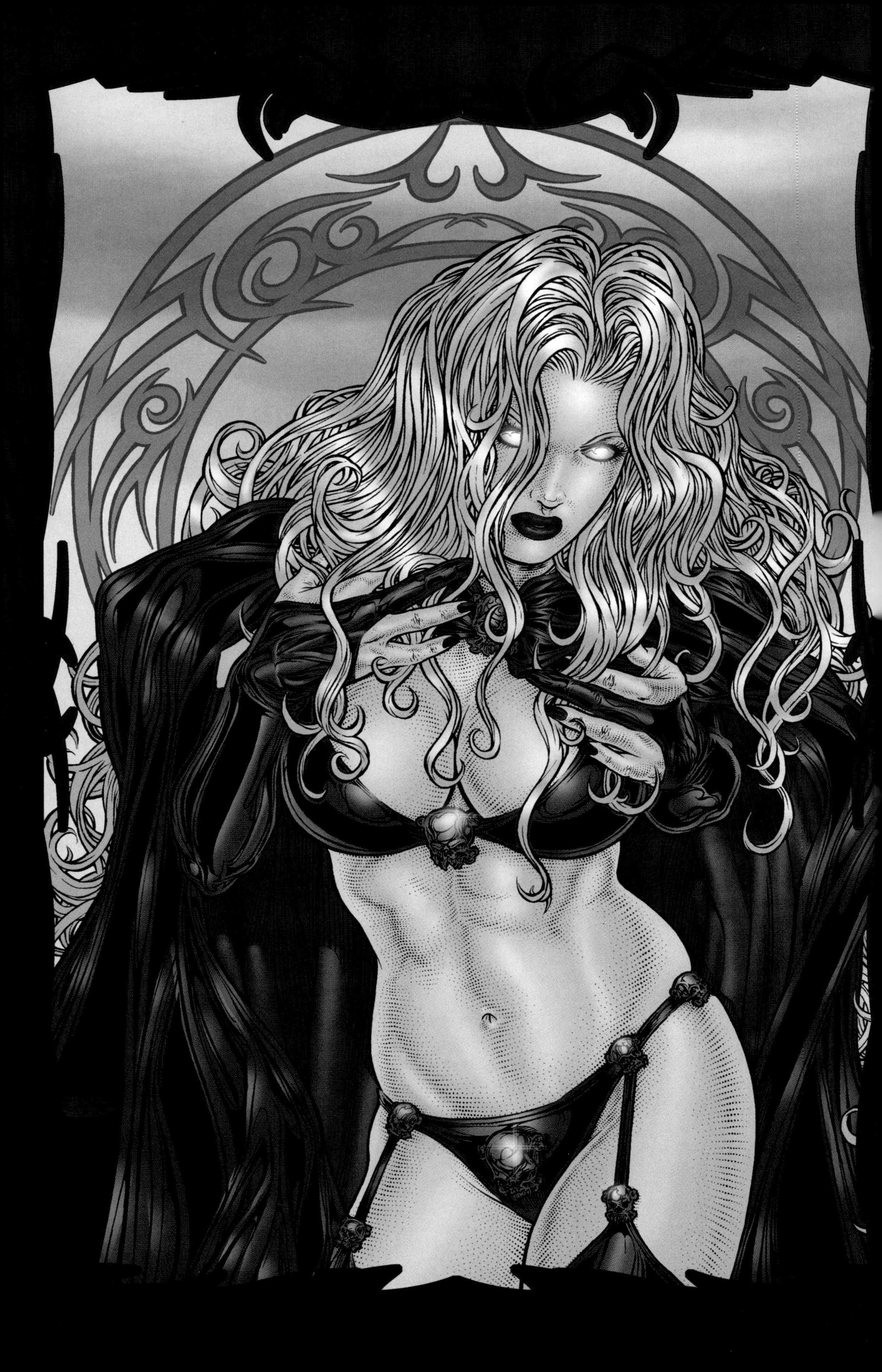

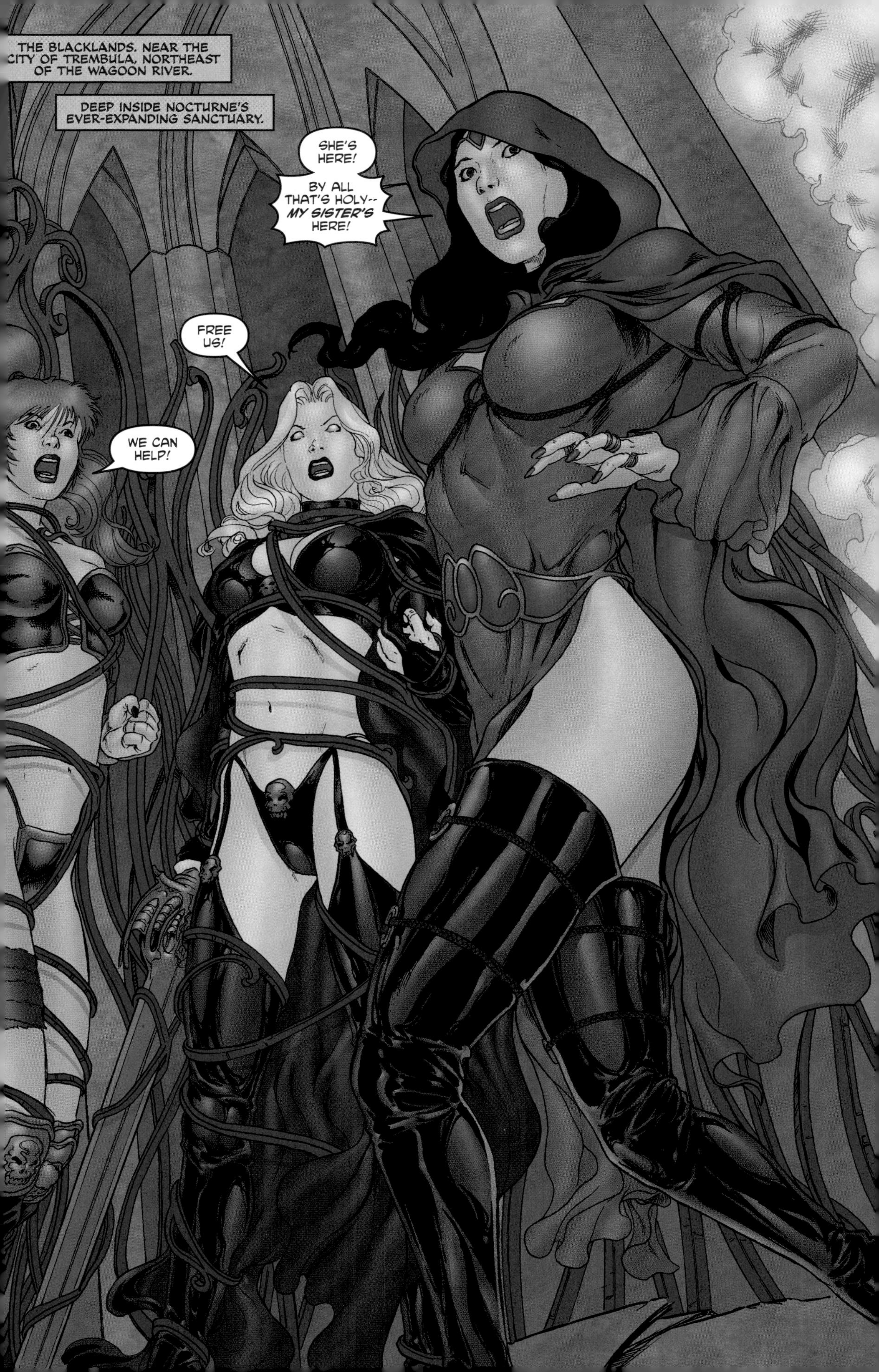
THE BLACKLANDS. NEAR THE CITY OF TREMBULA, NORTHEAST OF THE WAGOON RIVER.
DEEP INSIDE NOCTURNE'S EVER-EXPANDING SANCTUARY.
SHE'S HERE!
BY ALL THAT'S HOLY-- MY SISTER'S HERE!
FREE US!
WE CAN HELP!

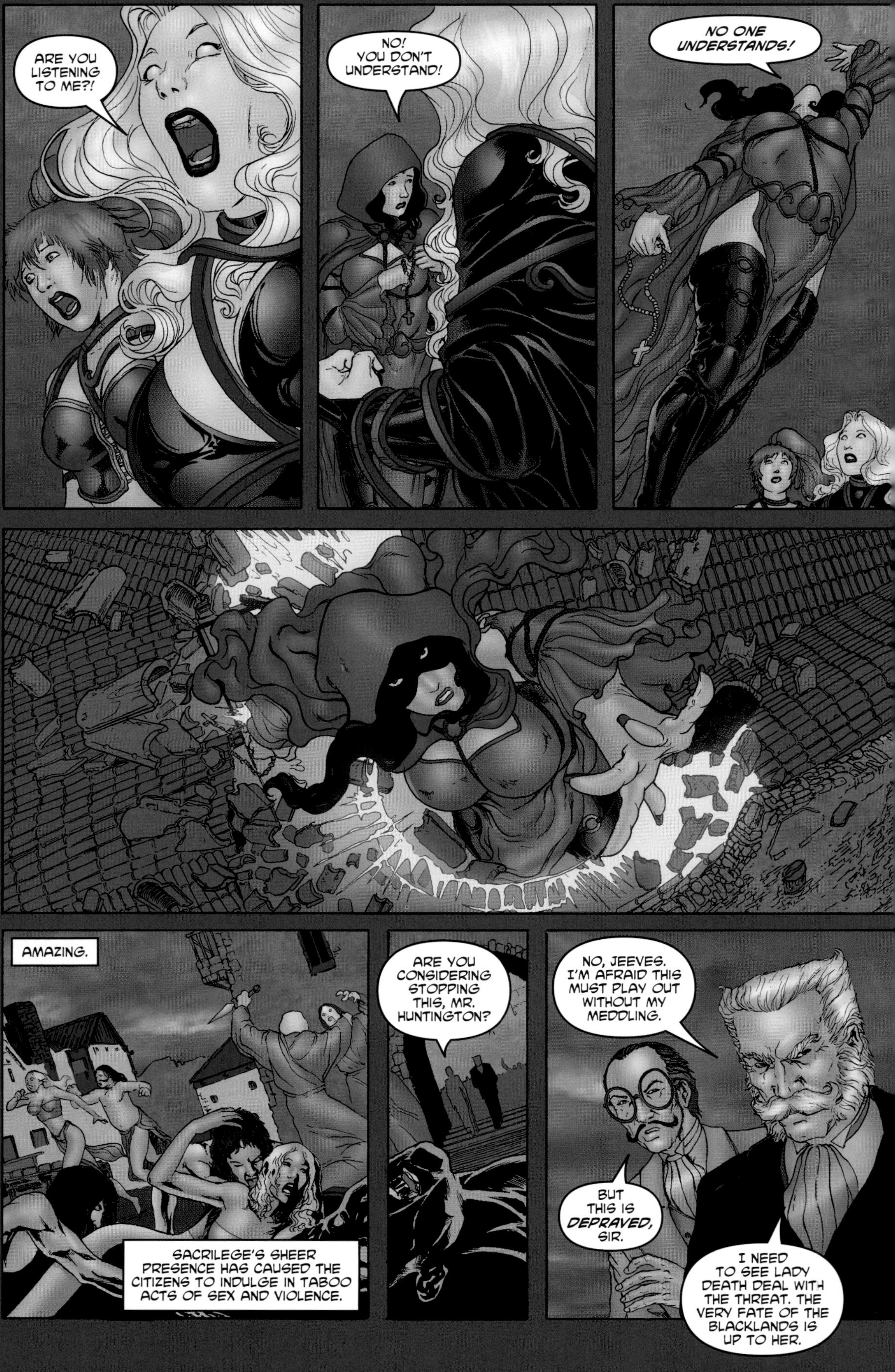

ARE YOU LISTENING TO ME?!
NO! YOU DON'T UNDERSTAND!
NO ONE UNDERSTANDS!
AMAZING.
SACRILEGE'S SHEER PRESENCE HAS CAUSED THE CITIZENS TO INDULGE IN TABOO ACTS OF SEX AND VIOLENCE.
ARE YOU CONSIDERING STOPPING THIS, MR. HUNTINGTON?
NO, JEEVES. I'M AFRAID THIS MUST PLAY OUT WITHOUT MY MEDDLING.
BUT THIS IS DEPRAVED, SIR.
I NEED TO SEE LADY DEATH DEAL WITH THE THREAT. THE VERY FATE OF THE BLACKLANDS IS UP TO HER.

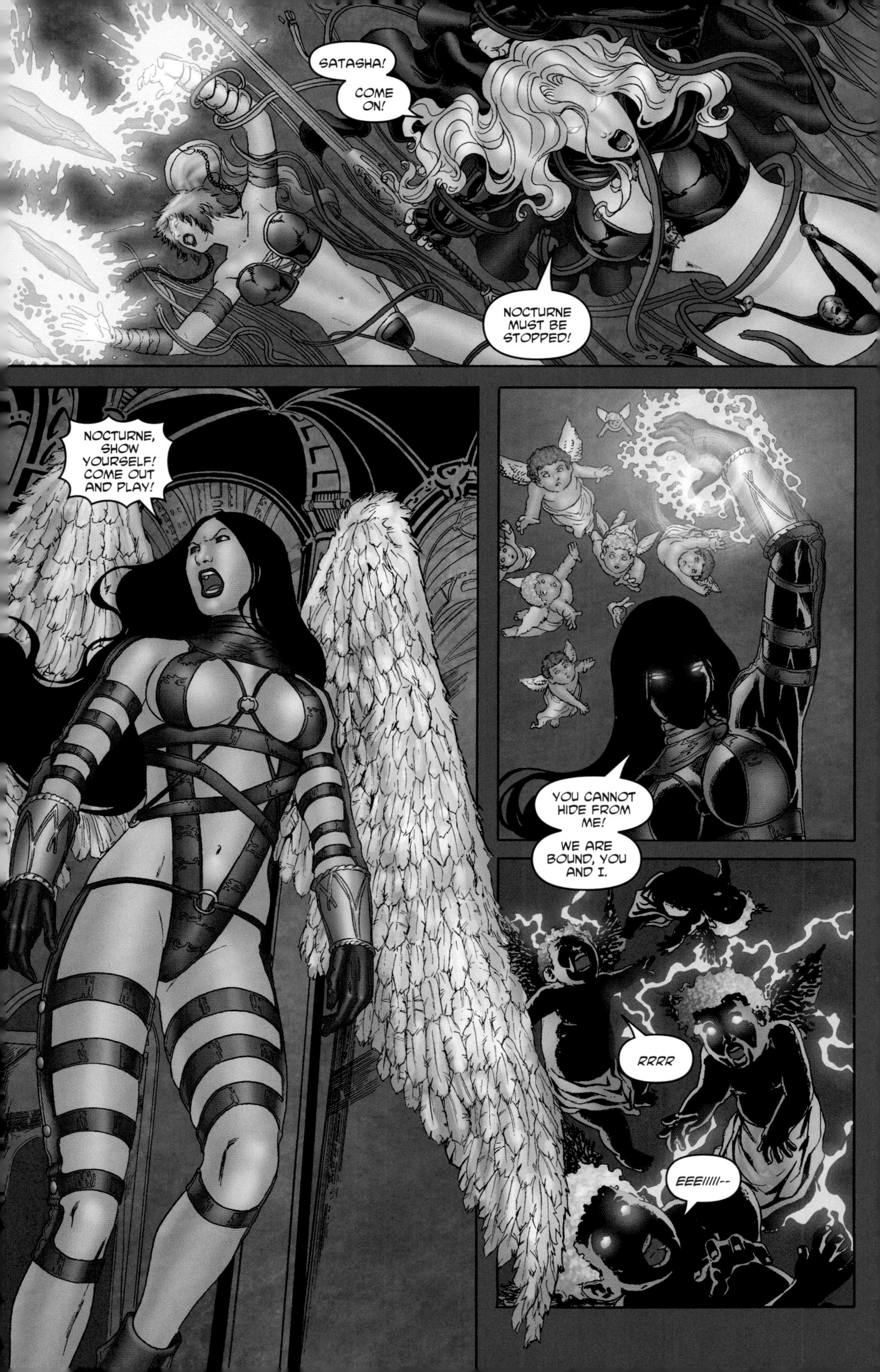
SATASHA!
COME ON!
NOCTURNE MUST BE STOPPED!
NOCTURNE, SHOW YOURSELF! COME OUT AND PLAY!
YOU CANNOT HIDE FROM ME!
WE ARE BOUND, YOU AND I.
RRRR
EEEIIIII--

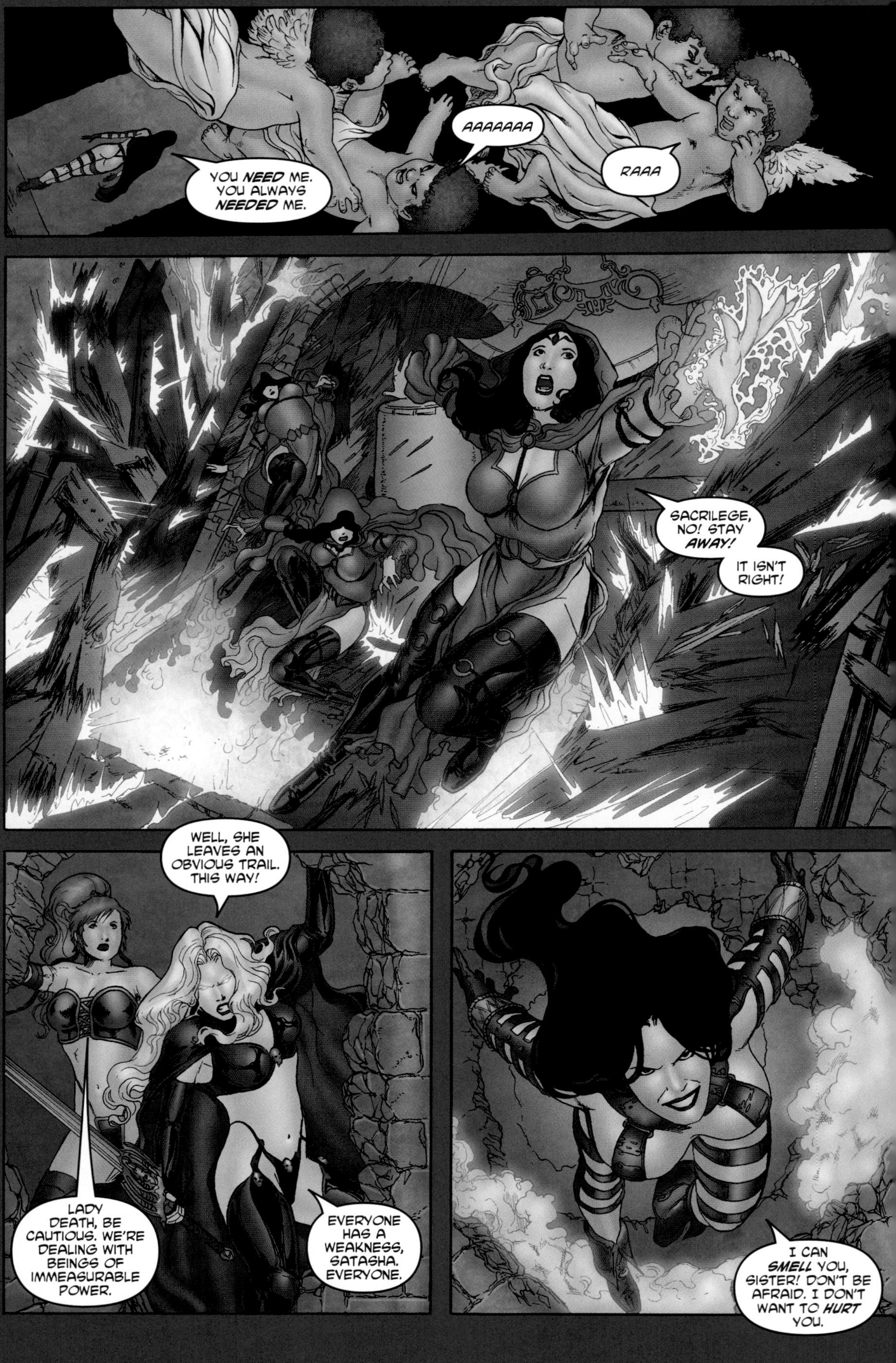
YOU NEED ME. YOU ALWAYS NEEDED ME.
AAAAAAA
RAAA
SACRILEGE, NO! STAY AWAY!
IT ISN'T RIGHT!
WELL, SHE LEAVES AN OBVIOUS TRAIL. THIS WAY!
LADY DEATH, BE CAUTIOUS. WE'RE DEALING WITH BEINGS OF IMMEASURABLE POWER.
EVERYONE HAS A WEAKNESS, SATASHA. EVERYONE.
I CAN SMELL YOU, SISTER! DON'T BE AFRAID. I DON'T WANT TO HURT YOU.

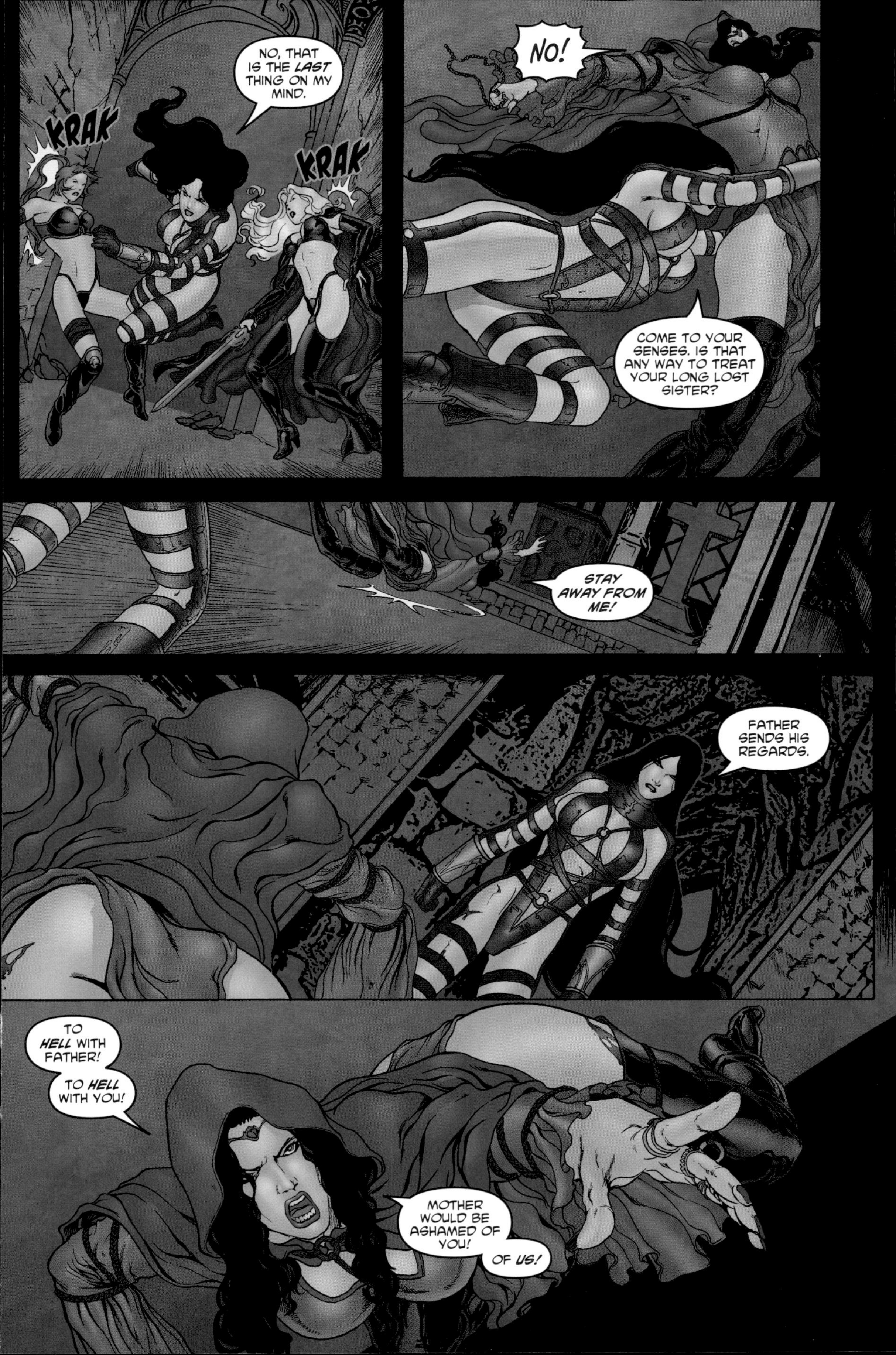
NO, THAT IS THE *LAST* THING ON MY MIND.
KRAK
KRAK
NO!
COME TO YOUR SENSES. IS THAT ANY WAY TO TREAT YOUR LONG LOST SISTER?
STAY AWAY FROM ME!
FATHER SENDS HIS REGARDS.
TO *HELL* WITH FATHER!
TO *HELL* WITH YOU!
MOTHER WOULD BE ASHAMED OF YOU!
OF *US!*

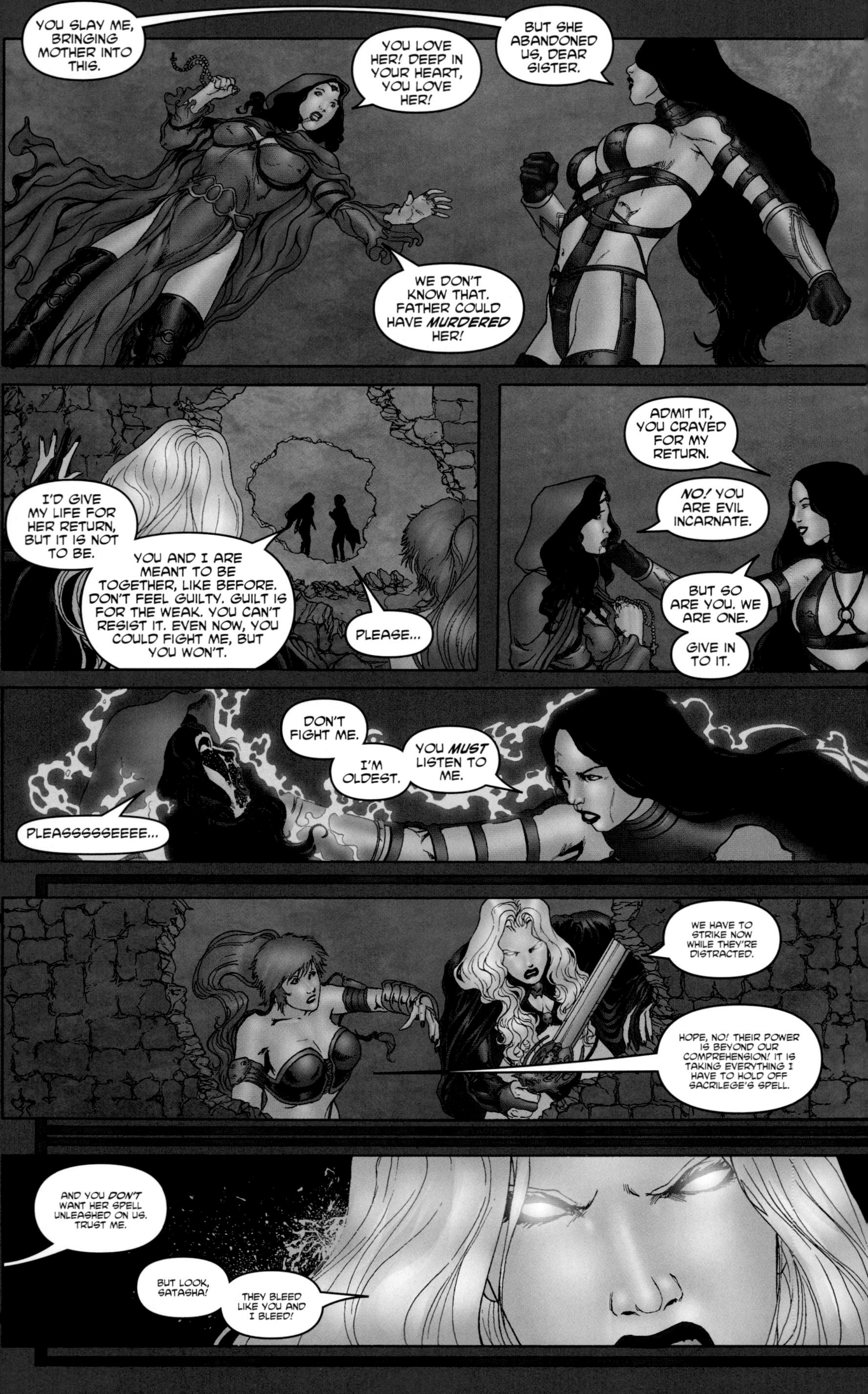
YOU SLAY ME, BRINGING MOTHER INTO THIS.
YOU LOVE HER! DEEP IN YOUR HEART, YOU LOVE HER!
BUT SHE ABANDONED US, DEAR SISTER.
WE DON'T KNOW THAT. FATHER COULD HAVE *MURDERED* HER!
I'D GIVE MY LIFE FOR HER RETURN, BUT IT IS NOT TO BE.
YOU AND I ARE MEANT TO BE TOGETHER, LIKE BEFORE. DON'T FEEL GUILTY. GUILT IS FOR THE WEAK. YOU CAN'T RESIST IT. EVEN NOW, YOU COULD FIGHT ME, BUT YOU WON'T.
PLEASE...
ADMIT IT, YOU CRAVED FOR MY RETURN.
NO! YOU ARE EVIL INCARNATE.
BUT SO ARE YOU. WE ARE ONE.
GIVE IN TO IT.
DON'T FIGHT ME.
I'M OLDEST.
YOU *MUST* LISTEN TO ME.
PLEASSSSSEEEE...
WE HAVE TO STRIKE NOW WHILE THEY'RE DISTRACTED.
HOPE, NO! THEIR POWER IS BEYOND OUR COMPREHENSION! IT IS TAKING EVERYTHING I HAVE TO HOLD OFF SACRILEGE'S SPELL.
AND YOU *DON'T* WANT HER SPELL UNLEASHED ON US. TRUST ME.
BUT LOOK, SATASHA!
THEY BLEED LIKE YOU AND I BLEED!

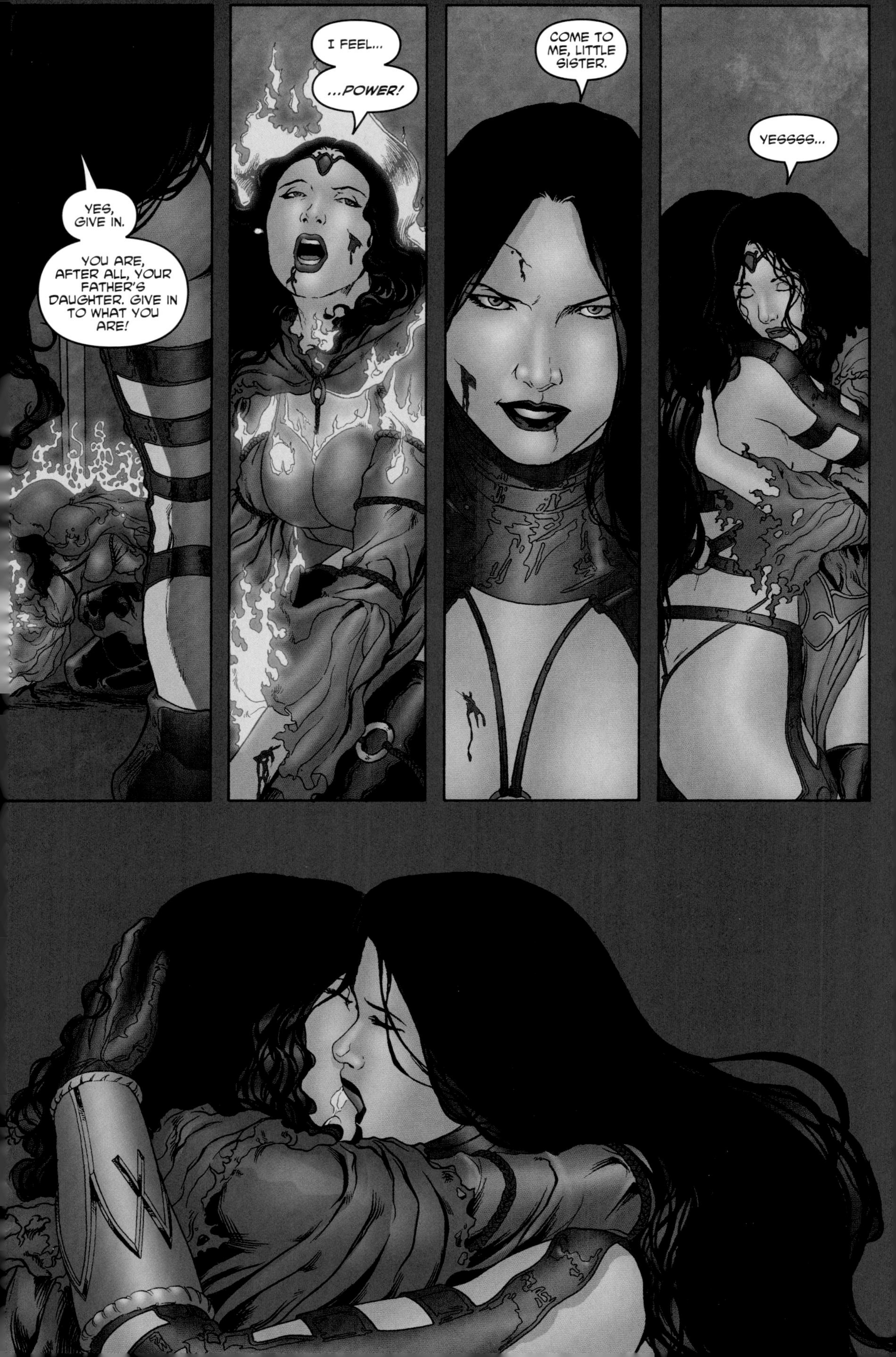
YES, GIVE IN.
YOU ARE, AFTER ALL, YOUR FATHER'S DAUGHTER. GIVE IN TO WHAT YOU ARE!
I FEEL...
...POWER!
COME TO ME, LITTLE SISTER.
YESSSS...

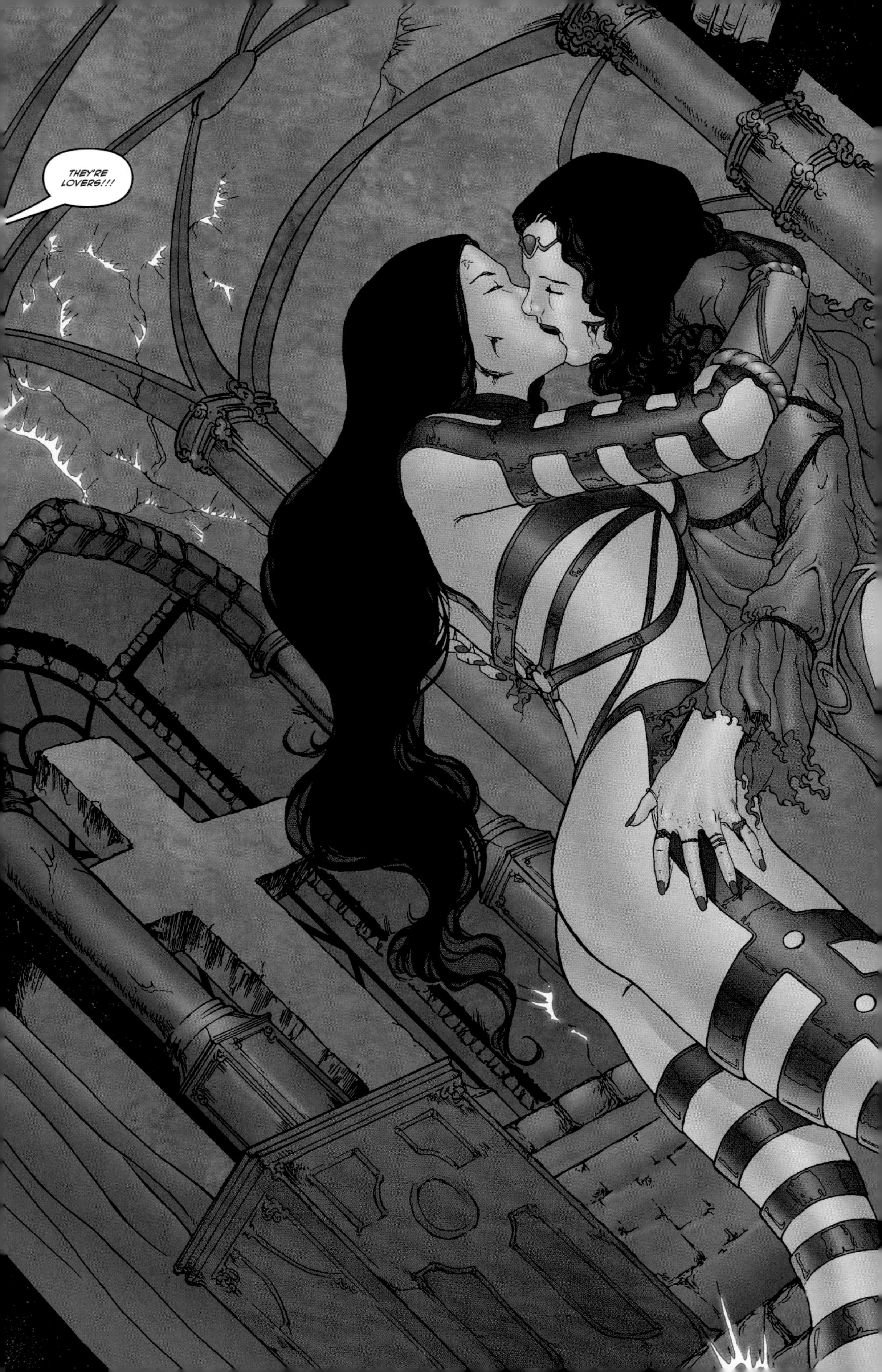
THEY'RE LOVERS!!!

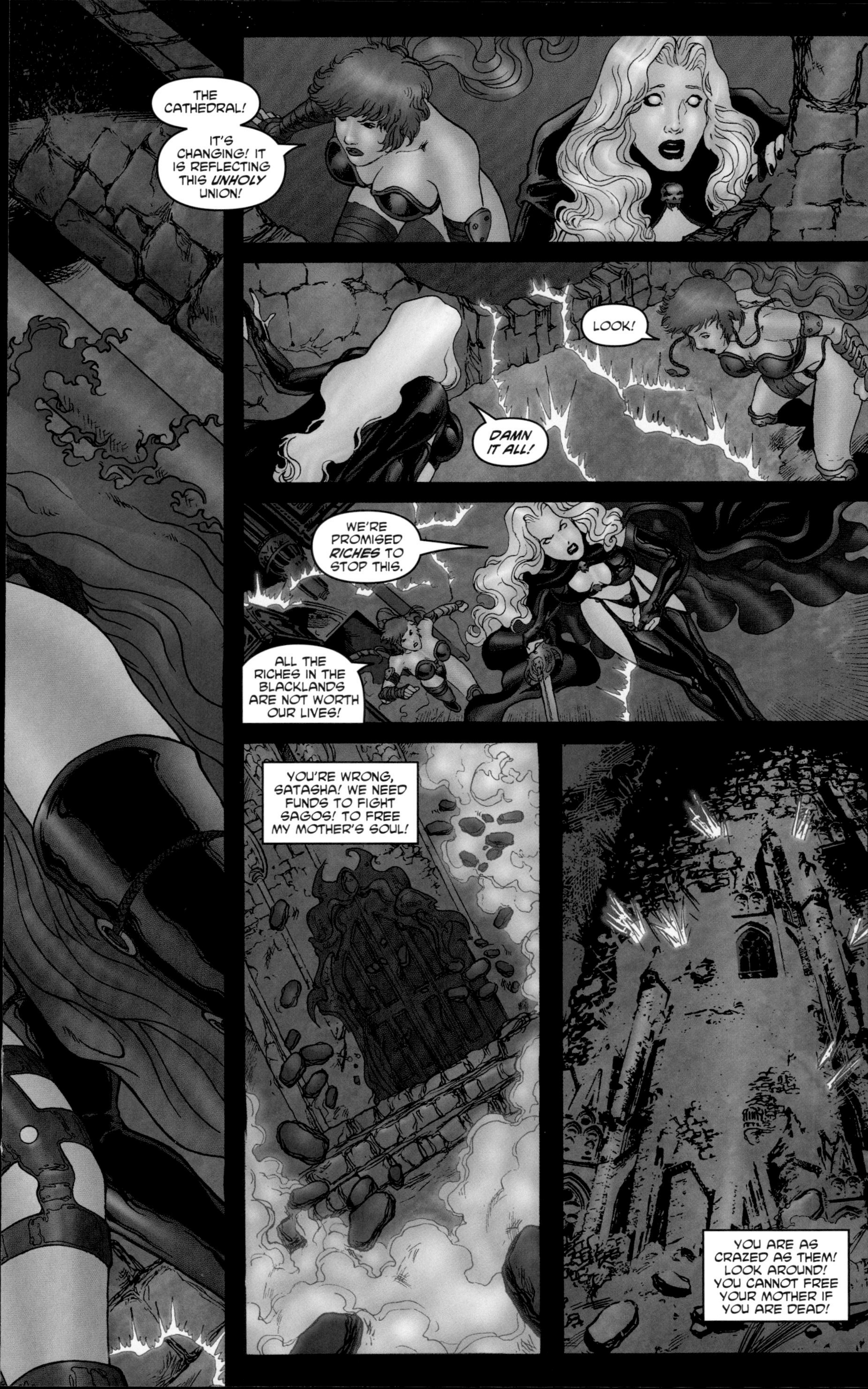
THE CATHEDRAL!
IT'S CHANGING! IT IS REFLECTING THIS UNHOLY UNION!
LOOK!
DAMN IT ALL!
WE'RE PROMISED RICHES TO STOP THIS.
ALL THE RICHES IN THE BLACKLANDS ARE NOT WORTH OUR LIVES!
YOU'RE WRONG, SATASHA! WE NEED FUNDS TO FIGHT SAGOS! TO FREE MY MOTHER'S SOUL!
YOU ARE AS CRAZED AS THEM! LOOK AROUND! YOU CANNOT FREE YOUR MOTHER IF YOU ARE DEAD!

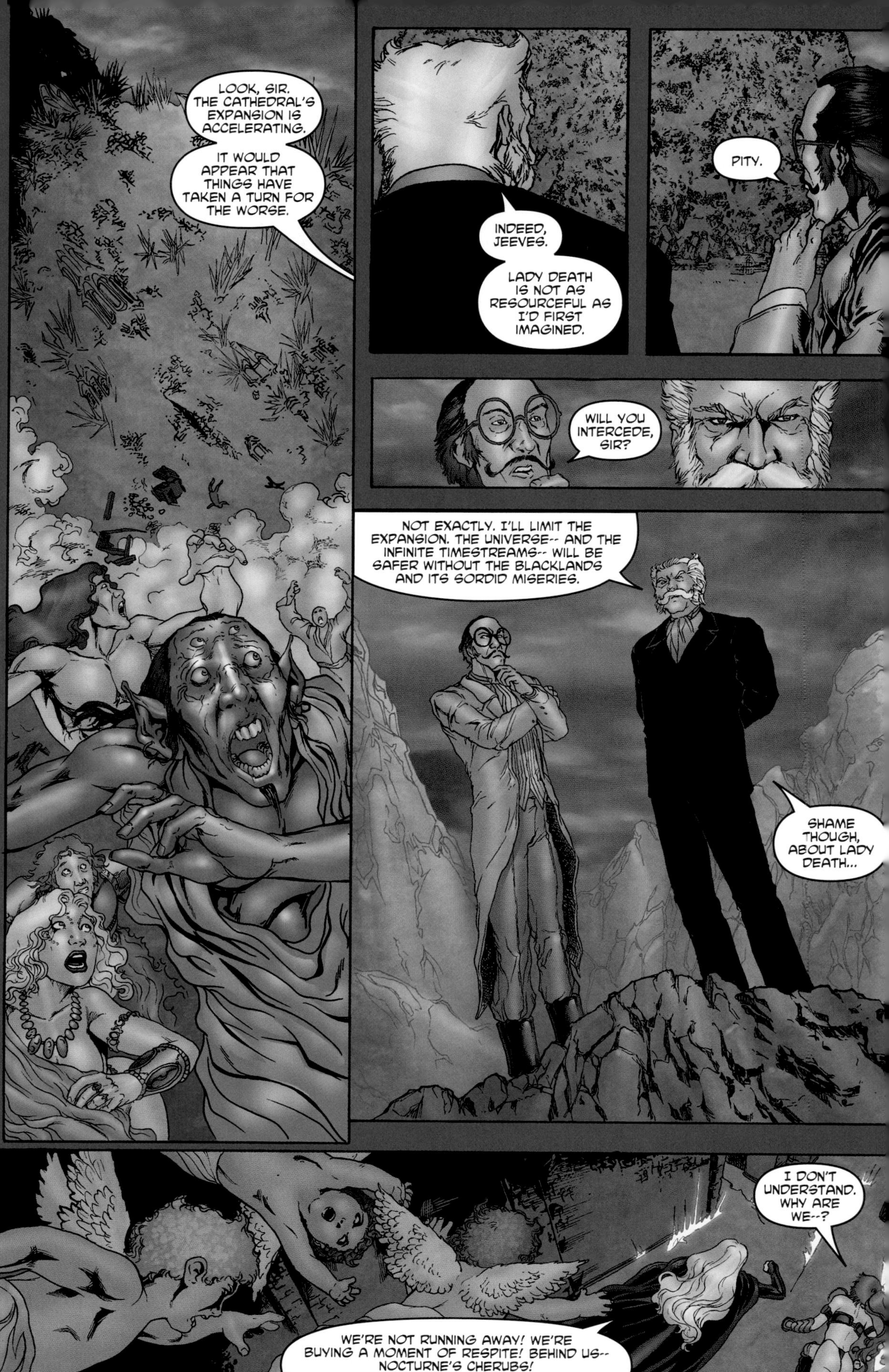
LOOK, SIR. THE CATHEDRAL'S EXPANSION IS ACCELERATING.
IT WOULD APPEAR THAT THINGS HAVE TAKEN A TURN FOR THE WORSE.
INDEED, JEEVES.
LADY DEATH IS NOT AS RESOURCEFUL AS I'D FIRST IMAGINED.
PITY.
WILL YOU INTERCEDE, SIR?
NOT EXACTLY. I'LL LIMIT THE EXPANSION. THE UNIVERSE-- AND THE INFINITE TIMESTREAMS-- WILL BE SAFER WITHOUT THE BLACKLANDS AND ITS SORDID MISERIES.
SHAME THOUGH, ABOUT LADY DEATH...
I DON'T UNDERSTAND. WHY ARE WE--?
WE'RE NOT RUNNING AWAY! WE'RE BUYING A MOMENT OF RESPITE! BEHIND US-- NOCTURNE'S CHERUBS!

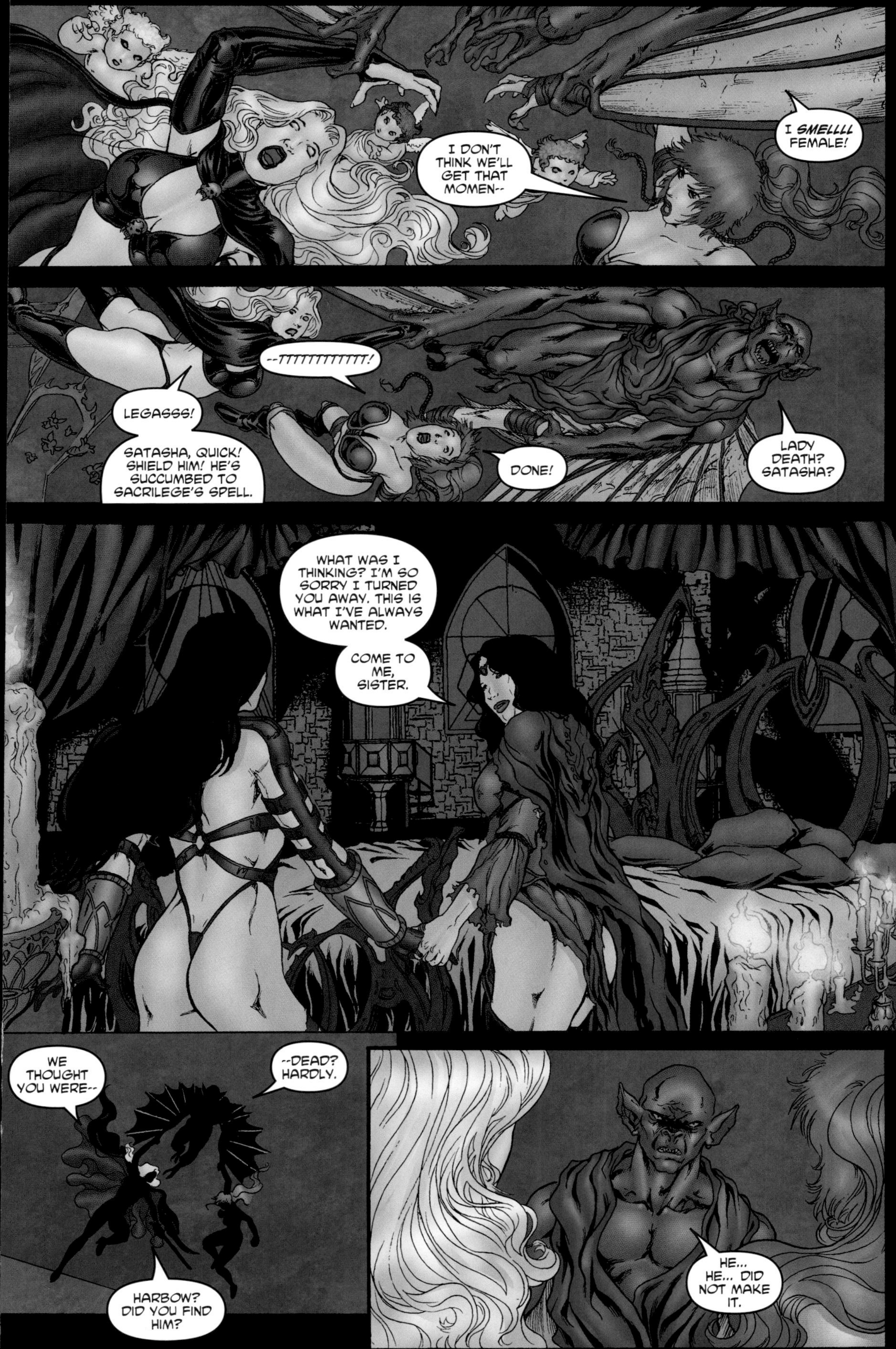
I DON'T THINK WE'LL GET THAT MOMEN--
I SMELLLL FEMALE!
--TTTTTTTTTTTTT!
LEGASSS!
SATASHA, QUICK! SHIELD HIM! HE'S SUCCUMBED TO SACRILEGE'S SPELL.
DONE!
LADY DEATH? SATASHA?
WHAT WAS I THINKING? I'M SO SORRY I TURNED YOU AWAY. THIS IS WHAT I'VE ALWAYS WANTED.
COME TO ME, SISTER.
WE THOUGHT YOU WERE--
--DEAD? HARDLY.
HARBOW? DID YOU FIND HIM?
HE... HE... DID NOT MAKE IT.

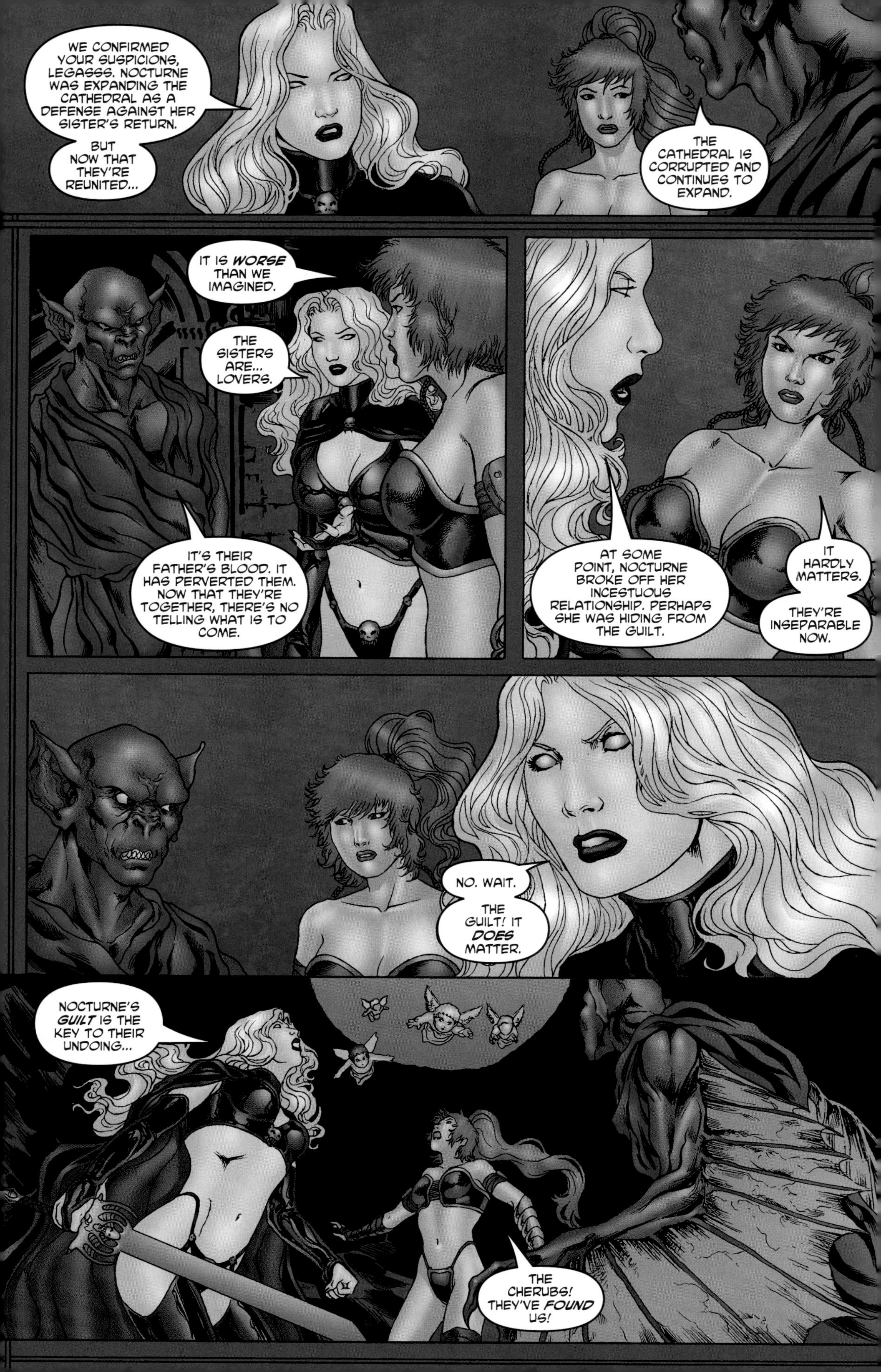
WE CONFIRMED YOUR SUSPICIONS, LEGASSS. NOCTURNE WAS EXPANDING THE CATHEDRAL AS A DEFENSE AGAINST HER SISTER'S RETURN.
BUT NOW THAT THEY'RE REUNITED...
THE CATHEDRAL IS CORRUPTED AND CONTINUES TO EXPAND.
IT IS *WORSE* THAN WE IMAGINED.
THE SISTERS ARE... LOVERS.
IT'S THEIR FATHER'S BLOOD. IT HAS PERVERTED THEM. NOW THAT THEY'RE TOGETHER, THERE'S NO TELLING WHAT IS TO COME.
AT SOME POINT, NOCTURNE BROKE OFF HER INCESTUOUS RELATIONSHIP. PERHAPS SHE WAS HIDING FROM THE GUILT.
IT HARDLY MATTERS.
THEY'RE INSEPARABLE NOW.
NO. WAIT.
THE GUILT! IT *DOES* MATTER.
NOCTURNE'S *GUILT* IS THE KEY TO THEIR UNDOING...
THE CHERUBS! THEY'VE *FOUND* US!

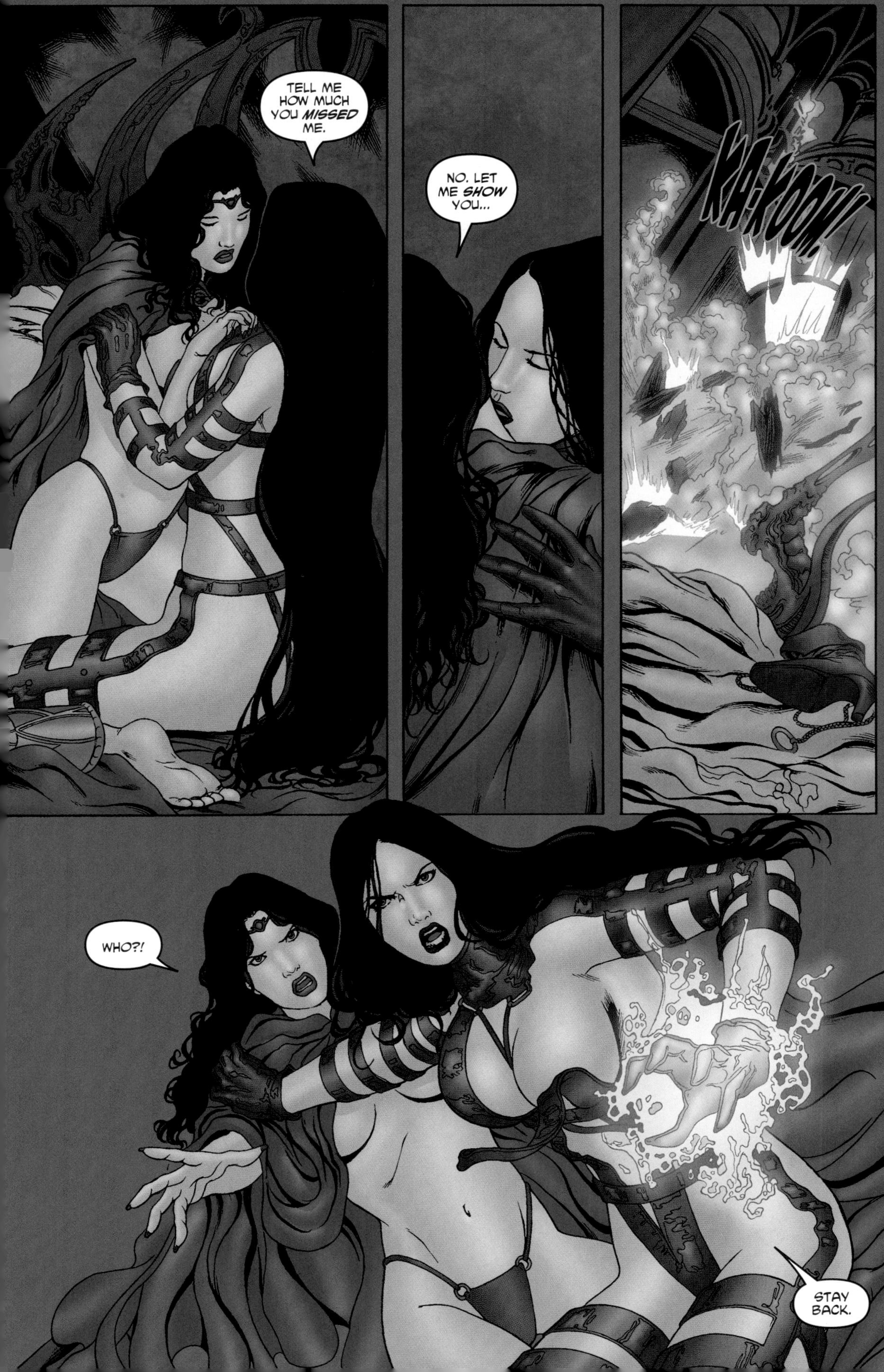
TELL ME HOW MUCH YOU *MISSED* ME.
NO. LET ME *SHOW* YOU...
KA-KOOM!
WHO?!
STAY BACK.

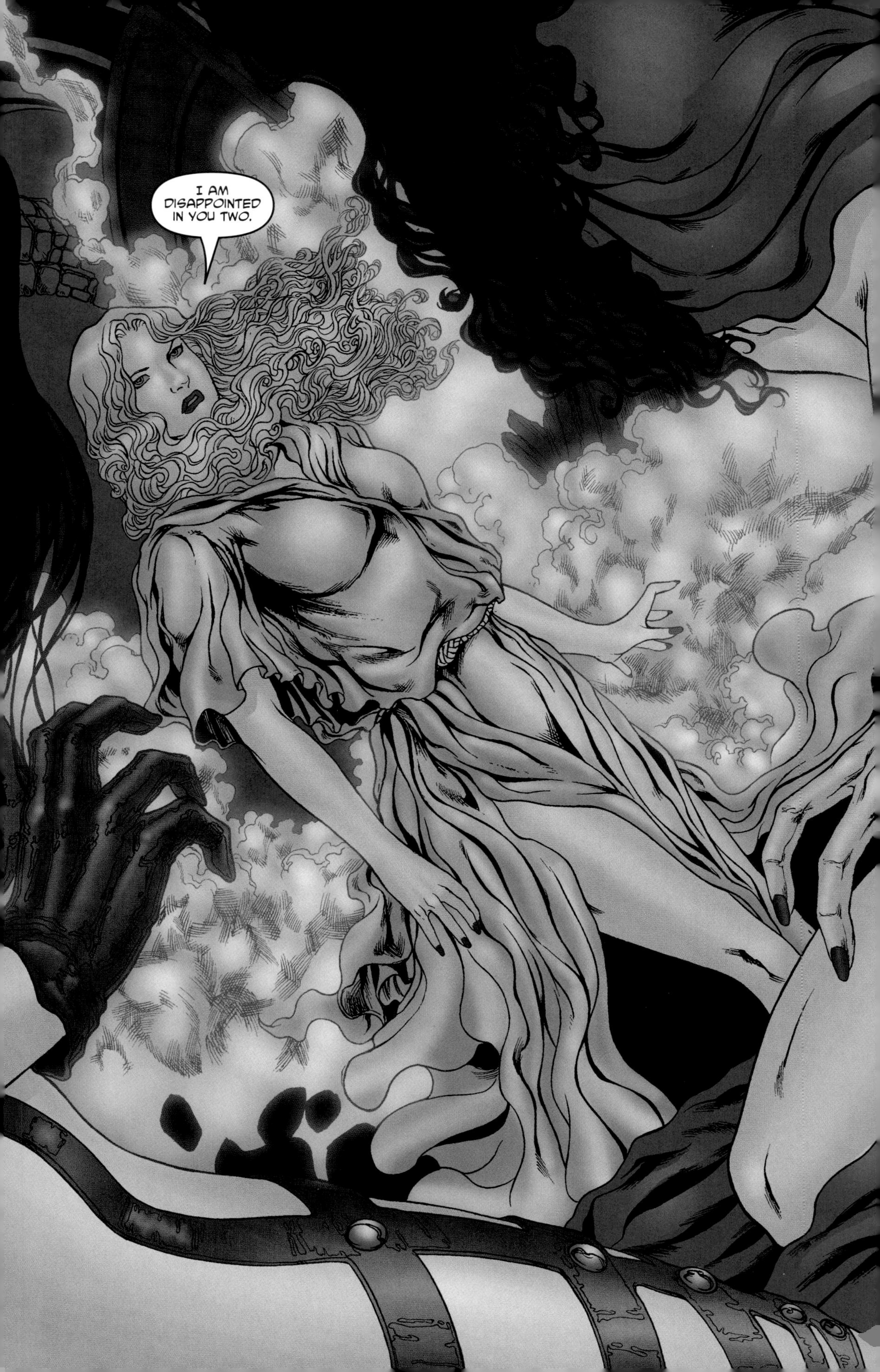
I AM DISAPPOINTED IN YOU TWO.

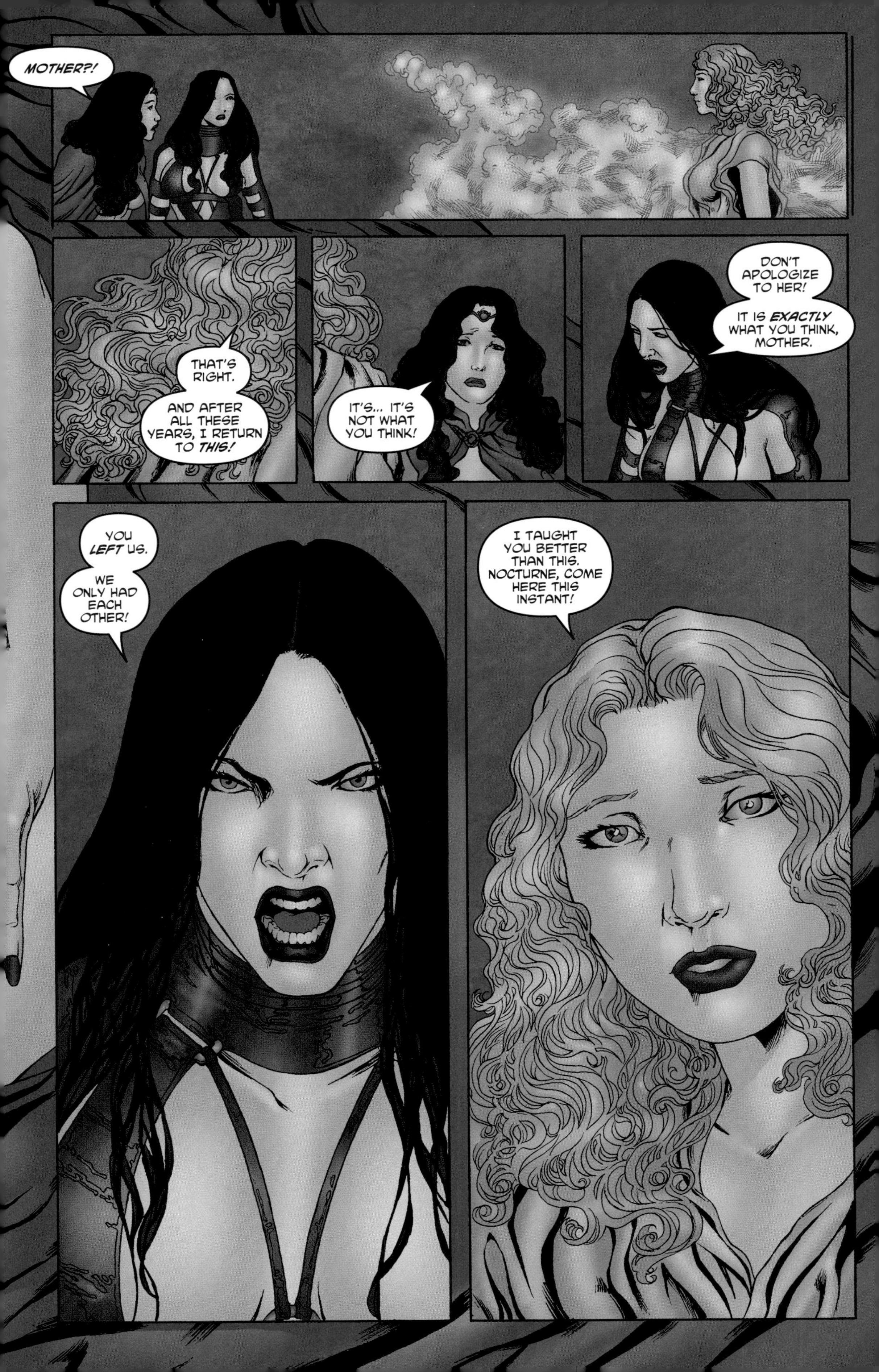

MOTHER?!
THAT'S RIGHT.
AND AFTER ALL THESE YEARS, I RETURN TO *THIS!*
IT'S... IT'S NOT WHAT YOU THINK!
DON'T APOLOGIZE TO HER!
IT IS *EXACTLY* WHAT YOU THINK, MOTHER.
YOU *LEFT* US.
WE ONLY HAD EACH OTHER!
I TAUGHT YOU BETTER THAN THIS. NOCTURNE, COME HERE THIS INSTANT!

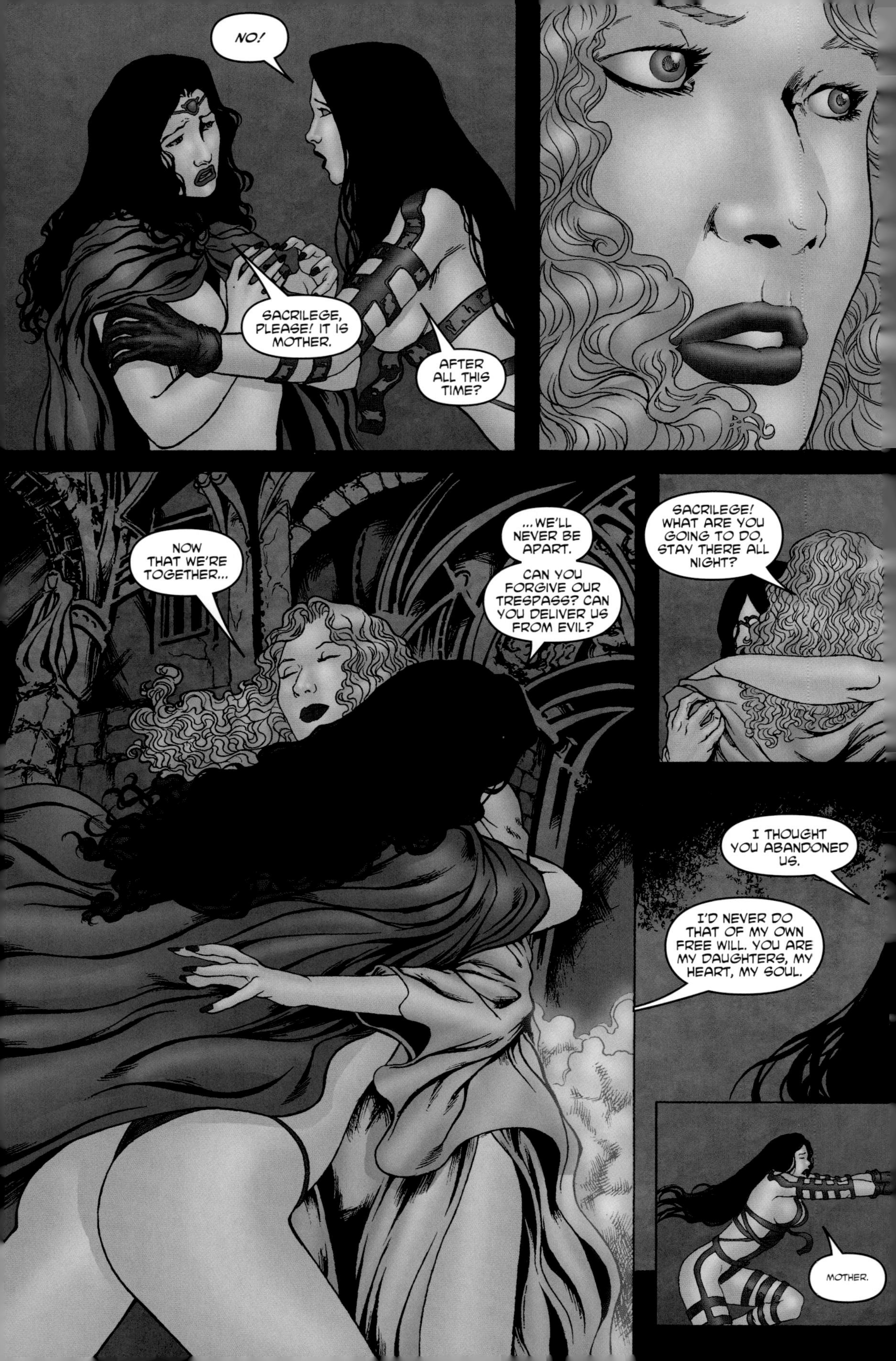
NO!
SACRILEGE, PLEASE! IT IS MOTHER.
AFTER ALL THIS TIME?
NOW THAT WE'RE TOGETHER...
...WE'LL NEVER BE APART.
CAN YOU FORGIVE OUR TRESPASS? CAN YOU DELIVER US FROM EVIL?
SACRILEGE! WHAT ARE YOU GOING TO DO, STAY THERE ALL NIGHT?
I THOUGHT YOU ABANDONED US.
I'D NEVER DO THAT OF MY OWN FREE WILL. YOU ARE MY DAUGHTERS, MY HEART, MY SOUL.
MOTHER.

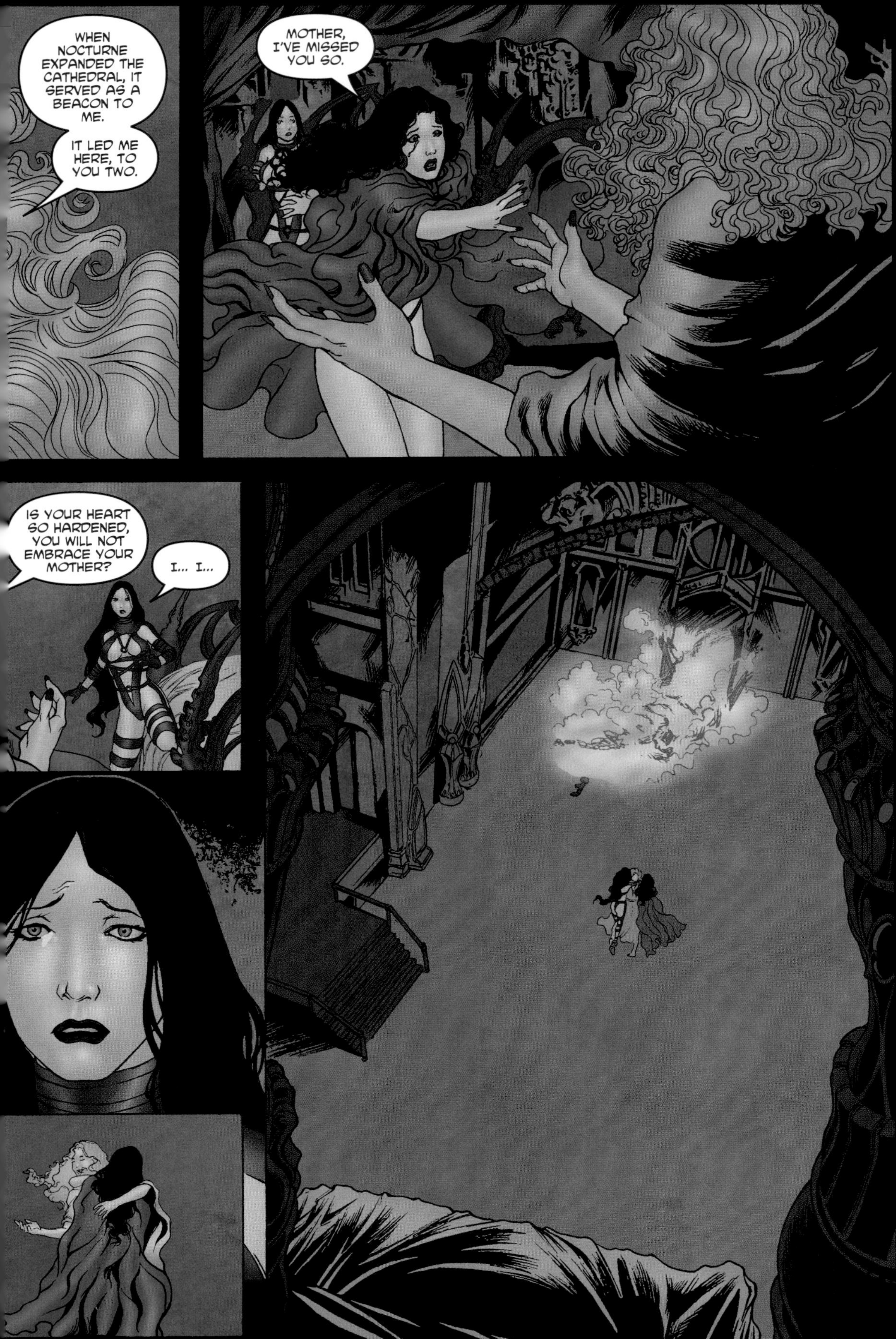

WHEN NOCTURNE EXPANDED THE CATHEDRAL, IT SERVED AS A BEACON TO ME.
IT LED ME HERE, TO YOU TWO.
MOTHER, I'VE MISSED YOU SO.
IS YOUR HEART SO HARDENED, YOU WILL NOT EMBRACE YOUR MOTHER?
I... I...

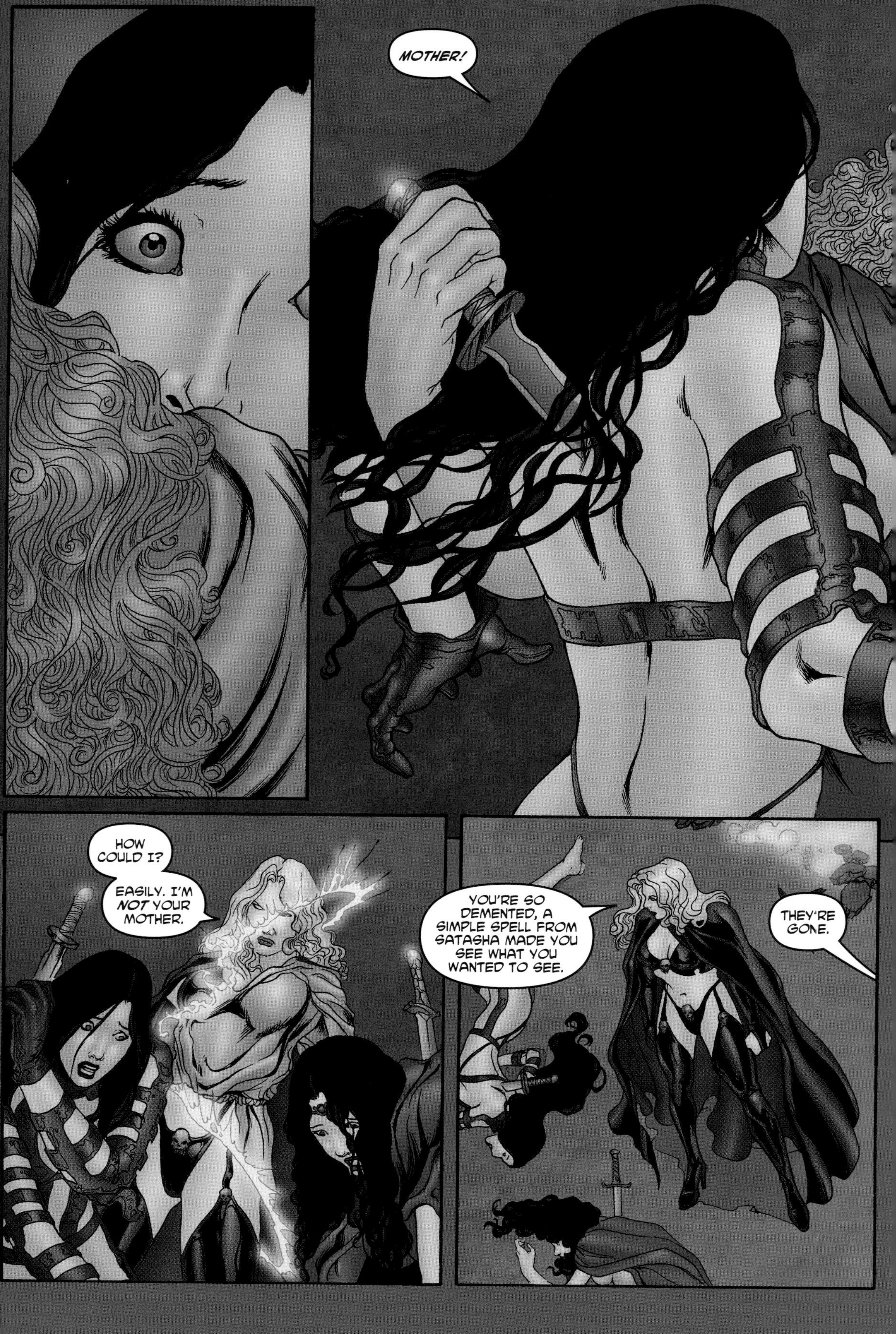
MOTHER!
HOW COULD I?
EASILY. I'M NOT YOUR MOTHER.
YOU'RE SO DEMENTED, A SIMPLE SPELL FROM SATASHA MADE YOU SEE WHAT YOU WANTED TO SEE.
THEY'RE GONE.

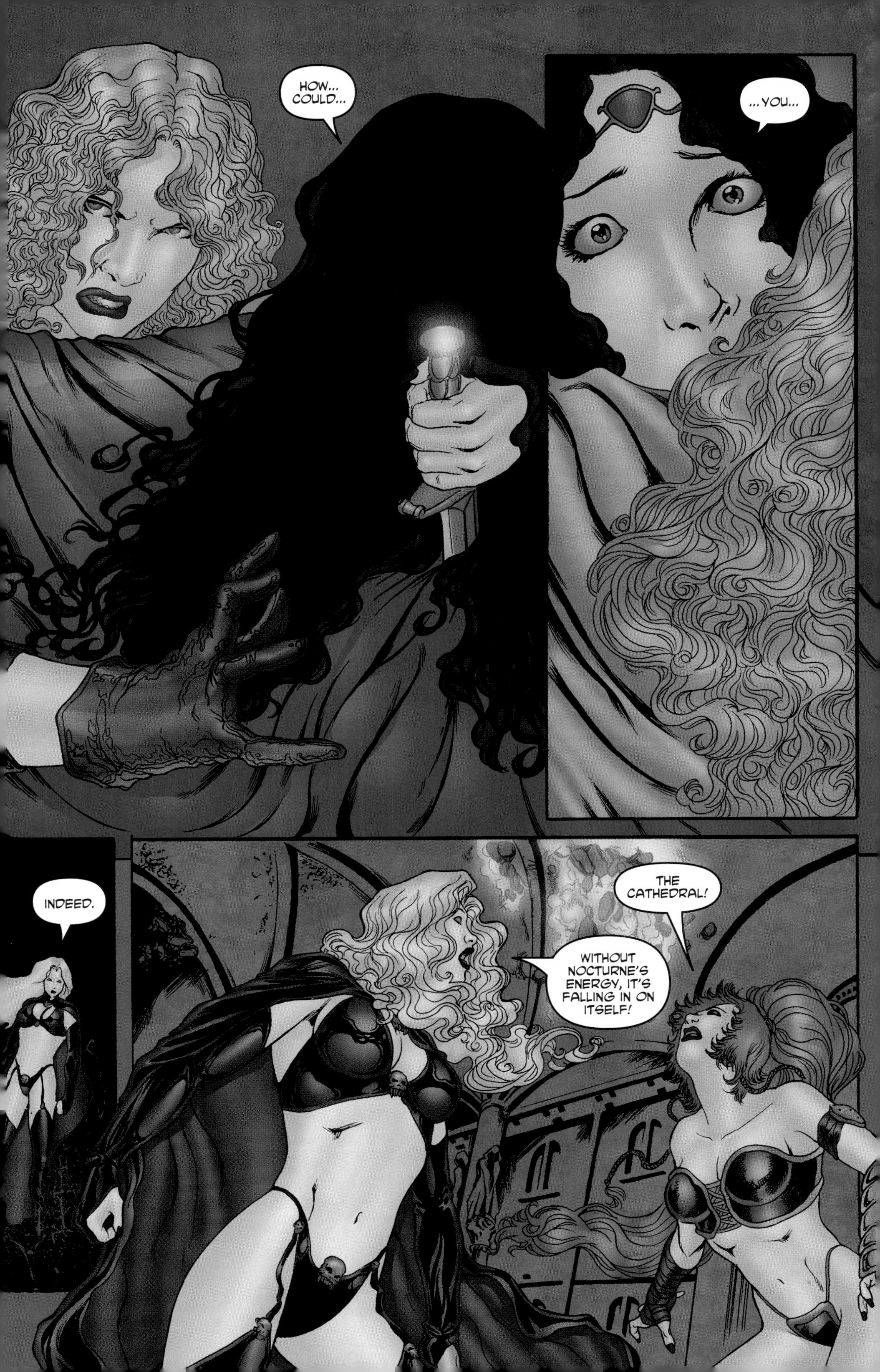
HOW... COULD...
...YOU...
INDEED.
THE CATHEDRAL!
WITHOUT NOCTURNE'S ENERGY, IT'S FALLING IN ON ITSELF!

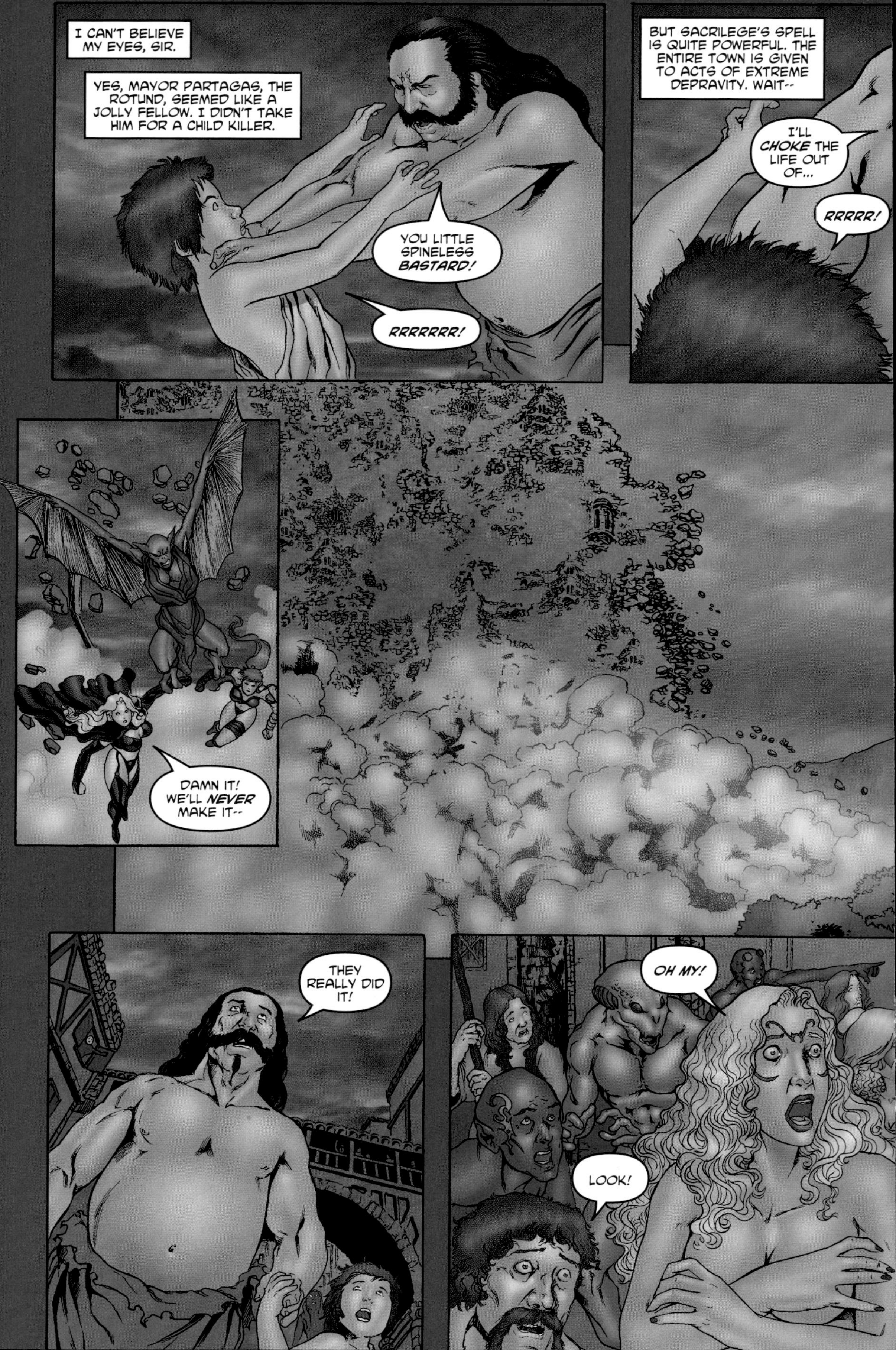

I CAN'T BELIEVE MY EYES, SIR.
YES, MAYOR PARTAGAS, THE ROTUND, SEEMED LIKE A JOLLY FELLOW. I DIDN'T TAKE HIM FOR A CHILD KILLER.
YOU LITTLE SPINELESS BASTARD!
RRRRRRR!
BUT SACRILEGE'S SPELL IS QUITE POWERFUL. THE ENTIRE TOWN IS GIVEN TO ACTS OF EXTREME DEPRAVITY. WAIT--
I'LL CHOKE THE LIFE OUT OF...
RRRRR!
DAMN IT! WE'LL NEVER MAKE IT--
THEY REALLY DID IT!
OH MY!
LOOK!

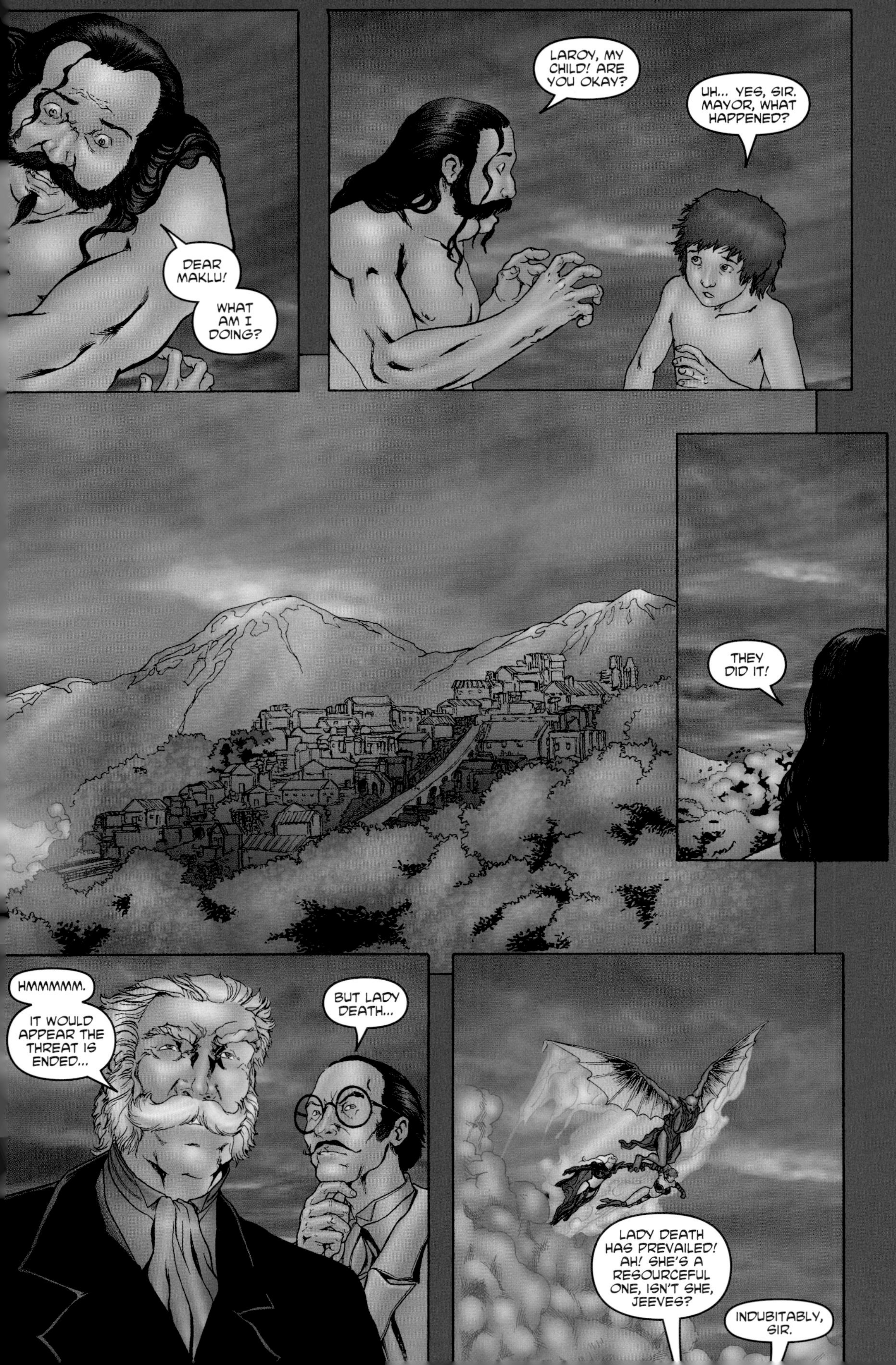
DEAR MAKLU!
WHAT AM I DOING?
LAROY, MY CHILD! ARE YOU OKAY?
UH... YES, SIR. MAYOR, WHAT HAPPENED?
THEY DID IT!
HMMMMM.
IT WOULD APPEAR THE THREAT IS ENDED...
BUT LADY DEATH...
LADY DEATH HAS PREVAILED! AH! SHE'S A RESOURCEFUL ONE, ISN'T SHE, JEEVES?
INDUBITABLY, SIR.

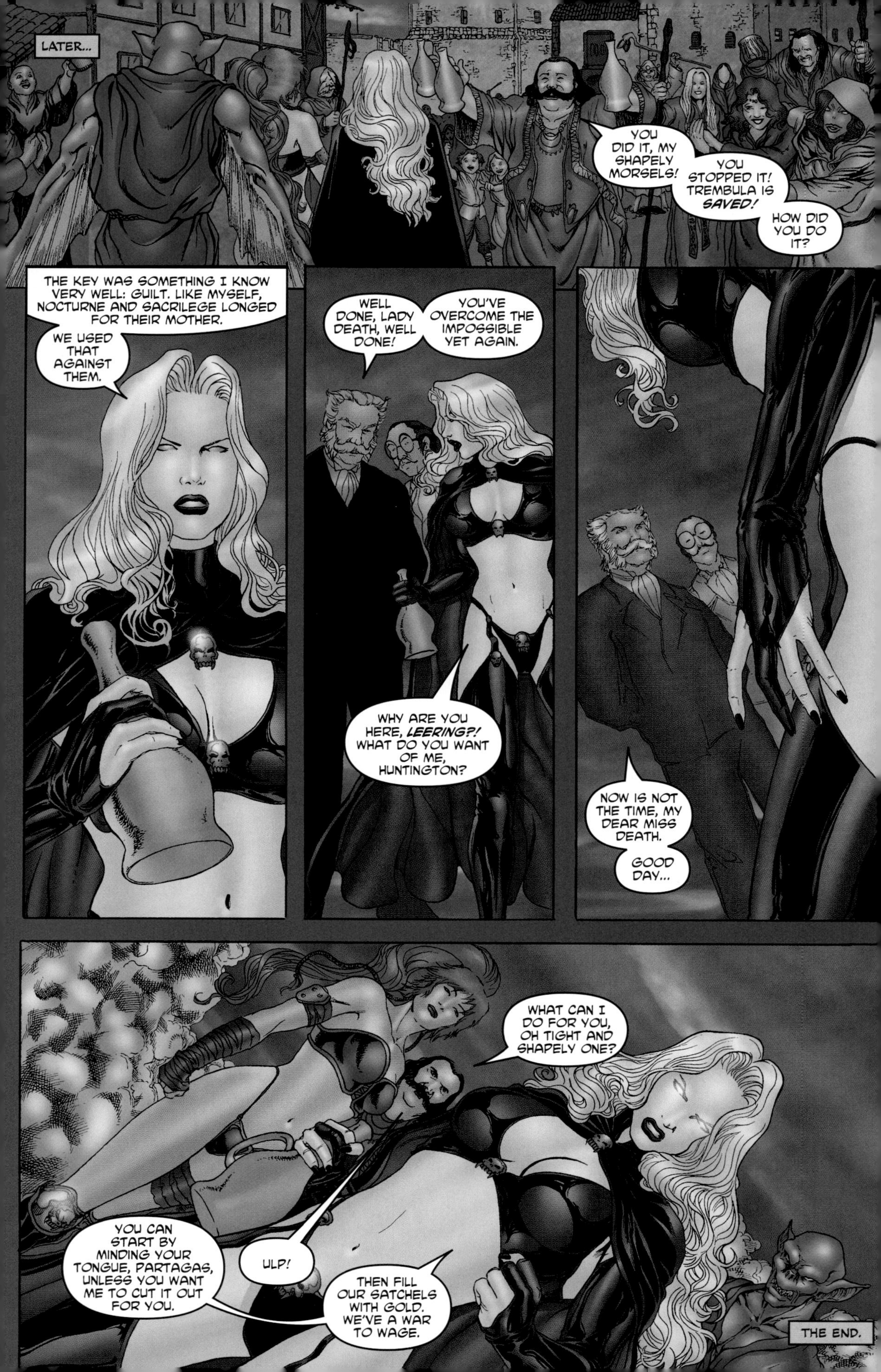
LATER...
YOU DID IT, MY SHAPELY MORSELS!
YOU STOPPED IT! TREMBULA IS SAVED!
HOW DID YOU DO IT?
THE KEY WAS SOMETHING I KNOW VERY WELL: GUILT. LIKE MYSELF, NOCTURNE AND SACRILEGE LONGED FOR THEIR MOTHER.
WE USED THAT AGAINST THEM.
WELL DONE, LADY DEATH, WELL DONE!
YOU'VE OVERCOME THE IMPOSSIBLE YET AGAIN.
WHY ARE YOU HERE, LEERING?! WHAT DO YOU WANT OF ME, HUNTINGTON?
NOW IS NOT THE TIME, MY DEAR MISS DEATH.
GOOD DAY...
WHAT CAN I DO FOR YOU, OH TIGHT AND SHAPELY ONE?
YOU CAN START BY MINDING YOUR TONGUE, PARTAGAS, UNLESS YOU WANT ME TO CUT IT OUT FOR YOU.
ULP!
THEN FILL OUR SATCHELS WITH GOLD. WE'VE A WAR TO WAGE.
THE END.

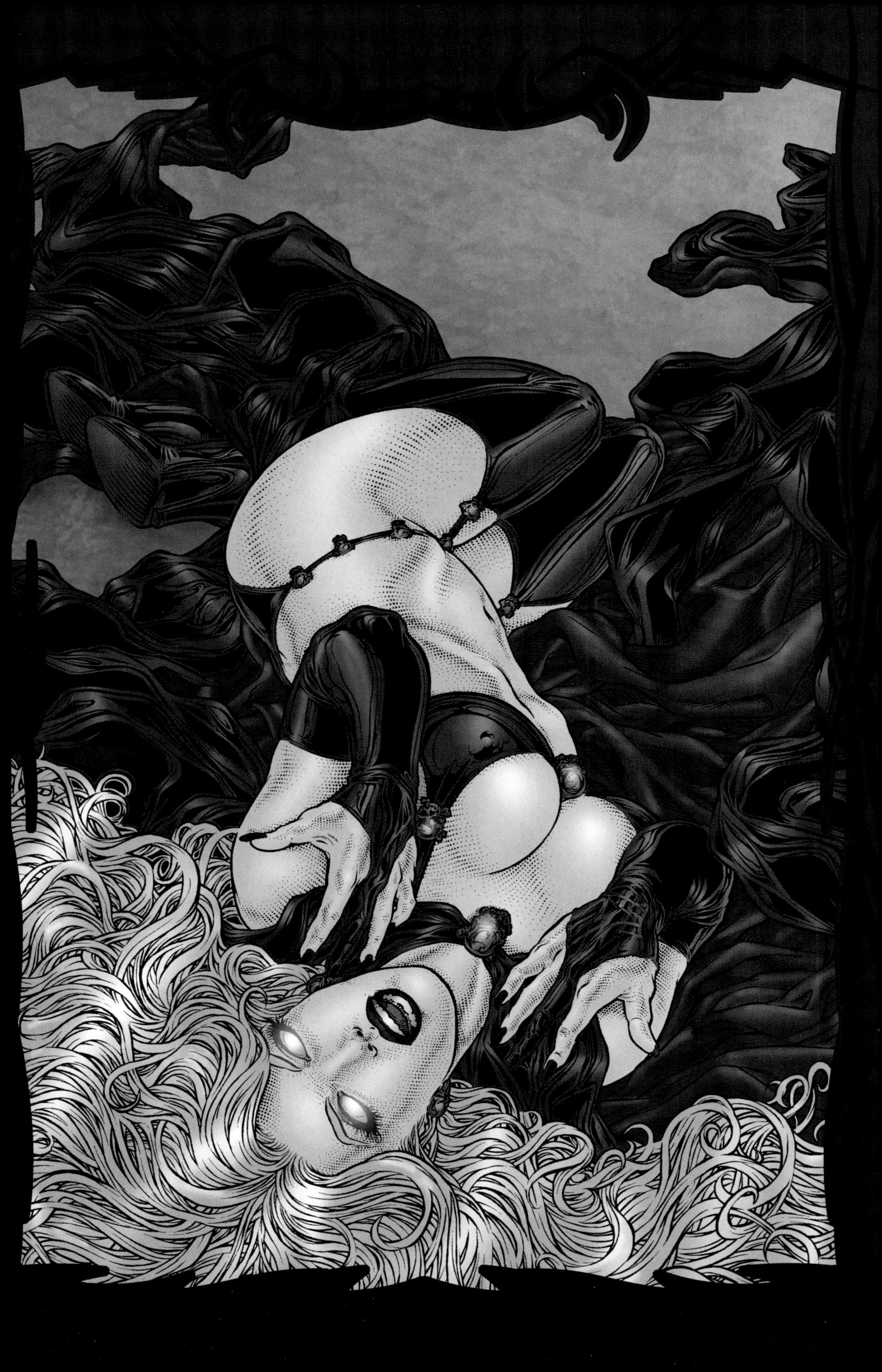

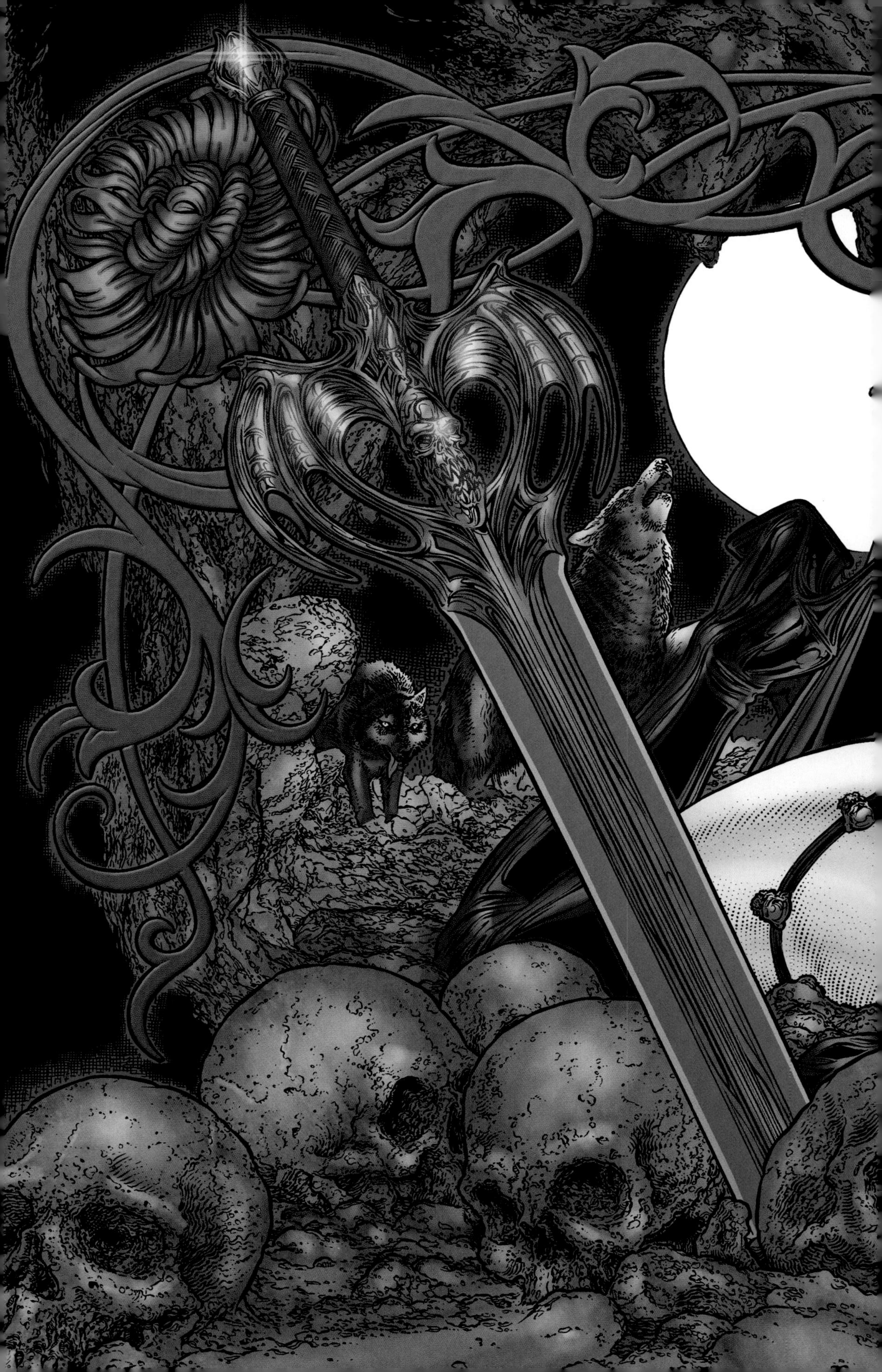

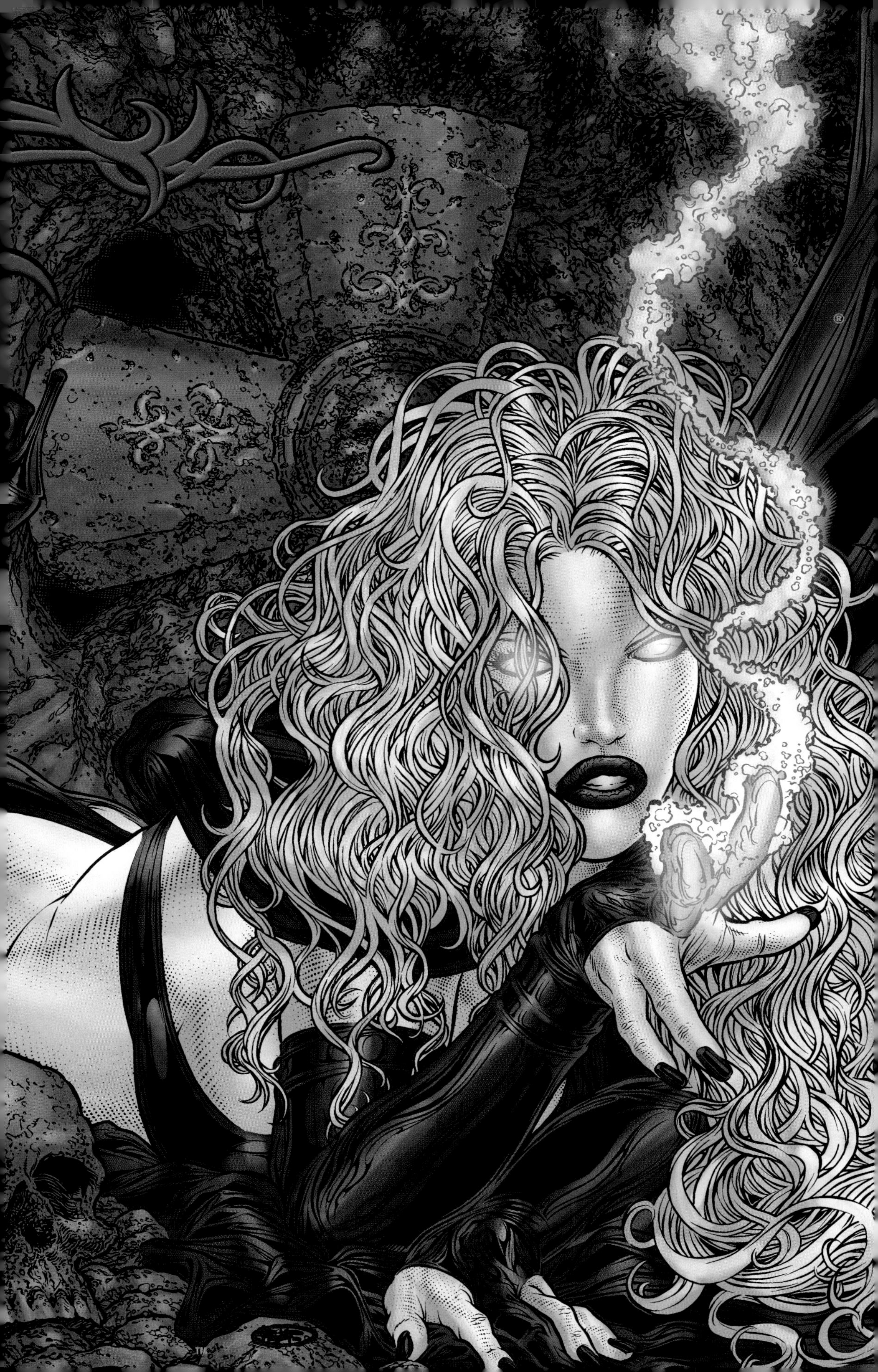

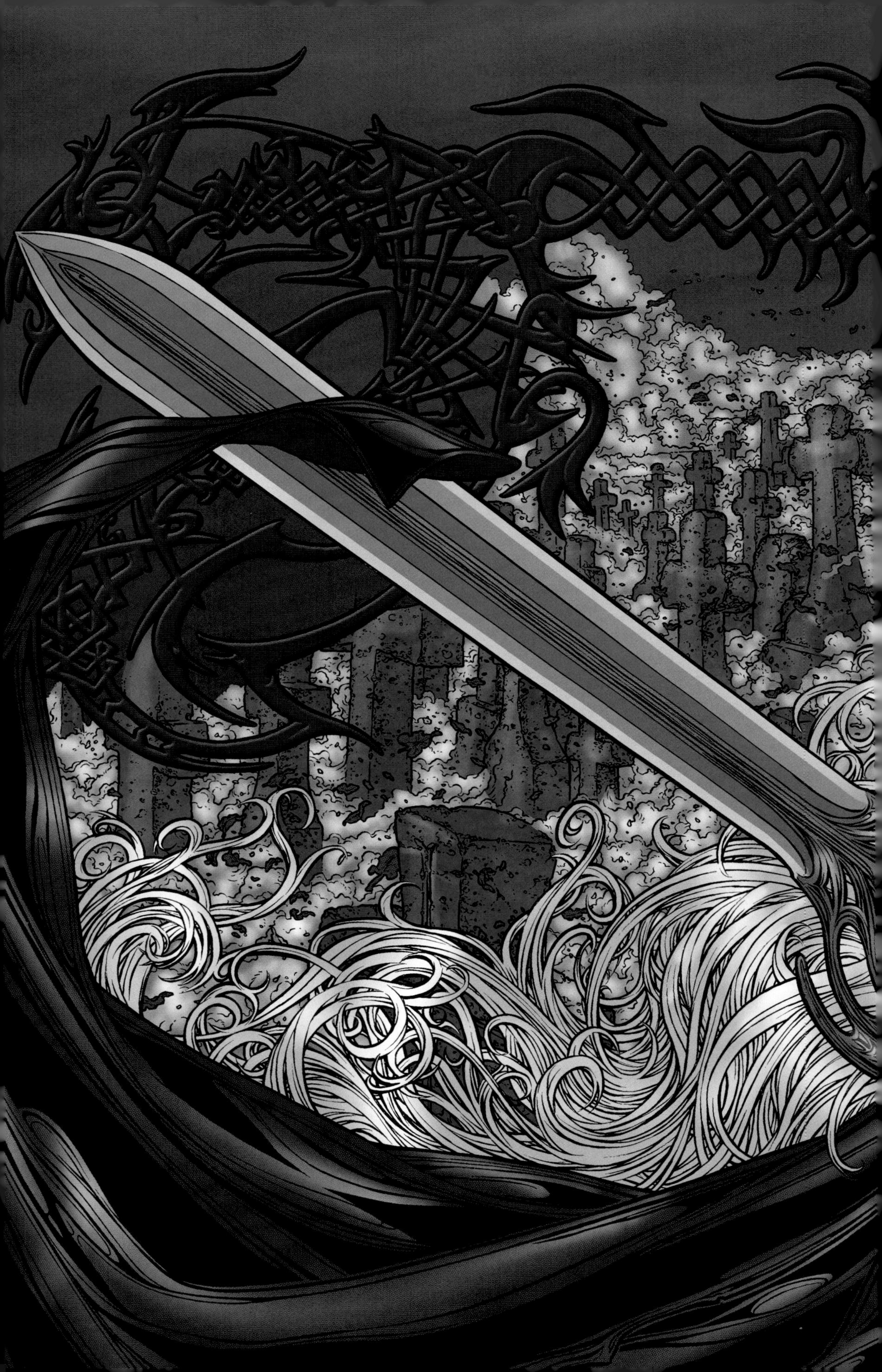

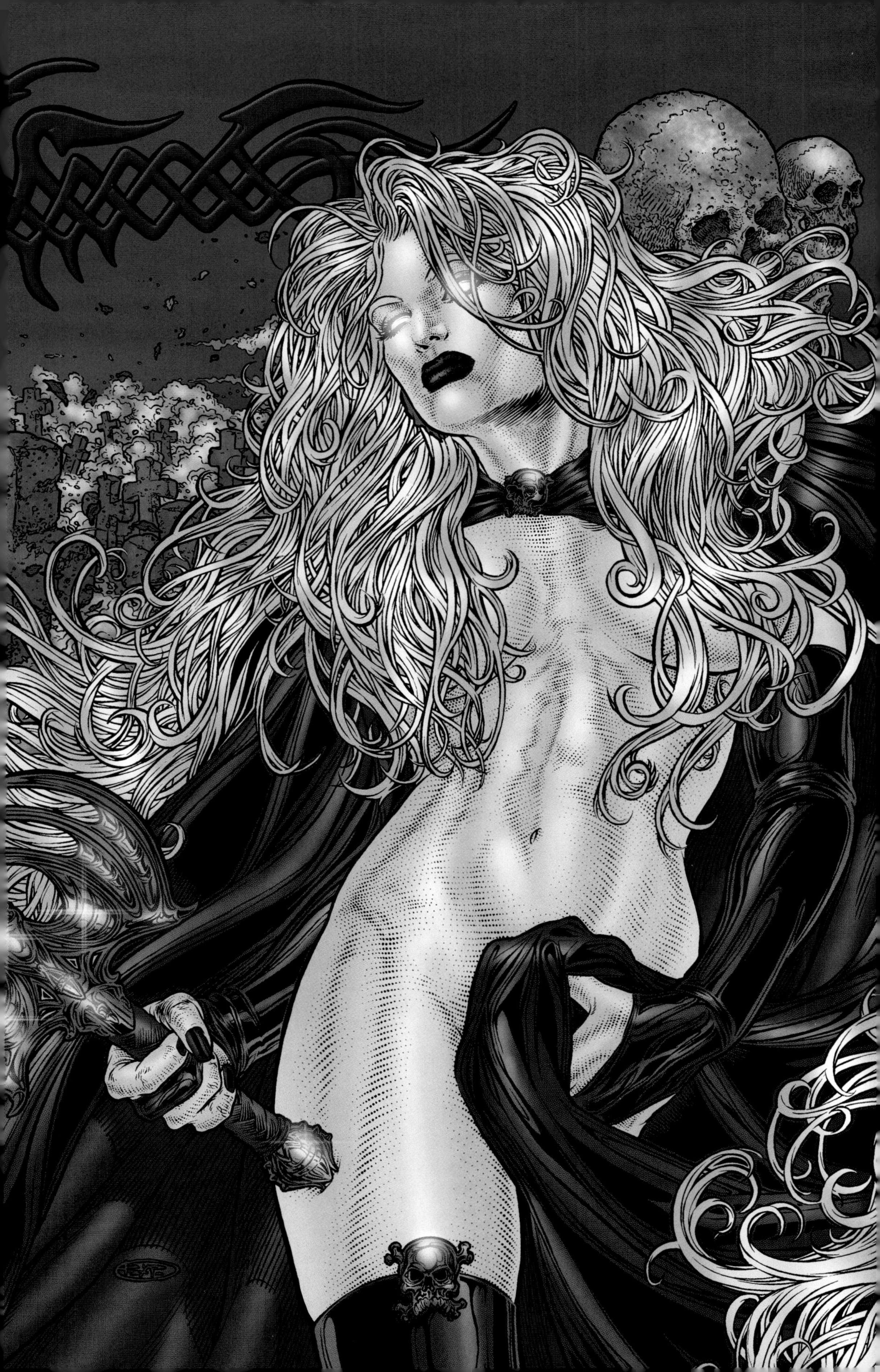

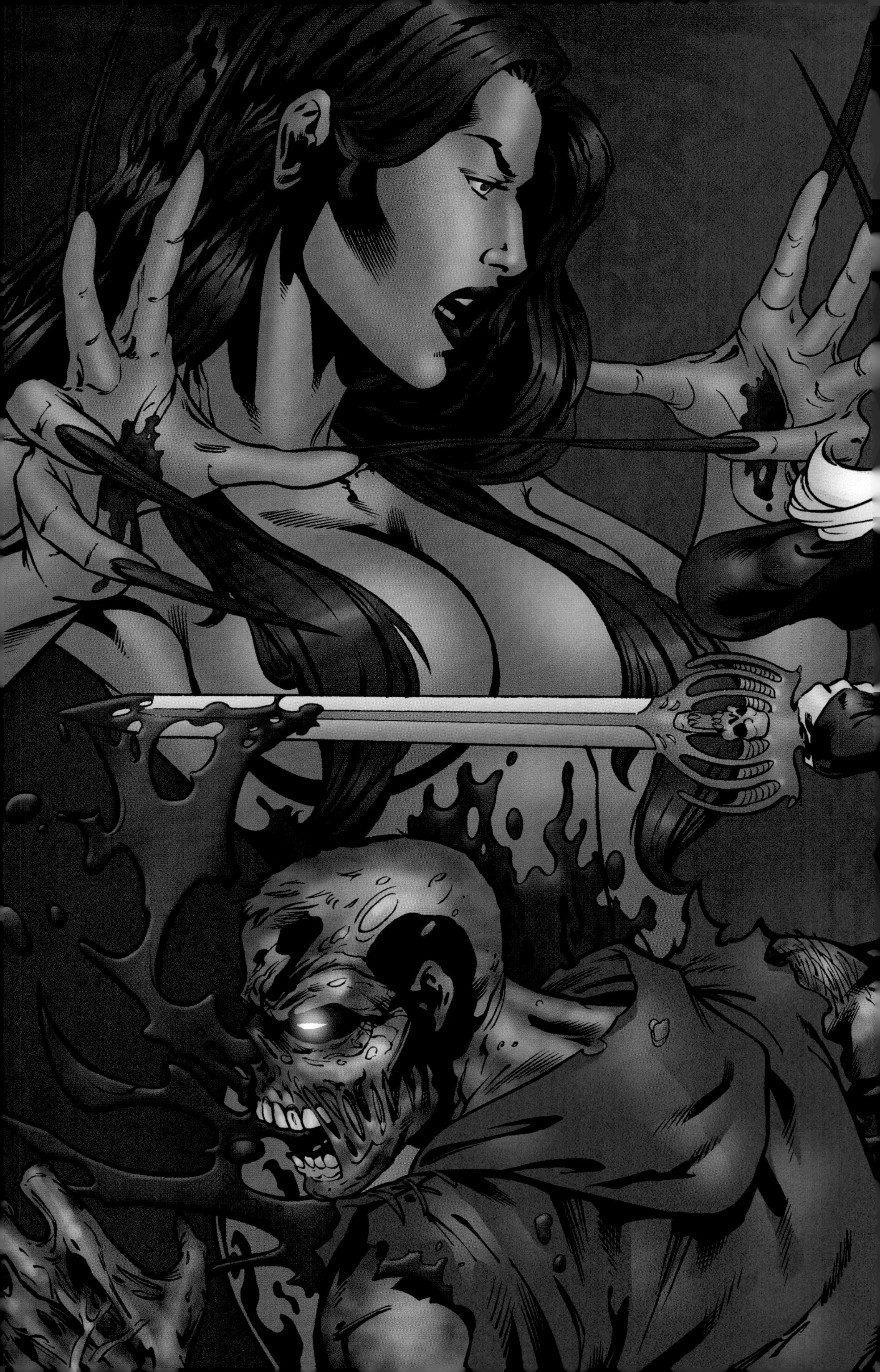

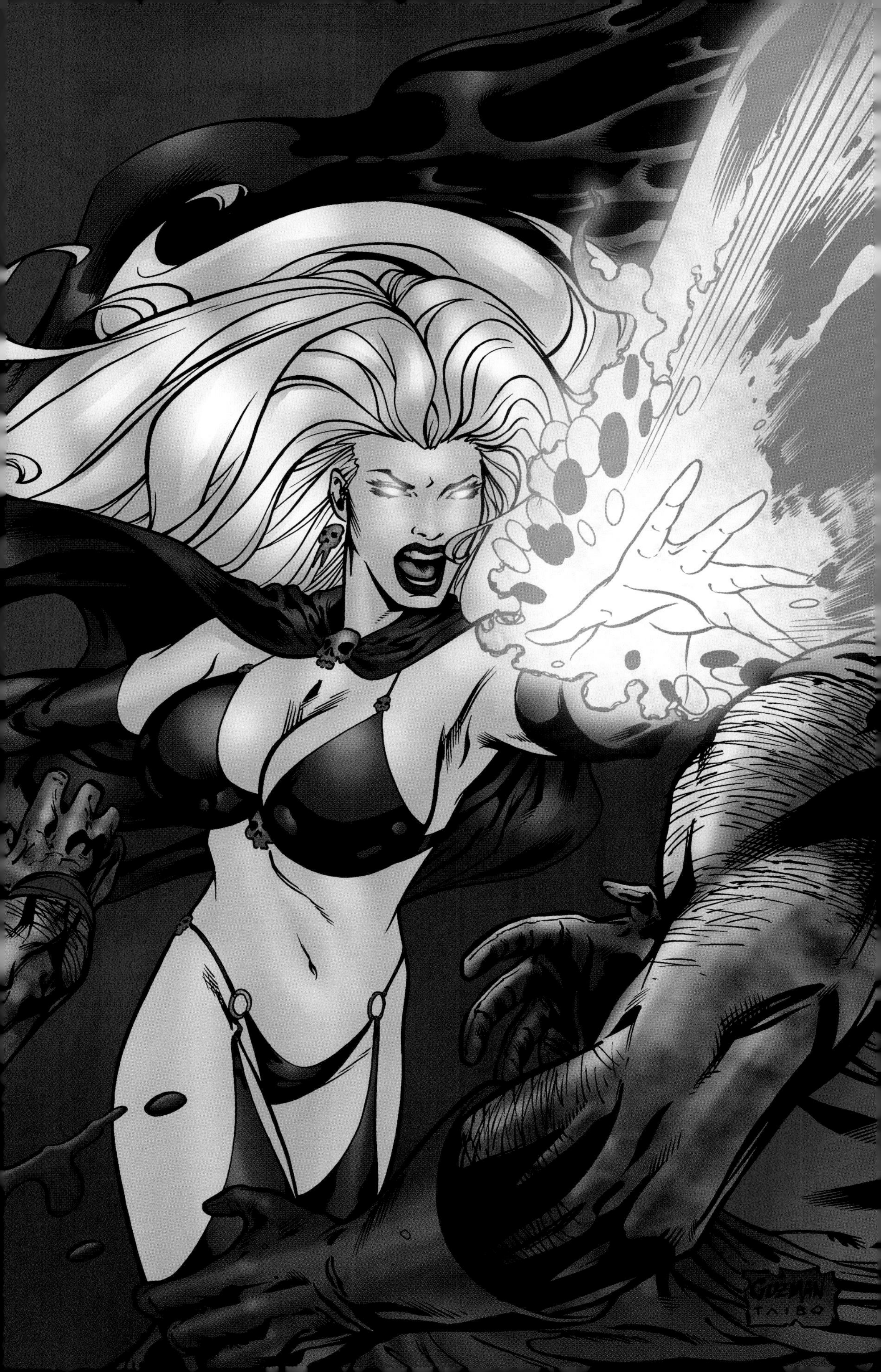
GUZMAN
TAIBO

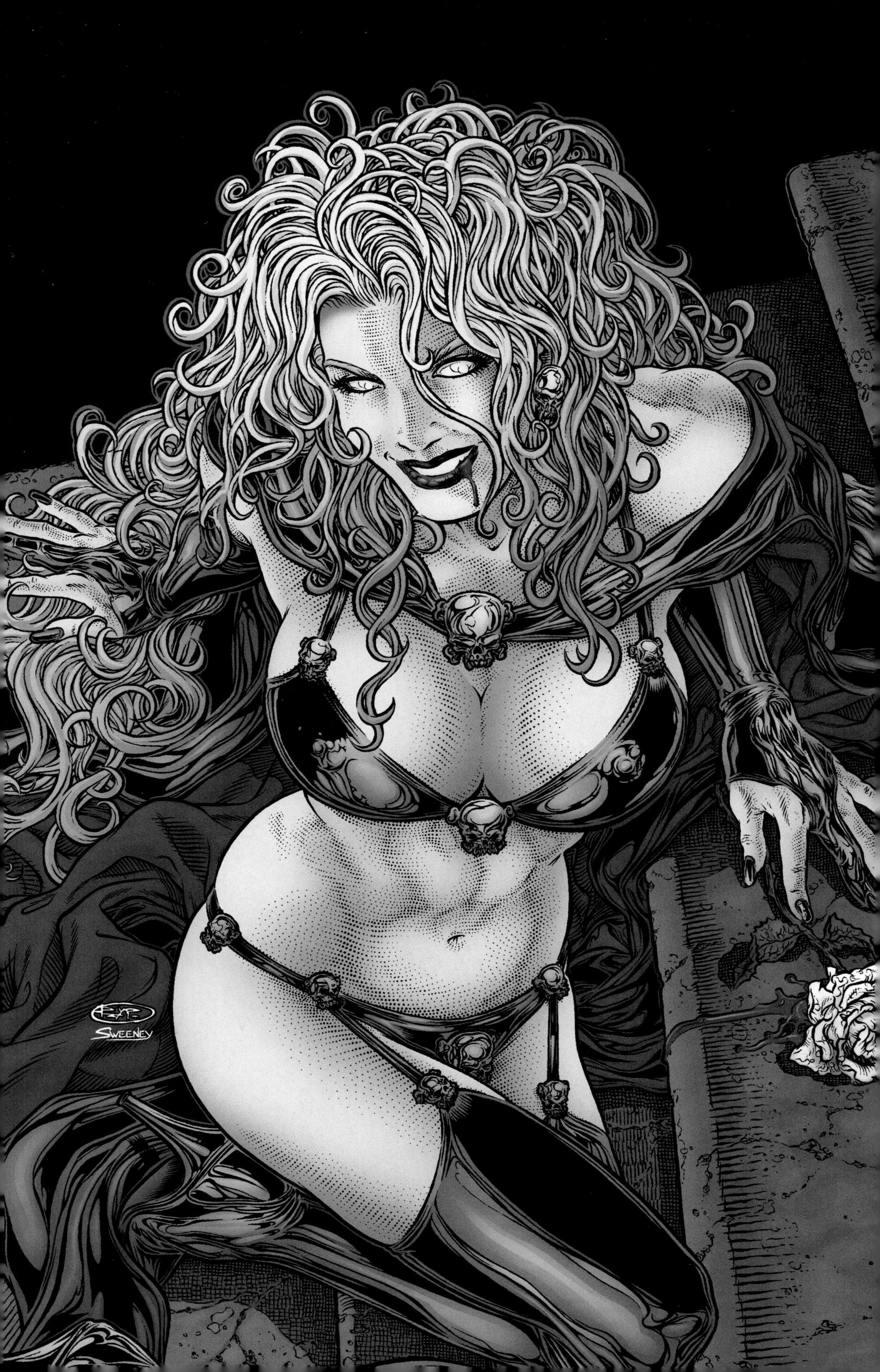
SWEENEY